D1555842

Otto Kiefer

Sexual Life
in
Ancient Rome

translated by
Gilbert and Helen Highet

Panther History

Sexual Life in Ancient Rome

A Panther Book

First published in Great Britain by
Routledge & Kegan Paul Limited 1934
reprinted seven times

Panther edition published 1969

*Printed in Great Britain by Cox & Wyman Ltd.,
London, Reading and Fakenham, and published
by Panther Books,
3 Upper James Street, London, W.1.*

Contents

Translators' Preface

We have verified and corrected the references in this book wherever possible; the numbering is that of the Oxford Classical Text, where such a text exists, and otherwise that of Teubner. We alone are responsible for the index.

All our translations of classical authors are from the original Latin or Greek. Where the reading varies, we have generally taken the variant adopted by Herr Kiefer.

The verse translations are intended to give the meaning and spirit of the originals without departing from the form in which they were written. The Latin poets generally used only three or four metres, and it might give a wrong impression of their essentially conservative technique if they were translated into a greater number of verse-forms. We have not used rhyme, because its possibilities nowadays are limited to the obvious or the reminiscent. The long-short couplet to render elegiacs seems to us more appropriate than anything like the heroic couplet: the second line in Latin is shorter than the first, and is as often as not in a position of dependence on it; that relation cannot be conveyed by the use of two equivalent lines in couplet form.

Sexual Life
in
Ancient Rome

Introduction

The Ideals of Rome

To reach a correct estimate of the position and importance of morality in the life of a nation we must first know the ideals to which that nation directs the efforts of its life. It is true that the characters of all nations and all races in the world are founded on the common basis of human instinct. But in practice the sexual morality of a nation would take very different forms if it were governed by the philosophy of Nietzsche's last period (which is not impossible) or by the doctrines of the medieval Christian church.

Historians and philosophers have constantly endeavoured to explain the character of the ancient Romans by comparing and contrasting them with some other general type – the Greeks, for example, or the Germans. Even today, if we follow the trend of modern thought, we explain the greatest achievement of the Romans, their state, by reference to their national character; and assist our explanation by classifying that character under one definite type. And there seems to be some justification for this, since Roman writers (especially in the Augustan age) often speak as if the Romans could be so classified. In the sixth book of Vergil's *Aeneid* (851) the spirit of Anchises looks into the future and foretells the task of the unborn Roman people: 'Roman, remember, – these shall be your arts – to rule the empire of the world, to impose the custom of peace, to spare the defeated and to crush the proud.' Livy, the great Augustan historian, says in the introduction to his gigantic work: 'If any nation can have the right to hallow its own origin and to attribute its foundation to gods, the Romans

11

are so renowned in war that when they call the war-god
Mars the father of their founder and their people, the world
accepts the Roman boast as contentedly as it accepts the
Roman empire.' In these proud words the function and the
character of Rome were described by the Romans of the
Augustan age. But we must remember that they were describing an ideal whose realization was yet to come. To conclude from the assertion of the ideal that it discloses the real
nature of the Romans would be as mistaken as to infer from
Nietzsche's *Zarathustra* that Nietzsche himself was a powerful and domineering character. We constantly find that
philosophers and poets proclaim as ideal that character from
which they themselves are most remote. We cannot, then,
conclude from the words of Livy and Vergil that the character of the Romans fulfilled itself in violence and conquest.

The poet Horace describes the old Roman stock more
cautiously. 'A manly breed,' he calls them in *Odes*, III, 6,
'of yeoman soldiers, taught to turn the clods with Sabine
mattocks and to carry cut logs at the bidding of a stern
mother, when the sun changed the mountain-shadows and
lifted the yokes from the tired oxen, bringing the kind
evening in his departing chariot.' That is the stock which
Horace praises, even as he condemns the degenerate weaklings of his own time: that was the stock which overthrew
Pyrrhus, and Antiochus, and powerful Carthage, which laid
the foundations for the empire of the world. Livy agrees
with Horace on that vital point. 'There was never a nation
which greed and extravagance invaded so late, nor one
where poverty and thrift were honoured so long and so
greatly.' It would be easy to cite other authors who confirm this description of the early Romans as a race of
simple and homely farmers. To sum up: the earliest Romans
whom we see, faintly, in the dawn of history cannot be
described as a nation striving for power, still less as a nation
striving to conquer the world. They were a sober, hard-
working, practical nation of farmers.

It was natural for such a nation, whose instincts were
healthy and primitive, to multiply till its numbers were
greatly increased, and to seek to extend its territory for
that very reason. This led inevitably to conflicts with neighbours – neighbours who were at first more powerful than

Rome. In addition, we are told that the farming nation turned its hand to trade also and even concluded commercial agreements with Carthage, who must then have been the mistress of the western Mediterranean. But still we see absolutely no trace of the domineering type, the born conquerors and empire builders, whom we are told to see among the Romans. We cannot then assert that the Romans were psychologically a race of conquerors.

We may infer, therefore, that in the earliest historical times the Roman was above all a practical man, with a primitive and healthy mind, who saw his world as a place for the simplest and oldest activities of a civilized race – agriculture and stock-rearing. His whole thought must have been as primitive as his life. All theoretical activities – art, science, philosophy – were beyond his reach. His race could not produce thinkers like Thales and Heraclitus, artists like Phidias, poets like Alcaeus and Sappho. But it must have had, from very early ages, a primitive belief in divine powers – especially in the personified forces of nature and in the religious character of certain acts and activities. It is easy to understand how such a nation, passing its whole life in the narrow circle of primitive practical duties, acquired an immensely strong *will to life*, unqualified by any trace of abstract thought. If such a will to life is crossed by external opposition, it resists with all its might, doubles and redoubles its intensity, takes pleasure in defending itself successfully, turns at last from defence to attack, and seeks and finds wider spheres and further possibilities of realizing itself, fulfilling its task, forcing itself upon the weaker and the defeated everywhere. That is the process: a nation fighting for the right to live becomes a conqueror, and conquest leads to empire.

But a nation which has used its strength for many centuries has no difficulty in learning how to misuse it. That is in the nature of the case – or, rather, it is in the nature of humanity. From the first appearance of man upon this earth he must always have been more of a beast of prey than an angel. We may here refer to Spengler's latest work, *Man and Technics* – especially to these sentences: 'Man is not a good-natured simpleton, not an anthropoid with a taste for technics, as Häckel describes him and Gabriel

Max paints him. That is a caricature, which is still darkened by the plebeian shadow of Rousseau. On the contrary, the life of a man is the life of a brave and splendid, cruel and cunning beast of prey. He lives by catching, killing, and consuming. Since he exists, he must be master.' These bold sentences contain only half the truth; but we shall discuss the matter elsewhere. It is certainly true to say that these words of Spengler apply less accurately to humanity in general than to the Roman nation as it developed in the course of history.

After the gradual rise of Rome to power, after she had attained the brilliant summit of her development, she constructed the greatest thing possible for her – a proud and seemingly eternal empire. Yet we must not forget how a thing so magnificent was created. It was built out of cruel tyranny, savage murders of men and nations, vast and incessant bloodshed. I have said above that the misuse of power is only a natural extension of the use of power by a ruler and conqueror. Such misuse will appear more rapidly and inevitably if the conqueror's own spiritual constitution cannot prevent it – that is, if he has within him few or none of the elements of a finer intellectual or spiritual life to balance a will directed only to the practical ends of self-preservation and the attainment of power.

About the time of Hannibal's final defeat, the Romans began to come into contact with the kingdoms of the eastern Mediterranean. As these contacts became more frequent, Rome learnt to know Greek culture – which, as we shall see, was to influence her in various ways, not always for the better. It was her contact with Hellenism and her overthrow of great kingdoms rich with treasure which first allowed Rome to express her ambition in a new way – in greed and avarice. Thenceforward, the conqueror of the Mediterranean lands became also their ruthless exploiter. Thenceforward, as we shall later show, Rome began to be thronged with those millions of slaves on whom the whole superstructure of society was built. (That superstructure, from an economic point of view, contained a deadly danger to its own existence; for it was bound to collapse as soon as the foundations were removed – as soon as the constant supply of slaves ceased.) In addition, 'wealth brought avarice to Rome, and the multiplication of pleasures brought the desire to ruin oneself and one's country by luxury and lust,' as Livy well says in his introduction. On one side, Rome's ideal of power led her to the gross exploitation of the world, and on the other to something more sinister – a degeneration unknown to the Greeks – to sadism, that peculiar feature of Roman sexual life which was so widespread in the time of the emperors.

We do not wish to assert that the life of Rome found its only fulfilments in sadism and avariciousness. Contact with Greece gradually produced a Roman literature which grew more refined as the centuries passed. And there was a small class of wealthy men who lived that life of ease and culture which we should not despise – the amiable life which we sometimes glimpse in the poems of Horace or the letters of the younger Pliny. Yet we must remember that the mass of the people cared for nothing but *panem et circenses*, food and sport; and that in many of the cultured rich men of Rome culture was only a veneer which easily broke and easily disclosed the coarse and brutish instincts of the peasant. All these generalizations are amplified and discussed in detail in succeeding chapters of this book.

It was natural, then, that the sexual life of the Romans should assume cruder forms than that of the Greeks. The Romans were originally uncouth farmers, chained to the plough and the stall; they became rough soldiers; and at last a few of their best and most gifted became statesmen. But a nation with that history, a nation which had seldom any real interest in art, history, or philosophy, could not produce a lofty and spiritualized sexual life, or conceive its further possibilities with the vision of Plato. It was enough for the Roman, with his primitive character, to direct his sexual instincts into simple channels. For many centuries marriage meant to the Romans a severe and pure, but prosaic, union; it was under the firm authority of the husband, who had little feeling for the subtler possibilities of sex. Besides marriage, there was in Rome from early times a coarse and unpleasant type of prostitution, directed more or less exclusively to the satisfaction of purely sensual desires. There is a significant passage in Horace's satires. He says (i, 2, 116):

> And when your lust is hot, surely
> if a maid or pageboy's handy, to attack
> instanter, you won't choose to grin and bear it?
> *I* won't! I like a cheap and easy love!

If Licht, in his *Sexual Life in Ancient Greece,* is right to speak of the 'predominance of sensuality in Greek life', we are even more justified in asserting the same predominance of sensuality among the Romans.

Still, our picture of Roman life would be one-sided if we ignored the poets. The dramatists Plautus and Terence, the lyric poets Catullus, Tibullus, Ovid, Propertius, Horace, the epic poet Vergil, all tried, and often with success, to unite Roman strength with the charm and formal perfection of the Greeks. And they produced many works which memorably and impressively reflect the love-life of their nation. Pictorial art in Rome, however, produced no great and independent works which told of love as clearly as the Greek vases or breathed the same subtle and enchanting eroticism as the splendid figures of Praxiteles and other masters of Greek sculpture. The only really ideal figure in Roman sculpture, Antinous, may have been created by the homosexual affection of the emperor Hadrian. Coarse and undisguised sensuality was expressed in numerous wall-paintings in Pompeii and elsewhere.

We may sum up our discussion as follows. The Roman character was fundamentally practical. Their practical spirit compelled the Romans to be farmers, soldiers, and statesmen, and thereby to create their greatest achievement, the Empire. Later, through contact with the spirit of Greece, it produced the philosophical thought of Cicero and Seneca and the historical genius of Livy and Tacitus. But the intellectual and spiritual bases of a real and original civilization were absent from the Roman character, as they had been present and active in the Greek. Roman sexual life ran a parallel course to this development: at first fulfilled in simple, severe, and prosaic married life, then developing into more sophisticated forms of sensuality, and degenerating into sadism, but always instinctive and always unspiritual. Yet, like its mighty Empire, Rome's sexual life sometimes displayed a greatness which may be repellent but is always impressive.

Chapter One

Woman in Roman Life

1. Marriage

MOMMSEN says, in his book on Roman penal law: 'If we investigate the beginnings of human development, we shall find that no nation provides so little traditional information as the Italians. Rome was the only representative of the Italian race to reach historical development; and at the time when her real traditions begin she is already a highly developed nation, strongly influenced by the superior civilization of Greece, and presiding over a great national league of city-states. And there is absolutely no non-Roman tradition about the early history of Rome. Even for the Romans themselves, those past ages are lost in darkness. It is vain to seek for any memory of the origin and rise of Rome, either among its impersonal and mythless deities, or in those legal fables, found in the chronicles, which are so strongly national despite their narrative form. Rome is a manly nation, and never looks back to its own childhood.'

Mommsen's remark is perhaps more applicable to the sexual life of Rome than to any other aspect of its history – by sexual life we mean the relations of the sexes. In historical times, we find among the Romans both monogamous marriage and various extra-marital relationships (which range from what we should call the basest up to the most refined); but we really do not know how any of these relationships developed.

From considerations of space our work on the history of Roman civilization cannot undertake to present or to criticize all the opinions which have been held about Roman

marriage and extra-marital relationships. Still, we shall
endeavour to reproduce a few of the more important views
on the matter – views which now once more occupy the
foremost place among the discussions of the learned world.

In the time of the early republic, the foundation of
Roman social life was monogamous marriage, entirely
dominated by the husband. The *patria potestas*, the
father's authority, rules the whole life of the Roman family
in historic times; we shall meet it again when we come to
deal with education. But it would be wrong to assume that
sexual relationships were confined to this marriage which
was based on paternal domination. On the contrary, as we
shall see, free sexual relationships co-existed with marriage,
even in the earliest times known to us – whether they are to
be described as 'free love' or 'prostitution'. But how can we
explain the co-existence of monogamous marriage and such
relationships?

Freiherr F. von Reitzenstein says, on page 28 of his little
book, *Love and Marriage in Ancient Europe*: 'It is certain,
in the first place, that the people had no complete *connubium* or legal marriage; and, secondly, that marriage
by capture was customary in the earliest times. But the
evidence of Roman law and history is especially valuable
for the further development of marriage. The legal genius
of the Romans makes it possible for us to pause at every
stage of their development, although that same genius
obliterated the earliest epochs in such a way as to make it
impossible for us to form a picture of them. We cannot
doubt the existence of matriarchy, which was constantly
encouraged by the Etruscans ... Marriage as a binding
union was certainly unknown to the plebeians; accordingly
their children belonged to the mother's family. This agam-
ous or marriageless relationship still existed at Rome in
later times, and was the basis of a widely developed system
of free love, which soon changed into different kinds of
prostitution.'

These opinions, in which there is a good deal of probability, really date back to the profound researches of the
Swiss scholar Bachofen. While Mommsen's school of
thought prevailed, Bachofen was long relegated to almost
complete obscurity; but now he is again universally re-

spected. In his important work, *The Legend of Tanaquil – An Inquiry into Oriental Influence on Rome and Italy*, he sought to prove that in ancient Italy the reign of strong paternal authority had been preceded by a state of exclusive matriarchy, chiefly represented by the Etruscans. He considered that the development of exclusive patriarchy, which we find to be the prevailing type of legitimate relation in historic times, was a universal reform, a vast and incomparable advance in civilization. On page 22 of his principal work, *The Right of the Mother,* Bachofen distinguishes three stages in the development of marriage. The primitive stage is indiscriminate sexual intercourse; the intermediate stage is marriage dominated by the wife; and the last and highest stage is marriage dominated by the husband. His words are: 'The principle of marriage, and the principle of an authority in the family which sustains marriage, are part of the spiritual *ius civile* (civil law). This is the intermediate stage. Finally, above this stage, appears the highest stage of all – the purely spiritual authority of the father, by which the wife is subordinated to the husband, and all the importance possessed by the mother is transferred to the father. This is the highest type of law, and it was most purely developed by Rome. Nowhere else did the ideal of *potestas* (power) over wife and child reach such complete maturity; and so nowhere else was the corresponding ideal of a unified political *imperium* (supreme power) so consciously and persistently pursued.' And Bachofen adds: 'The *ius naturale* (natural law) of ancient times is not mere philosophical speculation, as the later *ius naturale* is. It is a historical event, a real stage of civilization, older than the purely political statute law – an expression of the earliest religious ideals, a record of a stage through which humanity has passed. ... But the destiny of the human race lies in an increasing conquest of the laws of matter, in a transcendence of that material side of its nature which connects it with the rest of the animal world, and in an ascent towards a higher and more purely human life. The Romans banished from their laws the physical and materialistic view of human relationships, more completely than other nations; for Rome was from the first founded on the political aspect of the *imperium*; in conscious adherence to this aspect Rome pursued her destiny. . . .'

Thus Bachofen, whose opinions I shall neither endorse nor oppose. Still, he could appeal to such passages as Cicero *de inventione*, i, 2, where Cicero speaks thus of the primitive state of mankind: 'No one knew of lawful marriage, no one had seen legitimate children of his own.'

Moreover, even modern scholars like Hans Mühlestein (in his notable books *The Birth of the Western World* and *On the Origin of the Etruscans*) followed Bachofen in tracing a very strong Etruscan influence in the whole prehistoric development of Rome. And they find substantially stronger support for this view in the results of recent excavations. We can perhaps agree with them in concluding that a sort of matriarchy prevailed for many centuries before that real development of the Roman family and the Roman state which was based on the *patria potestas*; and that vestiges of this matriarchy survived in the various forms of free sexual intercourse which co-existed with the monogamous marriage recognized by the state. Of course, on the basis of our present knowledge of history, these are still more or less insecure hypotheses; later, perhaps, and especially when we understand the Etruscan language, they may solidify into historical certainty.

After these introductory remarks, let us describe marriage as it was in Rome of historic times.

Until the year 445 B.C. a regular marriage (*iustae nuptiae*) could be contracted only between patricians – members of the ruling class. Between patricians and plebeians there was no *connubium*: that is, there was no intermarriage which could be recognized as binding in a civil court. Later historians write as if the wicked Decemviri had been the first to put this ban on marriage between patricians and plebeians (Cic., *De rep*., ii, 37). But, as a matter of fact, the ban was one of the old laws which had until then been observed by custom only, and which were in 445 recorded at the codification known as the Twelve Tables. Eventually, after long and painful struggles between the classes, the ban was removed by the tribune Canuleius.

In this connection it may be interesting to quote the story of Virginia. It is probably a fable without historic authenticity, but it is important from the point of view of its influence in literature (Lessing's *Emilia Galotti* is an example). We quote the story as told by Dionysius of Halicarnassus – a version which is less widely known than others (Dion. Hal., xi, 28).

'There was a man of the common people named Lucius Virginius: he was one of the best soldiers in Rome, and commanded a century in one of the five legions which were campaigning against the Aequi. He had a daughter named Virginia, the most beautiful girl in Rome, betrothed to an ex-tribune called Lucius. (Lucius was the son of Icilius, the man who had instituted the office of tribune and had been the first to hold it.) Appius Claudius, the head of the Board of Ten, saw the girl reading in her school – at that time the children's schools were round the market-place – and was caught by her beauty; for she was of marriageable age. Being already enslaved by his passion, he was made worse by being obliged to pass the school many times. He could not marry the girl, for she was already betrothed to another man and he himself had a wife; also he despised her rank, and disdained to take a wife from the common people; and such a marriage was made illegal by the very law which he himself had inscribed in the Twelve Tables. So he first tried to seduce her by his money. She had no mother, and Appius kept sending messengers to the women who had brought her up; he gave the women large sums of money, and promised to give still more. He directed his agents not to tell the women who was in love with the girl, but only to say that he was one of those who could harm or help anyone he wished. However, he did not persuade them, but found that they guarded the girl even more carefully than before. He was now on fire with love, and decided upon a bolder course. Sending for one of his kinsmen named Marcus Claudius, a bold man who was ready to help in any deed, he told him of his passion. Then, after telling what he was to do and say, he sent him off with a number of shameless men to accompany him. Marcus went to the school, laid hold of the girl, and tried to lead her away through the market-place before the eyes of the citizens. There was an uproar and a huge growd assembled at once, so that he was prevented from taking the girl to the

appointed place. He therefore went to the magistrates. At
that moment Appius was sitting alone on the judges' bench,
giving advice and dispensing justice to those who asked for
it. When Marcus tried to speak there was a shout of protest
from the crowd of bystanders, all demanding that he should
wait until the girl's kinsmen arrived. After a short time her
uncle arrived, Publius Numitorius, who was highly respected among the commons; he brought with him many
friends and kinsmen. A little later came Lucius, to whom
Virginia had been betrothed by her father. He was accompanied by a strong force of young men belonging to the
common people. As soon as he reached the judges' bench,
still panting and breathless, he demanded to be told who
had dared to lay a hand on the daughter of a free citizen,
and with what purpose. There was silence. Then Marcus
Claudius, the man who had taken possession of the girl,
made this speech: "Appius Claudius, I have committed no
hasty or violent act on this girl. I am her legal master, and
am taking her away in accordance with the laws. I shall
tell you how she comes to belong to me. I inherited from my
father a woman who has now been a slave for many years.
When she fell pregnant Virginius' wife – who used to visit
her as a friend – persuaded her to give her the baby if it
was born alive. The slave kept her promise, for this girl Virginia was born to her, but she told us the baby had been
born dead, and then gave it to Numitoria. Having neither
sons nor daughters, Numitoria adopted the child and
brought it up as her own. This escaped my knowledge for
some time; but now I have been informed of it. I have
many reliable witnesses, and I have questioned the slave-
woman. I now appeal to the general law by which children
belong to their real parents, not to their adoptive parents,
and by which the children of free parents are free, while the
children of slaves are slaves to the owner of their parents.
By that law I claim my right to take away the daughter of
my slave. I am prepared to take this case to court if anyone
will provide adequate security that she will be brought into
court then. But if anyone wishes a quick decision, I am
ready to put forward my case before you immediately,
without delay and without security for the girl. Let my
opponents decide between these alternatives."

'After Marcus Claudius had stated his case, he was opposed by the girl's uncle in a longer speech. He said that it was only when the girl had reached marriageable age and her beauty was obvious that a claimant had appeared – a claimant who had an impudently false claim, and was prompted not by any purpose of his own but by another man who thought all his own desires should be satisfied in whatever way it was possible. As for the claim, he said that the father would answer it when he came home from service with the army; he himself, the girl's uncle, would lay the formal counterclaim to possession of her and would undertake the legal obligations.

'This speech excited the sympathy of the audience. But Appius Claudius made a cunning reply: "I am well acquainted with the law which deals with deposits for the security of persons who are claimed as slaves – it forbids those persons to be in the custody of their claimants until the case is heard. I shall not undo a law which I myself enacted. This, however, is my decision. There are two counter-claimants, the uncle and the father. If they were both present it would be right for the father to have custody of the girl until the case is heard. However, since he is absent, I adjudge that the girl's owner shall take her with him, and give trustworthy securities that he will bring her to the case when her father returns. As to the securities and the fine and fair treatment for you at the hearing, Numitorius, I shall pay great attention to all these matters. Meanwhile, hand over the girl."

'The women and the whole assembly broke out into loud complaints and lamentations. Icilius, the girl's betrothed, swore that as long as he lived no one should be allowed to take her away. "Cut off my head, Appius, and then take the girl wherever you wish, and all the other girls and women, too, so that the Romans may understand that they are no longer freemen but slaves. ... But be sure of this: my death will be the beginning of great unhappiness for Rome, or of the great happiness!"

'Virginia was seized by her pretended owner; but the behaviour of the crowd was so threatening that Appius was compelled to give in for the time. Her father was brought from the camp. As soon as he arrived, the case was heard.

He produced the most striking proofs of her legitimacy; but Appius declared that he had long known her to be suppositious but had been unable to follow up the matter in the press of business. He himself threatened to use force on the crowd, and directed Marcus Claudius to take the girl away, escorted by the twelve lictors with their axes.

'When he said this the crowd dispersed, groaning and striking their foreheads and unable to keep back their tears. Claudius started to lead the girl away, but she clung to her father, kissing and embracing him and calling him endearing names. In his anguish Virginius determined on an act which was bitterly hard for a father, but right and proper for a brave and free-born man. He asked for permission to embrace his daughter for the last time and to say a word to her alone before she was taken away from the marketplace. The consul allowed him to do this, and his enemies withdrew to a little distance away. He held her in his arms, drooping and fainting and clinging to him; he spoke her name and kissed her and wiped away her streaming tears; meanwhile, he moved gradually away from the others. When he came near a butcher's shop he seized a knife from the table and stabbed his daughter through the heart, saying: "My child, I send you free and chaste to your ancestors in the world of the dead; for while you live the tyrant allows you to have neither freedom nor chastity!" '

The story ends with the deposition of the tyrannous Decemviri; but we need not pursue it further. Whether it is based on fact or invented to illustrate the deposition of the tyrants, it is enough to show the pride of the rising commoners and their hatred for a caste of noblemen which they felt to be tyrannical; in this case especially with regard to marriage relationships. Appius thinks it beneath him to take a girl of a lower class in legitimate marriage, and for that reason attempts the outrage described above; Virginius is a commoner, proudly conscious of his class, and refuses to tolerate the outrage, preferring to kill his daughter rather than allow her to enter what he considers a dishonourable union with a member of another caste – and a cast whose privilege he can no longer recognize.

If we wish to understand the nature of regular marriage in Rome (*iustum matrimonium*) we must first differentiate between marriages in which the woman comes 'into the hand' (*in manum*) of her husband and those in which she does not. What is the meaning of this singular phrase? It is this. The woman stood while she was a girl under the parental authority of her father, as all children did. Her father had *patria potestas* over her. If she is married to a man 'into whose hand' she goes, that means that she leaves the authority of her father and enters the authority, the *manus*, of her husband. If she is married *sine in manum conuentione*, without entering the authority of her husband, she remains under the authority of her father or of his legal representative – in practice her husband is given no rights over her property. In later ages, as Roman women gradually emancipated themselves, it was to their advantage to be independent of their husbands with regard to property rights; accordingly, they made a point of avoiding marriages where they entered the *manus* of their husbands.

Marital authority, *manus,* was acquired only through the three forms of marriage recognized by a civil court – *confarreatio, coemptio*, and *usus*. We must now examine these forms in detail, in so far as they appear to bear on our subject; the more intricate details – some of which are the subject of much dispute – properly belong to a history of Roman law.

The oldest and most ceremonious form of marriage, corresponding to our church wedding, is *confarreatio*. The name is derived from a sort of meal-cake, *farreum libum,* which was used in the ceremony. Dionysius speaks of *confarreatio* as follows (ii, 25): 'The Romans of ancient times used to call a wedding which was confirmed by ceremonies sacred and profane a *confarreatio*, summing its nature up in one word, derived from the common use of *far* or spelt, which we call *zea* ... Just as we in Greece consider barley to be the oldest grain, and use it to begin sacrifices under the name *oulai*, so the Romans believe that spelt is the most valuable and ancient of all grain, and use it at the beginning of all burnt offerings. The custom survives still; there has been no change to some more costly initial sacrifice. From the sharing of *far* was named the ceremony whereby wives share with their husbands the earliest and most holy food, and agree to share their fortune in life, too; it brought them into a close bond of indissoluble relationship, and nothing could break a marriage of that kind. This law directed wives to live so as to please their husbands only, as they had nowhere else to appeal, and husbands to govern their wives as things which were necessary to them and inalienable.'

We need not describe the rites in detail: chief among them was a sacrifice performed by the High Priest (*pontifex maximus*) and the priest of Jupiter (*flamen Dialis*) in the presence of ten witnesses. Some of the rites are now almost unintelligible. Bachofen's interpretation of the whole ceremony may be found in his book, *The Legend of Tanaquil*. In later ages this form of marriage was still obligatory for the parents of certain priests, but it was felt to be burdensome (Tac., *Ann.*, iv, 16). Certainly it was the oldest and most aristocratic; it was originally the customary form for patricians, and it long survived beside the other simpler and less ritual types.

The relation of the other forms of marriage to the old *confarreatio* is still a subject of dispute among scholars. It is now generally assumed that the second form, *coemptio*, was originally introduced for the marriages of the common people among themselves, since the plebeians could not employ the aristocratic *confarreatio*. The distinguished legal authority, Karlowa, in his book on the history of Roman law, asserts that *coemptio* dates back to Servian times, and was invented as a legal form of marriage for plebeians. At first a marriage by *coemptio* did not cause the wife (if she were a plebeian) to enter the family (*gens*) of her husband. This aroused the animosity of the commons, resulting in the law of the tribune Canuleius, which made the effects of *coemptio* similar to those of *confarreatio*. But *confarreatio* survived as the prerogative of the patrician class.

The third form of marriage was that by custom, or *usus*. It was laid down in the legislation of the Twelve Tables that cohabitation lasting for a year without interruption should be considered as a regular marriage. The peculiarity of this type of marriage lies rather in the exception than in the rule. For the effect of an interruption of cohabitation for

three nights running (the *trinoctium*) was that *manus* did
not exist; that is to say, the marriage was regular enough,
but the wife did not leave the authority of her father and
enter that of her husband. This was established by the legislation of the Twelve Tables (Caius, *Inst.*, i, 111). This form
of marriage by custom was intended, in the opinion of Karlowa, to regularize unions between foreigners and Romans
where they were intended to be permanent. It was only
later that it was used to emancipate the wife from her subjection to the husband. As Karlowa says, the widespread
popularity of this form, whereby a wife could remain free
from her husband's authority by an annual *trinoctium*,
dates to a 'time when, after the conquest of Italy, Rome
began to look about for foreign conquests, to abandon her
religious outlook, and break down the old morality'. We
shall give more detailed consideration later in this book to
what may be called woman's struggle for emancipation
in Rome; we shall therefore discuss Karlowa's opinion no
further here. No one knows whether this type of marriage
'without *manus*' was first introduced by legal enactment or
simply by naturalization through time. It is certain that the
poet Ennius knew it in the time of the first Punic war.

The three forms we have discussed differ in this point.
In *confarreatio* the High Priest was present and marriage
and *manus* came into being together. In *coemptio* the husband acquired *manus* by a special legal ceremony which
was not in itself necessary for the celebration of the wedding. In *usus* a year's cohabitation was equivalent to
marriage, but there was no *manus* unless that year had been
unbroken by the separation called *trinoctium*.

The legal ceremony of *coemptio* was a mock purchase:
the husband bought his wife for a trifling sum like a pepper-
corn rent. The prefix *co* emphasizes the fact that the husband acquires his rights over the wife as a kinswoman
co-ordinate with himself (Karlowa). By it the wife gives
herself into her husband's power – she is not a passive
figure in the ceremony, but takes an active part in it.

Marriage by *coemptio* was the commonest form in later
times. We know that *confarreatio* was archaic, and fell into
disuse because it was so troublesome to perform. The
jurist Caius tells us that marriage by *usus* had become

obsolete in his day, partly by legislation and partly by
custom (*Inst.*, i, 111).

It is not within the scope of our inquiry to discuss in
greater detail the relationship of these three forms. It is
certain, however, that the rites observed at all three were
almost identical. It lay within the discretion of the con-
tracting parties to decide which should be used. Modern
scholars (e.g. Reitzenstein, *loc. cit.*, and elsewhere) believe
that the ceremonies by *coemptio* and *usus* are derived from
the ceremony used at a marriage by *confarreatio*, and are
only modifications of it. We shall try to give a short summary of the most usual rites in so far as they can be corroborated by evidence.

At a marriage by *confarreatio* the High Priest and the
priest of Jupiter were present; from this we may infer that
the holy act took place in a holy place, probably the *curia*
or senate-house. But no special place was necessary for the
celebration of the other types, and they took place in the
house of the bride. A wedding was generally preceded by
a betrothal, but if that were dissolved there was (at least
in later times) no possibility of a suit for breach of promise
(Juv., vi, 200; *Cod. Just.*, v, 1, 1). At the betrothal ceremony the bridegroom gave the future bride a settlement
or an iron ring which she wore on the fourth finger of her
left hand. Later, a marriage contract was usually drawn up
at the betrothal. The whole betrothal ceremony generally
took place in the presence of guests, and ended in a banquet.

On certain days of the year a wedding could not be celebrated. The whole of May, the first halves of March and
June, the Kalends, Nones and Ides of every month, and the
numerous Roman festivals were avoided on religious
grounds. The rites actually began on the day before the
ceremony, because on that day the bride laid aside the dress
she had worn as a girl and dedicated it to the gods along
with the playthings of her childhood. She now put on her
bridal dress: a specially woven *tunica* and a woollen girdle,
and – most important of all – the *flammeum*, a large red
veil which covered her head. Particular attention was paid
to the dressing of her hair. It was the custom to part the
bride's hair into six plaits with an iron spearhead whose
point had been bent. One authority actually tells us that

later this was done with a lance taken out of the dead body
of a gladiator—perhaps because such a weapon was held to
have some mysterious power of its own (Becker, *Roman
Private Antiquities,* v, I, 44). Beneath her red veil the bride
wore a crown of flowers which she had gathered herself.
The other persons at the ceremony also wore wreaths of
flowers.

According to Cicero (*de div.,* i, 16, 28), the marriage
began by the taking of auspices early in the morning; this
was done in ancient times by observing the flight of birds,
and later by examining the entrails of a sacrificial victim.
Meanwhile the guests were assembling, and were duly
informed of the result of the auspices. The marriage contract was now completed, in the presence of ten witnesses –
although it was not an essential preliminary to a marriage
(Cis., *ap.* Quint., v, II, 32). This was followed by a solemn
declaration by the bride and bridegroom that they were
agreed on their marriage. In a marriage by *confarreatio,*
or *coemptio* the woman said: 'Quando tu Caius, ego Caia' –
a much-disputed formula, which, according to Reitzenstein, means 'Where you are the father of a family I shall
be the mother'. The words certainly meant that the wife
was ready and willing to enter the *manus* of her husband
and thereby to enter his family (*gens*). After this declaration the bridal couple were led up to each other and their
hands brought together by the *pronuba.* (The *pronuba*
was usually a married woman, and represented the goddess
Juno. In Claudian, ix, 284, Venus herself appears as *pronuba* and clasps the hands of the bride and bridegroom.)
The ceremony had now reached its climax, and the newly
married couple moved towards the sacrificial altar to offer
the chief sacrifice themselves. This sacrifice must not be
confused with that which was made early in the morning.
In the most ancient times it consisted of fruit or of the meal-
cake mentioned above – in conformity with the rites of
confarreatio; later, it was an animal, generally a pig or a
bullock. During the sacrifice the bride and bridegroom sat
on two seats which were tied together with a sheepskin. The
auspex nuptiarum or, at *confarreatio,* the attendant priest
recited the words of the prayer and the couple repeated
them, walking round the altar. There remained the congra-

tulations and good wishes, and the banquet then followed
(Juv., ii, 119, e.g.).

Meanwhile night had come. The last stage in the ceremony now began – the *deductio,* the procession escorting
the bride to her husband's house. Ancient custom dictated that she should be torn by her husband from her
mother, to whom she had fled for protection. (Festus, 288,
says quite clearly: 'They pretend that the girl is torn away
from the protection of her mother, or, if her mother is not
present, from the protection of her next-of-kin, when she
is dragged (*trahitur*) to her husband.') The custom obviously points to marriage by capture in primitive times. Now
the bride was escorted to her husband's home by a gay procession – flute-players and a boy with burning torches went
ahead, then (according to many vase-paintings) the bridal
couple in a carriage, surrounded and followed by the guests
and any members of the public who happened to be near.
The procession sang Fescennine songs – originally phallic
songs, for *fescenninus* is to be derived from *fascinum,* the
male genital organ. It is not impossible that there was
also a phallic dance in the most ancient times – the custom
appears among primitive peoples (Reitzenstein, *loc. cit.*). It
is certain that the songs contained some very obscene jokes
(one such song is in the *Acharnians* of Aristophanes: cf.
Reitzenstein, p. 46). There is an interesting picture of such
a procession in Catullus's famous marriage song. It shows
us a chorus of young men who have dined with the bridegroom, and a chorus of girls who are the bride's friends. It
begins:

> Arise, evening has come – in heaven
> at last, at last its lamps are lit.
> Arise and leave the ample feast:
> the maiden comes, the songs are sounding.
> Hymen, come to us, holy Hymen!

The chorus of girls answers:

> See them, maidens, and rise to face them!
> The evening star now shows its beacon,
> 'tis sure – but see their eagerness;
> boldly they rise, to sing against us.
> Hymen, come to us, holy Hymen!

When the procession reached the husband's house, custom demanded that the wife should anoint the doorposts

with fat or oil and bind them with woollen threads. Then the husband lifted her over the threshold, for it would have been a bad omen if she had touched it. Inside, she was received by him into common possession of fire and water: together with him she lit the new hearth-fire, and she was then sprinkled with water. She was thereby admitted to share the domestic and religious life of her husband.

The consummation of the marriage, which now followed, was governed by certain sacred customs. The *pronuba* had already prepared the marriage-bed and given the bride all necessary instruction. The bride herself now prayed to Juno Virginensis and to Cincia, the goddess to whom the loosening of the girdle was consecrated. The husband loosened his wife's girdle, and she sat down (probably naked) on the phallus of a god of fertility, named Mutunus Tutunus. In the most ancient times the first sexual intercourse probably took place in the presence of witnesses. Originally, perhaps, the husband's friends had intercourse with the bride first. According to Bachofen, this was a survival of the free prostitution which preceded marriage in primitive times. 'Natural and physical laws are alien and even opposed to the marriage-tie. Accordingly, the woman who is entering marriage must atone to Mother Nature for violating her, and go through a period of free prostitution, in which she purchases the chastity of marriage by preliminary unchastity.' In later times, the husband's friends threw nuts into the bridal chamber. Finally, we must remark that the sexual intercourse of the newly-married couple was superintended by a series of deities, whose names show that they represented the various moments of the sexual act.

On the day after the marriage, the bride received her relatives and made her first sacrifice to the gods of her new home.

(We may say that one of the most important sources for the information contained in the above account is Becker-Marquardt's *Private Antiquities of Rome* [1864].)

A further question may now be asked. What were these marriages really like? What do we know of the married life and home life of the Romans, at various stages of their history? In old and new works on Roman morality, we often read that marriage in Rome had begun to break up early in Roman history, and at latest by the beginning of

the Imperial age. It is asserted that to this degeneration we
must attribute a great share in the eventual fall of that Empire which seemed to be established to eternity. For
example, here is a quotation from a great authority on
Roman married life, A. Rossbach. It occurs in his *Roman
Wedding-monuments and Marriage-monuments* (1871). 'If
we consider these monuments in connection with the time
when they were made, they appear as reminiscences of the
glorious past, of the disciplined family life of Rome, with
its domestic rites, its severe paternal authority, and the
morality and self-sacrifice to the community, which contributed so powerfully to the development of the state.'

Perhaps there is some reliable description of married
life among the Romans from which we can construct a
reasonably accurate picture of it. For such a description
we should consult Dionysius of Halicarnassus. He says in
ii, 25: 'Romulus did not allow the husband to arraign his
wife for adultery or desertion, nor the wife to take her
husband to court for ill-treatment or unjust repudiation.
He made no law to fix the amount of dowry which should
be brought by the wife or given back to her. He made no
laws for any of these matters, except one – which proved
itself to be suitable for all occasions: it guided the wife to
rigid chastity and morality. It reads: "A wife who is joined
to her husband by the sacred ordinances shall have all
property and all rites in common with him." ' Although
Dionysius speaks of a law given by Romulus, his remark
does not contradict the probability that Roman marriage
(in the oldest times of any historical importance) was a
simple affair, regulated by an inflexible *patria potestas*. But
it is difficult for modern minds to see anything distinguished
or noble in the life of a woman of ancient Rome: it was
passed within the narrow confines of immutable custom
and severe authority, and its ideal was *austeritas*, a noble
gravity. Her life was morally immaculate, but 'it lacked the
grace which the women of Greece possessed, and had nothing of that gay charm which makes a husband happy'
(Becker-Marquardt). Seneca says with justice that at the
time of the first Punic war 'immodesty was not a vice but a
monstrosity'.

Besides that, a Roman wife who came from a rich or

noble family had a reputation for a haughty, arrogant, and domineering character – which was a common subject for jokes in Roman comedy. The Roman matron was well enough off in her home: she did no cooking and no menial tasks. Her only occupation was spinning and weaving with the maidservants, the management of the entire household, and the education of the young children. There was not (as there was in Greece) a woman's apartment where she remained concealed from the eyes of all except other women and a few male relatives. She shared her husband's meals, sitting at table. She was forbidden to drink wine, however, which ancient Roman morals considered a misdeed punishable by death. She was called *domina*, 'mistress', by all the members of the household, including her husband. Her presence ensured a specially high standard of politeness in manners and conversation. In those early times she was not expected to make any effort to acquire culture, and her only intellectual stimulus came from her husband. Her education was chiefly directed to practical ends. If she left the house (which she could not do without her husband's knowledge and without a companion) she wore the long *stola matronalis*, matron's dress. Still, she could appear at the theatre, at a lawcourt, or at a religious ceremony; and everyone had to make way for her in the street. It was absolutely forbidden to touch or molest her.

On the whole, the picture of Roman family life which Plutarch gives in his life of the elder Cato is scarcely too idealistic. He says (20): 'Cato married a wife with more nobility than wealth; he thought that both nobly born women and rich women were proud and arrogant, but noble women had more shame of base conduct and suffered their husbands to lead them more easily towards virtuous actions. He used to say that a man who struck his wife or his son was laying violent hands on what was most sacred. In his eyes it was more creditable to be a good husband than a great statesman; and he admired the ancient Socrates for nothing but for behaving decently and kindly to a scolding wife and crazy children. When his son was born he held no business (except the business of the state) so important as to watch his wife bathing and dressing the baby. She suckled it herself, and she often put the slaves'

children to her breast also, so that when they sucked the
same milk they would have a natural affection for her son.'
Cato's behaviour after his first wife died was very significant. Plutarch says (24): 'Cato had such a sound and strong
constitution that he was able to have intercourse with
women even when he was old and to marry a wife much
younger than himself. This was the cause of his marriage.
After the death of his wife, he married his son to the
daughter of Paulus Aemilius, Scipio's sister; he himself
used to make love to a young girl who came to his house in
secret. But the house was small and there was a daughter-
in-law in it, so that the affair became known: once the
young woman seemed to pass through it a little too boldly
and Cato's son looked bitterly at her and turned away in
silence. The old man saw this and understood that his conduct was disliked. He did not find any fault or make a
complaint, but went down as usual to the market-place with
his friends. Now, a man called Salonius, who had been a
clerk under him, met him and joined his retinue. Cato addressed him aloud, asking if he had married off his daughter
yet. The man replied that he would not do so without con-
sulting Cato. "Well," said Cato, "I have found you a suitable husband for her, unless she objects to his age. He has
no other faults, but he is very old." Salonius urged him to
attend to the business and to marry the girl to the man of
his preference, because she was Cato's dependant and
stood in need of his patronage. Cato then told him without
prevarication that he was asking the girl in marriage for
himself. Naturally, the man was at first astonished by this,
because he thought Cato was beyond the marrying age, and
thought he himself was beneath an alliance with a man who
had been consul and celebrated a triumph. But when he
saw that Cato was in earnest he accepted the offer with
pleasure, and they both went down to the market-place
and completed the bargain. . . . From this marriage he had
a son, who had the by-name Saloninus from his mother.'

Another picture of family life in the good old times appears in Tacitus's *Dialogue on Oratory* (28): 'In former
times every man's son was born of a chaste mother and
brought up, not in the room of a hired nurse, but in the
arms and on the breast of his mother. It was the greatest

honour for her to have charge of her household and to
live for her children. Also, an elderly relative was chosen,
a woman of tried and tested virtue to whom all the children
of one family could be entrusted. Before her nothing could
be said which was disgraceful, nothing could be done which
was dishonourable. And not only the education and work
of the children, but their games and hours of amusement
were superintended by her with piety and modesty. In this
way we have heard that Cornelia, the mother of the
Gracchi, Aurelia, the mother of Caesar, and Atia, the
mother of Augustus, took charge of their sons' education
and brought them up to be great men in the state.'

These accounts, especially Plutarch's, show us this at
least – what we call love had hardly any part in these marriages. In addition, the husband and wife were very often
betrothed to each other by their parents in early youth,
for one motive or another; the reason was usually an
economic one. The earliest age at which a man could marry
was 15 to 16; a woman could marry when she was 12.
Tacitus married a girl of 13 when he was in his middle
twenties. If real love developed between husband and wife
in these conditions it was generally a fortunate accident
rather than the general rule. Cato the elder is said to have
made the remark: 'All nations rule their wives, we rule all
nations, but our wives rule us.' Tacitus himself says somewhere: 'The true Roman married without love and loved
without refinement or reverence.' Above all, the Romans
married to have children to succeed them – that was their
free and natural way of regarding sexual matters.

Still, the wife in a Roman household did not occupy a
humble position. Far from it. She was not bound to her
husband by any sentimental affection; for such a thing did
not lie within the Roman character, especially in the 'best'
times, that is in the period of the old Republic. But she
shared the direction of the large household with her husband for better or worse. That filled her life, though it
may seem to have been a prosaic life. Columella describes
it vividly in these words (xii, *praef.*): 'Among the Greeks,
and later among the Romans till our fathers' time, the care
of the household was the duty of the wife, while the father
came to his home as if to a place of recreation from the

anxieties of the forum. The home was ruled by dignity and respect, with harmony and diligence; the wife was filled with the noblest emulation in her efforts to complete the husband's work through her own industry. There was no discord in the house, and nothing was claimed by husband or wife as a particular right: both worked hand in hand.'

In this connection we must also speak of motherhood in the life of a Roman woman. We know already of Coriolanus' mother, Veturia, that woman of the legendary past before whose pride even her son's prowess dwindles to nothing. Livy (ii, 40) writes: 'Then the married women came in crowds to Veturia, Coriolanus' mother, and Volumnia, his wife. It is uncertain whether this was a plan of the government or an effect of womanish terror; certainly they induced Veturia (who was advanced in years) and Volumnia, taking the two little sons she had borne to Coriolanus, to go with them to the enemy's camp – so that the women might by their entreaties and tears defend the city, since the men had been unable to defend it by force of arms. When they reached the camp, Coriolanus was told that a huge procession of women had come: he had not been affected by the majesty of the state, personified in the envoys, nor by the religious awe which priests cast on eyes and heart – and he was much more firm to resist the tears of women. Then one of his friends recognized Veturia by her heavy mourning, standing between her daughter-in-law and her grandchildren; he said "Unless my eyes deceive me, your mother, your wife, and your children are there before us". Coriolanus, almost demented, leapt from his chair and attempted to embrace his mother. But she, turning from prayers to anger, said: "Tell me, before I accept your embrace, whether I have come here to see my son or an enemy, whether I am your prisoner or your mother in this camp. Have my long life and my unhappy old age brought me to this – that I should see you an exile and then an enemy of the state? Had you the heart to ravage this land which gave you birth and fostered you? Although you came to it with threats of war in your heart, did your anger not slacken as you crossed its frontiers? When you came in sight of Rome did you not think 'Within those walls are my home and my household goods, my mother, my wife, and my children?' If I had never been a mother, Rome would not now be suffering the attack of an enemy; if I had no son, I should have died a free woman in a free country. But now nothing can happen which brings more unhappiness to me than disgrace to you; though I am heavily burdened with grief, I shall not bear my burden long. You must think of your children here, for if you go on in your way they are doomed either to an early death or a long slavery." His wife and children embraced him; the whole crowd of women burst out weeping and lamenting their fate and their country's doom; and at last his will broke down. He embraced his dear ones and sent them back to Rome, and then moved his camp away from the city.'

Veturia is a legendary figure; but Cornelia, the famous mother of the ill-fated Gracchi, stands in the full light of history. As Birt says, she is 'the Niobe of Rome"; she lost her other sons by early death, and then saw the two remaining sons, the reformers, perish in furious street-fighting in the city of Rome. A tragic mother of a later age is Agrippina, Nero's mother, whom we shall discuss in a later chapter.

But, besides these great historical figures, we can see the simple perfection of Roman motherhood and wifehood in many touching and eloquent funeral inscriptions. It is very significant that most of them commemorate women, not of high rank, but from the middle and lower classes of society. We cannot, of course, quote them all: Friedländer's great *History of Roman Morals* includes a number of them (8th ed., 1910; vol. i, pp. 521 ff.). But we shall reproduce a few characteristic examples. A tombstone of the Republican period reads: 'Short is my say, wanderer: stop and read it through. This poor stone covers a beautiful woman. Her parents called her Claudia. She loved her own husband unchangingly. She bore two sons. One she left behind on earth, the other she buried in the earth's bosom. She spoke kindly and walked nobly, cared for her house and her spinning. I have finished: go.' Here is another, from Imperial times: '. . . She was the guardian spirit of my house, she was my hope and my only love. What I wished she also wished, what I shunned she shunned also. None of her inmost thoughts was ever hidden from me. She lacked no diligence in spinning wool, she was thrifty, but she was generous in love to her husband. She tasted neither food nor drink without me. Good was her counsel, quick her mind, noble her repute.' A sarcophagus bears these words:

> Here lies Amymone, the wife of Marcus:
> good she was, and lovely, and industrious,
> a careful housewife, too, thrifty and neat,
> chaste, honourable, pious, and discreet.

These few examples are scarcely enough to typify the mass of such inscriptions.

But the most magnificent of all memorials to Roman women is the 'Queen of Elegies', which Propertius wrote for Cornelia, the wife of L. Aemilius Paullus Lepidus. (This is the last elegy of Book IV.) After her pitifully early death, the poet imagines her to address the elegy to those who are mourning her, as a consolation for their grief. No work in the whole range of Roman literature gives us a lovelier and simpler picture of the heights to which marriage could rise in Rome. We shall end our discussion of marriage in early Rome by quoting this noble and profoundly human work.

> Cease, Paullus, to oppress my grave with weeping:
>   no prayers will unlock the gates of night;
> when once the dead enter the nether kingdom
>   inexorable steel bars their return.
> The dark divinities may hear your prayers;
>   your tears break hopelessly on the deaf shore.
> Vows move heaven's will; when Charon has his obol,
>   the sombre portals lock upon the tomb.
> Thus mourned the gloomy horns, when the hateful torches
>   brought me the fire that lit me to the grave.
> My Paullus could not save me, nor the triumphs
>   of the great dead, nor the pledges of my name.
> The Fates remained implacable and cruel,
>   and I am but three fingers' weight of ash.
>
> Night of the damned, dolorous swamps and shallows,
>   and you, river that ravels up my feet,
> I come here early, but I come here guiltless:
>   Pluto, give kindly verdict on my shade,
> or if King Aeacus sits to give justice,
>   let him draw lots, pass sentence on my soul;
> and let his brothers listen, while the Furies
>   glare on the crowd that fills the dismal court.
> Sisyphus, rest; and pause, whirling Ixion;
>   and Tantalus, snatch your deceitful draught;

let Cerberus attack no trembling phantoms,
   his chain shall hang in quiet from the bar.
Hear my defence. If I am false, my shoulders
   shall bear the Danaids' eternal urn.

If ancient victories mean present glory,
   Africa's kingdoms tell of my grandsire.
My mother's sires were the superb Libones.
   Both houses stand secure in old renown.
Now when I put off childish things for marriage,
   and the strange wedding-ribbon bound my hair,
your home I entered, Paullus – soon to leave it:
   this stone proclaims that I was one man's bride.
Witness, ye noble ashes loved by Romans,
   upon whose tombs lies conquered Africa . . .
that not for me the censor paused, that never
   misdeed of mine brought my own home to blush.
Cornelia was no shame to those old victors –
   she set a pattern in a noble house.
This was no change: my lifetime all was spotless,
   pure from the bridal to the funeral torch.
My nature gave me laws from the blood within me –
   terror of justice could not better them.

Let any grave assembly judge my pleading:
   no woman is disgraced who seconds me –
not you, whose virtue moved the slow Cybele,
   Claudia, rare servant of the tower-crowned Queen,
nor you, whose linen raiment could rekindle
   the sacred flame which failed on Vesta's hearth.
Scribonia dear, my mother, have I shamed you?
   what could you bid me change, except my fate?
Your tears and Rome's laments – these are my praises,
   and Caesar's grief has sanctified my bones
sad that a sister worthy of his daughter
   should die, the god was human, and shed tears.
Still, I have earned the mother's dress of honour –
   I was not reft away from a barren home.
You, Lepidus, you, Phallus, are my comforts,
   it was your love that closed my dying eyes.
And I have seen my brother twice ennobled:
   when he was consul, I his sister died.
Daughter, in you the censorship is imaged:
   go, copy me, cleave to one husband's love.
Maintain our stock: I go to death's dark river
   willingly, if my children swell my fame.
That is a woman's triumph, her last guerdon,
   that frank tongues honour her and bless her tomb.
Paullus, keep safe the pledges I have borne you –
   among my ashes, love for them lives on –
and fill a mother's place for them: my loved ones
   must all be cherished next your very heart;

kissing them when they weep, add my caresses;
    now all our household rests upon your arms.
And if you grieve, let them not see you grieving;
    when they approach, receive them with dry eyes.
Enough for you to wear the nights with sorrow,
    to dream of phantoms with Cornelia's face;
and, when you talk in secret to my image,
    speak every word as if I might reply.
But if another marriage-bed should enter
    and bring a wary stepdame to our home,
my children, praise the marriage and endure it –
    your kindly ways will take her prisoner.
Praise me not overmuch: if you compare us,
    your thoughtless words will turn to her offence.
If he abides, contented with my phantom,
    and if my ashes can fulfil his love,
attend his older years in the close future,
    admit no troubles to his widowed heart:
the years bereft from me add to your lifetime,
    let him age happily among my sons.

Yes, it is well: I never mourned my children,
    they stood united at my funeral pyre.
My plea is spoken. Friends, arise, and mourn me,
    while grateful earth rewards my life above.
Virtue can win to heaven: may I be worthy
    to mount in death among my honoured sires.

2. *Divorce, Adultery, Celibacy, Concubinage*

A marriage concluded by *confarreatio* could not, in early
Rome, be dissolved. But in early Rome *confarreatio* was
the only recognized form of marriage. It follows that
divorce was unknown at that period. Dionysius says (ii, 25):
'Authorities are agreed that no marriage was dissolved at
Rome for the space of five hundred and twenty years. But
in the 137th Olympiad, in the consulship of M. Pomponius
and C. Papirius, one Spurius Carvilius (a man of some
distinction) is said to have separated from his wife, being
the first who did so. He was obliged by the censors to swear
that he could not live with his wife for the purpose of having children, since she was barren – but for the divorce
(although it was necessary) he was always hated by the
commons.' Dionysius tells us also that if the wife committed adultery or drank wine, she was punished with death
by a family council attended by the husband. But according to Plutarch (*Romulus*, 22): 'Romulus made several laws

– one a severe one which forbids a wife to leave her husband, but allows a husband to divorce his wife for poisoning her children, for counterfeiting his keys, and for adultery.'
It is certainly true that (since Rome was in those early days a state ruled by men for men) wives could not divorce their husbands, but husbands could divorce their wives, chiefly for adultery.

In the legislation of the Twelve Tables, dissolution of marriage occurs in the form of a repudiation of the wife by the husband; and according to Valerius Maximus (ii, 9, 2) such a dissolution occurred in 306 B.C. The following were the misdeeds which gave a husband the right to divorce his wife: adultery, drinking wine, and a *peruerse taetreque factum* (perverse and disgusting conduct) which cannot be described more particularly. Much was left to the husband's discretion; but, as the above-mentioned passage in Valerius Maximus shows, he was obliged to summon a council of his family or friends before repudiating his wife. Here is Gellius's comment on the first divorce (iv, 3): 'Tradition says that for about five hundred years after the foundation of Rome there was no form of legal process concerning marriage nor any stipulation contemplating divorce, either in Rome or in Latium – there was no call for such a thing, since no marriages were dissolved in that period. Servius Sulpicius writes in his book on Dowries that the first legal injunctions dealing with marriage had to be made when Spurius Carvilius (also called Ruga), who was a distinguished man, divorced his wife because she was physically unable to bear children.' This account shows, then, that the first dissolution of marriage in Rome was occasioned by the wife's barrenness. According to Becker-Marquardt, it was not the first; but it was the first which did not involve the disgrace and condemnation of the wife. In this case the wife would keep her dowry, while the husband would retain it after the divorce if she had been guilty of misconduct. (The juristic formula for repudiation without misconduct was *tuas res tibi habeto*: 'keep your property for yourself'.)

All these accounts seem to agree in making it certain that in early Rome marriages were very seldom dissolved. But can we infer from that to a high degree of morality in

married life? That is another question. We must not forget
that the husband could commit no action which the law
recognized as a breach of his marriage-tie; he had an entirely free hand. And the liberty of wives was so restricted
that they seldom had the opportunity to commit misconduct – especially since they were faced with terrifying punishments if they were convicted. Her punishment was not
only to be driven with disgrace and infamy from the home
in which she had lived, as well as that, she could be put to
death by the family council in co-operation with the husband.

In those early times there were no statutory penalties for
adultery – probably because the husband took the matter
into his own hands, or called on the family council to inflict
the punishment. For example, Valerius Maximus (vi, 1, 13)
mentions several cases in which a detected adulterer was
flogged, or castrated, or handed over as *familiae stupran-
dus* – which last penalty meant that the servants and re-
tainers of the injured husband inflicted sexual dishonour
on the adulterer. Accordingly, a husband who committed
adultery with a married woman was liable to severe punishment; but not if he made love to slaves or prostitutes,
although we should consider that also to be adultery. For
instance, Valerius Maximus (vi, 7, 1) tells this story of the
elder Scipio Africanus: 'Tertia Aemilia, his wife . . . was so
kind and patient that when she knew one of her maids
pleased him she pretended to notice nothing, in order that
she should not cast guilt on Africanus, the conqueror of
the world.' And in Plautus (*Men.,* 787 ff.) a father meets his
daughter's complaints thus:

> How often I've told you to honour your husband,
> not to watch what he does, where he goes, what he thinks of?

When she complains further of his fickleness, he replies:

> And wisely!
> Since you watch him so closely, I'll help his lovemaking.

And later he adds:

> He keeps you well jewelled and dressed, and he gives you
> your food and your maids. Better come to your senses!

Cato, in concise and prosaic language, describes the contrasting situations of an adulterous wife and an adulterous
husband (*ap.* Gell., x, 23): 'If you take your wife in adultery

you may freely kill her without a trial. But if you commit
adultery, or if another commits adultery with you, she has
no right to raise a finger against you.' Yet if a husband committed adultery with a slave, a determined wife knew what
to do. That is shown by passages like Plautus, *Men*., 559 ff.,
Asin., v, 2, and Juvenal, ii, 57; Juvenal speaks of the 'uncouth concubine' who is 'sitting in the stocks' and working
at the bidding of the wife.

Early Christianity was severely idealistic in its attitude
to sexual relationships. This sentence was at least theoretically true: 'Among us, what is forbidden to women is
equally forbidden to men' (Hieron. *epist*., vol. i, p. 72). On
the other hand, Augustine is forced to make this admission: 'Banish prostitutes from society and you reduce
society to chaos through unsatisfied lust' (*de Ord*., ii, 12).

We have seen, then, that in early Rome there was no
statutory punishment for adultery, whether committed by
the wife or by the husband. That is corroborated by Cato's
remark (*ap*. *Quint*., v, ii, 39) that every adulteress was
a poisoner. Since there was no law aimed directly at adultery, the crime was attacked in this curious indirect way.
The first legal penalties for adultery occur in Augustus's
moral reforms, of which we shall speak later. The penalties
were banishment and loss of certain property rights; corporal punishment could be inflicted on members of the
lower classes. In later times, as the tendency was, these
penalties were increased. Constantius laid down that adultery should be punished by burning alive or drowning in a
sack, and Justinian compelled adulterous women to be shut
up in convents. These further developments can be described in Mommsen's words as 'pious savagery'.

In the later Republic, divorce became easier and more
general as the status of women improved. An important
point was that a marriage without *manus* could be announced simply as an agreement between two parties. This,
of course, led to many frivolous results. Valerius Maximus
(vi, 3, 12) speaks of a marriage which was dissolved because
the wife had visited the games without her husband's knowledge. And Cicero in one of his letters* relates that a wife

---

* The letter was written by Caelius, but is printed (with his others) in
Cicero's works, *Ad fam*., viii, 7. *Translators' note*.

obtained a quick divorce before her husband came home from the provinces, simply because she had made the acquaintance of another man whom she wanted to marry. There is no reason to be surprised when we hear that Sulla was married five times, Pompeius five times, and Ovid three times. We cannot say, then, that easy divorce came in only with the Empire. Still, marriage and divorce were then regarded with ever increasing frivolity. Seneca writes (*De ben.*, iii, 16, 2): 'Surely no woman will blush to be divorced now that some distinguished and noble ladies count the years not by the consuls but by their own marriages, and divorce in order to be married, marry in order to be divorced!' Of course, such practices would not escape the lash of Juvenal's bitterly exaggerated satire. He writes (vi, 142 ff., and 224 ff.):

> Why does Sertorius dote on Bibula?
> He dotes – look close – on the face, not on the wife.
> Give it three wrinkles, parch and pouch the skin,
> dim the bright teeth, and make those big eyes smaller –
> 'Pack up your traps!' his message runs, 'and go!
> You bore me, and you sniff too often. Go
> at once! I'll get a wife without catarrh.'

And thus of the wife, who gets rid of her husbands just as easily:

> She queens it there. But soon she leaves her empire,
> changes her house, wears out the bridal veil, and
> flies back again to the bed she left, still warm.
> The gates are garlanded – she leaves them, leaves
> the awnings up, the bouquets yet unwithered.
> Her score is mounting: she has had eight husbands
> in five short winters – put that on her tombstone!

Since there is no doubt that the increasing frequency of divorce had some far deeper cause than the 'degeneracy of the age', we shall leave the matter here, and discuss it later, in the section dealing with the emancipation of Roman women.

But it would be very unfair to blame only the women for this so-called decline in marriage. We know that even in early times the men had no great enthusiasm for the responsibilities of fatherhood. If this were not so, we could not understand why a man who obstinately refused to marry should be punished by the censors with the infliction of certain pecuniary disadvantages. Cicero says (*De leg.*, iii): 'The censors are to prevent celibacy.' According to Valerius Maximus (ii, 9, 1) there was a censorial decree against it as early as 403 B.C. Livy (*epit.*, lix) and Gellius (i, 6) tell us that in 131 B.C. the censor Metellus made a famous speech on this matter; it contains some very significant words, which throw a lurid light on the Roman conception of marriage: 'If we could live without wives we should not have all this trouble. Since nature has brought it about that we can neither live with them in peace nor without them at all, we must ensure eternal benefit rather than temporary pleasure.' The most interesting thing about this remark is that the speaker was happily married, and had four sons, two daughters, and eleven grandchildren; he spoke from experience. From Gellius (i, 6, 6) we know the official point of view: 'The state cannot be safe unless marriages are frequent.'

After the war with Hannibal, the poorer classes increased in numbers. Writers now spoke frankly about the flight from marriage. Plutarch writes (*De amore prolis*, 497e): 'The poor do not rear their children, because they are afraid that if they are badly fed and educated they will grow up to be slavish and boorish and to lack all the graces.' Besides that, there was the consideration stated thus by Propertius (ii, 7, 13):

> How can I furnish boys for family triumphs?
> My blood will never breed a soldier son.

Seneca adds another discouragement (*fr.*, xiii, 58): 'The most fatuous thing in the world is to marry to have children so that our name is not lost, or so that we have support in our old age, or certain inheritors.' In the end even the state lost its strongest motive for encouraging marriage; it ceased to need a constant supply of young soldiers for its interminable wars. In the long peace of the first centuries of our era Rome demanded no such quantities of spear-fodder to maintain its position or extend its power. At that time it was much easier to live like the man whom Pliny describes (*ep.*, iii, 14) – he was an ex-praetor who lived in his villa with some concubines. (He was, of course, unmarried.)

And, finally, if a man had leanings to philosophy, a family was nothing but a burden to him. Cicero said so (*ap.* Sen. *fr.* xiii, 61): 'Cicero was asked by Hirtius if he would marry Hirtius's sister now that he was separated from Terentia; he replied that he would never marry again, for he could not cope with philosophy and a wife at the same time.' And Cicero says in his *Paradoxa*: 'Is he free who is subject to a woman? who is ruled and regulated by her, who is told to do or not to do whatever she wishes?'

We see, then, that as the individual was gradually freed from the bonds of traditional morality and the demands of the community, his reasons for not marrying increased. This repeats itself throughout history.

Naturally, the state sometimes endeavoured to check this development through legislation; its existence was at stake. Augustus was the first to make the endeavour. His moral ordinances were bold and radical, but had little effect, for state legislation has little effect in such matters. Mommsen describes them in remarkable language: they were, he says, 'one of the most impressive and long-lasting innovations in penal law which is known to history'. They were known as the *Juliae rogationes*, and included the *lex sumptuaria,* the *lex Julia de adulteriis et de pudicitia, the lex Julia de maritandis ordinibus*, and the *lex Papia Poppaea* – passed between 18 B.C. and A.D. 9. We may sum up their purpose in the words of Becker-Marquardt: 'to impose property disqualifications for celibacy on men between twenty and sixty and on women between twenty and fifty and for child-lessness on men over twenty-five and women over twenty; to confer various rights and privileges as encouragements on parents of three or more children; to bring about suit-able marriages between people of senatorial families; and to regulate divorce by certain rules and ordinances.'

Augustus rigidly enforced these laws. What effect did they produce? Let us hear the evidence of a few of his contemporaries. Suetonius (*Aug.*, 34), writing of the law to encourage marriage within the various social classes, says: 'He had emended this law far more severely than the others, but so many protested that he could not carry it through, unless when he abolished or relaxed some of the penalties granted three years' general immunity and increased the rewards. But even so, once at a public show the knights shouted for its total abolition: Augustus called the children of Germanicus to him and took them into his own embrace and gave them to their father's arms, signifying by gesture and look that the grumblers should not be reluctant to follow the example of the young Germanicus.' We read in Cassius Dio (54, 16): 'Loud complaints were raised in the senate about the disorderly conduct of the women and young men; to that conduct they attributed the prevailing reluctance to marry, and they tried to induce Augustus to correct it by personal abuse, hinting at his many love affairs. His first reply was that the essential points had already been settled, and that it was impossible to regulate everything in that way. Then when they still held him to it he said: "You yourselves ought to give orders and directions to your wives as you wish; I certainly do." When he said this they pressed him all the more, and demanded to know what the directions were which he said he gave Livia. So he was compelled to make a few remarks on women's dress and finery and public appearances and modest conduct – not caring that his actions did not agree with his words.' In another passage Cassius Dio tells us that the emperor made a very full and detailed speech in defence of his legislation. Although the oration as given by Dio may not be authentic in every word, it contains the fundamental ideals and purposes of the Julian legislation: we shall therefore quote a few extracts from it (Cassius Dio, 56, 1 ff.): 'During the triumphal games the knights insisted vehemently that he should repeal the law about celibacy and childlessness. Augustus therefore assembled in different parts of the forum those knights who were unmarried and those who were married, including those who had children. When he saw that the married men were much fewer than the others, he was grieved and addressed them something after this fashion:

' "... Rome was at first a mere handful of men; but when we bethought us of marriage and had children we came to excel the whole world not only in strength but also in numbers. We must remember this, and console our mortality by handing on our stock like a torch to a never-ending line of successors – so that we may help one another to

change our mortality (the one side of our nature which
makes us less happy than the gods) to eternal life. It was
for this end above all that our Creator, the first and greatest
of the gods, divided the human race into two sexes, male
and female, and instilled into both of them love and the
desire for sexual intercourse, and made their association
fruitful – in order that new generations might make even
mortal life immortal. ... Surely there is no greater blessing
than a good wife who orders your house, watches over
your possessions, rears your children, adds happiness to
your days of health and tends you when you are ill, shares
your good fortune and consoles you in trouble, controls
the wild passion of your youth and softens the harshness of
old age. ... These are some of the private advantages enjoyed by those who marry and have children. As for the
state – for whose cause we ought to do many things against
our inclination – without doubt it is honourable and necessary (if cities and peoples are to exist and if you are to rule
the others and the whole world is to obey you) that a large
population should in peace time till the soil and sail the
seas and practise arts and apply themselves to handicrafts,
and in war defend their possessions with all the more zeal
because of their families and raise up others to replace
the slain. ..."

'He now addressed the unmarried men as follows:

' "What am I to call you? Men? You have not yet
proved yourselves to be men. Citizens? As far as you are
concerned the city is perishing. Romans? You are doing
your best to destroy the very name. ... A city is men and
women, not buildings and colonnades and empty market-
places. Consider the righteous anger which would seize
great Romulus our founder if he compared the time and
circumstances when he was born with your refusal to beget
children even in lawful marriage. ... Those old Romans
begot them even on foreign women, but you disdain to
make Roman women the mothers of your children. ...
You are not such recluses that you live without women:
not one of you eats or sleeps alone. All you wish is to have
liberty for sensuality and excess. ..." '

That was the anti-Malthusian ideal which lay behind
Augustus's legislation. But it found no enthusiastic sup-

porters; all classes of society had long been endeavouring to increase their personal freedom. The measures were bound to miscarry – especially since everyone knew that the princeps himself had till then done little to live up to an austere moral code. The results were, in sum, the introduction of a hitherto unheard-of police espionage into the most intimate details of private life – and a number of marriages contracted from purely mercenary motives. Seneca says: 'What shall I say of the men of whom many married and took the name of husband in order to make fun of the laws against the unmarried state?' And according to *Dig.*, xlviii, 5, 8, husbands must often have benefited by the adultery of their wives, and actually been their procurers. Tacitus writes (*Ann.*, iii, 25): 'More and more citizens came into danger, since every household was shaken by the inferences made by spies; people now suffered by the laws as they had once suffered by their own crimes.' In addition, a law was passed which we shall discuss elsewhere – that no woman whose grandfather, father, or husband was a knight should sell herself for money. So small was the real effect of Augustus's legislation.

One of the principal facts which kept it from real achievement was the circumstance that the law applied only to freeborn citizens. It did not, therefore, cover slaves and the various classes of women who did sell themselves. This allowed the men to find sexual satisfaction outside marriage quite as freely as before. Also the freedom of prostitutes must have had great attractions for the so-called respectable women, who now fell under legal restrictions, so that many of them assumed the prostitute's dress in order to live undisturbed by the law. (Cf. *Dig.*, xlvii, 10, 15, 15).

We may conclude our discussion of Augustus's legislation by noticing that it gave the first legal recognition to concubinage, that is, to cohabitation without the status of husband and wife. The code had had, as one of its chief aims, the encouragement of suitable marriages among the senatorial families. It was necessary that the law should take into account marital relationships which were not 'suitable' – a senator, for example, might desire to marry a freedwoman or a former prostitute, or have lived with her as husband and wife. All such cases were legally recognized

as concubinage. A man could live in concubinage with the
woman of his choice instead of taking her to wife; but he
was compelled to give notice of this to the authorities. This
type of cohabitation was externally in no way different
from marriage, and its practical results were purely legal;
the children were not legitimate, and could not make the
claims of legitimate children on their father. Therefore,
men of high rank often lived with women in concubinage
after the death of their first wife in order not to prejudice
the claims of the children they had had by her. For instance, the emperors Vespasian, Antoninus Pius, and Marcus Aurelius lived in this way. The principle of monogamy
was not affected by concubinage, since (Paulus, ii, 29, 1) it
was impossible to have a wife and a concubine at once.
Accordingly, the title of concubine was not derogatory,
and it appears on tombstones.

3. The Emancipation of Roman Women

As we have often said, the early Roman republic was, as
far as antiquity allows us to see, a masculine state, a state
run by men for men. We may refer here to the important
propositions established by Dr. M. Vaerting, in his book
*The Character of Women in a Masculine State and the
Character of Men in a Feminine State* (Karlsruhe, 1921).
When he says (p. 35) that the 'standards of social conduct
in a masculine state are inverted in a feminine state', his
remark can be applied without reservation to early Rome.
The ruling sex – men – had all property rights; at marriage
the wife brought a dowry to her husband; the man had the
'tendency to assign to the subordinate sex, woman, the
house and the home as her own province'. But Dr. Vaerting
establishes many other peculiar marks of a masculine state,
in connection with married life; and they may all be applied to early Rome – especially the regulations on feminine chastity, the 'double standard of morality'.

Now Vaerting lays down that if one sex frees itself in a
state dominated by the other sex, 'simultaneously with the
loss of power by the ruling sex, the peculiar functions and
natures of the sexes also change'. That is to say, the man
has hitherto appeared only as a stern lord and master, as a

rough soldier, and as a powerful and energetic statesman. He now becomes softer and more human – although softness and humanity would once have been regarded as unmanly. The woman has hitherto been nothing but a chaste and discreet housewife and mother. She now shows herself as an independent personality; she disregards the ties which once bound her, vindicates her own right to happiness and pursues it with all her might. When she does, her actions are regarded as degeneracy by those who know only the masculine state and its ideology.

That is exactly the change which occurred in the history of Rome. And it prompts us to ask why the old republic, which was dominated by men, should have evolved into the state which we see fully developed under the emperors.

Vaerting believes that the truth lies here: 'As a general rule, the pressure of the ruling sex produces complete dominance and complete subordination as its first effect. This dominance and subordination leads the rulers to increase the pressure – until the moment when it becomes so strong that it arouses opposition instead of creating obedience.' In this way, he thinks, the course of history is an oscillation between the predominance of men and the predominance of women.

These opinions are doubtless attractive. But in ancient Rome the case was different. The old republican institution of the family gradually altered its nature; but in our belief the cause of that alteration was purely economic. We shall expound our reasons.

It can hardly be an accident that all ancient writers mark the end of the second Punic war as the turning-point of morality and social tradition – and so as the beginning of the emancipation of Roman women. That was the period when Rome ceased to be a state of yeomen-farmers. A well-known passage of Appian describes the beginning of that ominous change (*Bell. Civ.*, i, 7): 'As the Romans gradually conquered Italy, they took portions of the conquered territories and built cities on them, or sent their own citizens to colonize previously existing cities. These settlements served to garrison the conquered countries. They took the cultivated land which they had won, and immediately divided it up among their settlers, either gratis or for purchase-money, or for rent. But they did not take time to draw lots for the great areas of land which were uncultivated because of the war; they made public proclamation that anyone who wished might cultivate it, the rent being a yearly percentage of the crop – 10 per cent of the seed crops and 20 per cent of the fruit. Those who engaged in stock-rearing were obliged to pay a proportionate rent for large and small stock. This they did in order to help the spread of the Italian population; they saw that the Italians were a hard-working race, and wished to have them as friends and allies.

'But the result was the opposite of their intentions. The rich seized most of the unoccupied land. Circumstances made them confident that no one would deprive them of it, and so they acquired the land surrounding their own, and all the small farms owned by poor men, partly by purchase and partly by force, until they were farming wide plains instead of estates. They used slaves to till the land and raise the stock, so that they should not be mobilized to serve in war, not being of free birth; also, the possession of slaves brought great profit to their owners, since slaves, being immune from war-service, multiplied with impunity.

'Consequently, the ruling class accumulated all the wealth for themselves, and the slave-population filled the country, while the real Italian population decreased terribly, worn out by poverty, taxation, and military service. And when there was a respite from these things they found themselves unemployed, because the land was owned by rich men who used slaves instead of freemen on their farms.'

Whatever the origin of this passage may be, it shows the necessary result of the military expansion of Rome. The real representatives and furtherers of that policy – the old Roman families – were gradually eliminated, and replaced by slaves; and such small farmers as survived the numerous wars sank to the position of an unemployed proletariat in the cities.

And the great conquests in the West and the East had other results, which are described by other authors. Farmers found it unprofitable to grow grain in Italy since the Roman market was flooded with masses of imported grain which forced down the price (Liv., xxx, 26). And the victorious armies had brought home (especially from the East) enormous wealth and luxuries. Livy writes as follows (xxxix, 6): 'The beginnings of foreign luxury were brought to Rome by the army from Asia in 186 B.C. They were the first to import couches of bronze, costly draperies, tapestries, and other woven things, as well as one-legged tables and sideboards, which were then considered costly articles of furniture. At that time banquets were first graced by their additions of girls to play the lyre and the harp, and other entertainments; and more care and expense were devoted to the banquets themselves. The price of cooks rose – although they had formerly been the cheapest and least regarded of slaves – and what had been a menial office was now regarded as an art.' Polybius corroborates this (xxxi, 25, as quoted by Athenaeus, 6, 274 f.): 'Cato gave vent in public to his displeasure that many people were introducing foreign luxury into Rome: they bought a keg of salt fish from the Black Sea for three hundred drachmae, and paid more for handsome slaves than for estates.' Again, we read in Velleius Paterculus (ii, 1) of a slightly later period: 'The elder Scipio prepared the way for Rome's power, the younger for Rome's luxury. When the fear of Carthage was removed and Rome's rival cleared from her path, the passage from virtue to vice was not a gradual process but a headlong rush. The old moral code was abandoned and a new one supplanted it. Rome gave herself up to sleep instead of watching, to pleasure instead of the use of weapons, to leisure instead of business. It was at that time that Scipio Nasica built the colonnades on the Capitol, Metellus those others we have described, and Cneius Octavius the handsomest of all in the Circus; and private luxury followed hard on public ostentation.'

If we examine all these accounts without prejudice we must come to this conclusion: what happened was the economic conversion of a small and limited state of simple farmers into a powerful oligarchy of prosperous but uneducated landowners, merchants, financiers, with a class of proletarians. It is easy to understand that in the course of this economic change there should have been civil disturbances and the usual battles between the classes; for the new wealth and luxury blinded men's moral perceptions,

and opened up unimagined possibilities for those who could
seize and retain power. The civil wars of Marius and Sulla,
of Pompey and Caesar, were bound to follow. Although
the two Gracchi made one more vain endeavour to set the
old Roman farmer-state on its feet, the contest in Sulla's
time was only a wrangle for power and the wealth of Rome.
Velleius writes (ii, 22): 'A new horror appeared in later
times. Greed was another reason for cruelty, and a man's
guilt was measured by his possessions – anyone who was
rich was a criminal, and paid the price of his own life and
safety; nothing was dishonourable if it was profitable.'

The old organization of the family, with all its restrictions on individual freedom through the predominating
patria potestas, was bound to break up – although it had
guaranteed a certain limited standard of manners and morals. No one can wonder at its dissolution; think of the
parallel instances of the boom in Germany after the
Franco-Prussian war, or even of the period after the Great
War. When an entire economic epoch is breaking up, it is
impossible for women not to change their nature and outlook; especially since new wealth and new opportunities
have a more powerful effect on the spirit of women than
on men. The average woman at that time in Rome saw new
and unprecedented possibilities of satisfying her innate
vanity, ambition, and sensuality. But women of deeper
natures welcomed the opportunity to acquire a new and
better education, to develop their talents for dancing,
music, singing, and poetry. There are some examples of this
in ancient literature. Sallust has left us a brilliant picture of
an emancipated woman of this kind (*Cat.*, 25). He says:
'Among the women who supported Catiline was Sempronia, who had often shown herself as brave as any man.
She was blessed by fortune in her rank, her beauty, her
marriage, and her children. She was learned in Greek and
Latin literature; she played the harp and danced with more
grace than an honest woman should; she had many other
accomplishments which pertain to a luxurious life. But she
valued her honour and her chastity least of all. It was difficult to decide whether she cared less for money or for
reputation. Her lust was so overpowering that she courted
men more often than she was courted by them. In the past

she had often committed perjury, misappropriated property entrusted to her, and been accessory to murder; she had sunk to terrible depths by her extravagance and poverty. Still, her talents were considerable. She could write verses, make jokes, and talk modestly, tenderly, or daringly; she was full of high spirits and very charming.' There is a certain partiality in Sallust's account of the lady; but we can see that Sempronia must have been an unusually cultured woman, far above the level of the average Roman matron. She was such a figure as we read of in the German romantic period. In fact, she had become conscious of her rights as a woman, and cared nothing for the prejudices of her honest but dull sisters. Naturally, such a woman sometimes acquires the reputation of immorality, extravagance, debauchery; it happens today. To judge her properly we must remember that she came from a distinguished family, and was the wife of the consul D. Junius Brutus, and mother of D. Junius Brutus Albinus, one of Caesar's murderers.

It is certainly wrong to hold that education and culture were responsible for making the serious matron of ancient times into a voluptuous and frivolous hetaira. That is proved, for example, by a charming passage in Pliny. He is praising his wife for her intellectual alertness (*Ep.*, iv, 19): 'Her mind is keen and her tastes simple. She loves me, which proves her chastity. Besides, she likes literature, to which she was led by her affection for me. She keeps my books, reads them, and even learns passages from them off by heart. She is painfully anxious when I am to conduct a case, and delighted when I have completed it. She appoints people to tell her what applause and shouts I have received, and what the verdict was. If I am reading my work in public she sits near by, behind a curtain, and drinks in the praise of my audience with expectant ears. She also sings my verses, and even sets them to music, taught not by a musician but by love, the best master.'

But the accusations of immorality against Roman women were of old standing. It is not by chance that one of the first complaints dates almost exactly to the period when the emancipation began. The elder Pliny (*N.H.*, xvii, 25[38]) tells us that the consul L. Piso Frugi lamented that chastity had disappeared in Rome. That was about the middle of

the second century B.C. And the oldest Roman satirist,
Lucilius (who lived in the same period), is said to 'have
blamed the excesses and vices of the rich' (*Schol.* Pers., 3,
1). Similar complaints continued for centuries. We could fill
books with them; a few characteristic examples will be enough.

Sallust (*Cat.*, 13) observes that after Sulla's time 'men
gave themselves to unnatural vice, and women publicly
sold their honour'. There is a famous jeremiad in Horace's
sixth Roman ode (iii, 6):

> Ages fertile in crime defiled
> first pure marriage, the home, the breed:
>   thence a deluge of sheer disaster
>   burst on the land and people.
> Each ripe maiden has learnt to love
> soft Greek dances, and knows the arts
>   taught by shame, and is early practiced
>   body and soul in lewd loves.
> then seeks younger adulterers,
> while her husband's at wine; she gives
>   any man the forbidden favours
>   hastily in the dark room,
> nay, she rises obediently
> (not unknown to her husband) when
>   pedlars call, or a Spanish sailor
>   purchases her dishonour.

Ovid says with shocking frankness (*Am.*, i, 8, 43): 'She's
chaste, who has no wooers.' And Propertius writes in the
same way (ii, 32, 41 ff.):

> But who will ask, in such a sink of lewdness,
>   'What makes her rich? who gave her wealth? and whence?'
> Ah, Rome, this age would rise and call you blessed
>   If only one woman transgressed the rule!
> Before my lady, Lesbia sinned, and boldly –
>   now surely imitation is less blame.
> In search of the old stock of noble peasants
>   an honest fool has lately come to town:
> but you could sooner dry the roaring ocean
>   and cull the stars from heaven with your hand
> than keep our women from their peccadilloes –
>   that was the rule in Saturn's golden age.
> But, while the world suffered Deucalion's deluge
>   and after he climbed his Mount Ararat,
> tell me, what husband had a chaste bedfellow!

It is interesting to see that Propertius does not believe
in the higher morality of ancient Rome. He says frankly
(ii, 6, 19):

> You made us guilty,
> you, Romulus, who suckled the harsh wolf.
> You taught your men to rape the Sabines freely:
> now love dares anything, and rules your Rome.

Under the emperors these complaints against women's immorality are redoubled. Seneca says (*Ad Helv.*, 16, 3): 'You have not joined the majority of women and yielded to the greatest evil of this age, unchastity.' Still, Seneca is too well-read not to know that 'it was the complaint of our ancestors, as it is ours, and will be that of posterity, that morality has changed, and wickedness rules, and mankind goes from bad to worse, and everything sacred is falling into disrepute. This one thing is and will ever be the same – changing its extent from time to time, like seawaves which the incoming tide drives on and the ebb keeps back and constrains. At one time adultery will be prevalent, and the ties of chastity will be broken; at another time there will be a rage for gluttony and the kitchen – the most disgraceful way of dissipating wealth. Then again come excesses of vanity where the adornment of the body displays the distortion of the soul. Again, misuse of freedom degenerates into arrogance and audacity, and finally into acts of horrid cruelty in private and public life, until the madness of civil war, when everything sacred and honourable is dishonoured. And times will come when immoderate drinking will be considered noble, and it will be a virtue to be able to hold one's liquor. Vices do not concentrate in one spot; they shift and change, they are in constant revolution, they fight and flee from one another. But we shall always be able to say the same thing of ourselves; we are, and we have been, sinful creatures – and (alas that I must add it!) we shall always be so' (*De ben.*, i, 10). He sums up his thought on this in Epistle 97: 'You are wrong, Lucilius, if you think that our age is peculiar for vice, luxury, desertion or moral standards, and all the other things which everyone imputes to his own time. These are the faults of mankind, not of any age. No time in history has been free from guilt.'

We must remember the words of this calm and dispassionate thinker, in order to view the complaints of Juvenal and the jests of Martial in their correct proportion. I am afraid that we have been too accustomed to listen to their glaring exaggerations rather than to the cool reflections of Seneca.

Tacitus, in his *Germania*, held up the pure and unde-generate morality of the Germans to the (so-called) de-praved manners of his contemporaries, for comparison and contrast (*Germ.*, 17–19). And he says elsewhere (*Ann.*, iii, 55): 'After murder had done its cruel work (in the civil wars of the Empire) and a distinguished name had meant death, the survivors turned to a wise life. At the same time crowds of men hitherto unknown were introduced into the senate from the Italian cities and even from the provinces. They brought with them the thrifty habits they had culti-vated at home; although most of them had made themselves rich in old age through good luck or diligence, their early outlook remained. But the emperor Vespasian was the chief apostle of a simpler way of living, he himself being a man who lived and behaved in the antique way. Hence came a general obedience to the emperor, and the passion to rival him was stronger than fear of the laws and punishment had been. But perhaps everything moves in a cycle, and morals revolve as the seasons of the year do; our ancestors were not superior in everything, and this age can boast of many achievements in art and life which our descendants well may copy. May we in Rome long strive to rival our ancestors in virtue.'

We can support these statements by many examples of truly heroic women from the times which are called de-generate; we must mention a few.

Velleius Paterculus (ii, 26) tells of a woman's fidelity in the time of Marius: 'The glory of a noble act must not be lost to Calpurnia, daughter of Bestia and wife of Antistius; when her husband's throat was cut she stabbed herself with the same sword.' Later, speaking of the period when Antonius was fighting Caesar's murderers and placing many of his personal enemies in the proscription-lists, he says (ii, 67): 'This we must point out – the men who were proscribed found their wives exceedingly faithful to them; their freedmen showed some loyalty, their slaves a little, their sons none at all.' The fact is confirmed and exempli-fied by a number of cases related by Appian (*Bell. Civ.*, iv, 36 ff.). He begins with the general remark: 'Here were seen

extraordinary examples of the love of wife for husband,'
and proceeds to numerous instances, of which we shall
quote only some of those in chapter 39 and 40. 'The wife of
Lentulus implored him to allow her to go into exile with
him, and watched him carefully in order to do so. But he
did not wish to expose her to the dangers he was running,
and secretly set out to Sicily. There he was appointed general by Pompey, and let his wife know that he was safe and
held a command. As soon as she knew where her husband
was she escaped from her mother (who was taking care of
her) and followed him with two servants. With these she
accomplished the journey, with much hardship and privation, as a slave-woman, and then sailed from Rhegium to
Messene in the evening. She easily found her husband's
tent; she found him not in his general's dress, but lying on
the ground with hair uncut and mourning dress, for the
yearning he had for his wife. The wife of Apuleius threatened that if he fled without her she would notify his enemies; he took her with him against his will, and he was
helped on his journey by the fact that he did not excite
suspicion – travelling as he was with his wives and slaves
and slave-women. The wife of Antius rolled him up in a
package of bedding, gave it to a firm of carriers and got him
from his house to the sea, where he sailed safely to Sicily.'

In later times we hear of wives who were no less loyal
than these – so much so that a condemnation of the whole
period is, to say the least, exaggerated. Tacitus writes
(*Ann.*, xv, 71): 'Priscus was accompanied into exile by his
wife, Artoria Flaccilla, and Gallus by his, Egnatia Maxi-
milla. Egnatia had once had great wealth, which was left
untouched at first, and later taken from her; both of which
facts increased her reputation.' The famous translator of
Tacitus, A. Stahr – one of the few scholars of an earlier
generation who did not take every word of Tacitus literally
– remarks on this passage: 'A community which valued
such qualities as much as they deserved cannot have been
altogether bad.' (This occurs towards the end of the reign
of Nero.) And, finally, the most famous of all these cases
of womanly virtue is the heroic courage of the elder and
younger Arrias. Here is Pliny's tale of the elder (*Ep.*, iii,
16): 'Her husband, Caecina Paetus, was ill, and so was her

son – both, it appeared, sick to death. Then her son died; he was a youth of amazing beauty and amazing purity; his parents loved him as much for his good qualities as for the fact that he was their son. Arria prepared the funeral and saw him to the grave without letting her husband know. In fact, whenever she entered his room she pretended that their son was alive and even that he was recovering; when he asked how the boy was she would say: "He slept well and he has taken some food with pleasure." Then, when the tears she was restraining rushed to her eyes and overcame her she went out, and gave herself up to her sorrow. When she had relieved her anguish she came back with dry eyes and a calm face, as if she had left her bereavement outside his room. But how marvellous her other action! – to draw the sword, to stab her breast, to pull the blade out, to offer it to her husband, to add the immortal and angelic words "Paetus, it gives no pain!" But as she did those things and uttered those words glory and immortality were before her eyes. It was greater to hide her tears without the reward of immortality, without the reward of glory, and to conceal her grief, and to act the mother though she was childless.' Tacitus speaks of her daughter thus (*Ann*., xvi, 34): 'Arria tried to share the death of her husband and follow the example of her mother Arria; but her husband bade her keep her life, and not to withdraw the only support their daughter would have when he was gone.'

As can be seen from these examples of 'good' and 'bad' morality in women, the emancipation of Roman women caused the development of very different types of character. This allows us to conclude that we cannot criticize that emancipation from an exclusively moral standpoint. We could, of course, see the whole development as nothing but the progressive sexual liberation of women; but the new freedom was not expressed in sexual life alone. It was principally an *economic* freedom which women then achieved.

Earlier in this book we have explained that in the old republic women were economically dependent on men. Originally, marriages ended in *manus*, which, as we saw, meant complete domination by the husband. As the old type of marriage, with its predominance of the husband, gradually changed into free marriage, women came to

achieve economic independence. In a free marriage the wife
kept all her property, except that her husband took her
dowry. If her father died she was *sui iuris* – for she had
hitherto been under his authority, but now she either remained sole mistress of her property or else took a guardian
to help her in its administration. The guardian frequently
entered an even closer relationship to her, and, as we know
from various cases, occasionally became her lover. In time
women must have come to own a very considerable amount
of property. If this were not so the attempt would never
have been made to decrease it by the *lex Voconia,* which
in the year 169 B.C. forbade women to receive legacies.
Gellius (xvii, 6) tells us that Cato recommended the adoption of the law in these words: 'First of all a wife brings you
a large dowry. Then she receives a great sum of money
which she does not make over to her husband, but gives to
him as a loan. And finally, when she becomes angry, she
orders her debt-collector to follow her husband about
and dun him.' The law is still a subject of controversy
among scholars. Certainly it cannot have had much effect,
for the laws of inheritance became constantly more and
more favourable to women, until finally, under Justinian,
the two sexes were given almost equivalent rights. Woman
had at last come of age, legally and economically. But these
last stages in her development lead into the period when
Christianity was supreme, and so fall without the scope of
our book.

Besides the sexual and economic freedom achieved by
women in early Rome, there was also a political emancipation. It is of less far-reaching importance than the emancipation in sexual and economic life; still, it is interesting
enough to merit a short discussion here, for the picture of
Roman womanhood would be incomplete without it.

Women in Rome had absolutely no political rights. We
read in Gellius (v, 19) that 'women are debarred from
taking part in the citizen-assembly'. But, in contrast to this,
the Roman matron enjoyed a much higher degree of personal independence than the Greek wife. She took part, as
we have seen, in meals with the men; she lived in the front
part of the house, and she could appear in public, as Cor-
nelius Nepos says in his preface. According to Livy (v, 25)

the women freely sacrificed their gold and jewels for the
state at the time of the Gallic invasion, and were consequently granted the right to drive to religious festivals and
games in four-wheeled carriages and to travel about on
ordinary festivals and working days in two-wheeled
vehicles. Besides, there were certain religious services which
were attended by women alone – we shall have more to say
of them later. We may remind our readers of the conduct
of the women when Coriolanus was attacking Rome. As
women freed themselves gradually from the restrictions of
the old patriarchal family they allied themselves with one
another to further their common interests. We have no
exact evidence on this stage of their evolution, but about
the time of Tiberius authors speak of a previously existing
ordo matronarum, a class, almost a society, of married
woman (Val. Max., v, 2, 1). In Seneca (*fr.* xiii, 49) we find
the words: 'One woman appears in the streets in richer
attire, another is honoured by all, but I, poor wretch, am
disdained and contemned in the women's meeting.' Suetonius (*Galba*, 5) also knows of the women's meeting,
as an apparently permanent institution to represent women's
interests. Under the emperor Heliogabalus (Ael. Lamprid.
Heliog., 4) an assembly room was built for the 'senate of
women' on the Quirinal, where the *conuentus matronalis*
(assembly of married women) had been accustomed to
meet. Lampridius uses the words *mulierum senatus*. However, he calls its decrees 'ridiculous', and says they were
concerned chiefly with questions of etiquette. It was, therefore, of no political importance. Friedländer's conjecture
(*History of Roman Morals*, v, 423) may be true: he thinks
that these assemblies dated back to some religious union of
women.

And there is no political significance in the event which
Livy (xxxiv, 1) describes so vividly; however, it is import-
tant for the comprehension of the character of the Roman
woman, and for that reason we shall discuss it in some
detail. In 215 B.C., during the terrible pressure of the
Hannibalic War, the Romans introduced a law, the *lex Oppia*, which laid restrictions on the use of ornaments and
carriages by women. However, after the victory of Rome,
these severe measures seemed to be less needful, and the

women exerted themselves to have the law removed. It was repealed in 195, in the consulship of M. Porcius Cato, although that conservative of conservatives backed it with all his influence and authority. Here is Livy's account:

'The anxieties of great wars impending or newly ended were interrupted by an affair which sounds unimportant but developed into a great and bitter struggle. M. Fundanius and L. Valerius, tribunes of the commons, proposed to the commons that the Oppian Law should be repealed. It had been enacted by C. Oppius, tribune of the commons, in the consulship of Q. Fabius and Ti. Sempronius while the Punic war was raging; it provided that no woman should possess more than half an ounce of gold, wear a garment of many colours, or ride in a carriage within Rome or a provincial town or within a mile of either of those places unless for public worship. The tribunes Marcus and Publius Janius Brutus defended the law, and said they would not allow it to be repealed; many distinguished men appeared to back it or oppose it; the Capitol was crowded with its supporters and opponents. Neither influence, nor modesty, nor their husbands' commands could keep the married women within doors. They beset all the streets in Rome and all the approaches to the forum, imploring the men who were going down to the forum that they should allow their former luxuries to be legalized, now that there was general prosperity in Rome. Every day the crowds of women grew, for they even came into the city from the provincial towns and market-boroughs. And now they dared to go to the consuls, the praetors, and the other magistrates and beseech them. But they found one of the consuls, M. Porcius Cato, quite inexorable.'

Livy now describes a great duel of oratory between the chief opponents – Cato the diehard, and the liberal Valerius; he states all the grounds which they adduced for and against repealing the law. The most interesting parts of their speeches are those in which they put forward entirely opposite views on the character and the ideal position of women in law and in public life. Cato says: 'Our ancestors laid down that women might carry out no business – even private business – without supervision from her guardian, and they confined them to the authority of their parents, brothers, and husbands. But we – save the mark! – are allowing them to take part in the government of the country and mingle with the men in the forum, the meetings, and the voting-assemblies. What else are they doing at this moment, in the highways and byways, except supporting a bill sponsored by the tribunes and voting for the repeal of a law? Give rein to that headstrong creature woman, that unbroken beast, and then hope that she herself will know where to stop her excesses! If you do not act, this will be one of the least of the moral and legal obligations against which women rebel. What they wish to have is freedom in all things – or, rather, if we are to tell the truth, licence in all things.' Later in his speech Cato condemns especially the fact that women want freedom in order to have more luxury. 'What honourable pretext can be adduced for this revolt of the women? "We wish to be resplendent in gold and purple," we are told, "to ride through the city in carriages on feast-days and working days as if we were celebrating a triumph over the law which we conquered and repealed and over your votes which we captured and carried off; we wish no limits to extravagance and display." '

The tribune Valerius meets Cato by declaring: ' "Before this, women have appeared in public – think of the Sabine women, the women who met Coriolanus, and other cases. Besides, it is right to remove laws without trouble as soon as the circumstances which called them forth have changed, as is done in other cases. ... Shall all other ranks and kinds of men," ' he says (and here we are again quoting Livy's version), ' "feel the benefit of the country's prosperity, while only our wives are deprived of the fruits of peace and tranquillity? We men shall wear purple on our official and priestly garments; our children will wear the toga with the purple stripe; we concede the right of wearing the purple stripe to magistrates in the colonial towns and to the lowest magistrates in Rome, the overseers of the wards – not only while they are alive, but even that they be burned wearing it when dead. Shall we then forbid the women to wear purple? When you can have a purple saddle-cloth, is your wife to be forbidden to have a purple cloak? and are the trappings of your horse to be more splendid than the dress of your wife?" ' He makes the point that even if this concession is made, the women will still be under the authority of their husbands and fathers. ' "As long as her kinsmen are alive, a woman is never free from her slavery; and she herself prays that she will never have the freedom brought by widowhood and bereavement. They would rather you should decide on their adornment than the laws. And you ought to keep them under your authority and guardianship, not in slavery to you, and you should prefer to be called fathers and husbands than masters. ... In their weakness they must accept whatever decision you make. The more powerful you are the more moderately you should use your power." '

(Cf. Teufer's excellent little book *On the History of Woman's Emancipation in Ancient Rome*.)

These speeches as given in Livy may not be authentic. Still, they reproduce the atmosphere and outlook of the opposition; even in Livy's time men of the ruling classes still opposed the emancipation of women thus. We may remind our readers that after this memorable meeting of the senate the women did not rest till the law they thought obsolete was repealed. But it should not be imagined that with this success women began to exercise any important influence on the government of Rome. In principle women were, and always remained, disqualified from taking part in politics. Notwithstanding that, intelligent and strong-willed Roman women still had great political influence over their husbands. We need not consider legendary figures like Tanaquil or Egeria; but think of Cornelia, the mother of the Gracchi, of Porcia, the famous wife of Brutus, or of the clever and discreet Livia, wife of the emperor Augustus. In later Roman history there were many women of fierce and immoderate ambition: Fulvia, for instance, dominated Mark Antony to such an extent that he had silver coins struck bearing her likeness and allowed her (Plutarch *Ant.*, 10) 'to rule a ruler and command a commander'. And the history of the emperors shows us ambitious and domineering women like the younger Agrippina, Nero's mother, Julia Domna, Caracalla's mother, and Julia Maesa, the grandmother of Heliogabalus.

4. Free Love

We have already said that in early Rome there were many
sexual relationships besides marriage. Scholars are still in
doubt as to their origin. Since there is no reliable evidence
for the period before the Gallic invasion, it is impossible to
state with accuracy how these sexual relationships arose
and developed in the first centuries of Rome's history. The
evidence of authors like the biased Livy is consciously or
unconsciously intended to display a better and purer past
to what they considered the degenerate present. We cannot
then consider that the story of Lucretia's chastity and death
is historically true – nor can we conclude that the early
Republic was much more morally upright than the early
Empire in which Livy himself lived and wrote.

There is an extremely important passage from Cicero's
speech for Caelius – a passage not read or known in schools
– (20): 'If there is anyone who thinks that young men
should be forbidden to make love, even to prostitutes, he is
certainly a man of stern righteousness – that cannot be
denied – but he is out of touch not only with the free life
of today, but even with the code and concessions which our
fathers accepted. For when was that not customary? When
was it blamed? When was it not allowed? When was it not
lawful to do what is a lawful privilege?'

In the same vein Seneca the elder writes (*Contr.*, ii, 4,
10): 'He has done no wrong, he loves a prostitute – a usual
thing – he is young; wait, he will improve, and marry a
wife.' And later: 'I enjoy the pleasures permitted to my
age and live according to the rules laid down for young
men.' And, according to Horace, even the severe moralist
Cato was liberal enough in these matters. Horace says in
Sat., i, 2, 31, ff.:

> Once, when a noble left a brothel, 'Blessed
> be thou for virtue!' quoth the wisdom of Cato:
> for when their veins are swelling with gross lust,
> young men should drop in there, rather than grind
> some husband's private mill.'

We can get an idea of the real truth about those early
times from passages such as these – and especially from the

emphatic pronouncement of Cicero that ancestral morality had not been so severe as to forbid young men to have
intercourse with prostitutes. In this respect, then, Rome
cannot have changed or degenerated much by Cicero's
time. Another interesting fact is that Livy (who elsewhere
says that the army from Asia first introduced *luxuria*) says
in his first book that according to some authors Larentia,
the fostermother of Romulus and Remus, was called *lupa*
by the shepherds. But *lupa* means she-wolf and also *unchaste woman*. And, again, soon after Porsena's time, Livy
relates this story quite calmly (ii, 18): 'In this year there was
a riot with fighting, and almost a battle, because some
young Sabines wantonly carried off some prostitutes at the
public games. Out of this little affair it almost seemed as if
a rebellion would arise.' This assumes that even then there
were such characters in Rome.

Paldamus, in his book *Roman Sexual Life* (1833), draws
attention on page 19 to the fact that 'no literary language
is so rich in words for the crudest of physical sexual relationships as early Latin. This can be proved by a glance
at the old glossaries, namely Nonius and Festus. All the
words are entirely lacking in a gay and frivolous charm;
they are dull sensual utterances.' We may also quote the
translator of Plautus, L. Gurlitt (Gurlitt was an honest and
unprejudiced student of the history of civilization; nevertheless, his work was contemptuously dismissed by a re-
viewer who disagreed with it, in the gratuitously insulting
phrase 'half-knowledge'. We are quoting from p. 15 of his
Erotica Plautina). He says: 'During the epoch when moral
degeneracy was obvious and infamous everywhere, the
Romans invented an ideal past for themselves. To this day
schoolboys are made to read passages from Roman poets
and prose authors which confirm those pictures of a noble
and primitive people. We may allow the pedagogues to use
the extracts, provided we do not forget that the truth had
quite another aspect.'

It is indeed the truth that prostitution and the frequenta-
tion of prostitutes by young men were an old and generally
recognized custom in Rome; the Romans had no need to
wait until that habit was introduced from Greece. As we
have said, the purity of marriage and the protection of

maidenhood were a different matter; but to demand con-
tinence from young men before marriage would have
seemed unnatural and absurd to the gross and sensual Roman.

We shall turn now to a detailed discussion of the phenomena which are grouped under the name of prostitution in
Rome – however one-sided that name may be from a modern point of view. But first we must draw attention to the
fundamental difference between what is called prostitution
today and the free sexual relationships of the Romans.
Today a prostitute is generally a woman who has actually
'fallen' – that is, she has dropped out of the class of respectable citizens. But in Rome a woman who was sexually
associated with a man without legal marriage was either a
slave (who had not higher social rank to lose) or a freedwoman (for whom the same thing was true) or else a free-
living woman of the upper classes, whose life did not deprive her of the respect due to her person and position. It
may be that she was regarded as morally unworthy in
particularly severe circles. But this one thing is certain:
everything relating to sex was regarded as completely natural, and was approached far more simply and innocently
that it is now. All these light ladies – from the mistress and
inspiration of a famous poet to one of the unknown thousands of her sisters – were all handmaids in the service of
Venus and Cupid; their hearts were not torn by the struggles of conscience, and therefore they did not sink so low
as the modern prostitute.

Among these free lovers we can distinguish various
classes – as Paldamus does. But it is obvious that a woman
who had the good fortune to be beloved by a celebrated
poet reached thereby a higher social position than her
many sisters, who were less fortunate, and now have disappeared silently into the abyss of the past. Is it really possible to single out a higher and a lower class among them?
It is doubtful. But always and everywhere the finer type of
men and women are in the minority: there are so few really
sensitive people. We cannot be surprised, then, if we hear
much of the women who served only for the transient sensual enjoyment of the average Roman, and little of those
who had some higher worth and were more esteemed.
Catullus's Lesbia – whoever she really was – was certainly

a personality; and (unless it was all an invention of the poet) she was equally certainly not an Ipsitilla.* And so it is perhaps fairer to say this: among the many women whom we know to have been sexual companions of Roman men, there were some with really memorable personalities, educated and refined, and a multitude of others of whom we know no more than that they satisfied men's sensual desires.

In another part of this book we shall speak in more detail of those women who were the inspirations of famous poets. Paldamus is without doubt right when he says: 'And who were the fortunate women who were honoured (eloquently or not) by the poems of their lovers? Certainly they were not matrons, married women of any class of society; and certainly they were not prostitutes. They were a peculiar class of women who were somehow analogous to the freedmen. For by their higher education and versatility they compensated the rights of citizenship and the privileges which they lacked. And sometimes they even rejected such rights as oppressive and burdensome, and created a middle class between the aristocracy and the underworld of women – between the *matrona* or *materfamilias* and the *meretrix*.' It is doubtful whether we should be justified in assigning women like Sallust's Sempronia to that class of women; she belonged to a noble family, and was wife of a consul and mother of D. Junius Brutus Albinus, one of Caesar's murderers. She was not, therefore, a woman who can be judged by her sexual life alone. I am much more inclined to see in her one of the emancipated women who are misunderstood by their neighbours – but not a prostitute. We meet women of her type both in history and in the present day; it is possible that they belong to a peculiar type, which Blüher (in his well-known book, *The Role of Sexual Life*, ii, 26) calls 'free womanhood'. As he says: 'Free women belong to an intermediate world. Their spirit is governed by a certain masculinity; their outward bearing shows that lively and excited character, just as the bearing of male artists shows a Hamlet-like tenderness and sensitiveness. A free woman finds her womanhood a problem; she shows that either by the conscious skill and sophistication with which she conducts her love-affairs, or by striving

* 'Little lady,' Catullus's name for a prostitute (32.)

for equality with the men who have hitherto oppressed
her sex by their own rules and regulations. But in her last
and purest embodiment the free woman is the student and
prophet of that which gives the female sex its greatest value
– Eros. ... But it is certain that nations of all ages have
always distinguished these two types of women very clearly
and decisively, and they proscribed them or glorified them
according to their fear of them. But because these types
are subject to social judgment we must not think that they
are social types. They are natural phenomena. One is born a
wife just as one is born a prostitute; and no woman who is
meant for free love becomes a wife by being married.'

Blüher's views are corroborated by the fact that among
the more distinguished Roman hetairai (to use the word
in Blüher's sense) were actresses and dancers, and, to go a
stage lower, harp-players and other musicians. (Such
women would share Blüher's title hetairai with the emancipated women who were liberating themselves from the
old morality and would be called degenerate by the old
Romans.) Sulla frequented such women (as we have said
elsewhere); Cicero had dinner with a certain Cytheris (*Ad
fam.*, ix, 26); and a remark in Macrobius seems to show that
philosophers especially loved to be with these 'educated
hetairai' – which is not hard to understand.

But the line of demarcation between a prostitute and a
free-living woman who did not love for profit must have
been very uncertain. That is shown by a decree of the time
of Tiberius, the beginning of the first century of our era. It
forbade a woman whose grandfather, father, or husband
was a Roman knight to make money by selling herself to
lovers (Tac. *Ann.*, ii, 85). In early times such things would,
of course, be much less frequent, because women had much
less opportunity to leave their old-established social position as *matronae*.

Now let us consider real prostitution in early Rome –
that is the cases in which a woman consciously sought
to earn money by surrendering her body for sexual purposes. We must first point out that for many centuries the
state took no cognizance of the matter. Mommsen says in
his *Roman Penal Law*: 'The lenient attitude which the
Roman Republic adopted to incontinence is closely con-

nected with the general decline in morality and the appearance of unchastity, shameless and unconcealed.' We cite
this remark only as evidence for the attitude of early Rome
to this matter, without sharing the opinion which it implies
– that laws might have been beneficial here. When Augustus passed his moral legislation it made not the slightest
difference; things were not, in Mommsen's sense, 'improved'. But it is a fact that originally the Romans had no
statutory prohibition of sexual relationships outside marriage. But according to Tacitus (*Ann.,* ii, 85) there was an
official register of prostitutes, kept by the aediles, 'in accordance with a custom which obtained among the early
Romans'. But the actresses, flute-players, and dancers who
lived in free love were not included in this register, and so
did not count as prostitutes. If women of rank (that is from
aristocratic circles) prostituted themselves they were liable
to a fine, as early as the Samnite war (Liv., x, 31). Later, in
the time of the Hannibalic war, they were actually punished
by banishment (Liv., xxv, 2.) Accordingly, anyone who
did not belong to the old aristocracy could conduct her
sexual life with as much freedom as she wished; with one
exception – professional prostitutes must have their names
on the list by the aediles. When the austere Tacitus says that
this enrolment as a prostitute was considered to be a punishment ('our ancestors thought that confession of guilt was
a sufficient punishment for unchaste women') he forgets
that very few of the women who gave their favours freely
or for money would have placed any value on her recognition by the ruling class as 'morally pure'. Otherwise it
would have been pointless to forbid women of noble birth
to enrol themselves on these lists as they did for the sake
of living a free life.

The real professional prostitutes on the lists were without exception slaves. The free-living women were generally
ex-slaves, freedwomen; at least, they were certainly not
Roman by birth.

We cannot decide when the first brothel was opened in
Rome. Certainly such establishments were known to
Plautus. We can dispense with a detailed description of
them, since one may be found in Licht's *Sexual Life in
Greece.* We can only add here that they lay in the second

district of Rome, in the Suburra quarter, between the
Caelian and Esquiline hills. But according to Juvenal and
others there were houses which served as brothels in the
Vicus Patricius, beside the Circus Maximus, and outside
the city walls. They are generally called *lupanaria* by
Juvenal, Catullus, and Petronius; Livy, Horace, and Martial use the word *fornices*. From the *lupanar* preserved in
Pompeii we can see that every considerable city in the provinces had its brothel. The dim little cubicles with their
obscene pictures above the doors give us an impression of
dirt and unhealthiness; still, even at that time, efforts were
made to take certain limited precautions against infectious
diseases by washing and bathing. (More exact information
can be found in Bloch's *Origin of Syphilis,* ii, 652 ff.)

The proprietor of the brothel was the *leno* or *lena,* pandar or bawd; his or her profession was *lenocinium*. The
girls in the brothels were slaves. There must have been a
flourishing trade in these servants of lust. In Plautus (*Persa*
665) £240 is paid for a girl who is said to have been ab-
ducted from Arabia. The elder Seneca (*Controv.,* i, 2, 3)
describes the sale of a kidnapped girl. 'She stood naked on
the shore to be criticized by her purchaser; all the parts of
her body were inspected and handled. Do you want to
hear the end of the sale? The pirate sold, the pandar
bought.' There are interesting details in one of Martial's
epigrams (vi, 66):

> A girl whose morals were doubtful
> (the kind who haunt the Suburra)
> was once for sale at an auction.
> The bids were rising but slowly.
> The auctioneer, to commend her,
> caressed her (though she resisted)
> and kissed her, showing her pureness.
> I'll tell you what the result was.
> A fiver offered was cancelled.

I attach a good deal of importance to the information
given in Rosenbaum's *History of Syphilis* (ed. 6, 1893, pp.
III ff.). He tells us that a multitude of prostitutes was
lodged near the Circus Maximus, with the purpose of solicit-
ing the men whom the sadistic pleasures of the games had
raised to a high pitch of sexual excitement.

Apart from the prostitutes lodged in brothels, there were

in Rome, and no doubt in provincial cities also, many girls who were kept for sexual purposes. Innkeepers and owners of bakeries and cookshops frequently kept slave-girls of this kind for the entertainment of their customers (Hor. *ep.*, i, 14, 21). There were also prostitutes who wandered about – the *scorta erratica*. These have very varied designations in Latin. They were called *noctilucae,* night moths; *ambulatrices*, strollers; *bustuariae,* grave-watchers, who plied their trade in cemeteries and combined it with the job of professional mourners; and *diobolariae,* the two-pennies who were the lowest stage of all. We could easily give further names. All these women practised their profession at street corners, in baths, in out-of-the-way corners of the city, and – according to Martial, i, 34, 8 – even on gravestones and in tombs.

The large numbers of these light women are sufficient evidence of a genuine demand. Who were their cusomers? We can reply, first and foremost, young men. We have already mentioned the liberal views of Rome about man's sexual life before marriage. It was not in the least remarkable that a young bachelor should satisfy his instincts with a prostitute. But we must not overlook another fact. According to Cassius Dio (54, 16), there were far fewer women than men of free birth in Rome at the beginning of the Empire. According to Friedländer the female population was 17 per cent less than the male. The necessary consequence was that many men could not marry at all, even if they wished, and therefore had to have recourse to prostitutes.

Besides young men the chief clients of the prostitutes were soldiers, sailors, many freedmen, slaves, and small businessmen like corn dealers, butchers, and oil merchants; and we learn from Plautus that creatures from the dark criminal underworld sometimes met in brothels. (Plaut. *Poen.,* 831 ff., *Pseud.,* 187 ff., and Hor. *epod.,* 17, 20, Juv., viii, 173 ff., Petronius, 7.)

Later authors, such as Suetonius and Tacitus say that those members of the imperial house whom they particularly detested used to visit brothels and have intercourse with prostitutes. But we can make no inference from this. That kind of sensational fiction cannot be accepted as historical truth – although it is accepted by Müller in his *Sexual*

Life in Ancient Civilization (1902), a book which is useless except as a collection of evidence.

We may cite the interesting work of Pohlmann, *Over-population in Ancient Cities in connection with the Collective Development of Urban Civilization* (1884). He has pointed out that 'the excessive crowding of human beings on top of one another was impossible without upsetting family life in many ways, without mingling the sexes and increasing temptations in a way which was bound to harm national morality all the more because it was counteracted by so little moral and intellectual education among the masses'. We may assume – although we have no exact figures – that prostitution vastly increased as the population of Rome reached the million mark. (In the time of the emperors, the population varied between one million and two and a half millions.) It is at least important that a tax on prostitutes was introduced in Caligula's reign (Suet. *Cal.*, 40), as brothel-keepers later had to pay tax also (Lamprid. *Alex. Sev.*, xxiv, 3).

Finally, the respective esteem or contempt in which classes of women were held is an important piece of evidence for Roman views on sexual life. Just as in the case of male homosexuality, anyone who sought sexual pleasure with prostitutes was not dishonoured by his action; but dishonour did attach to the woman who took money in exchange for her favours. By Roman law a free-born man could never marry a *lena* or a *lenone lenaue manumissa* (a bawd or the freed slave of a bawd or pandar); and a senator and his descendants could never marry any *quaestum corpore faciens* (woman whose livelihood was her body). (This is from Rossbach, *Researches in Roman Marriage*, 467). On the other hand, a procurer could become a Roman citizen (Juv., vi, 216) – yet another proof that Rome was a purely masculine state, and that it was only the woman who had prostituted herself, who was held to be for ever dishonoured. And there was an external difference: 'dishonoured women', especially prostitutes, were compelled to differentiate themselves from respectable girls and matrons by their dress: that is they had to wear as their outer garment the toga, which was strictly the dress of men (Hor. *sat.*, i, 2, 63, and 82).

Chapter Two

The Romans and Cruelty

In older histories of Roman morals the usual views appear
– that the Romans of earlier days were a rough people,
but simple, honest, and upright. They found, we are told,
no pleasure in cruelty as exemplified in hunting and gladiatorial games – such as are of general occurrence in later
Rome. They could not actually be said to take any pleasure
in the horrible. It was foreign influence which gradually
made a 'degenerate' race out of the 'noble' Romans of
ancient times. This element showed its worst qualities
more and more in the time of the emperors, and finally
descended so low that only a complete revolution – a complete reorganization of the nation's whole existence such
as was introduced by Christianity – could save mankind
from its total eclipse and complete 'immersion in the frightful degeneracy of morals' – or whatever else authors care
to call it.

I am unable to share this opinion, which chiefly originated among authors of Christian views. Since I have been
engaged in the study of Roman civilization, it has seemed
to me quite inexplicable that a nation whose predispositions
were so pure and upright should have been suddenly influenced by some singular and mysterious force so as to
develop into something very different – a brutish, immoral, and cruel nation. On the contrary, I have found it
increasingly clear that a nation whose development led it
from a rough and primitive sensuality towards the unmis-
takable signs of a lust for cruelty must always have possessed at least these characteristics which were evidence of

its inclinations. It may be objected, perhaps, that the
Romans who enjoyed such sadistic practices were an entirely different people: that there was no trace of the descendants of that simple and honest old peasantry which
had overcome the army of Hannibal, as the numerous subsequent wars had almost annihilated the old Roman stock.
However, it was the ruling classes themselves who arranged
these repulsive practices, and there were many illustrious
names and families (consider only the members of the various imperial houses) who are mentioned in Imperial times
as responsible for this degeneration.

But the facts are not as they have been hitherto represented. Even in those ancient times, which are alleged to be
so pure, the Romans displayed numerous traits which
would, if they had been directed to another end, have produced the same sort of sadistic actions as later fill us –
according to our outlook – with horror or surprise. The
basic disposition of the Romans was always the same. Nothing changed, except its field of action, the ends in which it
fulfilled itself. We shall see this exemplified in particular
details. My point, then, is that cruelty and brutality were
original Roman characteristics, and not later importations
into an originally different and 'better' disposition.

I have received considerable guidance in these researches from a work by the Viennese psychoanalyst Stekel
called *Sadism and Masochism*. According to this book,
'cruelty is the expression of hatred and of the will to power'.
In other words, cruelty often appears as the visible and
practical action of the will to power. But there is hardly
any better embodiment of the will to power than the
Roman State, and the best Romans of all had no other
conception of their state. One example may suffice. The
sentence quoted on page 1 comes from the work of Rome's
greatest poet, Vergil, the Aeneid: let other nations, he
says, devote themselves to art and science, but—

> *tu regere imperio populos, Romane, memento—*
> Roman, remember: thou shalt rule the world!

The most honoured and famous men of Rome – to whatever party they belonged – always acted in accordance
with this ideal. They always considered themselves to be

masters of the world by divine right. Could there be a
more obvious embodiment of the will to power? We shall
see in the course of our investigation that this people, which
in the earliest times had as its guiding purpose the conquest
of the world, never shrank from any means to power (however brutal) in order to reach its end. And it will be clear
that the whole social life of the Romans, their attitude
towards education of children, towards the treatment of
women and slaves, and towards the punishment of what
they considered a crime, is entirely determined by one
motive, their desire for power. If, then, it is true (as Stekel
says) that the will to power often expressed itself in
cruelty, we should not be surprised to find in the Romans
of early times a considerable number of characteristics
which later, when directed towards other objects, fill us
with horror.

Nietzsche describes the rise of an ancient aristocracy, and
his description can well be applied to the rise of the Roman
state. The passage is in his work *Beyond Good and Evil*
(Aphorism 262), and runs: 'An aristocratic commonwealth is a body of men dependent on themselves, who are
striving to perpetuate their type, chiefly because they *must*
perpetuate it or run a frightful risk of extermination. The
favourable conditions of prosperity and safety which encourage variation do not exist for such a community. The
type is necessary to itself as a type: as something which,
in virtue of its hardiness and homogeneity, can perpetuate
and establish itself through a constant struggle, either with
its neighbours, or with its subjects in active or threatened
revolt. It learns from its rich experience what particular
characteristics are responsible for the fact that it still exists,
despite gods and men, that it has always conquered. It calls
these characteristics virtues, and cultivates these virtues
alone. It does so with severity; severity is its aim – every
aristocratic morality is intolerant – in the education of the
young, in the control of women, in marriage customs, in
the relation of young and old, in penal laws (which bear
down only on variations from the type); it considers even
intolerance as one of the virtues, and names it "justice". A
type which has few but very marked characteristics, a
species of strong, warlike, canny, resolute, and reserved

men (and as such endowed with the most delicate feeling for
society's subtle charms) is in this way established beyond
and above the influence of type-variation. As has been
said, a type becomes firm and strong through the unceasing
struggle against constantly unfavourable conditions.'

Since these explanations of Nietzsche are relevant to the
rise of the Roman state, we are greatly helped by his next
remarks to understand the further development, the so-
called 'degeneration' of that people in later ages. Nietzsche
continues: 'But finally the nation reaches happiness; the
frightful strain is relaxed; perhaps no more enemies are left
among their neighbours, and there is an abundance of the
means to live and enjoy life. At one blow the constraining
bonds of the old discipline burst asunder – that discipline
no longer seems to be a necessary condition of the existence
of the race; and it can survive only as a luxury and an arch-
aism. Variations from the type, whether they be mere
deviation (towards something higher, finer, or rarer) or degeneration and debasement, suddenly appear in flourishing
life; the individual has the courage of his individuality and
dares to detach himself. At these crises of history we see, in
the closest juxtaposition and often in actual unity, magnificent growth and aspiration, crowding close like a primitive forest. There is a tropical eagerness in this race for
growth; stupendous collapse and self-destruction are
caused by the savage combat and explosion of these in-
dividualities which, as they strive for sun and light, recognize none of the restraints, limits, and forbearances of previous morality. That previous morality was responsible for
accumulating the enormous force which stands now so
threateningly with bent bow; that morality is now fast becoming a thing of the past.'

My view of Roman sadism would be similar to this. They
were inherent in the Roman character, these traits of a relentless will to power which, in order to assert itself against
other nations, shrank from no step which seemed in the
least degree necessary for its aim of mastery – necessary,
and as such 'good', with reference to Rome's development
into a world empire. Later, when this will to power had no
further end in view, it was compelled to turn against itself
or its enslaved subjects; or else it was aimlessly dissipated

in the constantly intensified thrills of the circus with its
combat of wild beasts and human beings. If the Romans
had naturally been, as the Greeks were, capable of ap-
preciating higher ends of civilization, they would, we may
suppose, have found other possible ways of fulfilling and
sublimating their will to power – perhaps by great works
of art or by constructing a socially perfect state. Since they
lacked these possibilities they created Roman law, that
subtly refined codification of the will to power; the mass of
the people, however, could create for themselves nothing
more than the cruel sensations of the games. It is no accident, therefore, that the wild orgies of sadism which we
discover in the games reached their highest point in the
later years of Rome. It was just then that the Roman will to
power had lost its original aim – the conquest of the
world and the assertion of that mastery against a constant
succession of attacks. And with the Principate the reign of
'eternal peace', secure at least for a time, had begun.

After this general introduction we shall now pass to the
separate phases in the development of what we may call
Roman sadism. We cannot, in this, attempt to give a complete survey of the innumerable authorities without writing a history of morals which would be only an anthology
from the voluminous work of Friedländer. Our aim is only
to give characteristic examples.

The ancient Roman whom we know faced the world
chiefly as its conqueror and foe. A foe can still be generous;
he can content himself with the defeat of those who oppose
his will, at the same time treating them with clemency. The
Roman was from the very beginning of his conquests always severe, at times harsh and cruel. So it is not by chance
that the external symbols of Roman power were the
lictor's *fasces* – the bundle of rods and with the axe in their
midst. But even apart from this official symbol, the sign of
power is, in Rome, an instrument of punishment. Thus, for
example, Cicero saw in his dream of the young Augustus
'that the boy was let down from heaven on a golden chain,
and stood before the door of the Capitol, and that Jupiter
gave him a scourge (*flagellum*)' (Suetonius, *Augustus,* 94).
Juvenal also (x, 109) says that Caesar kept the Romans
under his scourge after subduing them.

1. Education

EDUCATION in ancient Rome was carried on under the
scourge, symbolic of the will to power. In every human
community there is an eternal connection between the ideal
which dominates that community and the method of edu-
cating children, for ultimately they are educated to fulfil
this ideal. A people whose motto is power will therefore
rear its children under this influence – that is strictly, in-
exorably, without considering the real disposition of each
individual child. If the child's will is directed to other
ends it must therefore be suppressed; such education must
therefore employ punishments which are severe, even
brutal, if gentle admonition fail. By severe education we
must understand not only education by means of punishment: the child is introduced without delay to the sphere
of activities in which the desired characteristics may best
be acquired and practised. Hardened warriors and sturdy
farmers were needed – so anything else was needless and,
in fact, undesirable. This, at least, was the view held by
later ages of that early method of education which seemed
to them to be ideal. This is the preaching of Horace in the
famous Roman Odes, his admonitions to a degenerate age
(iii, 2):

> Youth must harden its limbs in war,
> bear harsh poverty like a friend,
>   learn to harry the savage Parthian,
>   riding him down at the spear-point,
> live life under the sky among
> urgent perils.

And elsewhere (iii, 6, 37 ff.):

> That was yeoman and soldier stock,
> skilled in turning the stubborn clods
>   highland mattock in hand, and bearing
>   logs at a mother's commandment.

In Dionysius of Halicarnassus (ii, 26) we are told: 'The
Roman lawgiver gave the father complete power over the
son, power which lasted a whole lifetime. He was at liberty
to imprison him, flog him, to keep him a prisoner working
on the farm, and to kill him. All this was possible even if
the son were already engaged in political affairs, even if he
held a chief magistracy and was already renowned for his

public spirit. In virtue of this law, it often happened that
illustrious men who acquired a great reputation by speaking on the public platform against the Senate and on behalf
of the people were pulled down from the platform by their
father and dragged away to meet the punishment which he
chose to inflict.'

This passage speaks without qualification of the right to
chastise and even kill a child. The father, as the absolute
master of the family, commonly possesses the right to
punish every member of the family, even to the fulfilment
of the death penalty. This absolute mastery is entirely appropriate for a state which is constructed on the principle of
power and conquest.

It is easily comprehensible that our sources do not often
speak of the physical punishments which a father could
inflict on his child. This was a daily event, commonplace
enough among these laws, and was taken for granted; only
especially striking cases were recorded. For example, Suetonius says in his life of the Emperor Otho that he as a
young man was much inclined to extravagance and vice, so
that he 'was often flogged by his father'.

If we know little of the imposition of these punishments
in the Roman family we have much greater information
about punishment in Roman schools. We cannot accurately
determine when the first school was set up in Rome. According to the saga, Romulus and Remus went to school
in Gabii. Livy and Dionysius speak of schools in Falerii
and Tusculum. It is certain that, in very early times, children were instructed by an elementary teacher in reading,
writing, counting, and the knowledge of the laws. Some
time after the Hannibalic wars instruction by a grammaticus
or litteratus was introduced. That meant a Greek gram-
marian, maintained at first only by a few prosperous and
specially interested families. Suetonius informs us (*De gr.*,
I): 'Grammar' (by which he means the whole teaching of
language) 'was not known, much less admired, for the city
was then uncivilized and warlike and not yet free for the
nobler branches of learning. When it was introduced, it was
still a modest affair; its oldest teachers – who were half-
Greek poets (I mean Livius Andronicus and Ennius, who
were known to have given instruction in both languages at

Rome and elsewhere) – confined themselves to expounding Greek literature.'

These so-called grammarians must have been introduced into Rome as the private tutors of noble families, and later must have attracted to themselves a growing circle of young pupils, which at last developed into a school. The state paid no attention to these schools, since there was no obligation to attend them. Nevertheless, there must have been, at later times, such a number of these schools in Rome that they competed with each other and pupils would transfer from an expensive master to a cheaper one.

Punishment in these schools must have generally been very severe, not to say cruel. All our sources agree with each other on this point. Suetonius says of the famous schoolmaster Orbilius, with whose cane young Horace was well acquainted: 'He had a bitter temper, and vented it not only against rival scholars, but also against his own pupils.' Horace implies this when he calls him a 'Thrasher', and so also does Domitius Marsus in the line:

> The victims of Orbilius' birch and strap.

The instruments of punishment which are described in our sources are, first, the *ferula* – a bundle of switches, made partly of birch branches like the nineteenth century birch rod, and partly from the branches of a sort of broom which grows in the south; secondly the *flagrum* or *flagellum*, a scourge of straps, generally employed only for the punishment of slaves; and, finally, the *scutica*, another scourge with a gentler stroke, being made of softer leather than the tough hard ox-hide *flagellum*. We can see from a passage in Horace (*Sat.*, i, 3, 117) that these instruments were classified according to their effect.

> But have
> some rule, to make the punishment fit the crime,
> not lash and mangle one who needs the birch.
> I don't expect you'll use a slender whip
> when scorpions are needed.

Does this not imply the sadistic thought – 'You will, of course, always prefer to inflict the sharper punishment'?

Finally, there was the *fustis*, a stick corresponding to our cane, which seems to have been less in use for the punishment of children. We possess in an Epistle of Ausonius (22) an interesting description of school punishments at a later period in Rome's history, which in this respect does not seem to differ at all from earlier days.

The poet dedicates this epistle to his grandson to give him courage on going to school. He says: 'Even the muses have their gaieties; the stern master's voice does not always hector his pupils. The times of study and rest come each in turn. . . . Thus the Thessalian Chiron did not terrify his pupil, Achilles son of Peleus, nor did the pine-bearing Atlas scare the young son of Amphitryon; but they both soothed their young pupils with gentle words. You also should not be afraid, even if the school resounds with thrashing and the master wears a scowl. "Fear proves a degenerate spirit." Be true to yourself and fearless. Neither the cry nor the resounding blows nor your fear will harass you in the morning hours. The sceptre which your master flourishes – his rod – his numerous stock of birches, the deceitful wash-leather which conceals the strap (*scutica*) – all these are only properties and shams to inspire terror.'

This passage is interesting for several reasons. The kind grandfather does not deny the fact that every school has various instruments of punishment – not only the expected birch, but also the cruel leather scourge, which in this case was evidently made of a softer material than the hard oxhide in order to diminish its cruel effects. Nevertheless, the poet calls it *fallax* (deceitful), because it was still capable, despite the soft leather, of producing pain enough. An early commentator on this passage remarks that this implement consisted of a wooden handle to which were attached three thongs as thick as a man's finger; these were used for chastisement *ad nates* (on the buttocks).

A fresco from Pompeii gives us a still clearer understanding of school punishments in Rome. The scene is under one of the colonnades which were numerous in all cities, where lessons were held in public. In the background are some boys, recognizable by their long robes. They are seated and absorbed in studying their rolls of manuscript, while an old bearded teacher of surly appearance stands in front to give them instruction. A few idle onlookers, or perhaps the other pupils, are standing in the background. In the

right foreground is represented a scene of punishment. A
fully developed boy of at least 14–15 years old, but with
childish features, quite naked except for a short loin-
cloth, is lying on the shoulders of a boy standing bent in
front of him and holding in his hands the victim's outstretched arms. Meanwhile, another boy kneeling behind
him grips his outstretched legs, so that the boy is held fast
and must let every blow of the rod strike him. A young
man standing behind this group is brandishing in his right
hand one of these implements, clearly the ferula which we
have described above. The victim's face is distorted for a
cry; it is purposely turned towards the spectator and shows
clearly that numerous violent blows have already been inflicted on him. This is also apparent from the position of
the heads of the boys who hold him; they are bent as if the
boys are afraid of being struck by the cruel rod. The whole
scene has an unintentional resemblance to the chastisement
of a slave; for it depicts the chastisement of the entire
naked body – a severe and cruel act which cannot have been
usual to such a degree of harshness. What end had the apparently primitive painter in view in painting such a picture?

Was it only the reproduction of an interesting scene from
daily life? Was it the record of a specially characteristic
scene distinguished by its uniqueness, was it a deliberate
striving for sadistic effect? In this case the shrinking from
nakedness which the Romans manifested on other occasions did not hinder the infliction of such punishments; they
were frequent enough in Germany in 'the good old times'.

Apuleius' novel (*Metamorphoses*, ix) contains an interesting literary parallel to this picture in its description of
the punishment of a young adulterer by the injured husband. It is interesting for its description of the thorough
flogging of the half-grown boy. The husband had surprised
him with his faithless wife, and, after using him for his
pleasure, thrashed him with the help of two of his slaves.
The words are *quam altissime sublato puero ferula nates
eius obverberans* – the boy was raised as high as possible
and his buttocks lashed with a rod. This, then, is the type of
punishment inflicted on boys and children. It must be emphasized that in this passage of Apuleius, the husband was
still treating the youth as a child, and intended chiefly to

dishonour him by this punishment, which showed that he did not consider him as a man.

In conclusion, we may ask if no protesting voices were ever raised in Rome against the infliction of such cruel punishments on children. At least, few of such protests survive. One of the most important is that of the rhetor Quintilian, who lived about A.D. 35–95. After giving much good advice on the spiritual education of young men, he writes in his *Institutio Oratoria*: 'I am entirely against the practice of corporal punishment in education, although it is widespread, and even Chrysippus does not condemn it. In the first place it is a disgusting and slavish treatment, which would certainly be regarded as an insult if it were not inflicted on boys. Further, the pupil whose mind is too coarse to be improved by censure will become as indifferent to blows as the worst of slaves. Finally, these chastisements would be entirely unnecessary if the teacher were patient and helpful. But nowadays teachers seem to be so slack that the boys are not induced to do what is right, but are punished for not doing it. Besides, if a boy is coerced by blows, what are we to do with youths who cannot be influenced by fear and yet must learn much more? And consider how shameful, how dangerous to modesty are the effects produced by the pain or fear of the victims. This feeling of shame cripples and unmans the spirit, making it flee from and detest the light of day. And if we do not take more care of the character of the teachers and instructors whom we choose, I blush to think how shamefully such contemptible fellows will misuse their rights. ... But I will spend no longer time on this matter – we know enough of it already.' As we read these words we are compelled to ask whether the scene represented in the picture we have discussed as taking place with all publicity should not be regarded as one of these shameful abuses of the right to punish: what else must have occurred to justify the words of Quintilian?

Boys who committed theft but were too young for the severer punishments of grown men could, if the judge so ordered, be thrashed with birch-rods. We read of this in Gellius (xi, 18).

2. Conquest

Everything which the Roman children, especially the boys, had to suffer from the severe discipline of school and home, was mild in comparison with the punishments which the Romans inflicted on their enemies, their slaves, and criminals.

We can give only a few characteristic examples from the abundance of extant material. Here again the sentence which we quoted from Nietzsche is relevant and important: 'There are men dependent on each other and themselves who strive to perpetuate their type chiefly because they *must* perpetuate it, or run a frightful risk of extermination.' As we know, the little Roman community was, during the first century of its existence, constantly beset by powerful enemies, against whom throughout centuries it fought for its life. We cannot wonder that such battles entailed dreadful slaughter; and we can easily understand that the Romans always used brutal means to keep in subjection a race once conquered. Similarly, although the fact has been too little observed in previous accounts of Roman life, we can easily comprehend that in this race which for centuries had lived at war, all the qualities were cultivated which eventually found a narrower fulfilment in sadism.

The Samnite people was one of the most dangerous enemies of ancient Rome. In his account of the wars with this race Livy gives many details which are important for us. For example, in the war which took place about 330–300 B.C., the city of Sora deserted to the Samnites and murdered its Roman colonists. (This city was a Roman military colony, that is a Samnite city garrisoned by Rome.) The Romans felt themselves obliged to inflict severe punishment on the city. They captured it; killed all the men who met them in battle, chose out 225 from those who had surrendered and took them to Rome. There the prisoners were publicly flogged in the Forum and then beheaded, *summo gaudio plebis*, to the great joy of the common people, as Livy expressly adds. Polybius (i, 7) describes a similar case, this time concerning 300 inhabitants of the city of Rhegium, who after their capture were all publicly butchered in the same way. The fate of Capua is well known. This unhappy city deserted to the Carthaginians during the war with Hannibal, and was reconquered by the Romans later. The city councillors were arrested and, before a reprieve could come from Rome, were tied to stakes in the old cruel manner, flogged, and beheaded. The remaining inhabitants of the city were sold into slavery, and the whole territory of the city was annexed by Rome.

If all the magistrates of a conquered city could be treated in this way, there was for the captured generals none of the mercy which might have been expected from a generous enemy. Think of the fates of Jugurtha or Vercingetorix. These men, as well as many others who are less generally known, were strangled by the executioner in the underground prison at the Forum, which can still be seen. After Titus had sacked Jerusalem, Simon bar Giora, the brave leader of the Jews, was exhibited in the victor's triumphal procession. Then, before the great sacrifice on the Capitol, which was the climax of the ceremony, he was taken to the edge of the Capitoline Hill, flogged, and then thrown over. Josephus says: 'When his death was announced there was a universal shout of joy, and the sacrifice began.' All these executions of captives took place in public. Above all, it was customary that the flogging, which proceeded every execution, should take place in public – this to be a warning and a deterrent. We learn from a passage in the Elder Seneca (*Contr.*, ix, 2, 10) that the citizens were summoned by a special trumpet call to be present at these executions. It is needless to expatiate on the psychological effects of regular attendance at these cruel executions. We must only insist on the fact that there is small difference between a nation which is accustomed to witness all executions and a people which gloats over the bloody combats of gladiators. Here are connections which have been too little observed in the past.

In those early centuries the Roman will to power aimed at the overthrow of all races and peoples which opposed Rome. When this aim was achieved by the subjugation of almost the whole known world, that will to power was compelled, as if were, to recoil on itself. This is correctly discerned by that profound psychologist Tacitus. He writes (*Hist.*, ii, 38): 'That old and deep-rooted human passion and the desire for power' (*potentiae cupido*, which we call *will to power*) 'grew in strength with the rise of the empire and broke into excess. For while the nation's power was limited, equality was easily maintained; but when the conquest of the world and the destruction of all rival states and princes gave the Romans leisure to strive for their now unchallenged power, then the first disputes flamed up between the aristocrats and the commons.'

In these internal conflicts, whether they represent the efforts of the enslaved masses to secure humane treatment, or the party struggles of the aristocrats and democrats by which the Roman state was torn asunder for a hundred years, the Roman's everywhere display the same characteristics of a will to power based on cruelty.

Here also we may confine ourselves with a few especially important illustrations. We know now how important was the policy of the brothers Gracchus, or would have been if the real value and necessity of their agrarian reforms had been appreciated in their bearing upon the future of Rome. In an age where they appeared to be no more than rebels and madmen, they were bound to meet with martyrdom. Exceptionally hideous examples of Roman sadism appeared at this period. Here is Plutarch's tale of the death of Tiberius Gracchus and his adherents: 'As Tiberius himself took to flight someone caught hold of his clothes. He left his robe behind and ran away in his shirt, but stumbled and fell over some of those who had been felled ahead of him. As he tried to stand up Publius Satureius, one of his colleagues, struck him with the leg of a bench. Lucius Rufus laid claim to the second blow as if he had some noble act to boast of. More than 300 others were killed by clubs and stones, but none with an iron weapon.' And Plutarch tells us this about the death of Caius Gracchus, the younger brother: 'The bodies of Caius, Fulvius, and more than 300 other citizens who had been killed, were all thrown into the river. All their property was confiscated; their wives were forbidden to wear mourning for them, and Licinia, the wife of Caius, was actually deprived of her dowry. But the climax of cruelty was reached in the execution of the younger son of Fulvius; he had neither taken up arms against the winning faction nor been present in the battle;

but when he came to ask for an armistice before the battle
he was arrested, and executed immediately after the battle.
But more than this and everything else, the commons were
indignant at Opimius for building a Temple of Concord;
because he seemed to display a triumphant pride in the
slaughter of so many citizens.'

The wars of Marius and Sulla were no less bloody. Velleius Paterculus (ii, 22) says: 'C. Marius entered the city,
bringing destruction for his fellow citizens. The cruelty of
his victory would never have been exceeded if Sulla's
triumph had not followed immediately. The fury of his
swords did not fall upon ordinary men, but it was the most
noble and illustrious in the state who met their deaths in a
hundred different ways.'

Sulla was especially distinguished for these acts of
cruelty. In him, a man who counted as cultured, they were
far less excusable than in Marius, who remained fundamentally a rough and gross soldier. After one victory,
Sulla had 8,000 prisoners done to death, and at another time
he caused 12,000 to be pierced with javelins. His proscrip-
tions are notorious – in them 90 Senators and 2,600 knights
were outlawed. The exact meaning of this is shown by
Appian in his *History of the Civil War* (i, 95):

'Some of these victims were caught unawares and done to
death wherever they were found, in houses, streets, or temples.
Others were taken to Sulla, carried hand and foot in the air,
and thrown down before him. Others were dragged along
and trampled underfoot. The terror was such that no one
who witnessed these cruelties dared to utter a sound.'

We may remark here that Sulla's character combined
many features which could well be ascribed to the Emperor Nero. Plutarch says in his biography of Sulla (2):
'He loved jesting so much that when he was young and still
obscure he spent his days with clowns and buffoons, and
joined in their ribaldry; and later, when he had reached
absolute power, he used to collect the wildest comedians
and actors, drink with them each day and bandy vulgar
jests. In this his conduct was not only unseemly for a man
of his years and disgraceful for his important position,
but often held him from his duty. For when he was at dinner it was impossible to make him attend to serious

business. Although he was so businesslike and serious at other
times, as soon as he sat down to drink in company he
changed completely; where comic singers and dancing girls
were concerned, he was weak and amenable, and would
refuse no one who approached him. Another defect aris-
ing from this way of amusement was his incontinence in
love and his inclination to voluptuousness; even in old age
he did not give this up. In his youth he was constantly in
love with a certain comic actor called Metrobius. He fell
in love also with a wealthy prostitute named Nicopolis. His
position and his youthful grace made her return his love,
so that when she died she left him all her money.'

In another passage this biography emphasizes Sulla's
capriciousness: it calls him naturally choleric and vindictive, and yet so soft-hearted that he could easily burst into
tears. Like Tacitus, Plutarch finds that the will to power
'does not permit a man's character to be consistent, but
makes him capricious, vain, and savage'. Again and again
he stresses Sulla's inhuman passion for revenge. But we
cannot now consider this to be self-contradictory that a
man of such qualities should still be considered by the
Romans to be a 'great' man, as much as to say he was a
great warrior. For even an old writer like Valerius Maximus can account for this contradiction only by saying: 'His
virtue broke through the bonds of vice surrounding him,
and cast them away. ... ' and 'if one carefully compares and
balances these huge differences and contrasts one may recognize two Sullas united in one person – a dissolute youth
and a really valiant man.'

Nowadays we may say this with more correctness. This
man's strong vital force allowed him to love men as easily
as women, to take as much pleasure in the buffoonery of
clowns as in the merciless slaughter of thousands of personal opponents. And it fulfilled itself thus in the most
diverse ways – but without reference to any sort of modern
moral restraint. Sulla is, then, a brilliant example of the fact
that the will to power is often fulfilled in acts of cruelty.

Later, when the gladiatorial fights increased in scope,
captives were no longer simply executed as they once
were, but delivered over to different cities for use in the
games. This was done for example in A.D. 44, under Claud-

ius, with some captured Britons; and later also after Titus
sacked Jerusalem, with a host of Jewish prisoners. It was
Constantine's regular practice; his panegyrists praised him
for the very fact that he 'delighted the people with the
wholesale annihilation of their enemies – and what
triumph could have been finer?' (*Panegyric* xii, 23, 3).

3. Law

Fundamentally, these acts of cruelty which were cus-
tomery against the enemy were only acts of severe military
justice. But apart from this penal justice in ancient Rome
was quite as cruel. Mommsen, in his book on penal law,
thinks it necessary to assert that Roman legislation confined
itself to a few traditional forms of penalty without elabora-
ting subtle torments. But, in the course of our exposition,
we shall show that this remark is valid only with essential
restrictions. Here, again, we can give no exhaustive history
of Roman criminal justice; we must content ourselves with
showing by suitable examples that cruelty which it often
shows in such gross forms.

   In the most ancient age – an age which we can understand more by inference from later conditions than by acquaintance through reliable sources – there is only one
punishment known to Roman law: death. By death the
criminal is eradicated from the community whose laws he
did not observe. That is the fundamental purpose of the
death penalty. But also there may always be something
sacrosanct about him. He may be conceived as being offered
in sacrifice to the god against whom he has sinned. Mommsen thinks that this ritual aspect of primitive executions
follows from the fact that the criminal was killed like a sacrificial animal. He says, with regard to this: 'At these executions the condemned man's hands were bound behind his
back. He was chained to a post, stripped, and flogged; then
he was laid on the ground and beheaded with an axe. This
proceeding exactly corresponds to the killing of the sacrificial animal as is demanded by the sacral character of
primitive executions.' From this primitive type of execution, it was obviously innate in Roman feeling to consider
death alone as insufficient punishment. Flogging must

precede it. The criminal must, as it were, experience death in advance through torture. For death is obviously felt as a sort of liberation. It is only a brief moment. But punishment should be a long drawn out pain, a torture to which a crowd of spectators were invited (as we have explained elsewhere), a torture which must always be presented openly like a play in a theatre. And, as we shall see, this flogging is ordained as the preliminary of every kind of execution. An interesting passage in Sallust's *Catiline* shows that flogging was regarded as the necessary intensification of every condemnation. We may perhaps recall the prosecution of the arrested adherents of Catiline and the speech of Caesar, who vainly sought to deliver them from death. He says: ' "As for their punishment, we can say what is really true; death, in misfortune and in grief, is a liberation, not a martyrdom. ... Why, then, did you not move that the prisoners should first be flogged?" ' Caesar, therefore, shares the old view that death in itself is not a punishment, therefore that a condemned criminal should first be flogged if he is to be really punished. Suetonius says about the cruel Caligula (*Calig.*, 30): 'He very seldom allowed a man to be executed without frequent and small blows, or without the well-known order: "Strike so that he feels he is dying." ' Perhaps we are scandalized by Caligula's notorious sadism, without thinking that it was the fundamental attitude of ancient Rome. Death in itself was no punishment, but every execution must be sharpened by a previous flogging. But this is the Roman penchant for cruelty, which we meet everywhere.

To be sure, it was felt at a comparatively early epoch that this form of punishment, which had been inflicted on free Roman citizens as well as defeated foes, was unworthy of a free Roman of the ruling class. Later it was represented that only the despotic kings of olden times could have dared to inflict such punishment on a free Roman. Thus Cicero says in his speech for Rabirius (3, 10): 'The honour of this belongs in the first place to our ancestors: after expelling the kings, they retained no trace of royal cruelty in a free people.' And, again: 'These formulas of torture which you in your merciful democratic way recall so readily came from the haughty and cruel king Tarquin: "Let his head be shrouded, let him be hanged on an ill-omened tree." These

words, citizens, have long been lost to view in the shadows
of antiquity and the light of freedom.'

In any case, it is true that since about the beginning of
the Republic every Roman citizen had the right to appeal
to the assembly of the people against a sentence of death
pronounced by a magistrate (Cic., *de Rep.*, ii, 31). The
tenacity with which republican law was maintained can be
seen from the fact that Cicero was driven into exile for
infringing it by executing the arrested Catilinarians.

Of course, we must not forget in criticizing this republican law that it is not a measure which proves any particularly humane feeling. It is, rather, a law passed by the ruling
class in the Republic to codify the autocracy of that class
and its independence of any individual governor or magistrate. Hence it follows that the popular assembly could
always pronounce a sentence of death. Also, none but free
citizens had this right of appeal. Again, the law did not
originally prohibit a general from flogging and executing
any of his command (up to the rank of captain) for cowardice in the face of the enemy (e.g. Livy, ii, 59). It was only by
later law that the general was deprived of this right as far
as it concerned Roman citizens.

Another type of death penalty – perhaps the most frequent among the Romans – is crucifixion. It also is very
old, and although it soon became the usual form of execution for slaves, it was originally not confined to them. Livy
(i, 26) relates a very striking instance. Even although the
story was perhaps invented to illustrate the old custom, the
custom itself is certainly described by Livy as it must often
have been practised in former times. The story tells how
the victorious Horatius murdered his sister, who had lamented the death of her betrothed, the Curiatius, who had
been slain by her brother. 'The bold youth's anger was
stirred by his sister's lamentations in the midst of his
triumph and the public rejoicings. He drew his sword and
stabbed her to the heart, with these words of rebuke: "Go,
you and your untimely love, to your bridegroom – you who
forget your brothers dead and alive and your country itself. And so let every woman of Roman birth go who laments the death of an enemy." Senate and Commons felt
the horror of this deed, but it was balanced by Horatius'

recent glory. Still, he was led before the King to be tried. The King, to avoid responsibility for a trial so unpropitious and unpopular, and for the condemnation which would follow it, called an assembly of the people and said: "According to the law I appoint a board of two men to judge Horatius for treason." The law had a cruel formula: "A board of two shall judge the traitor; if he appeals from the board the appeal shall be final; if it is refused let his head be veiled; let him be hanged on an ill-omened tree; let him be flogged either within or without the wall." The two men appointed by this law believed that it did not permit them to acquit him even if he were innocent. They found him guilty; one of them spoke, saying "Publius Horatius, I find you guilty of treason. Lictor, bind his hands." The lictor approached Horatius, and was already setting the noose about his neck, when he said "I appeal". He did this on the advice of Tullus, who took a more merciful view of the statute. The appeal was heard by the people. At the hearing the father of Horatius greatly influenced his hearers by saying that he considered his daughter to have been justifiably killed; and that if he did not he himself would have punished his son by his power as a father. Then he implored them not to make him, who had shortly before been the father of noble children, now a childless man. Meanwhile he embraced the young man, and, pointing to the armour of the Curiatii hung up as trophies ... said: "This is the man, Romans' whom you have just seen marching in with all the glory and triumph of his victory. Can you bear to see him bound in the pillory, scourged, and tortured? ... Go, lictor, bind those hands which have but now won power for Rome, with sword and shield. Go, veil the head of the liberator of the city; hang him on an ill-omened tree; flog him either within the city wall, among the spears and trophies taken from his enemies, or without the city wall, among the tombs of the Curiatii. Can you lead this young man to any place where his own glory will not defend him from such shameful punishment?" ' And so Horatius was set free. But his father, 'in order to purify his family, offered certain sacrifices whose observance is traditional in the Horatian house: he set a beam across the street and made the young man pass beneath it with his head covered, as if under the yoke'.

This story bears witness to an age when even Roman citizens were punished for murder by the disgraceful death on the cross. Here it is the type of crucifixion in which the criminal was not nailed on the cross to die slowly (the usual idea of crucifixion); this is the almost crueller method of flogging to death, which is mentioned in the ban passed on the Emperor Nero. The criminal was stripped, his head was covered up, and the fork (*furca*) was laid on his neck. Opinions differ about the appearance of the *furca*. Some believe that it was a simple crossbar, and that the condemned man's arms were tied to it. Others think it was a forked piece of wood, and that it was laid over the criminal's shoulders in such a way that his head fitted into the fork while his arms were tied to the two oblique prongs, making him defenceless against the scourging. Every flogging was performed in this way, even if it was not carried as far as death. Cicero tells of a slave who was led round the circus wearing the *furca*, being thrashed with rods all the time (*De div.*, i, 26, 55). If the flogging was meant to include death the condemned man was flogged continuously until he died. This type of execution was later described as *more maiorum*, 'according to the custom of our ancestors'. Still, by the beginning of the Empire it had become so unusual to inflict it on a free man that Nero, when informed that the Senate intended to execute him in this way, did not know what it meant (Suet., *Nero*, 49). As a form of scourging to death, this type of crucifixion occurs often enough in historical times, especially in the case of the seducer of a Vestal Virgin. Livy relates that in the time of the Hannibalic War a certain Cantilius, a priest's clerk, dishonoured the Vestal Floronia; he was scourged with rods by the high priest in the Forum so long that he died under the blows (Livy, xxii, 57).

But if this flogging were only the preliminary to that type of execution which we generally call crucifixion, another instrument was employed. This was called the *patibulum*. It was a divided log of wood, which was opened, placed round the neck, and fastened. At times this instrument so fastened could strangle its wearer. This was certainly the most merciful method of crucifixion. Usually, however, the operation was conducted differently – the wood was fastened on so that the criminal was not strangled. His hands were fastened, either by binding them or by nailing them, to the ends of the beam. The victim was then hoisted, hanging from the beam, on to a post planted in the earth; the beam made the transverse bar of the cross.

Finally, his feet were nailed to the post. So he hung and was allowed to die by inches, or else was killed at last by having his thighs broken. The difference between the *patibulum* and the real cross is defined by Isidore (*orig.*, v, 27, 34). 'The punishment of the *patibulum* is less than that of the cross, because the *patibulum* at once kills the man who hangs to it, while the cross tortures for long the man who is nailed to it.' But the constant use of the word *affigere* leaves no doubt that men were much oftener nailed than bound to the *patibulum*.

This was a dreadful method of execution; but it was sometimes not enough. There are always men whose sadism is so horrible that they can invent special tortures. Verres once had an innocent Roman citizen lashed on the face with rods; and Cicero implies that slaves could be put to death by being torn with redhot pincers. At all events, it is true that the executioner was left to decide how he would dispatch condemned slaves. This is illustrated by a passage from Seneca (*Ad Marciam*, 20, 3): 'There I see crosses, not of one kind alone, but built differently by different men. Some hang their victims head downwards, others drive the pole through the privy parts, others again spread their arms widespread on the gibbet. There I see wires and lashes, and machines invented to torture every limb and every joint.'

But the various methods of execution in Rome were not exhausted by beheading or crucifixion. In the Twelve Tables burning alive is known as a punishment for arson. And it was later a very widespread punishment in the army for desertion and treachery (*Digest*, xlviii, 19, 8, 2). This cruel method of execution was especially frequent under the Caesars; and to it belong Nero's famous 'living torches', about which there are more sensational reports than reliable evidence. Seneca speaks of 'the shirt which is woven and smeared with the food of flames' (*Ep.*, 14); Martial mentions the *tunica molesta*, the 'troublesome' shirt; Juvenal (i, 155) warns satirists not to attack Tigellinus, a well-known favourite of Nero, if they would avoid 'blazing at the tarred stake, where they stand with pierced breast in flames and smoke'. Even although we follow the school of the distinguished philosopher Drew, and believe that the whole passage of Tacitus dealing with Nero's persecution of the Christians is a later invention, we cannot doubt the true existence of death by fire in the manner of 'Nero's torches'. This form of execution, like every other, was preceded by scourging.

Another no less old method of execution was death by the sack. This was the punishment for the murder of a free man or woman, and especially of a relative. The Twelve Tables lay down that a thief of crops shall be crucified, and a murderer put to death by the sack. In this death the condemned man was first scourged with the greatest severity – it is expressly mentioned (*Digest*, xlviii, 9, 9) that he shall be flogged *sanguineis virgis*, with blood-stained rods – and then placed in an oxhide sack together with snakes, a cock, a dog, or an ape. The sack was then sewn up and sunk in the Tiber or in the sea.

From a speech of Cicero (*Pro Roscio*, 25) we learn something of the peculiar thought which was at the basis of this punishment. 'Our ancestors understood that there was nothing so sacred as to be kept safe from conscienceless attacks. Therefore they conceived an exceptional punishment for parricide in order that those who could not be held to their duty by the bonds of nature might be debarred from crime by the greatness of the penalty. They decreed that such men should be sewn into a sack and thrown alive into the river. What outstanding wisdom was this! Surely they seem to have banished such a man, to have torn him away from the world by denying him in one moment the air, the light, water, and earth; so that, for killing him who had given him life he himself might be denied all the principles of life. They would not throw his corpse to the beasts lest even the brutes which had touched a crime so terrible might become more savage. They would not throw him naked into the river lest he might be borne down into the sea and pollute that which is thought to purify all other defilements. ... He is to live his last moments without

T—D

breathing the air of heaven. He is to die, but the earth is not to touch his bones. He is to be tossed in the waves and never be cleansed. At last he is to be cast up against the rocks so that he may never have rest even in death.'

From immemorial times the punishment for theft by slave and for high treason and desertion to the enemy by a free citizen was to be thrown from the Tarpeian Rock. Livy (xxiv, 20) tells us that 370 deserters who had been captured were flogged with rods in the Forum, and then hurled from the Rock. Consider an event such as this, in all its real horror, as being a sort of brutal show; for such it was. Then you will understand that it is a short step from such a penalty to the fighting beasts and gladiators.

Today it must appear perhaps the strangest and most sadistic of these executions, which were also public festivals. But before we examine them more closely, we must briefly investigate the treatment of that class on which at all times sadism has been able to wreak its will most freely – the slaves.

4. Slavery

When Schopenhauer (*Parerga*, xi, 217) says that there is much evidence old and new to support 'the conviction that man surpasses the tiger and hyena in cruelty and pitiless-ness', he could have gathered much evidence from the accounts of Roman treatment of slaves. The distinguished classical scholar Birt takes much trouble to prove that on the whole the life of a Roman slave was not too dreadful. But we must assert that his picture is onesided, though correct as far as it goes. We must not make the same mistake on the negative side. We shall therefore admit the correctness of all that has been said about the better side of Roman slavery. But here we shall show the other side of the Roman slave's life, which might sometimes be so comfortable. It is of course easily understood that such a valuable piece of property as a slave would not be abused and tortured without respite – least of all in ancient times, when each man had few slaves and lived on simple terms with them. It is established that the first slaves in Rome were prisoners of war. Perhaps, as Mommsen held, this was the origin of the bond of pious duty between master and slave. In accordance with this sentiment, a slave was never admitted to give evidence against his master. On the other hand, the State always protected the master against his slaves, set public officials to capture runaway slaves, and imposed the death penalty on every slave in a household even if only one of them had murdered the master. There is a famous instance of this in Tacitus (*Annals*, xiv, 42), and this we must examine more closely, for it shows the real possession of the law against slaves, however gently they might be treated by any particular master. Here is the story: 'Pedanius Secundus, prefect of the city, was murdered by one of his slaves, either because he had been refused his liberty after paying for it, or because he was in love with a youth and could not bear to be supplanted by his master. But when all the slaves who had dwelt under the same roof were to be executed in accordance with ancient custom, a meeting of the commons (to save the lives of the innocent) grew into a riot. In the Senate itself many voices were raised against this excessive severity, although the majority held that no change should be made.'

The famous jurist, C. Cassius, made a burning speech in favour of the cruel law. Tacitus proceeds 'No one man dared to speak in opposition to Cassius; but a confusion of voices called for pity for the slaves – pity for their great number, their age, and sex, and general innocence. However, the majority were for the execution. But the order could not be carried out in the face of the massed crowds who were now brandishing stones and torches. Then the Emperor issued an edict rebuking them, and lined the way to the place of execution with armed guards.'

The brilliant scholar Stahr, in his admirable translation of Tacitus, rightly points out that the behaviour of the lower masses in strenuously opposing the brutal execution of 400 innocent persons makes a happy contrast to the cowardice and savagery of the rich and noble senators. It was fear of the multitudes of slaves who had suffered under them that compelled them to insist on this frightful penalty.

Inflexible law made the position of slaves in Rome as bad as it could be. A slave was not a man, but a thing, which his master could use as he will. The *Institutions* of

Caius (i, 8, 1) say 'Slaves are in the power of their masters; in all nations the masters have the power of life and death over the slaves.'

Hence we can easily understand that few masters felt obliged to care for slaves who were old or ill. Cato the elder says: 'You should sell old cattle, sick draught-animals, sick sheep, wool and hides, old carts and old iron, old slaves, sick slaves, and everything else which is superfluous.' Cicero once says that it would be better to lighten a ship in emergency by throwing an old slave into the sea rather than a good horse. It is true that the most appalling cruelties were practised on slaves in the later ages, when individuals possessed great herds of them; whence the proverb 'A hundred slaves, a hundred enemies'. But Plautus, living about two centuries before Christ, shows that slave-life was inseparable from floggings and the ever present danger of crucifixion.

The treatment of slaves in a besieged city is sketched by Appian (*Civil War*, v, 35) in his description of Perusia about 38 B.C.: 'Lucius collected the remaining provisions and forbade them to be given to the slaves; but he took care that the slaves should not escape to inform the enemy of the city's extremity. The slaves then collected in crowds and lay down within the city, or between the city and the defending wall, feeding on any grass or green leaves which they could find. Lucius buried those who died in long trenches, so that he might not inform the enemy of the fact by burning the bodies, nor allow stenches and disease to arise if they were left to rot.'

If the slaves had generally been treated like human beings, there would have been none of these slave risings which developed into wars. Diodorus saw this, and said: 'As power in use degenerates into cruelty and outrage, the morale of the subject races changes into wild desperation. Every man whose allotted station in life is inferior gladly relinquishes fame and magnificence to the man above him; but if he does not receive the treatment due to a human being he becomes the enemy of his inhuman master.'

These slave risings abounded in acts of sadistic cruelty. We must mention a few especially interesting events from these revolts. In Diodorus' account of the slave war, which broke out in Sicily about 240 B.C., we read (xxxiv, 2): 'For

sixty years after the power of Carthage had been broken,
the Sicilians were generally prosperous. Then the slave war
broke out, and this was its cause. Since their property had
greatly increased and they had collected great wealth, they
bought a multitude of slaves. The slaves were brought in
herds from the slave-pens, and immediately branded on
the flesh with special marks: the young ones were used as
drovers, and the others also had suitable duties. Their
service was very hard, and as regards food and clothing
they were almost uncared for. The majority kept themselves alive by banditry; murder was widespread, for armies
of brigands wandered about the country. The governors
tried to stop this, but since the masters of these slave-ban-
dits were too powerful, they were unable to punish them,
and were compelled to look on at the plunder of the whole
country. Most of the masters were Roman knights who
were feared by the governors as being the judges of all
officials who were impeached. Now the slaves were oppressed by their wretched condition and were often beaten
without good reason; they could endure it no longer. They
seized every opportunity to assemble and talk of revolt till
at last they brought their resolves into action.'

The history of this rising is one of unqualified horror.
Diodorus (*loc. cit.*) thus describes the acts of the rebellious
slaves: 'They broke into houses and committed wholesale
murders. They did not spare even children at the breast,
but tore them from their mothers and dashed them to the
ground. No tongue can tell what acts of abominable outrage
they committed on women before the eyes of their husbands.'

A Roman landlord named Damophilus and his wife
Megallis are mentioned for their exceptional cruelty. (It is
an interesting and significant fact that all our evidence
agrees in describing the cruelty which women practised on
slaves.) Diodorus says this: 'Damophilus treated his slaves
with excessive cruelty; his wife, Megallis, vied with him in
punishing the slaves and practising atrocities on them.' And
elsewhere: 'Since Damophilus was a man of no education
or breeding, in possession of great wealth without responsibility, he went from arrogance to outrage, and finally
brought destruction on himself and disaster on his country.
For he bought a multitude of slaves and treated them out-

rageously: he branded the bodies of those who had been free men in their own countries but had been made prisoners of war and enslaved. Some he fettered and imprisoned them in the slave pen, others he made herdsmen, without giving them suitable food or necessary clothing. No day passed without his mistreating some of his slaves for insufficient reasons – so remorseless and cruel was his nature. His wife, Megallis, took no less pleasure in outrageous punishments which she inflicted with great savagery on her maids and the slaves under her charge.'

All the hate of the rebellious slaves centred on Damophilus and Megallis first of all. She was handed over to the slave-women for her punishment, who tortured her and hurled her alive from a cliff; while Damophilus himself was hacked to death by swords and axes. With amazing rapidity the rising gathered enormous crowds of supporters – Diodorus talks of 200,000 men. They won several battles against Roman regular troops; but after being besieged in several cities (where they underwent such frightful tortures from hunger that they began to eat one another) they eventually surrendered to the soldiers of Rome. The prisoners were tortured in the old manner and then thrown down from precipices.

Everyone knows of the later revolt led by Spartacus. In this rising, the horrors at which we have hinted were repeated. Eventually these rebels also had to capitulate – about 6,000 of them – and died most cruelly on crosses along the Appian Way.

We have mentioned the fact that Roman women were distinguished for cruelty to their slaves. We shall adduce a few significant passages from the ancient evidence. Ovid speaks of the matter (*ars amat.*, iii, 235 ff.):

> But sometimes you may dress your hair before him,
>   and spread it hanging lightly on your back.
> And then take special care to show no temper :
>   you must not shake it out, to dress again,
> or strike the hairdresser. I hate the woman
>   who wounds her maid with hairpins, or her nails.
> The poor girl curses every hair she touches,
>   and weeps and bleeds behind her mistress's back.

In his *Amores* (i, 14) Ovid, referring to his mistress's hair, says:

> Your hair flowed easily in a hundred ringlets:
>   it never hurt you, or resisted you.
> It was not torn by comb or scratched by hairpin;
>   the maid who dressed it never had a wound.
> She often curled your hair before me; never
>   a savage hairpin wounded her soft arms.

Juvenal's account is still more unpleasant (vi, 474 ff.):

> But you should know what Everywoman does
> at home all day. Suppose her husband turns
> his back to her in bed. God help the housemaid!
> The lady's maids are stripped, the coachman's thrashed
> for being late (punished because another
> slept), rods are broken, bleeding backs are scourged
> and lashed: some women keep a private flogger.
> She scourges while her face is made up, talks
> to her friends, examines a gold-braided frock
> and thrashes, reads the daily paper through
> and thrashes, till the thrasher tires, and she
> screams GO NOW, and the inquisition's over.
> She rules her home more savagely than a tyrant.
> Has she an assignation, wants to look
> more beautiful than usual, quick, he's waiting
> under the trees, or in Queen Isis' brothel –
> poor Psecas combs the mistress's hair, her own
> tattered, with naked shoulders and bare breasts.
> 'This curl's too high.' At once the oxhide thong
> lashes the wretch: her crime was a coiffure.

If a slave-woman ever happened to let a mirror fall on her mistress's foot she was certain to be severely punished out of hand. In his treatise, *The Knowledge and Cure of Passions*, Galen speaks of a master who in fits of passion would rage against his slaves with his teeth, his feet, and his fists, knocking out their eyes or gouging them with his stylus. The mother of the Emperor Hadrian seems to have bitten her slave girls when she was in a rage. Chrysostom mentions a mistress who had her maid stripped and tied to the end of the couch and flogged in such a way that people passing in the street heard the poor girl's shrieks. The girl, who had suffered this, showed her bruised back for all to see when she accompanied her mistress to the baths.

Particularly cruel masters actually fed the lampreys in their fishponds with slaves. With regard to this Seneca writes (*De clem.*, i, 18, and *De ira.*, iii, 40): 'Although everything is permitted against a slave, the law which is common to all living beings refuses to allow certain things against any man. Surely everyone must have hated Vedius Pollio

even worse than his slaves did – for he fattened his lampreys with human blood and ordered anyone, who had
committed an offence, to be thrown into his tank which
was nothing but a pit of snakes? Surely he deserved a thousand deaths, whether he had his slaves thrown to the
lampreys which he was going to eat, or kept the lampreys
for no other purpose than to feed them in this way.' The
other passage is more circumstantial. 'Augustus was dining with Vedius Pollio. One of the host's slaves had broken
a crystal dish and Vedius ordered him to be put to death,
in an extraordinary way – by being thrown to the great
lampreys which he kept in his fish pond. Are we to believe
that it was gluttony which dictated this order, and not
cruelty? The boy tore himself away and fell at the Emperor's feet to ask him this only – that he should die by
some other death, and not to be fed to the fish. The cruelty
of this unusual order moved the Emperor to indignation,
and he ordered that the slave should be freed, that all the
crystal dishes be smashed in his presence, and that the fish-
pond be filled up. The Emperor was obliged to punish his
friend; he used his power in the correct way.'

But the gentle treatment of slaves, which the humane
Seneca commends, was always an exception, as we see from
the sentence which he himself uses: 'Everything is permitted against a slave.' The words of Galen (*de plac. Hip-
pocr. et Platon.* vi, extr.) seem to follow the truth only too
often. 'Such are they who punish their slaves for some error
by burning, slitting and maiming the legs of runaways, the
hands of thieves, the bellies of gluttons, the tongues of gos-
sipers—' (*exsecta lingua,* Cicero *pro Cluentio*) 'in short by
punishing each offender on that part of the body by which
he has offended.' It is true that Seneca advises Lucilius
(*Ep.*, 47) as follows: 'Fear and love cannot live together.
You seem to me to do right in refusing to be feared by your
slaves and chastising them with words alone. Blows are
used to correct brute beasts.' Columella and Varro speak
to the same effect. But the reports of evil treatment of
slaves are far more numerous; certainly it is true that the
suspicion and harshness of the masters grew with the
growth of the slave population, and that still subtler tortures were constantly invented.

As for the number of slaves in Rome, Aemilius Paulus is said to have brought back 150,000, while Marius imported 60,000 Cimbrians and 90,000 Teutons. Josephus tells us that at the end of the first century A.D. the number of slaves in Rome reached a million. A great traffic in slaves had developed in the Mediterranean, and pirates used to kidnap many of the coast dwellers to sell them into slavery.

Finally, we must not forget that Roman law did not admit the torture of a free man, but always employed this cruel method of extracting evidence from a slave. There was no such thing as a slave's evidence given without torture. Everyone not of free birth was always questioned under torture. The means used were all sorts of scourging, as well as the hideous torments which the middle ages took over from Rome and employed for centuries at every special investigation. Such were the *fidiculæ* – cords for wrenching the joints apart, the *equuleus* – a trestle in which the slave sat while his limbs were dislocated either by a windlass or by weights attached to his feet; so also red hot metal plates were laid on the slaves' bare flesh, and so the dreadful leather scourges were intertwined with spikes and knuckle-bones to increase their atrocity. To win a confession, the examiners did not shrink from torturing even women slaves in this way. Tacitus describes (*Ann.*, xv, 57) such a scene at the torture of a slave girl who was said to know of a conspiracy against Nero. It runs: 'Meanwhile Nero remembered that Epicharis was under arrest on the information of Volusius Proculus, and, in the belief that a weak woman could not resist pain, he ordered her to be torn by torture. But neither the lash, nor the fire, nor the fury of her torturers, which was redoubled to break down the woman's scornful resolution, could compel her to admit the accusations against her. In this way, the first day of the investigation was wasted. Next day, when she was being carried back to her torture on a chair – for her limbs were so wrenched that she could not support herself – she tied the girdle from her breast to the frame of her chair in a noose: she looped this round her neck and threw the weight of her body into it, and so crushed out what life she had left.'

We are told by Valerius of a case where a slave, who was 'still almost a boy', was subjected to hideous tortures –

lashing, burning with plates of metal, dislocation of the
limbs. Valerius mentions the case as an example of the
fidelity of slaves. From this story, as well as from that of
Tacitus, we see how little attention was paid to the age or
sex of those who were to be tortured, provided they were
not of free birth. It is very interesting to trace how the
Roman state began, from imperial times, to take measures
against the worst excesses of cruelty to slaves. This was no
doubt due in part to changing social conditions; but perhaps it also resulted from the spread of such humanitarian
ideas as we find in Seneca especially and later in the Christian writings. Just after the beginning of the Empire, a law
forbade masters to condemn their slaves to fight with wild
beasts, and transferred this right to a judge with statutory
powers (*Digest*, xlviii, 8, 11, 2). From the time of Antoninus Pius, a slave who felt himself too hardly treated could
complain to a municipal judge, and be sold in certain circumstances to another master. Claudius pronounced those
slaves to be free who were abandoned by their master when
they were ill. Hadrian abolished the master's right to kill
his slave at choice, or sell him to the arena, while Constantine put intentional killing of a slave on the same foot-
ing as murder (*Digest*, i, 12, 1; Spartian. *Hadr*. 18; *Cod.
Just*., ix, 14). And from the time of Hadrian dates the pregnant sentence: *patria potestas in pietate debet, non atroci-
tate consistere* – 'paternal power must consist of love and
not of cruelty.'

We must never forget that the spread of these gentler
views was in no small measure due to purely economic
changes. After the time when the Romans could extend
their conquests no further and confined themselves to im-
proving the organization and administration of their colossal
Empire, the principal sources of slavery (the importation of
prisoners of war and kidnapping) had sensibly diminished.
We know now that the slave population reached its greatest
extent about the beginning of Imperial times.

5. Public Executions

But the improvement in the attitude towards slaves forms
a marked contrast to the development of cruel punish-

ments. The last year of the Republic tended to abolish where possible the death penalty for a free Roman citizen. But, at the beginning of Imperial times, under Augustus, a general increase in punishments is noticeable – especially a more frequent infliction of the death penalty. As time goes on, these punishments are imposed more and more freely, they are inflicted for less and less serious offences, the executions are more severe, acts of tyranny grow and multiply. In the reign of the 'Christian' Emperor Constantine, horrible things make their appearance – tearing out of the tongue, pouring of melted lead into the mouth of the criminal. And it was during the Empire that what Mommsen called 'ceremonial executions' first took place in their full atrocity.

We must first signalize the difference between the real gladiatorial games which were not invariably considered as the punishment of condemned criminals, and, on the other hand, the throwing of criminals to wild beasts as a death penalty. We therefore shall treat separately the two kinds of shows in which men killed each other or were done to death to satisfy sadistic lusts. We shall, in fact, omit the real hunts of wild animals brought for that purpose to the arena – hunts which corresponded to the bull fights of today. We shall speak of the hunts which were at bottom no more than cruel methods of inflicting the penalty of death. Even during the Republic it was possible for a criminal (if not of free birth), when condemned to death after judicial examination, *bestiis dari*; that is, to be handed over to an amphitheatre in order to be torn to pieces by wild beasts as a public show. It is Valerius Maximus (ii, 7, 13) who mentions the earliest of these executions: 'After the overthrow of Carthage, Africanus the younger threw foreign deserters to wild beasts at the public shows which he produced in Rome, and Lucius Paulus after his victory over Perseus ordered such people to be laid down and trampled by elephants.'

These accounts show that this cruel method of execution originated from the law of warfare, which has always been the lowest stage in the development of law. They prove also that the Romans of the 'degenerate' imperial times were by no means the first to take pleasure in such cruel displays. Here again we see the truth of the psychoanalyst Stekel's remark: 'In the human soul, cruelty crouches like a beast, chained, but eager to spring.' If the earlier ages of Roman development had been able to throw their criminals before wild beasts, they would certainly have done so as freely as imperial times, when wild animals were imported wholesale. We cannot repeat often enough that the Romans were cruel by nature. Under Augustus, execution by casting to wild beasts was a statutory punishment. Mommsen says of it: 'It was quite as legitimate as the usual forms . . . its juristic regularity is beyond dispute.' We are told of the Emperor Claudius by his biographer Suetonius that he 'overstepped the legal penalty for serious frauds by sentencing such criminals to fight with wild beasts'. This remark shows that such a sentence depended on the will of the judge. Another passage in Suetonius gives us a picture of the character of these judges. Referring to Claudius, he writes: 'He directed that examination by torture and executions for high treason should take place in full before his eyes. On one occasion he wished to see an execution in the old manner, in the town of Tibur; when the criminals were already tied to the stake, no executioner could be found, but Claudius sent for one from Rome and insisted on waiting for him until the evening. At every gladiatorial game given by himself or another, he ordered even those fighters who had fallen by accident – especially the fighters with nets – to have their throats cut so that he could watch their faces as they died' (Suet., *Claud.*, 34).

But even apart from such natural sadists, there were many men in whom the same impulses slumbered, to be awakened by the sight of such cruelties. Augustine (*Confessions,* vi, 8) tells the following story: 'A young Christian was living in Rome as a student. He had long avoided the amphitheatre, but was at last taken to visit it by friends. He told them that they could drag his body there but not his soul, for he would sit with his eyes closed and so be really absent. This he did, but a great shout induced him to open his eyes in curiosity. Then, says Augustine, 'his soul was stricken more sorely than the bodies of those he yearned to see, and his fall was more lamentable than that which had caused the shout. For with the sight of blood, he absorbed a lust for cruelty; he could not turn away; his gaze grew fixed; he was drunk with the lust for blood. Why should I say more? He looked, his blood burned, and he took away with him a madness which goaded him to return again.' Modern psychiatry tells us that innumerable men have become conscious sadists in exactly the same way – even by witnessing a flogging at school, or by reading about such things or seeing pictures of them. As we have seen, the capability slumbers in the soul of almost everyone. In the course of centuries the receptive soul of the Roman people must have been terribly affected by numerous and varied public executions which reached extremes of cruelty in the arena. For it is certain that even minor criminals or slaves were sent to the arena to make up the numbers of the men whose death agonies delighted the Roman mob; and that mob comprised all classes of the people, even the chaste vestal virgins.

These victims of sadism were sent to their death in several different ways. Perhaps there was no way more dreadful than this: the criminal was chained to a stake, naked and unarmed, and so, defenceless, was mangled by wild beasts specially trained. A poem of Martial (*De Spect.*, 7) indicates that this was a frequent occurrence:

> Even as Prometheus on the Scythian mountain
>   fed with his growing breast the eternal bird,
> Laureolus, not in mimic crucifixion,
>   gave his bare flesh to a Caledonian bear.
> His frame still lived when all the limbs were mangled,
>   and all his body bore no trace of self.
> At last his punishment was just: the scoundrel
>   had stabbed his father's or his master's breast,
> or in his wicked madness robbed a temple,
>   or kindled Rome with sacrilegious fire.
> He had surpassed the crimes of ancient fable,
>   and now a fable was his punishment.

This poem is also an example of the execution of criminals as dramatic presentations of death scenes. This man Laureolus was compelled to portray Prometheus chained to a rock and gnawed by the eagle – except that here the criminal was chained to the stake and eaten alive by a bear. Similarly a man called Mnesthus, who murdered the Emperor Aurelian, was mangled by wild beasts at the stake.

And we learn from Ammian (xxix, 3, 9) that the Emperor
Valentinian kept two savage she bears to devour criminals.
'He looked after these brutes with such care that he had
their dens near his own bedroom; and set faithful guards
to see that they should not lose their murderous savagery.'
Many examples of such atrocities could be cited, since the
Acts of the Martyrs abound in them.

Again, it was always thought charming to connect mythological scenes with these executions – such as the castration
of Attis, the burning of Hercules (or of a criminal in his
costume), and the death of Orpheus by a bear (Tertullian,
apol., 15; Martial, *de Spect.*, 21; and elsewhere). Birt says
with reference to these shows: 'To our amazement the
philanthropic Emperor Titus perpetrated the wildest of
these excesses, or at least allowed it to happen. The arena
of the Colosseum is transformed into a forest – a criminal
is to die. Dressed as the bard Orpheus, he comes out of the
forest in rich robes, playing joyously on his lyre; as if enchanted, wild and tame animals follow his song. The old
legend has come to life, the public is astonished. Meanwhile, the bear advances; it attacks Orpheus and rends him
to pieces. What a perversion of the majesty of death and of
the real meaning of the condemnation! The execution becomes a fairy-tale, the dying criminal becomes an actor
playing a tragedy he does not know. And yet the rabble of
Rome must have its senses titillated in this way.'

It is our intention to illustrate by these instances the
fundamental difference between the souls of Greece and
Rome. In the Greek Theatre, when Oedipus fulfilled his
destiny in the hearing and sight of a really educated public,
the terror of pure tragedy, of real and great art gripped
everyone of his hearers. But in the Roman amphitheatre,
the most refined evocations of everything that was cruel,
atrocious, and abominable were used to charm the morbid
desires of a nation whose sadistic tendencies had been excited for centuries by sadistic sights and displays. The
Greeks listened with rapt attention to the profound words
of Sophocles. The Romans indulged their gross passions
with the shrieks of human beings tortured to death. Could
there be a more striking picture of the inner life of the two
nations?

6. The Arena

The amphitheatres, whose enormous ruins are still partly preserved, served another purpose. As well as the beast-shows, which we have described at their cruellest, there were the contests of gladiators. These contests were duels between two or more men who sometimes practised their bloody craft as a career, but were sometimes compelled to it as equivalent to a death penalty.

Inquiries about the historical development of these games lead us to two interesting accounts. The first comes from the history of Nicolaus of Damascus, who lived in the time of Augustus (*ap.* Athenaeus, iv, 153 f. and 154) It reads: 'The Romans, who inherited the custom from the Etruscans, gave gladiatorial shows not only at festivals and in theatres, but also during banquets. They often invited their friends to dinner, to enjoy among other pleasures the sight of two or three pairs of duellists; they were called in when the guests had eaten and drunk to their hearts' content. And when one of the fighters was cut down, the guests were delighted and applauded. A Roman once directed in his will that the most beautiful woman in his possession should fight a duel, and another ordered such a duel between boys whom he had loved. However, the commons did not tolerate such a transgression of the law, and found the will null and void.'

In the first place this interesting note points to the Etruscan origin of the gladiatorial games. But it is also strong evidence for the coarseness of the Roman character – the guests, stimulated by the banquet, delighted their senses with the spice of sadistic enjoyment. Finally, this note seems to me to show a peculiar correspondence with another account by Valerius Maximus. He says (ii, 4, 7): 'In the consulship of Appius Claudius and Marcus Fulvius, the first gladiatorial show was given in Rome in the cattle market. It was given by Marcus and Decimus Brutus to honour their father's ashes at the funeral ceremony. The contest of athletes was carried out through the generosity of Marcus Scaurus.'

There is no ground for doubting the historical correctness of these notes. It looks therefore as if these games were funeral games, borrowed from the dark and gloomy customs of the Etruscans. Perhaps they go back to a custom of many nations – the custom of putting into the grave everything which belonged to the dead man in his lifetime, especially his mistresses and favourite boys. To this custom the first note perhaps makes allusion. In addition, there is an Etruscan origin for the custom of dragging out the dead gladiators by slaves wearing the masks of an Etruscan god of death. At all events, we may certainly take as established the Etruscan origin of the gladiatorial games. The sadistic impulses which grew so deep in the Roman heart ensured the increasing popularity of this custom. The first gladiatorial show mentioned by the historians took place in the year 264 B.C. Livy (xxiii, 30; xxxi, 50; xxxix, 46; xli, 28) tells us that it gradually became a widespread Roman custom to honour the death of great men by spending ever greater sums of money on their funeral games. For instance, in 174 B.C., seventy-four men fought for three days in honour of the dead father of Titus Flaminius.

By the end of the Republic the practice of exhibiting gladiators had grown to such an extent that (although only private persons had hitherto given such exhibitions) the State took cognizance of it and issued regulations for it. Suetonius tells us (*Julius*, 10) that 'Julius Caesar while he was aedile gave a gladiatorial show, which contained fewer fighters than he had intended; for he had so terrified his enemies by the numbers of the troupe he had gathered that a decree was issued defining the maximum number which could be kept in Rome by any individual'. Plutarch, however, says that he exhibited 320 pairs (*Caesar*, 5). Ambitious men like Caesar made increasing use of these games to capture popular favour. The man who distributed corn and gave entertainment to the people could count upon its gratitude. Plutarch says in the same passage: 'By exhibiting 320 pairs of gladiators, and by other magnificent and costly theatrical displays, processions, and banquets during his aedileship, he overshadowed the ambitious efforts of his predecessors and made the commons so grateful that every man thought of new offices and honours with which to repay him.'

By this time sumptuous private displays, and displays arranged by the State itself existed side by side. The emperor Augustus laid down restrictions for public games and Tiberius did the same for games given by private individuals. But we can see from many accounts how little these regulations were observed. We cannot cite all the accounts; it is enough to allude to one passage in Tacitus (*Histories*, ii, 95): 'Caecina and Valens celebrated the birthday of Vitellius by gladiatorial shows displayed in every ward of the city with enormous and unparalleled expense.'

In the course of succeeding centuries these games multiplied so prodigiously that hardly any little provincial city lacked its amphitheatre. Inscriptions such as are found in Pompeii prove that the games were very often given by rich private citizens. Martial jokes about this (iii, 59)—

> One city had a show given by a cobbler,
> one by a fuller. An innkeeper's next!

On the other hand, officials of colonial towns and boroughs were obliged by law to give such games; as we learn from the charter of Urso in Spain, which dates roughly to the year 44 B.C. (cf. Friedländer's *History of Morals*, ed. 8, vol. ii, p. 427). But the games in Rome were by far the hugest. From the time of the Flavian Emperors they were held in the gigantic Flavian amphitheatre: and its arena was crowded with hordes of fighting men. In A.D. 107, at the games given by Trajan after the conquest of Dacia, 10,000 men fought for four months (Cassius Dio, 68, 15).

It is natural to ask where the organizers of these colossal games got their human material. The evidence shows that it came from very different sources. The fighters were partly prisoners of war and partly criminals (after A.D. 100) either sentenced to the arena or driven to it by Caesar's ordinance. The latter was commonly the case under emperors like the sadist Caligula and his successor Claudius (Dio, 69, 10; Sueton., *Calig.*, 35; *Claud.*, 14). Again, slaves were employed as gladiators: Cicero's friend, Atticus purchased a troupe of this kind. Finally, many men enrolled themselves as gladiators for one reason or another. A poet in the time of Tiberius says that these men sold themselves to death in the arena, and even if there was no war made themselves their own enemies.

Only the strongest of motives could have induced a man to enter this life of his own free will. Those who did so had to swear an oath to 'let themselves be scourged with rods, burned with fire, killed with iron'. The gladiators were lodged in special barracks, like that excavated at Pompeii. The oldest barracks of which we read dates to the end of the second century B.C., those in Capua to 63 B.C., and the largest were those which were attached to the Flavian amphitheatre in Rome. Life in these barracks was like the death to which it led – hard, rough, and cruel. Discipline was maintained by scourges, red-hot branding irons, and iron fetters. Escape was rare; so that we cannot wonder if suicide was common among the better spirits who had been forced into this life. Occasionally, a slave who was not in favour, perhaps if he had run away and been captured, would be sold to a gladiatorial trainer (*lanista*) or to a gladiatorial school. An odd case of this is related by Suetonius (*Vitell.*, 12). Vitellius was in love with a male slave called Asiaticus, with whom 'he had practised the defilement of lust'. However, Asiaticus grew tired of this in time (perhaps because he had other sexual impulses), and ran away from his lover. Vitellius recaptured him 'and enjoyed him again; but growing tired of his stubbornness and his rebelliousness, sold him to the master of a travelling troupe of gladiators'. But eventually he took him back and freed him from slavery, and 'on the first day of his reign gave the man golden rings'.

We have a vivid description of a gladiatorial fight in Seneca (*Ep.*, 7): 'I happened to go to a show yesterday at noon. I looked to find fun, wit, and relaxation, which would rest men's eyes from the sight of bloodshed. I found the opposite. All previous fights had been merciful: but this was a serious business – pure murder. The men have no defence: their bodies are open to every blow; every attack is bound to be successful. Most spectators prefer this to the regular duels of skill. They would! The fighters have no helmet or shield to resist the sword. What use is protection or training? These things only postpone death. In the morning men are killed by lions and bears, at midday they are killed by the spectators. The killer is sent out to be killed, and the victorious fighter is kept back for another murder. All the fighters meet one end – death. Fire and sword fight together until the arena is empty. "But," you will say, "one of them was a bandit." What of it? "He murdered a man." Then he deserves to be killed; but *you*, you wretch, what crime have you committed to make you deserve to see such a sight? "Strike him, flog him, burn him! Why does he shrink from the blade? Why does he strike so timidly? Why does he die so grudgingly?" They are lashed on to wound each other. They must strike and be struck with their breasts bare to the blows. This is an interval in the show – we must have some throat-cutting as an *entr'acte*. Do you not understand that evil examples have evil consequences for the men who provide them?'

Seneca's vivid account can be understood without further explanation. It describes an interval between the contests of trained fighters (which did not always end with death). But how is the interval occupied? In a truly Roman way, by setting condemned criminals to fight each other without defensive armour until they are all killed. In fact, by kill-as-kill-can fighting; which, as Seneca says, with bitter emphasis, the public enjoyed more than the regular battles between trained gladiators.

One final question. Rome produced many men of refined and philosophic natures – like Cicero, Tacitus, and Seneca. Was there no one to raise his voice against this passion for sadistic excitement? Any inquirer who shares our opinion that sadism was among the foundations of the Roman character will not be surprised to find that even the best men of that race did not in general oppose the gladiatorial system. Under the emperors, society must have taken the same interest in gladiators that it now takes in boxing-matches or films. The underlying reasons for enjoying such things are much the same now as they were then. We hear that children played at being gladiators; the younger generation keenly discussed the most important local fighters; the philosopher Epictetus warned his hearers against the tedious habit of gossiping about gladiatorial fights, while Horace already knew that to be a favourite subject of idle conversation. The general public, and women not least of them, raved about famous gladiators as we do about famous singers and actors. Inscriptions have been found on walls in Pompeii and elsewhere, calling a Thracian gladiator *suspirium et decus puellarum*, 'the maiden's prayer and delight', or *medicus puparum*, 'the doctor to cure girls'. Even great ladies of the court seem to have had occasional amours with gladiators. Marcus Aurelius' wife, Faustina, was accused of such intrigues, and her cruel son Commodus was actually described as the child of one of them (Julius Capitolinus, *M. Ant. Phil.*, 19). Distinguished gladiators were the subjects of many poems (Mart., v, 24); their portraits were on lamps, dishes, and pots.

But even the opinions which educated people held on the subject are almost unintelligible for modern minds. Cicero says (*Tusc.*, ii, 17): 'Many people are apt to think that the gladiatorial games are cruel and inhuman – perhaps rightly, as things now are. But in the days when criminals fought for their lives, sword in hand, our ears might find better lessons against pain and death, but our eyes certainly would not.' And in a letter he writes: 'What sort of pleasure can an educated man have in watching a weak man mangled by a powerful animal, or a noble beast pierced by a hunting-spear?' So it is only on the ground of the insufficiency of the pleasure that Cicero dislikes these cruel executions by the teeth and claws of wild beasts. And Tacitus – a man full of humanity and free from the prejudices of his time – cannot understand the repugnance which gladiatorial fights inspired in Tiberius, the emperor whom he describes with such prejudice and distortion. He writes (*Ann.*, i, 76): 'Drusus (son of Tiberius) presided at the games which he gave in the names of his brother and himself. He took too much pleasure in the slaughter, although it was of men who mattered nothing. This created dismay among the common people; even his father was said to have censured it. Tiberius himself was absent: various reasons were given for this: some said he disliked large crowds, others said it was his gloomy nature and the fear of comparison with Augustus' friendly participation in the games. I cannot believe that he gave his son the opportunity to show his native cruelty and offend the people, although that also has been stated.'

Seneca was the only ancient writer to attain the view of this and other matters which is now held by the whole of the civilized world. He writes (*Ep.*, 95, 33): 'Man is a thing which is sacred to mankind; but nowadays he is killed in play, for fun. It was once a sin to teach him how to inflict wounds or receive them; but now he is led out naked and defenceless, and provides a sufficient show by his death.'

Friedländer says (*loc. cit*., p. 420) with much justice, in summing up the whole matter of gladiatorial games, and we entirely agree with him, that 'Rome imported the Etruscan spectacle at a rough, warlike age. At first it was a rare thing, but gradually became more frequent, and after centuries had passed was common. By slow degrees, transmitted from family to family, and taking ever deeper root, habit exercised its irresistible power. And that power is enormous – it alone can change an original repugnance to cruelty into enjoyment of it, and there is no one who can avoid the influence of that spirit which penetrates his own era. Moreover, executions accompanied by torture have at all times been attractive shows.'

But Friedländer forgets to add that men acquire delight in cruelty, not only through the force of habit, but from the sadistic impulses which sleep more or less soundly in every man's heart, and which when once aroused always craves for stronger stimulus and stronger satisfaction. With these words we may conclude this chapter on Roman sadism. We have looked into the inmost heart of the Romans, and seen – what? The unrestrained impulse of the 'will to power' fulfilling itself in acts of cruelty.

But the unprejudiced inquirer will make another discovery. Out of this ocean of hatred, out of this madness of cruelty which raged with unequalled frenzy in the games of the arena, there appears the noblest word of religion. It rises like a delicate flower from a dark and sodden earth, the one truth which was strange to all the Roman nature: 'God is love.'

Until now, writers have always tried to show that the new religion, the gospel of universal love with all its innumerable social consequences, appeared by a miracle of providence as something strange and unheard of in the degenerate humanity of the 'declining ancient world'. Today we know that it was no miracle. Those orgies of hate and cruelty were *bound* to produce the gospel of love. It was their compensation: thus, in the life of an individual, cruel and hateful impulses often develop by compensation into the purest love of humanity. Seen in this way, the whole of Roman sadism is a necessary step towards a new, a truly noble state of humanity.

Chapter Three

Roman Religion and Philosophy in Relation to Sexual Life

(a) Religion

IN the second section of this chapter we shall discuss whether philosophy had any influence on the sexual life of the Romans, and how great that influence was. Here we shall investigate sexual life as reflected in Roman religion.

It is not at all surprising that primitive man finds something mysterious and divine in procreative power. Schopenhauer tells us that the sexual impulse manifests 'Nature's inmost being, and the strongest will to life'; while such old Greek poets and thinkers as Hesiod and Parmenides call Eros the Origin, the Creator, the Principle from which all things emerge. Many other nations deify the sexual impulse in this way – and the Romans not least among them.

Now, the vast difference between the classical and the Christian ideas of sexual life can be observed most clearly in this way. In antiquity, especially in Greece and Rome, the generative power was regarded quite ingenuously as the creator of new life, and so as something deserving honour and worship. But the Christian sees everything sexual as primarily unspiritual and unconscious, as something which must be conquered by the spirit lest it grows into such wild exuberance that it dwarfs all other expressions of the spirit. In this, Christianity derives from Plato. For Plato, as we shall see later, was one of the first to distrust the senses and preach a holy war against them. We may agree with Nietzsche's later opinion, that 'degeneration' began with this sophisticated attitude to the senses; or we may say that this change of opinion was part of 'the progress of civilization'. It is in the last resort a matter of personal opinion. At least it is certain that in antiquity men still approached sex in an ingenuous and primitive way, if they were not influenced by Platonic doctrines or others of the same kind: in sex they saw something essentially natural, which yet contained and exercised a power which was divine.

In this connection we may note a misconception which occurs in many books on the subject. It is quite mistaken to draw inferences from the constant occurrence of sexual symbolism in ancient art, and from the exaltation of sex in some ancient festivals, to some peculiar 'immortality' or 'depravity' in ancient times. Even the scholar Burckhardt, in his book on Constantine, speaks of 'infamous cults' – a remark which shows that he is prevented, by starting from Christian assumptions, from doing any real justice to these cults. The earliest Christian writers criticized in exactly the same way the cults which they could no longer understand. Augustine, for instance, in his great work *De civitate Dei* (vi, 9) criticizes from his own point of view all the Roman marriage customs connected with sex, and pronounces them partly ridiculous and partly horrible. In particular, he names the custom which shocks him most of all *mos honestissimus et religiosissimus matronarum*, the 'most honourable and profoundly religious of the customs of married women'; but he himself admits it was not an obscene and abominable practice like those found in degenerate nations. It is natural, of course, that all such primitive religious customs should in time develop into the practice of pure sensuality, and should be prized only as pandering to the grosser appetites. Bloch says with much justice, in the book we have quoted elsewhere (p. 514): 'This ceremony was only a primitive way of paying honour to the sexual principle and an equally primitive sexual exercise performed in reference to the deities of procreation. But it often changed, and became really a sexual debauch; and in such a case it was naturally apt to assume eccentric and unnatural forms, to express itself in obscene talk, onanistic practices, and perverted sexual acts.' However, we must never forget that such perversions are not the real nature of such customs.

1. Indigenous Roman Deities

To proceed to particulars. We may first lay down the principle that a great number of the deities connected with
sexual life which were later introduced into Rome, were
not originally Roman, but imported from other lands.
Which, we may ask, were of Roman origin?

Almost all the old Roman gods were part of the primitive
life of a nation living by laborious agriculture and stock-
rearing and engaged in constant warfare with its neighbours. Such, for example, were Jupiter, the sky god who
encouraged the growth of the crops by rain and sunshine;
Janus, the god of the house; Saturn, the god of sowing;
Ceres, the goddess of growth; Faunus, the god of the forest;
Mars, who protected the community in their annually recurring wars; and Terminus, the guardian of the boundary
stone in the field. There must have been other stages of
religious belief which preceded these deities; but they are
the oldest Roman gods whom we can know. Among them,
we can see hardly any deities connected with the love life
of the Romans. Even the name of Venus does not occur
in the oldest priestly records. On the contrary, we find
among these old gods the sexual deity whom we have
mentioned in the section on marriage. This deity was known
by the double name of Mutunus Tutunus: and had a sanctuary in ancient Rome visited by veiled women, according
to Festus (p. 155). He must have played a great part in
every marriage ceremony. Scholars have sought to derive
the signification of a sexual deity from the god's name by
referring the stem of *Mutunus* to *mentula*, the male sexual
organ; but this derivation is not certain. Augustine, who has
transmitted much information on marriage customs, connects Mutunus Tutunus with the later importation, Priapus.
But Lactantius seems to come nearer the truth (i, 20, 36):
'Tutinus (*sic*) also is honoured: brides seat themselves on
this god's genital member in order to make the first offering
of their virginity to the god.' This is the custom which
occurs among many other primitive peoples – the virginity
of every woman is offered to the god, or else a symbolic
act is performed to signify that offering. At the basis of this
custom is the primitive notion that the god should lend his

magic assistance to the coming marriage, in order to make it fruitful. For primitive man does not suspect the real connection between cohabitation and pregnancy, or has at least very vague ideas about it. From these considerations we can draw an inference about the great age of these sexual deities. It is, of course, not certain that this old custom was carried out at every Roman marriage. Still, various Christian writers mention it, which means that they knew it as still in existence.

To the same species of divine beings belong the deities connected with the further course of the first cohabitation in marriage. About them, Augustine says (*de civ. dei,* vi, 9): 'There are present the goddess Virginiensis, the divine father Subigus, the divine mother Prema, the goddess Pertunda, and Venus and Priapus. What does this mean? If a man really needed help from the gods at this task, would one god or goddess not be enough? Would not Venus alone be amply sufficient? They say that she is named Venus because a woman only loses her virginity *vi*, by force. The gods have no sense of modesty; but if men have any, will the bride and bridegroom not be so overcome by shame when they believe so many gods of both sexes to be present and interested that the groom will be less ardent and the bride be more reluctant? And surely, if the goddess Virginiensis attends to loosen the bride's girdle; if the god Subigus attends to surrender her to the groom; if the goddess Prema attends so that the bride after surrendering may be embraced without struggling – if so, what is the goddess Pertunda doing? She should blush. She should leave the room. The husband should have something to do! It would be very improper for anyone but him to perform the duty after which she is named.'

This interesting passage shows us not only the names and functions of the sexual deities, but also the important fact that at the time of Augustus all these deities were really misunderstood – they were a subject of amusement. In the distant times when men believed in the necessity of divine help in these intimate matters, the deities were never given such solid humanity. They were not considered as a crowd of inquisitive people, whose presence must disturb the important act of marriage, who deserved to be viewed with

indignation or raillery. The malignant criticism of the
Christian author puts him on the same level as the jester
Lucian with his *Dialogues of the Gods*.

We gather then from other passages of Augustine's work
that in very ancient times there were other Roman gods of
marriage. Juno is the guardian of woman's sexual functions; but she is also the goddess of marriage in particular
and as such has a different name for each function. As
Iterduca she brings home the bride; as Unxia or Cinxia she
superintends the anointing of the bride; as Pronuba she is
the bridesmaid; and as Lucina she attends the birth of the
child.

To Juno in woman's life corresponds the Genius in man's
life. A certain scholar has said with justice: 'Genius and
Juno are connected in the same way as procreation and
conception.' The word *Genius* is directly derived from the
root *gen*, meaning *generate* or *procreate*. Of course, the
significance of the Genius was gradually extended to mean
the deity which guards the whole personality and spiritual
existence of every man. And here we see the underlying
notion that every man has his own particular Genius (as
every woman has her own Juno) – a notion which recurs
only in the house deities, especially the Lar, who is bound
in the same way to one particular house. But, however
interesting this may be, we cannot go further into it here.

According to Augustine, other deities also, not really
connected with sexual functions, were in some way considered to be related with them. For example, Janus, the
god of beginnings, attended at the function 'in order to
open the way for the conception of the seed, when the fruit
of the body is conceived'. And Saturn, whose province is
seed and sowing, protects the seed of the husband. Augustine says with justice about these gods that 'unimportant
functions were allocated one by one to the numerous gods'.
But this is characteristic of all Roman theology.

So much then for the oldest known Roman gods connected with sexual life. We may apply to them the remark
already made about the development of Roman love life.
The love life of the most ancient Romans must have been a
primitive thing. Marriage was deeply reverenced as the
centre of sexual satisfactions; but such a subtle and refined

eroticism as the later Romans practised must have been
quite unknown in these early ages. And, especially, the cults
of Dionysos, Venus, and Priapus, which were so readily
invaded by orgiastic ceremonies, were entirely lacking. I
could not assert that their absence justified us in concluding that even the man's sexual life found its fulfilment only
within the monogamous marriage which he himself maintained. We saw elsewhere that prostitution occurred in early
times at Rome; and in addition, both male and female
slaves, whichever happened to be present, served to fulfil
the sexual needs of their masters.

Through contact with other nations, the Romans gradually became acquainted with other gods, whom they introduced among their own religious ideals. It is astonishing
that the Romans were so susceptible to new influences. If
this were a work of severe scholarship, it would have to
show which deities were imported from Italian nations and
which from the Greeks. It is much debated whether any
particular god originated in Italy, or should be referred
ultimately to the Greeks. We cannot here touch upon
scholarly minutiae of this kind; especially as they are discussed in every large work on Roman mythology. (See, for
example, Wissowa's profound treatment of this subject in
Pauly-Wissowa's *Handbook of Classical Antiquity,* which
we have to some extent followed in this account.) It is
chiefly important for us to have a correct picture of the
most important gods which were in course of time imported by the Romans as sexual deities.

2. Venus

We must first allude to the real goddess of love – at least
according to popular conceptions; that is, Venus, the goddess who acquired great fame after Vergil had in his Aeneid
shaped many old legends into a national epic.

Although her name is strangely absent from the oldest
priestly records, modern scholarship considers her to be a
primitive Roman deity, connected – like so many of their
old gods – with the agricultural life of the nation. She appears in some of her evidence to be literally the guardian
of gardens and flowers. Later she becomes the goddess of

race and beauty; and eventually coalesces with the Greek importation, Aphrodite, thus becoming principally the Aphrodite of Rome. In Sicily, the cult of Aphrodite on Mount Eryx was very ancient; and it was the source of the later Roman worship of Aphrodite. Even in Imperial times, under Tiberius and Claudius, the temple on Eryx was restored, for it was considered the sanctuary from which the Roman cult of Venus originated (Tac., *Ann.*, iv, 43). As early as the second Punic War, the first sanctuary of Venus Erycina appears on the Capitol in Rome (Liv., xxii, 9, 7).

The cult of Venus had several quite different meanings. The goddess was the guardian of honourable marriage, and as such her worship was celebrated by the *matronae*, the mothers of families. On the other hand, she was the goddess of *meretrices*, harlots. Finally, Venus in some way the mother of the Roman nation. Sulla honoured her as his patroness under the name *Venus Felix* (fortunate). Pompey decorated a temple to *Venus Victrix* (victorious). Last of all, Caesar, after his famous victory at Pharsalus consecrated a sanctuary to Venus; and gave her her permanent title of *Venus Genetrix* (mother) – the divine mother of the descendants of Aeneas, to which family the Julii belonged. Caesar liked to boast of his descent from Venus: he himself says 'The Julian clan, to which my house belongs, is sprung from Venus' (Suet., *Jul.*, 6). And Velleius Paterculus (ii, 41) says that Caesar 'came of a very illustrious family, descending as from Anchises and Venus, as is agreed by all students of antiquity'.

Finally, Augustus, in his efforts to reform Roman religion by reviving old cults, did not let slip this opportunity of employing the cult of Venus to glorify the Julian dynasty. Thenceforth, Venus and Mars, in particular, were adopted as ancestral gods of the Roman race. They appear as pre-eminent among many less important deities, in the Pantheon built by Augustus's famous general, Agrippa. The connection of Mars and Venus was really much older than this. They appear together as early as 271 B.C., the year of the dreadful defeat at the Trasimene Lake, when they were honoured by a *lectisternium* (sacred banquet) on the advice of the Sibylline books.

We may notice an especially interesting form of the worship of Venus, where she appears under the title of Verti-cordia. In the year 114 B.C., three Vestal Virgins were condemned to death for transgressing with Roman knights the rigid law against sexual intercourse. To atone for their misdeeds, a shrine was dedicated to Venus Verticordia in the hope that she would turn the hearts of women and girls against licentiousness and towards chastity. Hence her name *Verticordia,* which means the turner of hearts. Under this title she was especially worshipped by married women, and on the 1st April, when Venus Genetrix, also her festival. The patroness of harlots whom Lucretius calls Volgivaga (street-walker) was adored on the 23rd April (Ovid, *Fasti,* iv, 863 ff.) After Caesar's time male prostitutes had their own love festival, celebrated on the 23rd April.

In the chapter on Roman Literature we shall see more of the important part which Venus plays in Roman literature, especially under the amplifying influence of the Greek poets.

There is a peculiar sexual deity who seems to belong to the early age of Rome, but whose real origin is still unknown. This is the *Fortuna virilis* (man's fortune), who is held by many scholars to be a prehistoric Latin deity, although others think her synonymous with Venus – an opinion which will hardly hold. She was worshipped by women of the *poorer* classes and significantly enough in the men's baths – because as we are naïvely told, 'there, those parts of the male body are uncovered, which seek women's favour' (*Fast. Praen.,* 1st April). This goddess can never have been a protectress of female modesty, as is shown by a remark of Quintilian about such baths: 'It is characteristic of the adulteress to bathe along with men.' For this reason her picture was hung beside the altar of Venus.

In contrast to her (the same contrast that existed within the cult of Venus) there was a *Fortuna Virginalis* (maiden's fortune), to whom maidens dedicated their clothes at their marriage ceremony. Finally, Fortuna appears as *Fortuna muliebris* (woman's fortune), the deity of wives who lived within the bonds of strict monogamy. Her shrine could be entered by women living in their first and only marriage (Dion. Hal. viii, 56, 4).

3. *Liber*, *Phallus*, *Priapus*

The god Liber was originally an old Roman patron of growth and fertility, and the seed of plants and animals; but he was identified with the Greek importation Dionysus. In various parts of Italy, Liber – obviously a real Italian fertility god – was honoured by Phallic cults. In these, a large phallus, probably carved from wood, was carried on a cart about the fields and through the city, and eventually crowned by a matron. Augustine's *De civitate Dei* contains a very interesting reference to this (vii, 21): 'Varro says among other things that the rites of Liber were celebrated at the crossroads in Italy so immodestly and licentiously that the male genitals were worshipped in honour of the god – and this not with any modest secrecy but with open and exulting depravity. That shameful part of the body was, during the festival of Liber, placed with great pomp on waggons and carried about to the crossroads in the country, and at last into the city. In the town of Lanuvium, a whole month was dedicated to Liber. During it, all the citizens used the most disgraceful words until the Phallus had been carried across the market place and put to rest again. It was necessary that the most honourable of the matrons should publicly place a wreath on that disgraceful effigy. The god Liber had to be propitiated to ensure the future of the crops, and the evil eye had to be repelled from the fields by compelling a married woman to do in public that which not even a harlot might do under the eyes of married women in the theatre.' Thus Augustine. But as we can see, the fact that this ceremony was performed by an honourable woman shows that it was not a piece of debauchery, but an old custom of religious significance to avert destructive 'magical influences'.

The phallus (or as the Romans called it, the *fascinum*) was employed on all sorts of occasions to avert magic. Preller's *Roman Mythology* speaks with justice of the 'frequent employment throughout Italy of the *fascinum* as an amulet and a charm against magic: this expressed a belief in the protection of the eternal divine creative force'. For this reason, the phallus in various forms was hung round children's necks; set up above the doors of shops, even attached to the triumphal chariot of a general. Pliny (*N.H.*, xxviii, 4[7]) says in connection with this: 'The phallus is the protector not only of little children, but also of generals.' This god (the phallus is correctly called *deus*) 'is worshipped by the Vestal Virgins in Rome; and also helps to avert envy from the chariot of the triumphant general while it hangs below it'. A phallus was sometimes set up above city gates as a protection against ill-luck. Sometimes, under a phallus appears the inscription *Hic habitat felicitas* – 'happiness dwells here'. This, of course, does not mean that the place guaranteed any sort of sexual happiness, only that the phallus expelled unhappiness by its magic. Phallic amulets of this kind are in almost every museum of antiquities throughout Europe; but they are generally removed from public view, since the man of today views these things almost with the eyes of Augustine – and so, as we can now understand, does no justice to the deep original meaning of the symbol.

Another being of this kind is the garden god Priapus. Priapus is really nothing but a giant phallus, connected in some way or other with a human face. Naturally it was often enough to add a phallus at the correct place to a Hermes, that is a pedestal surmounted by the head of the god. Modern observers naïvely imagine this to be the height of indecency: as if the sculptor had wished to emphasize his interest in the head and erected member. Readers, who have followed our exposition know by this time that these phallic statues have an entirely different significance.

The usual view of scholars is that this god Priapus was introduced to Rome from Greece, or even from Asia Minor. I make bold to assert that the customary employment of the phallus as an apotropaic symbol is Italian in origin; in fact, since it is found among other nations, it is a custom of all primitive peoples. Still, it is conceivable that the phallus was combined with the phallic god Priapus of Asia Minor, after the Romans came into contact with Asiatic races – that is, after the war with Hannibal. In any case, the later Romans always knew Priapus as a garden god who kept away thieves and birds as a sort of scarecrow. That is how Horace describes him in *Satires*, i, 8: –

Once I was a fig-stump, useless wood:
a carpenter, wanting a stool or a god,
preferred me Priapus. I am a holy
scaregod for birds and thieves; my strong right hand
scares thieves, and the strong stump between my thighs.

(Almost all these statues had a male genital organ of tremendous size – the phallic symbol of the eternal procreative Power of nature.)

The phallus appears also as a sort of weapon or instrument of punishment with which chastisement is inflicted through gross sexual acts. There is a well-known collection of Latin poems called *Priapeia*; it is obscene doggerel by unknown poets, who speak with a good deal of wit about this function of Priapus. Those who have read the poems will remember the strongly sadistic tone of the acts and descriptions to which I allude.

Priapus was not only a garden god. As guardian of fertility, he was also the patron of human fecundity. Therefore, people whose marriage was barren implored his special help; and, in the same way, his assistance was sought in all sexual difficulties.

The phallic god was often portrayed in ancient art; either in the form mentioned above of a phallic Hermes, primitive or aesthetically elaborate, or in phallic amulets of various types. Juvenal (ii, 95) mentions 'glass Priapi', that is, vessels of phallic shapes. These were sometimes made of other materials such as gold or silver, and according to Petronius (*Sat*. 60) there were Priapi of pastry, like gingerbread men and chocolate easter eggs nowadays.

The priapic poems mentioned above show that the coarse imagination of the people seized upon a deity who was originally neither comic nor obscene, and in so doing emphasized his purely sexual aspect. We shall say more of this on the chapter on the Roman stage.

In later ages, the cult festivals in honour of Priapus must have been extremely bold and crude. Petronius's description (*Sat*. 26 ff.) may be purposely exaggerated, dealing as it does with the deflowering of a little girl. But Augustine also writes 'was it only the clowns and not also the priests who gave Priapus genitals of such enormous size? Or is his appearance in the holy places of his worship different from his guise in the theatre where he rouses so much amusement? ... In the past we had good reason to be thankful to play-actors for sparing their audience and not revealing in their plays everything which is hidden behind the holy temple walls. What good are we to think of the ceremonies which are hidden in darkness, if what is revealed is so damnable? ... What sort of ceremonies are those which worshippers approach with piety, but which are not admitted on the lewdest stage?'

We can see how widespread among the common people these things must have been from the fact that in the year 1834 excavations near Xanten on the Rhine disclosed great quantities of phallic amulets, musical instruments with phallic pictures, and similar objects. All these had obviously been brought to Xanten by the Roman legions.

4. Bacchanalia

Closely connected with the god Liber are the Bacchanalia. This was a cult which apparently originated in South Italy, and attempts were made to introduce it into Rome. It seems to have developed in the south under Greek influence, and to have been encouraged by the Etruscans in the north. Since sexual manifestations were frequent in its ritual, we must include it in our investigation. To quote Preller's *Roman Mythology* again: 'To the simple worship of the god of vineyards and vintages another cult was linked. This was the fanatical and mystical religion of Bacchus which was primarily connected with the Thracian and Theban Dionysus, the son of Semele or of Persephone, the symbol of Nature's periodic death and resurrection. His secret festivals and worship were enacted generally at night by women in the wildest frenzies of religious excitement.'

The cult was apparently introduced to Rome soon after the Hannibalic wars, perhaps, as a refuge from national emergencies. Livy shows clearly that it was at first tolerated. His words are (xxxix, 15, 6): 'You know well, senators, that the Bacchanalia, which have long been widespread in Italy, are now flourishing in Rome: you know this not only by hearsay but by the noises and shrieks which resound through the city by night.' Clearly the cult had assumed

a form and reached an extent which filled all serious-
minded Romans with anxiety and even terror. Livy (xxxix,
9 ff.) relates at some length an extraordinary tale, which we
shall here abbreviate.

A young man called Aebutius had formed a liaison with
a freedwoman, Hispala, who had been a notorious harlot.
His stepfather, having administered the boy's property dis-
honestly, wished to 'do away with him or else to gain some
power over him. The boy's mother was under the stepfather's influence. The only way to ruin him was through
the Bacchanalia. The mother called the boy, and told him
that while he was ill she had sworn to initiate him in the
Bacchic rites as soon as he recovered ... He was to observe chastity for ten days, and on the last day, when he had
bathed and purified himself after supper, she would take
him to the shrine.' His mistress learned of the mother's
intention, because 'the young man jokingly told her not to
be surprised if he passed several nights away from her ...
he was to be initiated in the Bacchic rites. As soon as the
woman heard this she cried out in dismay: "God forbid!
It would be better for both of us to die! I wish that all the
dangers of this may fall on the heads of those who persuaded you."' Aebutius was surprised by her excitement,
and questioned her. 'She told him that she had accompanied her mistress to the shrine of Bacchus when she was
a slave, but had never gone there since she was freed. She
knew the shrine for the abode of all kinds of corruption. It
was known, she said, that for two years no one older than
twenty had been initiated. Whenever a man was introduced,
he was handed over to the priests, like a beast for the
slaughter. They took him to a place which resounded with
cries, hymns, and the beating of drums and cymbals – so
that no one could hear the victim's cries for help while he
was violated.'

The young man allowed his mistress to persuade him to
have nothing to do with the initiation. 'When he reached
home his mother began to remind him of what he must do
each day in preparation for the rite. But he said he would
do none of these things, and did not intend to be initiated.
The stepfather was present and heard this. The woman at
once cried out that he could not sleep away from Hispala

for ten nights, that he was hypnotized and poisoned by that snake, so that he no longer respected his mother, his step-father, or the gods. His mother and stepfather, abusing him together, drove him from the house with four slaves. He betook himself to his father's sister, and told her why his mother had expelled him from his home. On his aunt's advice, he went next day to the consul Postumius and told him the story. . . .' The consul established the young man's trustworthiness, and then interrogated, among others, the woman Hispala. At first her terror made her deny every-thing, but eventually she told all she knew. 'She said that the shrine had at first been reserved for women, and that no men had been admitted. There had been three special days every year on which initiation took place. Married women had taken it in turns to be priestesses. Then a Campanian woman had changed the whole ritual, ostensibly at the command of the gods: she had begun by initiating two men, her sons . . . After, the rites had become open to everyone, so that men had attended as well as women, and their licen-tiousness had been increased with the darkness of night; there was no shameful or criminal deed from which they shrank. The men were guilty of more immoral acts among themselves than the women. Those who struggled against dishonour, or were slow to inflict it on others, were slaugh-tered in sacrifice like beasts. The holiest article of their faith was to think nothing a crime. The men prophesied like madmen with their bodies distorted by frenzy. The women, dressed as Bacchantes, with hair unbound, ran down to the Tiber carrying burning torches which they plunged into the water and brought out still burning, be-cause they had been smeared with sulphur and lime. They said "The gods have taken them", when certain men were bound to a windlass and snatched away out of sight into secret caverns. Those were the men who had refused either to take the oath or to join in the crimes or to be violated. The society had a huge membership – almost half the popu-lation – and among them were men and women of noble birth. It had been customary for the last two years to init-iate no one over twenty.' The Consul put both witnesses in safe custody, and reported the matter to the Senate. The Senate was horrified, but thanked the Consul, entrusted him with further investigation, and promised the witnesses immunity and rewards.

It was further determined that all the priests of this cult, men and women alike, should be traced. 'A special court of investigation was to deal with those who had assembled or taken an oath to do immoral or criminal acts.' Guards were posted throughout Rome, whose especial duty was to prevent meetings by night and to keep watch against arson. Finally, the consul made a speech before the commons, in which Livy makes him say: ' "A great number of the ad-herents are women, which is the origin of the whole trouble. But there are also men like women who have joined in each other's defilement, fanatics maddened by night-watching, by wine, by nightly shrieking and uproar. The conspiracy has no power yet, but its power can vastly increase because its numbers grow every day. Your ances-tors forbade even you to hold assemblies without good reason. They allowed them only when the standard was hoisted on the Citadel and the army marched out to vote, or when the Tribunes had proclaimed an assembly of the Commons; or when one of the other magistrates had called a meeting. And wherever there was a crowd, it was decreed that it should be under the presence of a legally appointed authority. What then do you think of these assemblies which take place late at night, which are attended by men and women indiscriminately? If you knew the age at which the men are initiated, you would be filled not only with pity for them, but with shame. Do you think citizens, that young men who have taken this oath can be made soldiers? Are they to be trusted with arms when they leave this ob-scene sanctuary? Are they, defiled by their own and others' sins, to fight in defence of the honour of your wives and children? ... Every offence prompted by lust, deceit, or violence, which has been committed in these last years, originated in that shrine ... The evil grows every day ... It affects the whole commonwealth of Rome ... If any man has been drawn into that gulf by lust or madness, judge him to belong not to you but to those with whom he has conspired to commit every shameful and criminal act ... Nothing is more specious and deceitful than superstition. When the will of the gods is made a pretext for crime, our hearts are invaded by the fear of infringing some divine law while we defend the crimes of mankind. You are absolved from these scruples by countless edicts of the High Priest, decrees of the Senate, and decisions of soothsayers. Our fathers and grandfathers often gave the magistrates the duty of forbidding foreign rites, banning fakirs and prophets from the market place, the circus and the city, of collecting and burning prophetic books, and of forbidding all sacrificial ritual which was not Roman. For they were skilled in human law and divine law alike; they judged that true religion was never destroyed so quickly as when the old rites were abandoned and foreign ones introduced. I have thought it necessary to give you this warning so that you may not be disturbed by superstitious scruples when you see us, the magistrates, destroying the Bacchanalia and breaking up their unlawful assemblies. All that we do is done by the favour and will of the gods, who were angry at the defilement of their godhead by lust and crime, and dragged these things to light, disclosing them not to go unpunished but to be avenged and exterminated." '

The senate's measures must have had great effect; for a large number of those who were involved in the scandal attempted to leave Rome despite stern prohibitions; but they were arrested, one by one, and taken before the authorities. Some killed themselves. The total number of those connected with the affair was perhaps seven thousand men. The investigators disclosed one fact of particular interest – not only lust and murder had been practised, but other crimes also, such as falsification of evidence, and forgery of signatures and of wills. All those involved in serious crimes were put to death: according to the ancient custom, the execution of the death penalty on the women was assigned to their kinsmen. Finally, there was issued the senatorial decree of 186 B.C., which has come down to us on an extant bronze tablet: it prohibits the Bacchanalia for ever throughout Rome and Italy, but for a few unimportant local cults and other small exceptions, of which the praetor was to be informed.

That, in brief, is Livy's account of the case and its consequences. He has perhaps given it a romantic colouring after his fashion, but in general he has done justice to the facts. But we must add one note: the immoralities associated with this cult, whose actual occurrence we cannot discuss or verify, did not chiefly cause the authorities to interfere; they interfered because they suspected some danger to the existence of the state from these essentially mysterious conspiracies – especially when their investigations revealed regular crimes like murder and forgery. At that time the Roman state did not permit the coexistence of any other power within itself which it did not know or could not direct. As soon as it lost the power to prevent the formation of such unions, it lost its whole authority and the Civil War began.

Nevertheless, the senate and the consul took such severe measures against these degenerate and criminal Bacchanalia that they blotted them out for ever. It seems that Caesar introduced a new worship of Bacchus, but we cannot depend on that piece of information. Certainly, we know from the inscriptions of Bacchic societies, that the cult reappeared in later times in connection with other foreign cults such as those of Isis, Mithras, and the Magna Mater.

5. Cybele

In this connection, it is well to turn to Bachofen, although, as we have pointed out, he receives little or no attention from scholars in general. He says, somewhere: 'It is by its religions that the East seeks to impose a second yoke on the West.' But when Rome opposed so strongly the first introduction of this originally Asiatic cult, it showed its consciousness of the movement of universal history. Bachofen says in that connection that Rome represented and fulfilled the ideal of higher morality in opposition to the sensualism of Asia; and in this, he thinks, Rome was performing its real task. This conception of history is strongly influenced by Hegel. I cannot give it unqualified assent, but I believe that these far-reaching thoughts must stimulate us to deep reflections on Roman life and history. We must perhaps think of Bachofen as we do of Nietzsche, who on the whole is certainly wrong, but is certainly right in many details, and as such is a constant stimulus to thought. But let us return to our argument. We shall resume by quoting another remark by Bachofen. He says in his book, *The Legend of Tanaquil*: 'To cure Italy of the ulcer of Hannibal, the shapeless meteorite was brought from the Phrygian home of the Romans. Rome, the city of Aphrodite, was terrified by her long neglect of the mother, and her exclusive preoccupation with the father's rule as a political principle.'

To what is Bachofen referring? It is the importation of the cult of Cybele from Asia Minor, the goddess whom the Romans called *Magna Mater,* the 'mighty mother'. This cult certainly had some sexual features; and although we do not know the exact details, we must speak of it here. Livy gives a naïve account of the rise of this cult in Rome. It took place in the year 204 B.C., a short time before the last crisis of the Hannibalic war, that is, at a time when the nation was broken down by the long arduous years of war and the disasters which they brought. If we remember similar conditions in the World War, we shall see that Rome was easily accessible to the spread of new cults with many mysterious customs. The Decemviri found in the Sibylline books a prophecy to this effect: 'Whenever a foreign foe brings war to Italy, he can be conquered and driven out if the Idaean mother is brought from Pessinus to Rome' (Livy, xxix, 10). This referred to a sacred meteorite, a fetish of Cybele, which had been brought by King Attalus from Pessinus to Pergamum, where it was set up in a shrine called the Megalesion (Varro, *de l.l.* vi, 15). The symbol of the goddess was accordingly brought to Italy in state. Livy tells us (xxix, 14): 'Publius Scipio was ordered to go to Ostia with all the married women in order to meet the goddess: he was to take her off the ship and carry her to land; then he was to give her to the matrons to carry. When the ship arrived at the mouth of the river Tiber, he sailed out as he was ordered, received the goddess from the priests, and took her to land. There the first ladies of the state received her. Among them the name of Claudia Quinta is pre-eminent: her reputation had been doubtful, but she made her chastity famous in succeeding ages by this holy service. These ladies carried the goddess in succession to Rome: the whole city poured out to meet her: lighted incense-burners were placed in front of the doors which she passed: and they all prayed that she should enter the city with good will and great favour: she was carried to the temple of Victory on the Palatine.' Other accounts say that miracles occurred as soon as the goddess reached the Tiber. For example, Claudia's prayer refloated the ship carrying the image after it had grounded on a shoal in the Tiber; and so on.

Finally, in 191 B.C., the goddess was given a special temple on the Palatine; and she was soon afterwards honoured by theatrical shows, which became a regular institution in Rome under the name of the *Ludi Megalenses*. In aristocratic Roman houses she was honoured by banquets given in common, and attended with great splendour. But the cult of this foreign goddess was by decree celebrated only by the priesthood called the Galli, who had immigrated with her. This is a sign that she was originally viewed with as much suspicion as the Bacchanalia which had been polluted by orgies. Certainly her ritual was strange enough. Dionysius of Halicarnassus (*Rom. Ant.*, ii, 19) says: 'Every year, according to the Roman law, the praetors conduct sacrifices and games in her honour. She is served by a Phrygian man and a Phrygian woman, who take her through the city asking alms for her, as is their custom; they wear little images on their breasts, and are accompanied in their hymns to the goddess by a procession with flutes to the beat of drums. But no one of Roman birth goes round the city to beg or play the flute wearing these bright coloured clothes, nor worships her with the orgiastic Phrygian rites: this is prohibited by a law and a decree of the senate.'

We learn from other sources that these priests were eunuchs; in this, they followed the legend of Attis. Attis was the young lover of the goddess for whose sake he castrated himself in a frenzy, died, and rose again. His legend was early connected with the cult of the Mighty Mother in some way not altogether clear to us.

We read the story in Ovid's *Fasti* (iv, 223 ff.): –

> Attis, the lovely boy of the Phrygian forest,
>   bewitched the goddess with the crown of towers.
> To keep him for herself, her temple-guardian,
>   she said 'Canst thou not always be a boy?'
> He gave his pledge, and said 'If I am perjured,
>   by an embrace, may it be my last love.'

But he was perjured, and gave up his boyhood
    in a nymph's arms. The goddess took revenge.
She hacked the tree, and with it killed the Naiad,
    for with the tree the Naiad lived and died.
But Attis, mad, thinking the roof was falling,
    rushed out, and ran to Dindyma's high peak,
crying 'Ah, the torches!' crying 'Scourges!'
    swearing the Furies drove him to his death.
And now with a sharp stone he cut his body,
    dragging his long hair in the filthy dust,
and crying 'I deserve to bleed and suffer!
    Perish the member that made me forsworn!
Away with it!' he cut away his manhood –
    leaving no sign to show he once was male.
His madness still is copied, and his servants
    cut their vile bodies while they toss their hair.

That is Ovid's version of the old legend. Catullus gives
it a different rendering : –

Over the billows Attis fled swift on a hurrying keel,
till with eager step he hastened into the Phrygian grove,
to find the hidden sanctuary deep in the holy forest.
There the madness whipped his mind, there his spirit raved,
there with the flintblade's heavy blow he cut away his manhood.
Now when he saw his body stripped of all that made it man,
and the blood-gouts dripping freshly on the soil beneath,
he grasped (his hands were woman's hands) the rapid kettledrum,
the kettledrum and the trumpet, the sacred rites of Cybele,
shaking and sounding the hollow hide of a bull in his tender
        hands,
and thus he sang, trembling and pale, before his wild company.
'Up and away to the tall groves of holy Cybele!
away, priestesses, wandering sheep of the Lady of Dindyma,
you men-women, exiled folk, strange in a strange land,
following my leadership, companions of my worship.
With me you bore the rush of the brine and the wild ocean
        savagery,
with me unmanned your bodies in your hatred of love and Venus.
Rejoice your hearts with cymbal-clash and rapid wanderings,
abandon slow delays and lingering, follow, follow swift
to the Phrygian home of Cybele, to the holy Phrygian forest,
where the cymbal sounds again, where the drums rattle and roar,
where the Phrygian piper plays loud and deep on the clarion,
where the Maenads rave and toss their heads ivy-entangled,
where with shrill Hallelu they rush and shriek in the rites,
where our Lady's servants lightly, rapidly range the forest,
there let us hasten with feet flying swift in the sacred dance.'
Thus he cried to his company, proud of his bastard womanhood,
as they raised a howling Hallelu shrill with trembling tongue;
roared the rapid kettledrum, clanged the hollow cymbal,

while the dervish chorus danced to the greenwoods of Ida.
And there went, panting and raving, his wild heart beating high,
Attis their leader beating his kettledrum through the black
    woods,
swift as a young heifer unbroken, avoiding the weight of the
    yoke,
swiftly the unmanned priests followed their leader's precipitate
    pace.

These quotations may be enough to make the myth clear.
I shall refrain from any attempt to interpret it. It would
be a valuable investigation for psychoanalysts. There can
be no doubt that the cult had sexual implications. We can
understand that the early Romans scorned to concern themselves with such things. There is a scourge (mentioned in
this connection by Apuleius and pictured on a relief) to
which knucklebones are fastened so as to make it a real
instrument of torture. This indicates a certain resemblance
to the flagellants of the Middle Ages. Flagellation to the
effusion of blood was probably undertaken later, in place
of castration. This occurred on the Day of Blood (generally 24th March) which was followed by the day of rejoicing to celebrate the resurrection of the dead Attis.
Some time after the end of the second century A.D. the
worship of the Great Mother was changed by the introduction of a peculiar sacrifice, of bulls and rams called
Taurobolium or Kriobolium; and the priesthood was now
opened to Roman citizens. The baptism by blood came to
play a great but mysterious part in the worship. The neo-
phyte was placed in a pit with a perforated covering, and
drenched by the blood of the bull which was sacrificed
over him. This act was thought to signify the rebirth of the
person baptized. Priests were obviously ordained in the
same way. In the sacrifices the bull's testicles had a special
significance – another indication of the innate sexual character of the whole myth. According to Pliny (*N.H.*, xviii, 3
[4]), the Roman peasants believed that the crops had grown
richer every year since the Mother came to Rome. Actually, this mysterious religion, whose ceremonies have a certain resemblance to those of Christianity, was very
widespread until the time of the late Caesars, and this is
shown by the innumerable altars and descriptions which
have been discovered. We might appreciate Bachofen's views

more if they were more securely established in all their details. Possibly further researches will bring greater certainty to the matter.

Apuleius (*Metam.*, viii) describes the priests of Cybele as very lewd and degenerate, and says that they gratified their gross lusts with strong young peasants. But in my opinion we cannot conclude from this that the whole cult of Cybele was a practice of homosexuality (as Bloch states, for example'). We cannot extend to all the priesthood of Cybele this melodramatic description of a few of its degenerate representatives, any more than we can characterize all the Christian ministry by the sins of an individual cleric.

6. Isis

Another religion introduced to Rome from the East, and generally regarded as a sexual cult, was that of Isis.

However, I cannot consider it as certain, from the available evidence, that the prostitution which occurred in her temples was an integral part of her worship, and that we can justly term it a sexual cult. Let us examine the matter more closely. According to Preller, Isis was 'the female goddess of crops and cultivation' in Egypt, as Osiris-Serapis (with whom she is often associated) was the 'male fertility god' of the country. She was therefore by origin a real Egyptian national deity, like her male partner Osiris. But through time her functions were widely extended: she became the patroness of journeys by sea, and the founder of laws and legislation (e.g. Diod. i, 27). She says of herself in a hymn found on the island of Andros: 'I first imparted to men the courage to sail over the sea; I lent them the power to administer the law; and I gave women to men, as the beginning of procreation' (quoted by Bachofen in *Primitive Religion and Ancient Symbols*, vol. ii). Bachofen says with much truth: 'We should observe that the principle of lawgiving is connected with the maternal principle which gives fertility and protects sea voyagers. The same mother who brings together man and woman, and brings their offspring to fruition in the tenth month, also founds the law. Fertility and law are part of the essence of motherhood;

they are a principle immanent in matter. The mother becomes an expression of the highest justice, dividing everything among her children with loving impartiality. Here we see again the First Mother as the bringer of peace, reconciliation, and plenty – as she appears in other manifestations. Isis puts an end to war, the work of man; instead of it she brings peace and prosperity through shipping and commerce.' The hymn we have quoted expressly says: 'I, Isis, have banished the sorrow and distress of war; I have raised to fame the royal power which brings prosperity and justice.'

It is quite certain that the worship of Isis was introduced to Rome by way of Lower Italy (especially from Puteoli) about the time of Sulla. However, the authorities were long hostile to it. In 58 B.C. altars of Isis on the Capitol were pulled down by public decree. But in 43 it was decided to build a temple to the goddess, although, as modern research shows, the resolution was not carried out. The cult was officially recognized only under Caligula. Tiberius had destroyed one of Isis's shrines, and thrown her image into the Tiber, because the priests had used the ceremonies to dishonour a noble lady (Joseph., *Ant.*, xviii, 65). This clearly refers to a sexual offence: does it allow us to conclude that the sexual element was inherent in the cult? That conclusion seems to be confirmed by other passages: e.g. Ovid (*A.A.*, i, 76) says: 'do not shun the temple of Isis – she makes many women become what she became for Jupiter.' (This is an allusion to Isis, who was identified with Jove's mistress Io.) Elsewhere Ovid says: 'do not ask what could happen in the temple of "linen-clad Isis".' Juvenal, who always paints in the darkest colours, calls the priestesses of Isis simply 'bawds'. And in the ninth satire he says to Naevolus (who lived on the earnings of his immoral acts with men and women) that he 'diligently defiled' the temple of Ganymede, Isis, the Altar of Peace, the secret home of the foreign Mother, and Ceres, 'for in every temple stand prostitutes'. What is the result to which we are led by a study of these passages? Are we to believe that the worship of Isis was a sexual act, as some scholars (diligently repeating each other) assert? I think not. But it does follow from these and other passages that it was customary to use the temples in search of love-adventures with men or women:

not, however, the temple of Isis alone, as the quotation from Juvenal shows. So much we can conclude, and no more. Of course, the priests and priestesses may very often have assisted in furthering such adventures – as the priests of the Mighty Mother sometimes exhausted their passion in sexual frenzies. But all this has nothing to do with the cult, or with the real nature of the gods. Actually, the worship of Isis was very widespread in the later Empire, and, like that of the Magna Mater, must have been deeply rooted among the lower classes. This explains the boundless hate with which it is pursued by such Christian authors as Firmicus Maternus.

We have little conclusive evidence on the nature of the ceremonies of consecration to Isis, of the details of her ritual, and of the deeper significance of its mysterious doctrines. But Apuleius has left us a vivid description of one of her processions, in *Metamorphoses,* xi.

'The procession sacred to the saviour (Isis) was marshalled onwards. The women, gleaming in white garments and blooming in spring garlands, proudly bore the holy things: with flowers from their laps, they strewed the ground where the sacred company trod. Others with glittering mirrors on their backs, showed the goddess reverence while she advanced; and others, with ivory combs, moved their arms and curled their fingers while they adorned and arranged the queenly hair of Isis. Others again sprinkled the streets with shaken drops of generous balsam and other unguents. After them came a great crowd of men and women, bearing lamps, torches, candles and other lights, to honour the mother of the stars of heaven. And there was a ravishing music of pipes and flutes with sweet harmonious tones. There followed then a joyful choir of chosen youths and maidens gleaming in white raiment and ritual robes, who ever repeated the lovely song made to music by a great poet, whom the Muses favoured and inspired ... with them, too, there went the pipers who served great Serapis, playing on a fife which slanted towards their right: they repeated an air familiar to their temple and their god. There were heralds too, calling "make way for the holy things".

'Then flowed on the crowd of initiates to the sacred

rites: men and women of all ranks and every age, shining
in the clear whiteness of linen garments. The women had
bound their anointed hair with lucid veils, while the men's
heads were shaven of hair and shone brightly, as the earthly
stars of the sublime worship of Isis. They made a clear
music with sistra of bronze and silver, even of gold. And
the high priests of their rites, in a close garment of white
linen weave flowing from their breasts to their feet, bore
the symbols of the mightiest gods. The first held outstretched a lamp with clear and flashing life – not like those
lamps of ours which light our evening feasts, but a golden
bowl which sent up a great flame from its midst. The
second wore the same dress, but bore in both hands an
altar, the altar of help, whose name comes from the provi-
dential help of the goddess. The third, as he strode on,
raised a palm branch cunningly fashioned with golden
leaves, and the serpent staff of Mercury. The fourth displayed the symbol of justice: it was a deformed left hand
with outstretched fingers, a hand which was by nature slow,
neither cunning nor artful, and seemed nearer to justice
than the right; the same priest bore a golden vessel, rounded
like a woman's breast, from which he poured offerings of
milk. The fifth had a winnowing fan made of golden laurel
branches; and the sixth bore an urn. And straightway came
the gods deigning to walk on human feet. There advanced,
first, the dreadful messenger of heaven and hell – Anubis,
raising his dog-head high, half black half gold. In his left
hand he bore the serpent staff, and in his right he shook a
green palm branch. On his steps there followed a cow,
standing upright, a cow, the image of the fruitful Mother,
borne on his shoulders by one of the priesthood moving
with proud and stately step. In the hands of another was
borne the ark of the mysteries, holding the secrets of the
wondrous worship. Another bore in his happy breast, the
sacred effigy of the mighty god – like neither beast nor
bird, wild nor tame, nor like a man, but hallowed by the
very strangeness of its fashion – the ineffable symbol of that
holy mystery, made of shining gold. It was a small urn,
skilfully hollowed out with a rounded base, and adorned
with strange Egyptian images. Its short neck stretched into
a long slender orifice, and opposite was a wide curved

handle round which clung knotting and twisting a scaly snake which reared high its swollen neck.'

We cannot here describe the further details of this fantastic procession. However, we see that it contained no symbol of sex, which it certainly would have done, had the worship of Isis been a sexual cult.

On the contrary, we find again and again that it demanded various ascetic observances from its adherents, especially the ten days' chastity kept by initiates. The sensual South obviously considered this a severe restraint, and we often hear of it in the Augustan poets. The sickly Tibullus complains (i, 3, 23): —

> What help to me is Isis, or the cymbals,
>   Delia, so often beaten by your hand?
> all your retreats, and all your pure ablutions,
>   and ritual nights spent in a lonely bed?

And Propertius says (ii, 33, 1): —

> Alas, again the evil ceremonies!
>   Cynthia serves the goddess for ten nights . . .
> The goddess who divides such eager lovers
>   so often, is a jealous deity . . .
> Be satisfied with Egypt's tawny children;
>   why travel over the long road to Rome?
> What benefit to you, if girls sleep lonely?

And Ovid, that sophisticated connoisseur of women's hearts, advises the mistress to increase her lover's ardour by often denying herself to him: and he says that Isis can be used as a pretext (*Am.*, 8, 73): —

> Often refuse a night. Call it a headache;
>   and Isis sometimes makes a good excuse.

It does not lie within the scope of this work to further investigate the cult of Isis, and its significance in the history of religion. We had only to show that though the cult may possibly have been a sexual cult, the probabilities are that it was not.

7. Bona Dea

An apparently similar religion was that of the Bona Dea (Good Goddess): This deity has been identified by many

scholars with the old Roman goddess Fauna. Others consider that she was introduced from Greece. Certainly she
was a god of woman, and women implored her help in
trouble and sickness. She was known in Rome as early as
the time of the Tarentine war (272 B.C.); it is possible, therefore, that her adoption was influenced by Roman contact
with Magna Graecia.

So much for these questions, which we cannot here discuss further. It is certain, as we have said, that the Bona
Dea was worshipped by women and women alone. Here is
a passage from Plutarch (*Caesar*, 9). 'The Romans have a
goddess whom they call the Good One, as the Greeks call
her the Woman's Goddess. The Phrygians say she belongs
to Phrygia, and was the mother of their King, Midas. The
Romans think she was a dryad who lived with Faunus. The
Greeks again say she was that one of the mothers of Bacchus who must not be named. Accordingly, when they
celebrate her festival, the women erect tents roofed with
vine twigs, and, in accordance with the legend, a holy snake
lies beside the goddess. It is unlawful for any man to come
to the festival, or even to enter the house. The women remain quite alone and are said to perform many rites like
those of the Orphic mysteries. When the time of the festival comes, the consul or praetor, in whose house it is held,
leaves the house with all the other men in the household.
His wife takes over the house and arranges the ceremonies. The greatest of them take place at night, and are inter-
spersed with gaiety and music.' This is Plutarch's simple
account of the cult. It is astonishing to compare it with that
given by Juvenal in the famous sixth Satire. Since Plutarch
and Juvenal were contemporaries, we are forced to conclude, either that women appeared to them in entirely
different lights, or that the authors drew from sources dat-
ing to quite different times. For Juvenal's description of the
festival is so revolting that we can only acknowledge, but
not explain, the difference between the two accounts.

This is Juvenal's picture in all its glaring colours:–

> The rites of the Good Goddess! Shrieking flutes
> excite the women's loins, wine and the trumpet
> madden them, whirling and shrieking, rapt
> by Priapus. Then, then, their hearts are blazing

> with lust, their voices stammer with it, their wine
> gushes in torrents down their soaking thighs . . .
> This is no mimicry, the thing is done
> in earnest: even Priam's aged loins
> and Nestor cold with age would burn to see it.
> Their itching cannot bear delay: this is sheer Woman,
> shrieking and crying everywhere in the hall,
> 'It is time, let in the men!' The lover sleeps –
> then let him snatch a greatcoat, hurry here.
> No? Then they rush upon the slaves. Not even
> slaves? Then a scavenger comes off the streets.

Finally, if a man cannot be procured, they content themselves with an ass! So ends this fearful description.

I am much inclined to consider it as fantastic as many other romantic and malevolent inventions – for instance, in Tacitus. It may be admitted that in this cult the women may have occasionally yielded to sexual excess, but the cult in itself had nothing to do with such depravities. Passages of this kind should not be taken over by one moralist from another without reservation, and this opinion of the serious moral character of the Bona Dea festivals could be supported by an assertion of Plutarch's (*Cicero*, 19): 'Every year, in the Consul's house, his wife or mother conducts a sacrifice to this goddess in the presence of the Vestal Virgins.' Could orgies such as those described by Juvenal be imagined in the house of a high official in the presence of the Vestal Virgins? I consider it much more probable that the Bona Dea is one of the many avatars of the Mother Goddess – who, according to Bachofen's brilliant interpretation re-entered or sought to re-enter the Roman religion at various times in the later age of Rome. This also might be an example of the war in the soul of the Roman women between the mother and the prostitute – as Bachofen describes it – and that, if true, would explain the astonishing difference between two accounts of the same worship.

This concludes our account of the gods of Rome and of those adopted by the Romans from elsewhere in so far as they are connected with sexual life. We could, of course, discuss the worship of Hadrian's mysterious favourite, Antinous*, or the pompous oriental cult of the boy Caesar,

---

* Cf. Gregorovius, *Splendour and Decline of Rome*, a biography of Hadrian.

Bassianus, who called himself Elagabal after his god. But these cults cannot be understood unless we know something of the men, Antinous and Bassianus, who produced them. We shall, therefore, discuss them in another place.

At the close of this chapter, we may consider once again the gods who were really important for Roman sexual life in its long development. It will perhaps be noticeable that among the numerous deities born on Italian soil, or introduced from abroad, there is no god to represent homosexuality – as the youthful god Eros did in Greece. The absence of such a deity allows us to conclude once more that homosexuality was at no time idealized by the Romans, even if they knew the phenomenon at an early time. The Roman sexual deities are intrinsically related always to sexual functions of woman or to love between man and woman.

(b) Philosophy

In a work which undertakes to depict the whole range of Roman sexual life, it is perhaps appropriate to inquire whether its development was influenced by ancient philosophy. We see, for instance, how deeply Christian thought affects sexual life in the Middle Ages, and among strict Catholics even today. As we said in the Introduction, the character of the Roman did not predispose him to reflect on life. He was a man of action, not of thought. But I believe Spengler to be correct when he says (in his famous *Decline of the West*): 'The true Roman is more strictly a Stoic than any Greek could be – even the Roman who would have opposed Stoicism most resolutely.' It is no accident that the Romans felt themselves so attracted to that creed. An exact description of the Stoic teaching would fall outside the scope of this work. But we shall briefly describe its essential features, in so far as it was real and important to Roman thought. Perhaps no thinker has grasped its inner meaning so well as Schopenhauer, who says (*The World as Will and Idea*, i, 16): 'As a whole, the ethic of Stoicism is actually a noteworthy and valuable attempt to use man's greatest privilege, Reason, for an important and salutary end – to raise him above the pains and sorrows to which every human life is subject.' And he adds, in Book ii, chap. 16: 'We can therefore conceive Stoicism as a spiritual hygiene; in accordance with it, as we harden our bodies against wind and weather by privation and exercise, we must also harden our spirits against unhappiness, danger, loss, injustice, malice, treachery, pride, and human folly.' Another writer says this creed is the very blood of Rome.

Stoicism is obviously based on the idea that the world is a unity, whose separate parts and manifestations are all necessary; and that each of us fills a necessary place within that unity, a role which he must fulfil without troubling about the satisfaction of his own personal desires. All the externals like wealth, prosperity, luxury, and even joy and sorrow, are powerless to rob us of our inner freedom – if we only use our reason correctly, remain masters of ourselves, make all our will harmonize with the inevitable course of things, and recognize that things never conform themselves to us. The Stoic ideal is the Wise Man whom nothing more can disturb, who preserves a calm soul in the face of every event, from utter happiness to utter sorrow. *Nil admirari* ('be never amazed') says Horace; and again, still more clearly, *si fractus illabatur orbis, impauidum ferient ruinae*, 'if the universe broke and fell, he would stand undismayed as its ruins struck him.' Stoicism teaches a manly firmness of will against pain and against the seductions of life. What philosophy could be more appropriate to the Roman outlook? And yet Rome's maturer spirits held themselves aloof from it when it was first presented to them by two Greek philosophers. Plutarch says in his biography of Cato (22): 'When Cato was an old man, an embassy came from Athens to Rome, which included the Academic philosopher Carneades and the Stoic Diogenes. Their mission was to appeal against a penalty of 500 talents which had been given against them by default; the Oropians had been the plaintiffs and the people of Sicyon the awarders. Immediately these philosophers were visited by the young men who were most desirous of learning; they assembled to hear their talk, which was greatly admired. Great numbers of admiring listeners were attracted by the charm of Carneades' character, his exceptional ability and his correspondingly great reputation; a great gust of talk about him blew through the city. It was said everywhere that a Greek of astonishing genius and charm had inspired the young men with a great passion for philosophy, which made them leave all their usual pleasures and pastimes. This pleased the Romans: they liked to see their sons becoming acquainted with Greek culture and meeting distinguished men. Only Cato was from the first indignant at the growing love for literature and oratory, for he was afraid that the young men's ambitions would be diverted, and that they would prize a reputation for speech rather than for action and for fighting . . .' 'He tried to put his son against Greek culture, and made a prophetic remark too violent for one of his age, that the Romans would ruin their state by filling it with Greek letters.' Finally, in the year 150, the Senate passed a decree banishing all foreign philosophers and rhetors from Rome. But this could not stop the course of things. We know that Cicero and Horace, among others, showed great interest in Stoic doctrines; and the most typical representatives of later Stoicism were three famous Romans – Seneca, Epictetus, and Marcus Aurelius.

For Romans like the elder Cato it was, of course, inconceivable that a man could employ the forces of his mind in reflecting on life. They saw no problem in life. They did not meditate. They acted. They worked on the land, they were soldiers and statesmen. They lived, we have said, as their strong instincts bade them. How could they be brought to reflect on life and happiness?

Yet, it is very significant that the later Romans felt themselves especially attracted to this creed. For it did not seek to solve theoretic problems so much as to find some method by which man could overcome the difficulties of life without denying his pride or sacrificing his inner freedom. It can be said with truth that the Romans of the Empire took Stoicism over into practical life. We can see the process as if recorded in a diary in Marcus Aurelius's famous *Meditations*. And we know that many a less famous Roman of the Imperial age put an end to his own life in conformity with Stoic heroism.

But the Stoic creed, especially in its Roman form, contained other elements. The older Stoa had taught that men

should be estimated not by his nationality but by his virtues and vices. So it became a fundamental principle of
Stoicism that all national boundaries were 'unnatural': the
whole world was a great social organism in which every
man must help every other. But it was expressly asserted
that help was obligatory not through any feeling of sympathy but through the fact that all men were members of
the same great organism. This 'cosmopolitanism' preached
by the later Stoa is strongly reminiscent of the Christian
doctrine of universal brotherhood – it even preaches love
for one's enemies. We cannot here discuss whether Christianity is descended from Stoicism (as some modern scholars
hold) or the doctrines of the New Testament, though similar to Stoic teaching, rest on deeper foundations. At all
events, the philanthropic theories preached by the Stoics
did not tend to strengthen the ideal of Rome's mastery over
the world. They could not make their way into her realms
until she had of her own accord abandoned her policy of
conquest and had become an international, cosmopolitan
empire based on what seemed to be an eternal peace.

The Stoic outlook perhaps found its strongest expression in the writings of Seneca. His letters and treatises are
full of sentences which look as if they were borrowed from
the New Testament. 'Every virtue is its own reward. Virtue
is not practised for profit – to have done well is the wages
of a good act' (*Ep.*, 81, 19). Again: 'How pleasant, how
valuable it is for a man who gives something to refuse
thanks: for him, at the very moment of giving, to forget
that he has given anything!' (*De ben.*, ii, 6, 2). Again: 'Think
of a kindness as you do of an offering to the gods. Nothing
good comes of it unless it is given with a good heart' (*De
ben.*, vii, 29, 1). Again, 'The man who knows God worships
him . . . God needs no servants. Why should he? He is the
servant of humanity; he is ready to help everyone, everywhere' (*Ep.*, 95, 47). We must, of course, not forget that
this Stoic god is not the 'loving father of all men' who appears in the New Testament. He is a more impersonal being,
almost a pantheist divinity. Seneca can say this also:
'Nature made us all kinsmen by creating us from the same
materials, for the same end. She implanted mutual love in
us and made us gregarious. She created equity and justice.

According to her arrangement of the world, it is more miserable to do an injury than to be injured. According to her command, those who need help will find helping hands ready' (*Ep.*, 95, 52).

But the Stoic outlook has another, deeper side. With it we return to our own subject.

The Stoic values reason above all things: he holds reason to be his better self. But he knows that besides reason there is another element in man – pure instinct, 'the flesh', which constantly hinders us from living in exact accordance with the decrees of reason. And so he is ready to draw the inference which leads to pessimism and at last to pure asceticism: I must combat or despise everything which distracts me from following reason. Such a line of thought will produce this remark: 'We must shake off the desire for life, and learn that it does not matter *when* we suffer, since we must suffer at some time' (*Ep.*, 101, 15). And this: 'If you will believe those who look deep into the truth, we live under sentence of death. We are cast into a deep and stormy sea: tossed by shifting tides, which now bear us up on a sudden flood, and now hurl us down on a steep ebb, we never have a steady landing-place; we hang suspended in the moving waves, dashed against one another, sometimes shipwrecked and always terrified. In this stormy sea, lying open to every tempest, the sailor has only one harbour – death' (*Ad Polyb.*, 9, 6).

The man who sees life like that cares little for it. And we read elsewhere in Seneca: 'I think Panaetius made a fine reply to the young man who asked him if a wise man would ever be a lover. He answered: "We shall talk of the wise man some other time. But you and I, who are still far from wise, must not commit the error of falling into a stormy passion which enslaves us to someone else and is of no value to ourselves. If the beloved does not reject us, we are encouraged by her kindness; if she despises us, we are kindled by her haughtiness. Love injures us when it is difficult as much as when it is easy: we are bewitched by its easiness, we wrestle with its difficulties. Let us therefore know our own weakness, and rest in peace. Let us not put our weak heart into the power of wine, nor of beauty, nor of flattery, nor of any pleasant attraction." That was Panae-

tius' answer to the man who asked him about love. I apply
it to all emotions. Let us keep back, as far as we can, from
slippery places: even on dry ground we do not stand too
steadily.' (*Ep*., 116, 5 ff.)

We need not add details to prove that the Stoics were the
first to despise and condemn all sexual satisfactions which
were not 'regular'. But they did not value even marriage
very highly: although the older Stoics like Zeno and Chrysippus had more positive views on the subject. But here we
are discussing Stoicism in the form which it assumed in
Imperial times. And then a contempt for the world, even
a rejection of the world became an essential characteristic
of the creed.

Here we come to a very interesting and important sphere
of human thought and feeling: I refer to that which can be
called, in the most general sense, asceticism. This attitude
to life was at that time widely prevalent among the Romans,
and not only among those influenced by Christianity. It
will be worth while to speak of it in more detail – especially since such practices have a decisive influence on man's
attitude to his sexual life.

If we wish to understand the general idea of asceticism,
and to see how it can be explained by studying the attitude
of the human soul to the world, we can even today turn to
Schopenhauer's pages on the subject. Asceticism plays a
decisive part in his immortal teachings. It must, however,
suffice us to show how these ideas and this outlook reached
the Romans of the later ages.

It was a very old Orphic and Pythagorean doctrine (perhaps introduced from India) that the soul 'sinks' out of a
mystical state of bliss, when it enters this earthly life: and
consequently, that this life appears to be a punishment,
a purgatory, after which the soul may return to the 'gods'
if it has passed through the purgation successfully. According to this view, the earthly life is traversed in distinct
stages – which explains the idea of the 'wanderings of the
soul'. The 'purer' a man has been in his life here, the sooner
he returns to his state of blessedness. But in this ideology
a 'pure' life is a life which turns away from everything
sensual, which cares only for the life of the soul. Plato has
described it with much beauty in the *Phaedo*: 'The body

fills us with passions, desires, fears, many images and much idle talk, and in actual truth (as the catchword goes) it never allows us to think . . . While we live (it seems) we shall come nearer to knowledge, if we put our body away from us as much as possible, and disavow the senses where we are not bound to them by absolute necessity, and do not fill ourselves with their nature, but keep ourselves pure from the flesh, until God himself sets us free. Then for the first time pure, and freed from the folly of our body, we shall meet our equals, and without an intermediary, we shall know everything which is pure – and that, perhaps, is the truth. For only a pure thing can touch that which is pure' (*Phaedo*, 66*c*).

This was the conception which made on Cicero – who can certainly not be described as ascetic in other respects – such a deep impression that he expresses agreement with it in the profoundest passages of his philosophical writings (e.g. in the *Dream of Scipio, De rep.*, vi). But it is only a step from this conception to the complete doctrine of conscious asceticism – abstinence from carnal pleasures, from all indulgences, and naturally from sexual intercourse. That step was taken by the later school, the Neoplatonists. Their chief representative was the sublime thinker Plotinus (*c*. A.D. 250). He considers the truly human life to be the *vita contemplativa*, the pure theoretic life, far from all the allurements of the senses. Consequently, he thinks that the 'social' virtues, which serve only to restrain lust as far as social life demands, are the least valuable; the 'purifying' virtues, which turn us away from sensuality, are higher; the 'spiritual' virtues, which lead men to thought, are still higher; and the 'ideal' virtues, which give us the power to see God, are the highest of all. Here we see man's practical life as the necessary basis of his spiritual life; and asceticism makes entry into that higher life possible. Every human act which deserves to be called virtuous is in some way a 'purification of the soul' from the defiling bonds of the world of sense; enthusiasm for beauty (this idea is inherited by Plotinus from Plato) is justified only in so far as it awakes Eros in us, Eros, the guide to the realms beyond sense. 'To lapse into carnal love is a sin' (Plot., *Enn.*, iii, 5, 1).

It is important to know that Plotinus actually lived in

accordance with his own doctrine: he did not roam the country as a beggar or wandering preacher, as the Cynics did, but he lived a life of culture and thought. His biographer Porphyrius tells us: 'Plotinus seemed to be ashamed of having a body. Therefore he never brought himself to say anything of his birth, his parents, or his country. He disliked the idea of sitting to a painter or a sculptor so much that he would say: "Is it not enough to carry about the shadow which Nature has given us? Is it worth while making a shadow of that shadow and leaving it to posterity as a notable thing?"' When he was ill, he ate and drank nothing which was made of animal flesh; for he never ate meat. (One of his friends, a senator, reached such a point of asceticism that he gave up all his property, freed his slaves, resigned all his honours, paid no more attention to state business, and entered a simple primitive life, in which he took only one meal a day. Plotinus had an extremely high opinion of this man, and set his life before others as a pattern.) He himself slept little, ate little, and was unmarried, but did not shun conversation with his fellow men. Many noble men and women, when they were near death, brought him their children (boys and girls alike) and entrusted them to him, with all their property, making over the whole to him as a pure and saintly guardian. So his house was full of boys and girls: among them there was an occasional one whose education would especially interest Plotinus. He administered their property accurately, saying: 'While these young people are not yet philosophers, we must take great care of their property.' He was always affable and ready to receive anyone who sought his society; and so he had no enemies, although he settled many quarrels by being arbitrator. Moreover, he was famous for his knowledge of men: he detected a thief at once among the slaves of a widow who lived in his house, and he could foretell what every one of the boys living with him would become.

He was no crude thinker: he conceived asceticism not as a violent annihilation of each and every natural impulse, but as the consistent conquest of the instincts, 'the body', by the spirit. The instincts as Plotinus understands them are closely related to Schopenhauer's *Assertion of the Will*

to Live; and he sees the physical nature as the real basis
from which the soul must rise upwards – he calls it somewhere 'a natural impulse towards the natural terminus of
marriage' (*Enn.*, iv, 3, 13). This attitude implies, although
not always consciously, a severe denunciation of sexual
impulses as almost sinful. Therefore every virtue is a 'purification' (Plot., *Enn.*, i, 6, 6). And everyone who means to
reach the pure spiritual contemplation of supersensual
things must, like Odysseus, 'hasten away from the witches
Circe and Calypso, even if his eyes delight in pleasure,
and delighting, are filled with sensual beauty'.

But Plotinus's thought and feeling are those of a true
Hellene. He cannot agree with the condemnation of the
world as something utterly evil and hateful, which is
preached by the Christian Gnostics of his age. In his famous
book against the Gnostics (*Enn.*, ii, 9), he says: 'If the world
is so made that we can reach wisdom and live a godly life
in it, that proves that it depends entirely on the spiritual
world.' And elsewhere: 'We may praise the Gnostics for
despising earthly beauty, if that means only the beauty of
women and boys – that despisal would keep them from
being overpowered by evil lusts ... But, we must observe
that individual things are less beautiful than the universe;
and also that even in the world of sense-perception, and in
individual things there, there is enough beauty to arouse
in us admiration for its creator, the origin of that beauty.
We may draw a further conclusion, and describe that sensual world as overpoweringly beautiful – provided that we
do not remain fixed in contemplation on the earth, but
raise ourself from it to the spiritual world without despising the earth we have left.' And again: 'When we see beauty
radiant in a face, we feel ourselves drawn towards it. And
when we gaze on the beauty of the world of sense, the sym-
metry and order of the vast spectacle played by the stars
despite their distance from us, who would be so dull and
insensitive that he could not gather from this the majesty
of these things and of their creator?'

But there is one point in which Plotinus is nearer the
original conception of Christianity than all his predecessors. He is never tired of praising beauty: but above it
stands goodness. He says, for example, 'the Good is gentle,

gracious, soft – it is present to every man as he wishes. But
the beautiful brings amazement and excitement, and
pleasure mixed with pain. It draws men away from the
good without their knowledge, as a son in love is drawn
away from his father. For beauty is younger while goodness is older, not in age, but in truth. And goodness has a
higher power – a power without limits ... God is Good
itself, not anyone good' (*Enn.*, v, 5, 12). The highest thing
in the life of a pure man is the ecstatic union with this
Good, with God. Plotinus himself reached this holy experience four times, and speaks of it in strange and mystical
language (*Enn.*, vi, 7, 34): 'When the soul by good fortune
reaches that Goodness, or rather when that Goodness appears and approaches the soul; when the soul shakes off
all its accompaniments and prepares itself to be as beautiful as it may, to resemble Goodness (the preparation and
adornment of the soul are known to those who are preparing themselves for this experience): then the soul suddenly sees Goodness, or God, within herself. There is
nothing between the soul and God – they are not two; they
are together, and one. While God is in the soul, they cannot be separated. (This union is imitated in our world by
lovers, when they try to become one flesh.) The soul no
longer perceives that it is in a body, no longer knows
whether it is a man, or an animal, or a being, or the whole
universe. The soul is unequal to thinking of these things –
it has neither time nor will to think of them, but seeks God
only, and meets him face to face and looks at him, not at
itself – nor can it even see itself as it does so. It would not
exchange this experience for anything that exists, not even
if the whole heaven were offered in exchange.'

I have purposely quoted a number of passages from the
wonderful work of that God-intoxicated mystic Plotinus,
in order to show the loftiness of the thought of the best
minds of his age. We can understand that such men considered politics, economics, and everything which satisfied the usual desires of the mob to be far beneath them.
The more a man of great gifts is beset and harassed by
external things, the more resolutely he retreats to the
secret depths of his soul. This was the spiritual life of the
Romans who had not yet reached Christianity. They met

life's imperfections gently, almost forgivingly: they were sure of the completeness of their inner experience.

And we must think of the attitude of educated Christians as very similar to this – perhaps even more ready to shun the 'world', especially since the world sometimes strove against the new faith by torture and execution. We cannot treat in detail the early Christian strivings towards asceticism, and so must content ourselves with examples.

Burckhardt says in his life of Constantine: 'In considering the moral effects of Christianity on deeper natures, we must not measure them by Eusebius' standards. Eusebius postulates no greater reward for conversion than earthly happiness and power. But deeper natures found an entirely new relation to all earthly things: some became more and some less conscious of them than before. Most converts arranged their life as comfortably as was possible and as was allowed by the moral supervision of their country; but earnest men entirely gave up many worldly pleasures.'

But Constantine himself was certainly not among these earnest men. He tolerated Christianity, but he was certainly not a Christian. Still, there were, in Burckhardt's words, 'many men and women, sometimes of the highest rank and accustomed to lives of luxury, who followed out to the letter Christ's advice to the rich young man. They sold all that they had and gave the money to the poor – so that they themselves amid the life of the world and the thunder of the great cities might live a life of voluntary poverty in the pure contemplation of the highest things.' Others went into lonely places, such as the deserts of Egypt. In this way grew the class of anchorites, which developed later into the monastic orders.

I am not sure whether we must, like Burckhardt, consider these phenomena as systems of the 'unsoundness of individual and social life'. Some critics have seen the same 'unsoundness' in the advent of Schopenhauer's philosophy. I should like to dissociate myself entirely from this vulgar and Philistine view. Its advocates consider that man's condition is 'unsound' unless he enjoys his life unthinkingly, is satisfied with all his fellow men, and like God on the Seventh Day looks on everything and says: 'Behold, it is very good.' But is it not always true that the finer, deeper

spirits of this world question life and all its appearances
more and more? – until, at last, they ask themselves: 'Is
the world rational? Would it not have been better if it had
never existed?' These questions are asked in widely different
times and places – by the philosophers of India, by the
Greeks, by the Christian mystics, and by the modern pessi-
mists who follow Schopenhauer.

Today, we must be secretly grateful to those first Christian hermits for practising asceticism in this way – for despising the world and exalting the spiritual life, for losing
themselves in the mysteries of religion. Burckhardt is right
to say: 'In our times, while we enjoy the free activity of the
mind we forget one thing too easily. That activity is lit by
the splendour of eternity – the inheritance of science from
the medieval church.' Yet these first hermits and monks
renounced the life of the senses with a violent austerity
which has hardly ever been paralleled in later Europe. They
took certain injunctions of the New Testament literally and
seriously. They refused to compromise, and in Burckhardt's words 'did not pave their way with half-measures'.
The injunctions of the New Testament may have been the
external motive which drove these men from the highly
civilized Roman cities to the loneliness and privation of the
primitive desert. But I suggest that they were not the real
cause. The real cause can hardly be understood in the light
of cold reason. It was the sudden light of a higher, better,
supramundane world – in the light which all the mystics
have striven to describe in the same faltering words, the
light which Schopenhauer calls a gleam through the darkness of the renunciation of the will to life. Schopenhauer
shows us clearly that this mysterious impulse can enter the
soul suddenly like an intuition. But more often it is awakened by the purifying flame of sorrow.

Fiercely driven on by the will to life, striving for eternal
pleasure and eternal fulfilment, we find at last 'the futility
and emptiness of all our striving'; as the mounting waves
of sorrow surge around us, we cry in sudden enlighten-
ment, 'Why should this be? Why can I not change the aim
of my will, transform my very will itself?' The savage thirst
for self-fulfilment, when it has obtained everything for
which it strove, is sometimes slaked by another's pain –

as many Romans may have found during the slaughters of the Circus. But, after conversion, as Schopenhauer tells us, this thirst tortures us no more. 'However poor, joyless, and impoverished our life may seem, it is full of an inner happiness, and a divine calm.'

It may be objected that if most people entered upon 'this ascetic life' our world would decay and perish. But we may reply to that: 'Do you know what is the real aim of this important world of ours? Is it not more than probable that all our momentous activity will one day be blotted out by some catastrophe over which we have no control?' But even apart from all this, does every thinking man not see that all we call ethical conduct, and everything which really deserves that name, originates in a denial of the will to life? We may confirm this by a remark of Schopenhauer: 'From one and the same root spring the assertion of the will to life, the world of appearance, the diversity of things, individuality, egoism, hate and wickedness. And from another root spring the denial of the will to life, the world of reality, the identity of things, justice, and love of humanity.'

Must all this lead to a mystical conclusion? Is it perhaps true that the man who lives ethically, that is, justly, and loves his fellow men, is striving for utter annihilation of self? Perhaps, when we have determined on the renunciation of the will to life, we find it to be the highest reality and perhaps the only true reality. Perhaps it is the secret source from which the only worthy actions of humanity draw their overwhelming power. Perhaps Goethe's line has another meaning here: 'Within thy nothing, may I find my all.'

But such experiences, and the men who really feel them, are rare, as all great and noble things are. We must not think that every man who has been converted to deny the will to life has entered a state of unshaken peace. The Christian anchorites tell us again and again that they win their inner place through a constant war against their desires of the flesh. As Schopenhauer says: 'that peace and blessedness are only the flower which blossoms over the conquered will. The soil, from which it springs, is eternal war with the will to life. No man on earth can have enduring peace.' And, significantly enough, we are often told that the anchorites were besieged by sensual visions – the bodies of naked women, tables set with appetizing food, battles of gladiators – in fact, visions of the city life which they had left. Finally, it cannot be denied that this arduously sought liberation from the world and its temptations developed into 'hypocrisy and abomination'. For, as Schopenhauer justly says: 'Such a life is impossible for the greater part of mankind.'

We may close our remarks on sadism by emphasizing this fact. The men who asserted their wills and their lusts so completely and repulsively in the cruel sport of the circuses naturally suffered as a reaction the inner light of renunciation. Many of them chose instead of their voluptuous enjoyments of costly baths the filth and privation of a hermit's cell, instead of constant sexual excitement complete sexual renunciation, instead of orgiastic banquets submission to hunger and thirst, instead of the brilliant poetry of the senses the devout reading of holy scriptures. Even if such entire conversions were rare, they were facts. Through them Christianity reached its victory – not the external victory won by a state religion, equivocal and imperfect, which replaced the Roman power, but the true mystical doctrine, the overwhelming love, the supreme self-sacrifice, the mysterious power which arose from the denial of the will to life.

Chapter Four

Physical Life

1. Dress and Ornament

WALK through one of the magnificent Italian museums – in Rome, Florence, or Naples – and feast your soul on the beauty of ancient sculpture. Do not look only at the later works, like the Apollo Belvedere and the Laocoon, which have become so popular with modern scholars. There are others, less known, less intelligible to the untrained eye, and perhaps for that very reason truer and purer works of art. Such, for instance, are the dying Niobid in the Thermae Museum, and the most spiritual of all female statues, the Psyche of Capua. After you have seen the sculptures in one of these museums you will be bound to admit that the nation which collected them, though it did not produce them, had a deep understanding of the beauty of the human body.

Therefore, it is even harder to understand the constant deprecation of nakedness which is preached throughout Roman literature. We may quote the blunt and straight-forward statement of Lucilius: 'Seeing others naked is the origin of vice.' But Cicero must have had many fine works of plastic art in his splendid villa – it is all the more astonishing that he quite agrees with the old poet's maxim. We do not begin to see light until we read Seneca, who condemns everything connected with gymnastics as unworthy of Roman citizens. Gymnastics, then, were suitable for a puny Greek; but only arms and armour were fit diversions for a Roman. This may remind us of the admiration for gladiatorial fights: the true Roman admired them, but never took part in them. Gymnastics make nakedness necessary. In that connection we also must consider and condemn gymnastics as improper for true-born Romans. The coarse sensual character of the nation made it impossible for them to see a naked body as anything but a sexual stimulus. Cicero believes that homosexuality is a natural product of nakedness (*Tusc.*, iv, 33); and Propertius and Plautus both show that the naked body of the beloved is admired from purely erotic grounds, but never as a work of art (Plaut., *Most.*, 289; Prop., ii, 15, 13; Sen., *Ep.*, 88).

It is very significant that in Latin the word *nudus*, 'naked', can also mean 'rough, uncouth' (as in Pliny, *Ep.*, iv, 14, 4). The Romans almost always took nakedness to be synonymous with indecency, impropriety.

Yet they were enthusiastic collectors of naked sculptures. Why? They filled their rooms with these figures, either to delight themselves with erotic fantasies, or – as I am more inclined to suppose – because they had subconscious thoughts and feelings which were truer, higher, and more human than we should guess from these few condemnatory quotations. There is a memorable remark in the elder Pliny (*N.H.*, xxxiv, 5[10]): 'The Greek habit is to conceal nothing, the Roman way and the warrior's way is to give the statues each a coat of armour.' If this were true, we should have no Roman statues without suits of armour: but that is not the case – there are countless naked statues of Antinous and many others. The remark can only mean this, that the Romans preferred to portray their great men, like Augustus and his successors, in a warrior's uniform rather than naked. The most useful explanation of the sentence is in Lesing's *Laocoon:* 'Beauty is the first purpose of art. Clothes were created by necessity – but what has art to do with necessity? I grant that there is a certain beauty in costume, but what is it compared with the beauty of the human body?' The true artist presents nature unclad. But the Roman was not a true artist. At least, he was never so conscious of the beauty of the naked human body as the Greek was. The only important Roman nudes are the portrait statues of Antinous; but Roman sculpture reaches greater heights in its interesting character-portraits of men and women. (Of course, it became more usual in later ages to see nakedness in public, with the growing fashion of frequenting great public baths.)

T—F

Let us turn to Roman costume. In modern times we cannot say without qualification that clothes are a product of necessity. Costume, and specially women's costume, is much more closely connected with sex. Nature instructs women to be sexually attractive to men: the existence of the next generation depends on that attraction: and it is not only understandable but right for women to do everything which can produce erotic excitement in men. The beauty of the female body serves to attract men; so that it would be natural enough for women to expose all their beauty without concealment. They are kept from doing that not by climatic conditions, but by the fact (which is a matter of experience) that an entirely naked body is less stimulating than one which is partly hidden and partly revealed. This explanation of the facts is universally accepted nowadays. These causes account for every variation in female costume and for many in male costume, and it can justly be said that without sex there would be no fashions. The healthy perceptions of an unperverted man will find a costume 'beautiful' if it is natural, and neither discloses nor completely hides the shape and the various parts of the figure. Accordingly, a female statue like the Callipygos, which reveals only the hips, must be peculiarly stimulating; whereas an entirely naked statue of a woman will be simply 'beautiful'.

It is therefore striking that the ancient peoples knew nothing of changes of fashion in costume. (The Greeks and Romans were alike in this.) After all, fashion is nothing but the revelation or concealment of various parts of the body. It is entirely a matter of erotic necessity. We could infer that it was so from the fact that women who wish to produce no erotic effect (nuns and sicknurses) never wear fashionable clothes; their clothes are always simple, and have no openings which reveal and emphasize any part of the body.

We have said that in ancient times there were no fashions as we know them. Colours often changed, but never cut, and seldom the general pattern. From earliest times, the Romans wore an undergarment, the *tunica*, and an upper garment, the *toga*; the women always wore a rather longer *tunica*, and an upper garment called the *stola*. It is not, of course, disputed that the toga was gradually replaced by a

more practical dress for everyday and travelling – cloaks of
various kinds borrowed from the Greeks and other foreign
nations – while in the third century of our era, the women's
stola was replaced by the *dalmatica* (a long tunic with
sleeves). But all these changes are comparatively small and
cannot be compared with the constantly altering modern
fashions. The fact remains that fashion is a modern invention. Its absence in ancient times cannot be explained by the
fact that the sexual life of ancient people was more un-
sophisticated and 'pure' than ours. We have already seen
that this was not the case. There is another reason. Ancient
peoples, especially the Romans, could produce erotic
effects without changing the cut of their costume, by variations in the attitude or drapery which were governed by no
hard and fast rules. There is an illuminating remark in this
connection on p. 260 of Lothar's stimulating travel book
Between Three Worlds: 'The artistry of ancient costume
lay in the fact that there was no prescribed style of draping
– each man and woman wore the costume and arranged its
material as he or she wished.' Accordingly, variations in the
arrangement of the same type of costume could give very
different impressions. A woman could show as much or as
little of her body as she thought correct and appropriate.
Respectable matrons of the highest rank appeared discreet
and stately in the long ceremonious folds of the *stola*. But
quite a different effect was produced by the light lady who
slipped into the room of her lover, Ovid, wearing only the
tunica, in the expectation that in his passion he would tear
it off her, as in fact he did. So also, in Apuleius' novel, the
charming frivolous Fotis appears in a thin light *tunica* and
excites the hero to immediate passion.

Women who wanted to produce equally striking effects
while wearing the stola, usually adopted thin delicate materials for it. Seneca preaches bitterly against this (*De ben.*,
vii, 9): 'There I see silken clothes, if they can be called
clothes which protect neither a woman's body nor her
modesty, and in which she cannot truthfully declare that
she is not naked. These are bought for huge sums from
nations unknown to us in the ordinary course of trade –
and why? So that our women may show as much of themselves to the world at large as they show to their lovers in

the bedroom.' These clothes, of airy delicacy, were called
Coan garments, because they were imported from the
island of Cos into Greece and Rome. (Plin., *N.H.*, xi, 22[26]).
Tacitus says that in the reign of Tiberius men also were forbidden to wear thin silken clothes (*Ann.*, ii, 33). For the
male sex also could produce erotic effects by wearing fine
and delicate materials. Handsome young slaves, kept as
male favourites, were purposely dressed in thin clothes, cut
as short as possible. Many Roman dandies must have affected this fashion otherwise the ban of which Tacitus speaks
would be incomprehensible. Juvenal derides a young fop
for wearing these clothes and advises him to appear naked
instead, since 'madness is less disgraceful'.

Again, these distracting garments of silk and fine fabrics were always used by those women who lived for love –
the freedwomen who as we saw made up almost the whole
class of prostitutes in Rome. We read in Horace (*Sat.*, i, 2,
101): 'No concealment here! You can see her almost naked
in her Coan dress, and make sure that her thigh is not mis-
shapen or her foot ugly; you can measure her flank with
your eye.' Horace is speaking of the freedwomen, who were
much easier to possess than married women, against whom
he always warns his hearers. We need not explain that the
respectable married women, the *matronae,* usually wore
the less attractive *stola* and later the tightly fastened *dalmatica* – neither being woven from thin transparent fabrics
but from plain wool. In accordance with unbroken custom,
a man married a wife not for love but for the procreation
of children and the government of his household.

Let us turn to the colour of Roman costume. The man's
toga was always white. At home and on journeys clothes
of subdued and darker hues were usually worn. In the Imperial period colours were much more varied. Seneca says
(*N.Q.*, vii, 31, 2): 'We men wear the colours used by prostitutes, in which respectable married women would not be
seen.' Even in early times, as can be seen from the dispute
over the annulment of the *lex Oppia*, respectable matrons
claimed and won the right of wearing purple dresses. The
frescoes of Pompeii and Herculaneum show that women of
later ages wore garments of many bright colours. The
freedwomen of course chose bright colours to harmonize

or contrast with their hair, as Ovid says (*A.A.*, iii, 162).

Our account of Roman costume would be incomplete
without reference to jewellery. The Roman women love
jewels, as all southern races do. We hear of bracelets,
necklaces, earrings, finger-rings, ankle-rings, hairpins,
buckles, and *fibulae* (ornaments like our brooches) – all
made of costly metals and decorated with even more costly
gems. But it would take a treatise to deal with these matters exhaustively. A few significant examples may be
enough. Pliny (*N.H.*, ix, 35[58]) tells us that the consort of
the Emperor Caligula possessed a set of jewels consisting of
pearls and emeralds, and representing a fortune of £400,000.
We read in Petronius that the wife of the purseproud mil-
lionaire, Trimalchio, wore golden armlets weighing more
than 6 lb. Women particularly favoured pearls, which, according to Pliny, they wore principally as earrings. Seneca
(*De ben.*, vii, 9) says that women sometimes wore 'two or
three estates in each ear'; in the same place he scoffingly
says that 'ears are used as beasts of burden'. The precious
stones which were chiefly used were diamonds (in rings
only), and opals, emeralds, and beryls. Next were the numerous semi-precious stones – onyx, rock-crystal, jasper, cal-
cedony – which were worked into popular ornaments such
as cameos and gems. These ornaments sometimes bore the
portraits of the reigning emperor. But this could on occasion lead to unpleasant results, as in the case of the praetor,
Paulus, of whom Seneca tells the following amusing anecdote (*De Ben.*, iii, 26): 'Paulus, a man of praetorian rank,
was once at a dinner, where he wore a portrait of Tiberius
embossed on a very striking jewel. I should be acting very
foolishly if I looked for phrases in order to tell you that he
took up a chamberpot. This was immediately noticed by
Maro, a well-known spy of those times. At the same moment the slave of Paulus (whose death was being com-
passed) slipped the ring away from his drunken master.
When Maro called the other guests to witness that the emperor's portrait had been dishonoured and started to write
a deposition, the slave produced the ring lying in his own
hand.' Women, especially freedwomen and prostitutes,
loved to wear long slender gold chains which hung from
their neck over their bosom and sides (Plin., *N.H.*, xxxiii,

3[12]). Juvenal (vi, 122) even speaks of *auratae papillae* – which would seem to indicate that certain women were so tasteless as to gold their breasts; but perhaps he means only that they wore these gold chains covering their breasts. Men wore no gems but the signet-ring; but effeminate dandies and emperors like Caligula and Nero took to wearing bracelets. Many articles of jewellery have been discovered by excavations in Pompeii even in the House of the Vestals. This shows how generally women felt bound to adorn themselves with jewels: they wished to be especially attractive to men in public – in theatre, in the circus, in the fashionable baths.

Finally, we must describe how Roman women dressed their hair. (It is not necessary in this place to discuss how men wore their beards at various times in Roman history.)

There is a very interesting passage in Apuleius's novel (ii) which shows us how a man prized his mistress's hair, how he was charmed by it if it was thick and beautiful, and how utterly he would have despised the modern fashion of cutting it short.

'The head is the noblest part of the body, so placed by nature that it is first to meet our gaze. Its natural sheen gives it that grace which is given to other limbs by the gay hues of rich garments. When a woman wishes to display her nature and her loveliness she throws off all her array, and puts away all her apparel: she appears in naked beauty, trusting that the roses of her skin will be more delightful than the gold of her dress. But – it is blasphemy to say it, and may such a dreadful thing never come to pass! – if you despoil the most peerless beauty of her hair you will strip her face of its natural beauty. Although she came down from heaven and were born of the sea and nursed by the waves, although she were very Venus companied by the choir of Graces, followed by the Cupid-folk, and girt with her own girdle, although cinnamon breathed from her and balm dropped from her – if only she were bald she could not please even her husband Vulcan. But what could be more enthralling than hair of lovely colour, gleaming with bright lights, glittering brilliantly in the sun or shining softly, varying its appearance into different beauties – now glistening gold shading into the gentle dusk of honey, now

raven blackness rivalling the blue bloom on the neck of
doves, or anointed with Arabian oils, divided by the slender tooth of the fine comb, turned back to meet her lovers'
gaze and like a mirror give back a lovelier image? or when
its wealth is heaped into a crown or flowing freely in abundant locks down her back? The hair is such a noble thing
that although a woman move in the beauty of gold, fine
apparel, jewels and all adornments, if she has not cared for
her hair she is not really adorned.'

The man who can hymn his mistress's hair in this way
must wish that she will give herself to him with hair unbound: and that is what the mistress in the *Metamorphoses* does for her lover.

But the Romans in general paid little attention to the
beauty of long hair in woman – they preferred to see it
dressed in all possible ways. How else can we explain the
huge number of styles of hairdressing, which Ovid mentions
(*A.A.*, iii, 139)? Ovid, the connoisseur of women, advises
them to dress their hair according to the shape of their
head. We shall not particularize here: Ovid says, however,
that there are as many styles as there are honey-bees in
Hybla and wild animals in the Alps. In the same connection
he mentions the common fashion of dyeing the hair, and of
padding it out by wigs of false hair. Ever since the auburn
hair of German women had become known in Rome,
Roman ladies were wildly eager to have such hair instead
of their own black locks. There was consequently a flourishing trade in wigs made of red or fair hair from the heads of
German girls (Ov., *Am.*, i, 14, 45). According to Juvenal (vi,
120) the empress Messalina wore one of these blond wigs.

The beautiful long hair of handsome male slaves was
much prized (e.g. Sen., *Ep.*, 119, 14; Petron., 27, I; and
many other passages). Boys of free birth also wore their
hair in long curls until they assumed the toga of manhood,
that is, until the beginning of puberty. Fashions of hairdressing among Roman men changed, like the styles of
wearing the beard; they had little to do with sexual life.

We must mention in closing that women did not only
coil their hair gracefully, but also used all kinds of gold and
jewelled pins to hold their curls together; bands, nets, pearl-
caps, and tiaras should also be mentioned. The possibilities

of these styles can be grasped by anyone who looks at the coins or portrait-statues of the Roman empresses and other noble ladies.

This account will perhaps be sufficient for our purpose.

2. The Toilet

In many modern accounts of the development of Roman civilization we meet the belief that the older Romans (the 'real' Romans, who had not yet degenerated into 'sickly urbanized weaklings') were healthy, simple, chaste and so on, not only in their thoughts but in the care they took of their bodies. They were, we are told, 'undegenerate', simple and healthy in the way they bathed, anointed and adorned themselves; but later, that is about the beginning of the Principate or even before, these noble characters developed into the effeminate voluptuaries who bathed for hours in the warm water of luxurious baths, who anointed themselves with fragrant perfumes, whose women painted their faces and tied their hair.

This idea seems to be supported by passages in Seneca and Tacitus: these two writers constantly refer to the simple manners of the early Romans or of the even nobler Germans.

I must admit that descriptions of this kind struck me as suspicious even at school when I first learned something of the ancient Romans and Germans. I could not understand how it could be taken for a sign of degeneration in a people if its citizens cleaned their bodies thoroughly every day, or even took an occasional hot bath. As for cosmetics and the like, I thought that people had really advanced if they paid some attention to their hands and fingernails, or treated their skin with some sort of fat or cream to make it whiter or more 'beautiful'. The same sort of advance is sometimes made today by farming people, but it has certainly nothing to do with degeneration.

When I grew older, I understood how a *bad smell* will always kill love, and will even turn it into disgust. With this general truth I connected the fact that every nation throughout the world has always tried to banish certain evil smells belonging to the natural body, or at least to

compensate them by other artificial odours. Then it occurred to me that I also might be 'degenerate' for thinking
these thoughts; and I searched the literature of the subject
without discovering anything like a Philosophy of Smells to
clarify my ideas. Then, a little time ago I found a remarkable book called *Egyptian Nights*. Its author is a well-
known doctor, natural historian, and philosopher, named
Hans Much. His book is distinguished from all other
Egyptian travel books by the fact that he does not weigh
up all the previous opinions of scholars on any subject, but
looks at everything with his own eyes, and produces opinions which are often bold and always original. All my views
were refreshed and illuminated by the following remarks
on the connection between love and the care of the body:
I shall quote them, therefore, at the head of this chapter
(Much, p. 176).

'Pure sensuality is always the slave of love in our life,
never its victim. Eros reserves himself with all his gifts for
the man who can use sensuality as an instrument of the
spirit, although it would be dangerous to use it otherwise.

'Few of us know the real Eros. In Egypt he was part of
the very being of the aristocracy for thousands of years.
And he demands that the lives of his subjects shall be luxurious, or at least immaculate ... So it is and so it has always
been. In the aristocratic Egyptian homes, the bath was an
important ceremony. Three baths a day were part of the
household routine. They knew how much beauty Eros
gives to life, and they built him a vast number of altars. A
house often had twenty bathrooms. Other altars were the
toilet rooms, and finally the splendid chambers reserved for
love and sleep.

'The Egyptian women knew that Eros does not favour
nature herself, but nature embellished and elaborated. For
love is akin to the spirit; and the spirit formalizes – that is
one of its greatest arts. In Egypt the man wears only an
apron. But the woman always appears veiled in a garment
which conceals her, and yet reveals her more subtly – slim,
yielding, exciting. Eros is served by cosmetics and colour:
the art of their application was excessively refined; and the
very spoons and jars were works of art; they were made of
gold, and the palettes of gold and enamel.

'Only the bodies of animals, and not those of most plants, give off unpleasant odours: and when these are not removed several times a day, how can Eros rule? But that is not all. The hair harbours these odours. So away with it – it must be removed from the whole body. The Egyptian ladies allowed no hair to grow anywhere on their flesh. Nor did the men, except for the hair on their head and sometimes that on their chin ... If we shave the chin for cleanliness' sake, we must shave all body hair for the same reason. Cutting and shaving the head and beard is formalization. For if we let nature take its course with our appearance, we would soon look like gipsies ... The fashions of Egypt are not a sign of degeneration, for degeneration cannot last for 6,000 years ... Eros commands that anything ugly in the body must be removed as far as it can be removed. And rightly!

'Even then, there is yet more to do. When the body is cleaned, it must be embellished and perfumed. It is embellished by artificial perfumes which must not conceal the natural odours of the body (as they did in the unwashed court of Louis XIV), but replace these natural odours when they have been washed away.

'Now the body is perfumed. Now it is painted with colours which add a soft gleam to its skin and emphasize all its beauties. Even the gleam of the eyes is enhanced by plant juices. And now the charming robe, itself a perfume, is moulded to breast and hips. And now the body is adorned by the master's loveliest gifts – gold, precious stones, and jewellery ... I have always found that bodily purity was spiritual purity ... Behind this cult of cleanliness, Eros need not appear. Cleanliness and care of the body are desirable in themselves. But Eros stands unseen behind them.'

When I read this my eyes were suddenly opened. The old Romans, whose simple life was famous, were, as seen by our eyes, no more than sturdy farmers and soldiers. They were simple and primitive and ignorant of the care of their bodies as they were of other such matters. This primitive outlook was a defect which later ages considered to be a special virtue of their ancestors. If they had not so considered it, we could not understand why a statesman like Cicero or a general like Scipio should imitate their rude forefathers, in washing little or seldom, using dirty water for the bath, and in other practices which Seneca and others considered especially characteristic of the true ancient Romans. In a discussion of the changes in the Roman attitude to this matter, Seneca writes (*Ep.*, 86): 'I am writing this letter from the villa of Scipio Africanus ... It is built of squared stone; its wood is surrounded by a wall; on both sides rise towers, like ramparts for its protection; there is a tank beneath the house and garden, big enough to water an army; and a narrow bath, dark as they usually were in ancient times – our fathers did not think a bath was warm unless it was dark. It was a great pleasure to me to consider Scipio's customs compared with ours. He, the terror of Carthage, he to whom Rome owes the fact that she was captured only once – in this corner he washed his body when it was tired of field work. For he took exercise by working, and as they did in those old times he turned the soil himself. He stood beneath this mean roof, this cheap pavement felt his footsteps. Nowadays who would bear to take a bath in such a place? Every man thinks he is poor and miserly unless his walls glitter with great costly plaques, unless he has Alexandrian marble set off by Numidian overlay, unless he has an elaborate frieze all round varied like a picture, unless the vault is concealed by a glass ceiling, unless Thasian stone (once a rare sight in an occasional temple) lines the pool into which we lower our bodies exhausted by long sweating, unless the water flows from silver taps. And I am speaking only of the ordinary man's plumbing. When we come to the baths of the freedmen, what a multitude of statues, what a host of pillars which support nothing but are merely expensive ornaments! What a rush of water, tumbling noisily down flights of steps! We have become so luxurious that we will not walk on pavements which are not jewelled.

'In Scipio's bath there are no windows, but rather thin slits cut in the stone wall to let in the light without decreasing the strength of the building. Nowadays we call a bath a cockroach-covert, unless it is arranged to let in sunlight all day by extensive windows, unless we can sunbathe while we are still in the water, unless the country and the sea can be seen from the pool. . . .

'In early times there were few baths, and those were not elegantly decorated. Why should a thing be decorated which costs a penny, and was invented for use and not for pleasure? There was no constant supply of water; it did not flow as if fresh from a warm spring; they did not think it was important to wash off their dirt in crystal clear water. But it is delightful to enter those gloomy baths with common ceilings, where you know that Cato as aedile or Fabius Maximus or one of the Cornelii regulates the heat with his own hand! That was the duty of the noblest aediles: they entered those places where the common people were admitted; they exacted cleanliness and a temperature which was useful and healthy – not this modern invention, which is so like a fire that you should condemn a slave found guilty of a crime to be washed alive. I really think that it makes no difference now whether a bath is hot or on fire. Nowadays they would accuse Scipio of being provincial because he did not let daylight into his steamroom by broad windows, because he did not stew in full daylight and want to be cooked in his bath. Unhappy man! he did not know how to live. He did not wash with filtered water – the water was often clouded and muddy when it rained hard. He did not care if it was. He came to wash off, not oil, but sweat. What do you think some people will say to that? "I don't envy Scipio: he was living the life of an exile, to have baths like that." And yet, if you knew it, he did not bathe every day! Historians of the customs of old Rome tell us that our ancestors washed legs and arms daily, from the dirt they had collected at work; but they took a complete bath once a week. I hear it said "I can see that they were very dirty, once upon a time. How they must have smelled!" They smelt of soldiering, of work, of manhood.'

This attitude reminds us of Cynicism, and it is with set purpose that the wealthy and luxurious Seneca adduces it. Can we share his views? I think not. When Roman civilization develops from that primitive condition in which they sang the praises of honest dirt, to a really cultured view of baths and washing (such as is found everywhere under the Principate), we should perhaps welcome that development rather than submit it to the pedantic judgments of Stoicism. But besides that development we must consder the eccentricities seen especially in the use of excessively hot water and in the colossal size and ostentatious luxury of the buildings. And these matters we must try to understand from our knowledge of the Roman character. When a man of coarse disposition suddenly gets power and money he becomes ostentatious, even today. We must notice that in the passage quoted from Seneca only 'plebeians' and 'freedmen' are mentioned as building themselves such magnificent baths. From this we cannot infer that the upper classes would behave differently. We can infer only that anyone who had the money could build himself baths of this kind.

Martial (vi, 42) speaks of such a bath with its refinement of situation and decoration: 'Oppianus, if you do not bathe in Etruscus' baths, you die unbathed.' The walls of this palatial bath were inlaid with green marble, mixed with a sort of alabaster; and beside the steamrooms there were basins into which water flowed from the Apennine mountains, brought in the channel constructed by Marcius Titius. At this period Rome was rich in such public water-courses. The water was laid on to the city in a very efficient system of lead pipes, and conducted thither on acqueducts (lofty channels carried on stone arches, the majority of which are still preserved). The best known were the gigantic *Aqua Claudia*, which was completed in Claudius' principate: it brought water from the Sabine hills, 45 miles away from Rome. To this day its colossal arches are one of the beauties of the Campagna. In Constantine's day, there were nine such supplies in Rome. From them, water was supplied to eleven large public baths, 850 other baths, 135 public fountains, as well as innumerable households. The most famous of all baths were those laid out under Carcalla, Diocletian, and Constantine. The enormous walls of these baths were used by such later architects as Michael Angelo to build great churches. Part of the baths of Diocletian became the Church of S. Maria degli Angeli. Another part has been converted to the finest of all museums of ancient culture.

But perhaps these details are enough. We cannot give a history of Roman baths and bathing: information can be found in any book on Roman antiquities. What interests us especially is the question whether this sphere of Roman manners had any connection with sexual life. We may quote

from Ovid (*Ars Am.*, iii, 633 sq.): 'What is the use of guard-
ing women? ... When, even although the girl's guardian
keeps her clothes in safety outside the baths, hidden lovers
lurk safe within?' This shows that assignations with lovers
must frequently have been made in one or other of the
baths. But this took place, not in the great baths of later
times, but in the smaller establishments built or rented by
private individuals, who managed them and charged
visitors a small sum. According to Martial (iii, 93) there
must have been special baths for prostitutes, which were
of course visited by no respectable woman. But they must
have been visited by men, wishing not so much to bathe as
to have a convenient opportunity of visiting their mistress
(*Mart.*, xi, 47). In particular, there were always baths
reserved for men, and others reserved for women. Baths
for mixed bathing were introduced about the time of the elder
Pliny. In these, the women alone wore a bathing costume,
like a short apron: objectionable incidents naturally followed. Hadrian was the first to ban these mixed baths; but
his prohibition had obviously little effect since it was renewed by later emperors. All the repeated prohibitions
were useless, as we can see from a piece of description in
Ammianus Marcellinus, who wrote about 370 A.D. (xxviii, 4,
9): 'When these nobles, with fifty servants following them,
enter the vaulted baths, where we common people are, they
shout in a threatening voice. If they suddenly hear that a
strange harlot has appeared or a prostitute from a provincial town, or a veteran hag of the streets, they compete
with each other to court her, and woo her with disgusting
flattery, as the Parthians flattered Semiramis, the Egyptians
Cleopatra, the Carians Artemisia, or the Palmyrenes
Zenobia. This they do, although in the time of their
ancestors a senator was stigmatized by the rebuke of the
censors for daring to commit the indecency of kissing his
wife in the presence of his daughter.'

In this connection we must mention the famous watering
place of Rome – Baiae the magnificent. Baiae had a
splendid situation between Naples and the Cape of Mise-
num: to this day it is a place of fabulous beauty, although
there are now only a few poor relics of the rich villas which
were so numerous in the Imperial period. According to the

general belief about Baiae, a wife who visited it without her husband was exposed to great temptations. Propertius mentions this (i, 11, 27) : –

> As soon as may be, leave the vicious Baiae;
>   those beaches part many a loving pair,
> beaches which hate and injure decent women –
>   a curse on Baiae and its guilty loves!

The moralist Seneca utters warning against the enervating effects of Baiae, in one of his letters (*Ep.*, 51): 'Baiae has begun to be the haven of the vices. Luxury and voluptuousness have fewer constraints there than elsewhere; there, as if they felt a certain freedom due to the place, they are far more boldly extravagant. We should choose a place which is healthy not only for our bodies but also for our morals ... Drunk men wandering along the beach, banquets in boats, the lakes echoing with the voices of singers, and the other acts of debauchery, displayed as though the laws had ceased to bind them – why should I see all these things? ... Do you think Cato would ever have lived in one of these houses, to count the adulterous women sailing past him, to watch the painted boats sailing on a lake amid a tide of roses, to hear the noise of singing every night?'

We can, then, picture these smart watering places as not unlike the modern Biarritz or Nice. Their hot sulphur springs, of course, had curative properties; but contemporary moralists preached against their easy hedonistic life as they do against their modern counterparts. The peculiar freedom which characterized the life of ancient Baiae must have been the outcome of an ease and freedom in the relations between men and women, such as was held to be improper in the highest Roman society. We cannot, of course, imagine that the life of Baiae resembled the life of the great cosmopolitan hotels at modern watering places. There was nothing like a hotel. The rich Romans had country houses of varying degrees of splendour, as homes for the summer months. As we saw from Seneca's description, there were numerous festivities; and the god of Love played his part in them. It could easily come about that (as Martial bitterly says) a Roman lady who was Penelope when she entered Baiae, was Helen when she left it. In later times, other towns possessing warm springs such as Aix-la-Chapelle, Ems,

Teplitz, and Pyrmont, became known for their cures, and were furnished with bathing establishments by the Romans.

The care of the body was not confined to bathing. As Seneca points out, the Romans knew all the arts of applying ointments and cosmetics to the care of the body. Massage before and after the bath or for gymnastic purposes was known very early; the habit was acquired from Greece. Plautus mentions, among the slaves of a concubine, an *unctor*, whose special duty was to anoint his mistress with the usual oil after her bath. The Romans originally used pure olive oil for this purpose, which was entirely hygienic. Later, however, these oils were mixed with various floral perfumes, obviously with the intention of removing the natural odours of the body and replacing them by others more agreeable. It seems indisputable that this change was almost consciously dictated by erotic developments. It was natural that moralists of Stoic origin should soon preach against this degeneration. Later legislation correctly distinguished ointments intended merely for health from those employed for pleasure (*Dig.*, xxxiv, 2, 21, I). Ointments and oil were applied not only to the head and beard but to the whole body, not only after every bath but also before festal dinners – ointments were distributed by the host, like garlands, when the guests arrived (Petronius 60, 3). We have said that perfumes were used to banish the natural odours of the body; it may be pointed out that there are many warnings in literature against permitting he-goat smells on one's body (e.g. Catullus, 69, 71: Ovid, *A.A.* iii, 193). These warnings applied to both sexes, although Ovid immediately adds that the warning is unnecessary for women, since he is talking of Romans, not of barbarians. It was a refinement to eat pastilles in order to perfume the breath (Hor., *Sat.*, i, 2, 27). The evidence on all this is abundant and cannot be explored in detail here; it is clear that the use of ointments, oils, pomades, perfumes, etc., was so popular in the Roman empire that their manufacture was a flourishing industry. Subordinate industries were preparations for the care of the skin's texture and colour, for dyeing the hair, for care of the teeth and nails. A lady of the Empire must have used at her daily toilet a battery of little pots, jars, and bottles. There is an amusing account of this from the days of Lucian: although a little over-emphasized and misogynistic, it may very well represent truth (? Lucian, *Amores*, 39). It runs:

'If one could but see women rising from their beds in the morning, one would think them worse than the beasts which one may not mention in the early morning in case of bad luck. That is why they keep themselves in seclusion at home, unseen by any man. They are surrounded by old women and maids who look no less hideous, all doctoring their unfortunate faces with elaborate treatments. They do not wash off the greasy night with the pure waters of the spring and go straight to some useful work. Instead, they beautify the ugly skin of their face with an array of cosmetics. As if at a public procession each maid carries something – a silver jar, a bottle, a mirror, or a chemists' shop of little jars, all vials of abomination, treasures to polish the teeth or blacken the eyebrows and lashes. But most time and energy is spent on curling their hair. This lady dips her hair in henna to redden it and dries it in the midday sun like some wool-dyer, because she despises its natural colour. That lady thinks black hair suits her, so she spends all her husband's money on it; all the perfumes of Arabia sweeten her little hair. With steel tongs heated in the fire's gentle flame, she forces her curls into shape. In front she carries them carefully down to her eyebrows so that only a small space of brow is left, while behind, her curls fall and ripple coquettishly.'

Many other authors speak of the various preparations for tinting the skin and hair. According to Cicero (*Or.*, 23, 79) they were occasionally used by men also. Tertullian wrote a whole treatise on women's toilette (*De cultu feminarum*); he and other Christian authors preach against the rouging of women's cheeks, which they thought would only lead to adultery. It was also a favourite practice to apply a mask of paste every night, and wash it off with asses' milk in the morning: this was thought to keep the skin fresh and unwrinkled. This custom was practised at times by foppish men. Suetonius mentions it as followed by the Emperor Otho (Suet., *Otho*, 12). Homosexual men in particular used these means to keep their skin looking fresh and young.

Finally, it was a widespread custom to remove all hair from one's body: it was considered ugly. No female statue of classical times has pubic hair, or hair in the armpits, for care was taken to eliminate it. The elder Seneca says (*Contr.*, i, *praef.*, 8) that effeminate young men 'tried to vie with women in the softness of their bodies'. This was especially practised by the creatures who served homosexual purposes. Marital writes with brutal directness (ii, 62): –

> You depilate your arms, your legs, your bosom,
>   and shave yourself, even your hairy loins.
> Of course you do it for your mistress, don't you?
>   Still, others might have your smooth end in view.

We may sum up thus. With the development of their Hellenistic civilization under Greek influence, the Romans became acquainted with the arts of caring for their bodies – arts which were partly a product of sophistication and partly suggested by natural feeling. We must recognize, finally, the close connection of these arts with sexual life.

3. Dancing and the Theatre

We often read that dancing is one of the activities which can be explained only in terms of sex. This generalization is certainly wrong. In every nation there are dances which have nothing to do with sex. It seems to me that there is much more in Schopenhauer's remark: 'Dancing is the purposeless employment of superfluous energy.' The philosopher is not expressing blame; he is stating a fact. If we take it as a fact we shall understand that dancing may well be the expression of erotic feelings, but that it often expresses quite different feelings.

In order to understand the attitude of the Romans to dancing we should proceed from Schopenhauer's definition. The Roman was a sober, practical farmer, soldier or statesman. At the time of his rise to world power, he had no medium for the 'purposeless employment of superfluous energy'. It was different later; but then, as we shall see, their views on the subject were changed. The Roman never consciously expended energy in a 'purposeless' way; he was always intensely purposeful, and expended his energy on the extension of his conquests. He could not understand how anyone could have superfluous energy or expend it without purpose. That is why the Roman is essentially in-

artistic. He lacks understanding of the real essence of dancing, that purposeless activity. The Greeks, those born
artists, practised dancing with artistic completeness. We
must begin any discussion of the Roman attitude to dancing
by quoting Cicero's famous remark (*Pro Mur.*, 13): 'No one
dances while he is sober, unless he happens to be a lunatic.'

We must not think that no one ever danced in Rome.
According to Plutarch (*Numa,* 13) one of the oldest institutions of Rome was the war-dance or spring dance of the
Salii – a sort of procession of religious character. Varro
makes an interesting comment on it (*ap.* Serv., *Comm. in
Verg. Ecl.*, v, 73). 'The meaning of dancing at religious rites
is that our ancestors felt that no part of the body should
be debarred from religious experience.' With this we may
compare the dances at the funeral services of nobles, or at
the *ludi juvenales* founded by Nero. After the Hannibalic
war, special instruction in dancing began at Rome. Macrobius (iii, 14, 4) tells us: 'Beginning with the time of highest
morality, between the two Punic wars, free-born citizens,
even sons of senators, went to dancing schools and learned
to dance and wave the castanets. I hesitate to say that
even married ladies thought dancing no disgrace. On
the contrary, even the most respectable took an interest in
it, although they did not seek to become experts. Sallust
says: "She played and danced more gracefully than a
respectable woman should." In fact, he censures Sempronia,
not for dancing, but for dancing well. The sons of noblemen and, what is worse, their unmarried daughters, were
engaged in learning to dance. This is proved by Scipio
Africanus Aemilianus who says ... ". . . boys and girls of
noble birth go to the dancing schools among degenerates"
. . . Scipio goes on to say that he had once visited such a
school and seen more than fifty boys and girls there.
Among them was a boy of about twelve years, the son
of a candidate for a magistracy: the boy danced "a dance
with castanets which not even a brazen slave could have
performed with decency".'

We have already quoted Cicero's deprecatory view. On
the other hand it is recorded that Cicero's friends, such as
M. Caelius Rufus and P. Licinius Crassus, loved dancing
and displayed great skill in it. The consul of 60 B.C. was

reproached with being a better dancer than he was a statesman. Roman opinions therefore contradict each other. This
may arise from the fact that the value of dancing as exercise
was not recognized; it was regarded – apart from war-
dances and religious dances – as more or less stimulating
to the sexual instincts. (We may explain in the same way,
the Roman dislike for nakedness.) The Romans liked to
watch dancing, but they condemned it when performed by
amateurs with professional skill, or by women of society
in public.

Still, opinions must have changed under the Empire,
especially in liberal circles. Horace speaks of the graceful
dancing of Maecenas' wife. Ovid recommends every girl –
in fact everyone who is in love – to learn to dance (*A.A.*, iii,
349). The poet Statius (about Domitian's time) mentions
as creditable to his daughter the fact that her dancing did
not offend against decency (*Silv.*, iii, 5). In Augustus' principate, a Roman citizen gave instruction in dancing for the
first time in history. Lucian wrote an essay on dancing; he
says somewhere that in his day the dancing teacher was
one of the regular tutors in noble houses. The Stoic Seneca,
of course, laments this fact; he asserts that these exercises
softened the body and made it difficult for young people
to give their attention to serious studies. His warnings have
some justification. For, as we saw, the Romans were
ignorant of the real essence of dancing; so that wherever
dancing was practised all kinds of immorality accompanied
it. Moreover, the professional dancing-girls played on the
sensuality of the spectators. As we learn from all sources,
they were extremely skilful. Ovid (*Am.*, ii, 4, 29) says : –

> Graceful her arms, moving in subtle measures;
> insinuatingly she sways her waist.
> I can be touched by any novel beauty,
> but she'd excite the pure Hippolytus.

(Literally, 'Hippolytus would become a Priapus'. Hippolytus is the chaste stepson of the amorous Phaedra, and
Priapus the spirit of the generative powers.) That is a frank
enough admission of the erotic effects of such dances. The
graceful women who danced them are pictured in many
Pompeian frescoes.

The dancing-girls were generally foreigners, from Cadiz (Gades) or from Syria. The Spanish dancers were distinguished for an especially exciting and sensual type of dance. The severe Juvenal says (xi, 162): –

> Perhaps you will expect the itching dances
> of Gades, while a band croons, and the girls
> sink to the ground and quiver to applause . . .
> a stimulus for languid lovers, nettles
> to whip rich men to life . . .

Martial agrees with him: he lives simply, for (v, 78, 22)

> my table's small, I acknowledge,
> but no one tells or repeats lies,
> you keep the face that God gave you.
> There is no poetry reading,
> no girls from infamous Gades,
> to wriggle, endlessly itching,
> and shake and quiver expertly.

Elsewhere (xiv, 203) he says: –

> She trembles, quivers, sways her loins, and wriggles –
> She'd make Hippolytus forget himself.

(In the text the simple word *masturbator* is used.)

The Syrian dancing-girls appear in Horace's satires (i, 2, I). Suetonius ranks them with prostitutes (*Nero*, 27). Propertius (iv, 8, 39) also mentions them as hired to enliven a banquet: they danced lascivious dances to the sound of flutes, and accompanied themselves with castanets. The culmination of a revel was reached when one or more of these hired dancers entered. We see this clearly in Cicero's speech for Murena, which we have quoted above. Cicero proceeds in the same context: 'Dancing crowns and completes a long dinner with sumptuous entertainment and delightful surroundings.' It is clear that Propertius's mistress Cynthia delighted her lover in this way (Prop., ii, 3). A truly Roman attitude to dancing is that of the poet Horace. He loves to evoke (*Odes*, i, 4; iv, 7) the springtime dances of the naked Graces and the nymphs; but he complains bitterly that young girls find pleasure in learning Ionic dances. At the basis of these contradictions lie two opposing facts: it was improper for a respectable Roman woman to pay serious attention to dancing, but the Romans enjoyed watching the frequently lascivious performances of hired

dancers, and were not averse to incorporating beautiful
dancing women in their poetry, their sculpture, and their
painting. And it is not difficult to understand later accounts
of the progress of dancing, such as that given by Ammianus
Marcellinus (xiv, 6: *circa* A.D. 350): 'In these circumstances
even the few houses which had once distinguished themselves by their love for serious learning were now filled with
light and indolent pastimes, and resounded with song and
loud music. Instead of keeping a philosopher, a household
now kept a singer, and instead of an orator a master of
the revels. Libraries were like graves – shut for ever.
Instead, people installed water-organs, gigantic barrel-
organs as big as carts, flutes also, and all manner of stage
properties. This absurdity went so far that when (a little
time before) strangers were hurried out of the city because
of an alarm of possible food shortage, the lovers of arts
and sciences were relentlessly banished, while the attendants of actresses and those who pretended to be such, and
three thousand dancers with their musicians, and three
thousand dancing masters were allowed to remain undisturbed.' Ammian complains in this context that women
who were old enough to be the mothers of three children
preferred to remain single 'in order to turn and twist with
practised foot upon the dancing floor, in portrayal of the
countless different characters who appear in different
plays'.

This leads us to a kindred subject – the Mime and the
Pantomime, whose popularity grew and spread enormously
in later Rome. We must speak of these matters in some
detail, because they are part of any discussion of Roman
dancing.

Livy tells us that the old stage plays were introduced into
Rome in legendary times, shortly before the Gallic invasion, about 400 B.C. We must quote the whole passage.
'Since the power of the pestilence was diminished neither
by the plans of men nor by the help of the gods, the Romans
gave way to superstition and, it is said, instituted stage plays
as one of several measures to appease the wrath of heaven.
This was a new thing for the warlike Romans, who had had
no spectacle except the circus. Like all beginnings, the plays
were of little importance at first; and they were foreign.

Players brought from Etruria danced graceful figures in their native manner to the flute, but did not sing nor represent songs with action. Thereafter, the young Romans began to imitate them, and at the same time repeated jokes in rude verses, with appropriate gestures. The thing became popular and grew in importance by repetition. Since the Etrurian word for an actor is *hister*, the Roman players were called *histriones*. Whereas before they had interchanged rude verses like the Fescennines at random, and extempore, now they acted medleys, or satires full of different metres, accompanied by a piper, with appropriate gestures. After some years, Livius first ventured on a play with a plot instead of a series of satires. Like all of his time, he was the actor of his own compositions. He is said to have lost his voice by giving frequent encores and, after asking leave, to have set a boy to do the singing in front of the piper, while he himself acted the song – his gestures being all the more vivid because they were not hindered by his singing. Thenceforth, a singer was put on to supplement the actors, who were left only the dialogue. Under these conditions, the play ceased to be concerned with laughter and random jokes: it gradually became an art. Meanwhile the young men left the actors to perform regular plays. They themselves began, in the ancient manner, to exchange jests set in verse, Hence arose what were later called the *exodia*, or farces, and are chiefly attached to the Atellane plays. These performances were taken over from the Oscans, and the young men did not allow them to suffer at the hands of professional actors. Hence the custom, which still survives, that those who act in the Atellanes may not be removed from their tribe and may serve in the army as if unconnected with the stage. Here, where the origins of other things are described, it seems necessary to recount the first beginnings of the Roman drama, in order to show the sober origin of a madness which is now almost ruinous for rich and powerful kingdoms.'

The word Fescennine is nowadays usually derived from *fascinum*, one of the many names of the phallus. The Fescennine songs were sung by farmers and vintagers, while they carried a phallus (symbol of Nature's generative powers) in procession on a cart to celebrate the vintage or the harvest. When we use the word *fascinate,* do we ever think of its real meaning – enchantment by the sight of the phallus? Enchantment of this kind performed with evil intent, and accompanied by certain songs, was expressly forbidden by law. (In Germany such songs are still sung to unpopular neighbours – they are called cat-concerts or charivari.) It is important to notice that our quotation from Livy indicates an Etruscan origin for all these dance-plays: another of Rome's countless debts to Etruria.

These mimic shows (closely related to dancing, and more or less dependent on sensuality for their effect) can be divided into three types. These are (1) the Atellanes, (2) the mimes, (3) the pantomimes.

The Atellanes (*fabulae Atellanae*) were coarse farces of South Italian origin named after the Campanian town of Atella. They were introduced to Rome some time after the Hannibalic War. Their language was originally Oscan – a tongue well-known for its abundance of coarse words and dirty expressions – and was later the vulgar Latin of Rome. The farces themselves were always crude and coarse, especially in their presentation of erotic subjects. Their characters were certain set types from the life of society and the family – the stupid old Pappus (Pantaloon), the ever hungry Parasite, the amorous Lover, the Peasant whose wife is seduced in his absence, the severe Schoolmaster who enjoys his canings, the jesting Fool. Originally no more than improvisations by glib-tongued amateurs, the Atellanes were gradually transformed (about 100 B.C.) into the 'literary Atellane'. This new form was a farce with a connected plot, but it was no less coarse than its predecessor: authors like Pomponius and Novius are connected with it. It was performed after a tragedy (when it was called *exodium*), just as in Greece the tragic trilogy was followed by the satyric play, though that was a far more artistic thing than the Atellanes. Among its many themes and characters some were erotic – the Prostitute, the Pregnant Girl, the Pandar. It is important and interesting for us to notice that these farces referred to adultery, incest, and homosexuality; the fact illuminates the suggested 'moral purity' of the early Roman Republic. (See especially Ribbeck's *History of Roman Poetry*, i, 215.) Unfortunately, only fragments of the Atellanes are extant, so that we cannot be certain of the plot of any one play.

About Cicero's time, the mime began to compete with the Atellane farce, and at last supplanted it – especially under the Empire, when mime had changed to pantomime. What was the mime? As its name shows it came from Greece. Mimos means 'imitation', imitation of real life. The actors also were called *mimi*, whence comes the modern word *mime*. The mime itself was a faithful reproduction of coarse and ludicrous situations and characters; it was distinguished from its origin by 'crass realism and clumsy indecency' (Ribbeck). The mime came from the Greek South of Italy, and gradually penetrated Rome, where it was always performed at the Floralia after the year 238. None of the actors wore masks. The female parts were played by women who had to appear partly or entirely naked at the end of the performance – which shows clearly enough the tendency and emphasis of the mime. We have in Ovid (*Trist.*, ii, 497) some plain-spoken evidence on these farces. The usual theme was 'the sinful intrigues of wives': the adulterous wife, therefore, with her maid as confidante, her lover and her deceived husband were among the regular characters.

In both Atellanes and mimes great importance was given to the dance. This was not like any modern social dance; it was a series of movements of the arms and body by which the player accompanied his speech. In earlier times, it had sometimes been customary for a player in mask and costume to recite beautiful and effective passages as monologues, while a dancer with a musical accompaniment expressed the sense in gestures. In time this mute action supplanted the verbal monologue. The Pantomime had been created.

It was no advance in civilization when audiences came more and more to prefer the pantomime to the real play with spoken words. We have seen a change of a similar kind – the theatre is being abandoned for the cinema, The Roman pantomimes appealed (like the cinema) almost entirely to the imagination and the senses and hardly at all to the intellect. (Of course, high and serious subjects could be presented in pantomime. The 'tragic pantomime' was introduced by an actor named Pylades from Cilicia, and the 'comic pantomime' by Bathyllus from Alexandria; both lived in the time of Augustus.)

In the end, pantomime entirely supplanted tragedy. The fact is well-known, and is described in more or less detail by every historian of Roman manners; but it has seldom been regarded as an advance in culture. A modern author, it is true, frankly says that 'this type of art offered more than classical tragedy and comedy to the citizens of Rome, with their thousands of immigrants from the whole world' (Fr. Weege, *The Dance in Antiquity*, 1925). However true this is, it is a shocking proof of the necessary results of complete internationalization of the world – a process which was completed under the emperors. These results certainly cannot be an advance in culture; and it was not so in Rome, where the better elements introduced by immigration were mingled with masses of worthless human material. The reader may draw the natural comparison between ancient Rome and many a great modern metropolis.

Tacitus mentions the pantomimes among the 'evils of the city'. Juvenal (vi, 63) says many women almost died of desire when they saw the beautiful young dancer Bathyllus 'represent Leda in pantomime'. That was the sort of material which the pantomimists used – nearly all scenes from mythology with some erotic colour, like Bacchus and Ariadne, Medea, Semele, and so on. The pantomimic performances did not necessarily aim at producing purely erotic effects. The effect desired was rather the imitation and reproduction of every conceivable emotion by movements of the hands, the arms, the head, and the whole body; and it is clear that many artists managed to do this with amazing success. However, in the end the subjects of the pantomimic performances altered – as always – in accordance with the desires of the public. As we saw above, high officials and noble ladies did not in the least object to witnessing the mimic performance of amazingly erotic scenes: it is easy, therefore, to imagine the development of taste among the uneducated masses of Rome. Friedländer's well-known *History of Roman Morality*, to which readers may refer for further details, says with justice (ii, 111): 'Lubricious scenes were the real spice of these mimes and pantomimes: they often combined a certain seductive grace with a shameless sensuality which shrank from nothing.' The vindications of pantomime which authors like Libanius have left us cannot conceal the main fact – only a nation whose civilization was on the down grade could have taken such a universal pleasure in dances of this kind, however 'beautiful' their presentation. And, not to mention Christian writers, the pagan Zosimus (i, 6) decides that the introduction of pantomimes under Augustus was a symptom of decadence.

The pantomimes were performed by male dancers, who paid great attention to the care of their bodies and to the maintenance of their slim and beautiful figures. They were able, by changes of costume and mask, to represent the most widely different characters. As we have said, it is perfectly possible that these dancers produced great effect without appealing to eroticism; many truly noble and beautiful dances must have been performed. If eroticism of the grossest kind eventually supplanted the nobler uses of the art, we must not blame the art itself but the greedy eyes of the public.

The dancers generally belonged to the lower classes, and were freedmen, if not actually slaves. Still, some of them gained great fame, wealth, and popular influence. The tragic actor Apelles was one of Caligula's court; and rumour even said that the pantomime Mnester had a love affair with Caligula (Suet., *Cal.*, 36). The actor Paris played a big part in Nero's court. Originally a freedman of Nero's aunt Domita, he gradually gained the confidence of the Emperor. He joined Nero (according to Tacitus) in all sorts of shameful acts – perhaps he was only Nero's dancing-master – and was at last made an entirely free citizen by him (Tac., *Ann.*, xiii, 20, 22, 27). Domitian separated from his wife for a time, because she was in love with a handsome pantomimist also called Paris (Suet., *Dom.*, 3). Lastly, we hear of pantomimists at the courts of Trajan, Antoninus Pius, Caracalla, and others. Famous and skilful dancers of this kind inspired the same popular enthusiasm as film-stars today; and their supporters sometimes split into opposing parties which fought, and even shed blood, for their heroes. So strong was the passion for the art among the common people. The governors of Rome were subject to the same influences: sometimes, like Nero, they granted pantomimes the most complete freedom, and sometimes, like Domitian, forbade them to perform and even temporarily expelled them from Italy.

In this connection we must mention another dance introduced from Greece to Rome: the Pyrrhic dance, which had a strong resemblance to a large modern ballet. Erotic material was used in this dance also, so that it is relevant to our discussion. But instead of detailed descriptions we shall transcribe a vivid description of one of these ballets, from Apuleius (*Met.*, x, 29).

'Boys and girls in the bright blossom of their youth, paragons of beauty, brilliantly clad and walking eloquently, came out to dance the Pyrrhic dance of Greece. They formed into rows and wove graceful patterns – now curving their line into an even circle, now stretching into a continuous slanting line or gathering into a hollow square, or breaking into scattered companies. After they had met and parted and met again in mazes of intricacy, a trumpet call resolved their complications and made an end: the curtain rose, the side-panels folded back and the stage was disclosed.

'There was a lofty hill made of wood, like that famous mount of Ida which the bard Homer sang: it was planted with greenwood and living trees, and from its topmost peak ran riverwater from a fountain made by an artificer. A few goats grazed on the grass; the goat-master was portrayed by a youth like a Phrygian herdsman, in fine garments, his head girt with a golden turban and his shoulders draped by the loose native dress. There entered now a lovely boy, naked but for the short cloak on his left shoulder; his head shone bright with yellow hair, and on it were two jutting golden wings alike on either side. His serpent-wand showed that he was Mercury. He danced his way forward, bearing in his right hand an apple overlaid with gold leaf which he offered to Paris, signifying the will of Jupiter by nodding his head: and straightway he turned back with nimble step and left our sight. After him appeared a handsome girl, in presence like the goddess Juno, for a white diadem clasped her brow and she bore a sceptre.

Then a second rushed in – you would believe her to be Minerva, whose head was clad with a gleaming helm, the helm itself covered with a crown of olive; she raised a shield and brandished a spear, and she was all like the goddess in battle. After them paced in a third, excelling them both in visible beauty, and proclaimed as Venus by the sweetness of her ambrosial skin: she was Venus when Venus was still a maiden: she displayed her perfect beauty by the naked-ness of her body, except that a fine slip of silk veiled her lovely loins. Yet an inquisitive wind, enamoured, blew this veil wantonly away and revealed the flower of her youth, or breathed voluptuously upon it until it clung straitly to her and modelled her delicious limbs. The goddess bore two colours: white her body because she came from heaven, blue her garment because she rose from the sea.

'Each of these maidens, seeming goddesses, was followed by her own attendants. Juno was served by Castor and Pol-lux – their heads clad in rounded helmets with proud starry crests – but these, too, were boys acting the gods. She ad-vanced to the changing Ionian melodies of a pipe; with calm and undisturbed gesture and gracefully bowing her head, she promised the shepherd to grant him the kingship of all Asia if he would adjudge to her the prize of loveliness.

'The maiden in armed array who was Minerva had two allies, Panic and Fear, the armed comrades of the battle goddess, leaping high and brandishing naked swords. Behind her a piper played the warlike Dorian strain; mingling deep blares with shrill squeals, like the voice of a trumpet, he kindled the energy of her nimble leaps. Tossing her head, rolling her menacing eyes, making swift and contorted ges-tures, she showed Paris that if he granted her the victory in beauty he would be brave and famous for his trophies won in war through her assistance.

'But now, amid the homage of the theatre, Venus stood smiling sweetly in the centre of the stage, surrounded by the laughing children, her subjects: smooth milk-white babes, who seemed real Cupids flown that very moment from the heavens or from the sea: for they were marvellously like, in their little wings, their tiny arrows, all their aspect, and they bore bright glittering torches as if their lady was going to a marriage feast. After them a lovely troop of young maidens flowed in – the gracious Graces, and the beautiful Hours – a nimble band doing homage to their goddess, by casting loose flowers or garlands and honouring the mistress of pleasure with the blossoms of Spring. And the pierced pipes lapped her in soft Lydian airs. But while they gently soothed the spectators' hearts, Venus herself, lovelier than all music, moved gently forward: her pace was slow and lingering, her back swayed gently, her head was bowed a little: she answered the soft notes of the pipe by delicate gestures, and her eyes were now mild and almost closed, now they themselves made spirited gestures: she seemed now and then as if she danced with her eyes alone. As soon as she came before the sight of the judge, she seemed to promise, by the movement of her arms, that if she were preferred to the other goddesses she would give Paris a bride like herself and of astonishing beauty. Then the Phrygian youth gave her the golden apple, which he bore, as the pledge of her victory ... When the judgment of Paris was over, Juno and Minerva left the stage in gloom and anger, expressing their indignation at defeat by their movements and gestures. But Venus, in happy rejoicing, showed her delight by dancing with her whole choir. Then from the topmost peak of the mountain, through a hidden pipe, wine mingled with saffron shot high aloft, and like a perfumed rain fell in drops upon the goats feeding along the slopes, until they were altered to a better colour and changed their native grey for the yellow saffron. And now, when the whole theatre was sweetly perfumed, the earth gaped, and the wooden mountain disappeared.'

Chapter Five

Love in Roman Poetry

If it is true that the magic of love makes every man a poet, then poetry must be the truest and clearest reflection of a nation's love-life. Men choose the language of poetry to record both the noblest and the basest of sexual experiences. The sublimest utterances of passion – the sonnets of Michael Angelo and Shakespeare, Plato's mystical revelations of Eros – spring from the inmost souls of their creators no less than the coarse and sensual poems of the Priapeia. Our love and our sexual experience have their roots in the remotest depths of the hidden unconscious life of the soul, in darkness unexplored by the rational mind; and from these depths spring the most precious and delicate flowers as well as the vilest poison-weeds. As we know, the ruling principle of life, Schopenhauer's mysterious Will to Life, is nowhere revealed more truly and powerfully than in that sphere of life which we name love. So it is that poetry, the clearest mirror of love, is also the brightest revelation of the heart of a people.

Today, under the levelling influence of European civilization, it is often difficult to distinguish whether any particular poem is the work of a German, a Swede, or a Norwegian. But the most important ancient poetry is usually so strongly national (in the best sense of the word) that even without being a scholar one can easily tell whether any poem is Greek or Latin. For example, the comedies of Terence are written in Latin, but their spirit and their affinities are so thoroughly Greek that we cannot study Roman life in them. Yet the coarser comedies of Plautus, though their material

is also borrowed from Greek comedy, contain much more
of the true Roman spirit. But the springs of Roman poetry
are clearest when their source is the personal experience of
the poet – that is, in the work of Catullus, Tibullus, Propertius, Horace, and occasionally in Ovid. Even although
the formal element of such poetry is derived from Greek
models, the content of it is more truly Roman than that of
Terence's comedies. We are therefore restricted to certain
poems of certain authors for our evidence in this chapter.
Further restrictions are imposed by the scope of the book.
It would be impossible to give an exhaustive account of
Roman erotic poetry without writing an extensive work on
that subject alone. For the whole of Roman poetry is im-
pregnated with eroticism, from its first faltering essays to its
end in the work of Ausonius. It is almost enough to distort
the proportions of this book if we discuss a few of the leading poets with reference to sexual life; we shall purposely
omit the many poets whose works are preserved only in
scanty fragments known to scholars alone. Our purpose is
not to write an exact survey of all Roman poetry; it is to
see how the most important Roman poets treat the problem
of love, which we have already seen in other spheres of
Roman life.

We must first lay down one basic principle. The Romans
were farmers and soldiers; their nature was prosaic and
practical; and they had no natural inclination to create
poetry for themselves, as the Greeks had.

We have already mentioned a little book on *Roman Sexual Life* by the brilliant scholar, H. Paldamus. He says in it,
with much justice: 'Every nation must pay for despising
common humanity and natural feeling; and the Romans
paid more dearly than any other nation. After they had subjected all their morality, all their feelings, and all their
habits to the supreme power of the state, after the earlier
moral code had become compulsory and legalized – then,
when the constraint was at last removed, their passions
(under the influence of Greeks and Asiatics) broke out with
redoubled violence; and soon they reached a height which
has been unequalled since the Roman Empire passed away.'

Paldamus differs from us on one point especially. We do
not believe in this 'earlier moral code'. As we have often

said, the Roman is *by nature* a coarse sensualist; in a sense he is brutish and savage; nevertheless he is a sober and steady citizen, anxious to find the way to a reasonable and efficient communal life. Such a nation cannot produce poetry spontaneously, far less love-poetry: it will have no geniuses of the love-lyric, like Sappho, Ibycus, Anacreon, and Mimnermus. The Romans lack the spiritual equipment for the finer types of love. As Tacitus says, 'they marry without love and love without respect or refinement'. And their love-poetry has the qualities we should expect: it is either imitation and almost translation of Greek models, or it reaches its best in the frank expression of sensuality. Perhaps the most truly original Roman work dealing with love is the sensual novel of Petronius (which survives only in a mutilated form); and next to it come the poems in which the poets speak of their own experiences, as did Catullus, Tibullus, Propertius, Horace, and to some extent Ovid also. Paldamus points out that much important Roman erotic poetry – especially that written before the time of Catullus – has been irretrievably lost. That is true, but we must not forget that the soil of the old Republic was unfit to bear the tenderest flowers of love-poetry.

Many passages from Plautus' comedies show us what love was in the Republic of the second century B.C. They always paint the same picture – wild sensuality. A few quotations may be sufficient. We read in the *Pseudolus* (64):–

> The constant love we share and wear so near,
> our fun and games and talking lip to lip,
> the closely strained embrace of our amorous bodies,
> the gentle little bites on tender mouths,
> the wanton pressure of tiptilted breasts –
> ah, all these pleasures which you shared with me
> are broken, wasted, ruined now for ever.

Elsewhere in the same play (1255), a banquet is thus described:–

Why talk in riddles? This
makes glad to be alive,
this has all pleasures, this has all life's treasures,
this is heaven itself.
When a lover holds his sweetheart, when he presses lip to lip,
when they catch and clasp each other, tongue with tongue,
when breast and breast are closely pressed, when bodies
    interlace,

T—G

then the white-handed girl pours cups of nectar for her love.
There are no frowns or hateful faces,
unwelcome guests or idle talk –
perfumes and unguents, ribbons and fine garlands,
gaily given and generously.

As we have said, Plautus was more or less indebted to
Greek models for all his material. It was inevitable that he
should confuse Greek and Roman elements in his represen-
tation of manners and customs. In the *Cistellaria* (22) we
may find a suitable example of this. The bawd is bewailing
the lot of prostitutes as compared with that of married
women:–

> Right it is and proper
> that women in our walk of life
> should be good friends and allies.
Look at the blue-blooded ladies, wives in lofty families,
see how close they keep their friendship, how they back each
> other up.
If we copy them and do the same, we have a hard life still.
They detest us! and they wish we needed all their help:
> never to stand on our own feet,
> always to need *their* backing,
> humble suppliants.
Go to them! you'll soon prefer to leave them, for they flatter us
openly at least; in private, if they get the chance,
> they pour cold water on us,
> say we catch their husbands,
> rival themselves in love.
> They keep us down – we're freedwomen!

We have seen that it was impossible for the daughter of
a patrician family to become a harlot without being stigmatized as dishonourable (*infamis*). It was different for the
daughters of freedmen. The Roman matrons particularly
hated these girls, suspecting (not without justification) that
they were temptations to married men. Accordingly, the
bawd says (*Cistellaria,* 78):–

> It may be profitable for a lady
> to love one man and spend her life with him.
> A prostitute is like a prosperous city –
> she can't get on without a lot of men.

A man's adventures were limited by the convention which
Plautus elsewhere describes (*Curculio,* 35):–

> No Stop sign here, no Notice To Trespassers.
> If you've the cash, buy anything on sale.

> The highway's free to all – walk where you like,
> but don't make tracks through any walled preserve.
> Don't touch a wife, a widow, or a virgin,
> a youth, or a freeborn child – take all the rest!

Perhaps even these few quotations from Plautus are not altogether appropriate; for our purpose is, after all, to show the nature of Roman love-life, and not merely the treatment of erotic subjects in the Latin language. We shall therefore follow the example of Paldamus, and discuss Plautus no further. Anything said of Plautus is equally true of Terence, whose work was more refined but still more Greek in spirit. And with that let us leave the early dramatists.

Among the poets whose work survives, the first to treat of love is Lucretius. His work is a didactic poem which attempts to expound the doctrines of his master Epicurus. He refers incidentally to love – not of course in personal reminiscence like Catullus, but theoretically, like Schopenhauer in his chapters on sexual life. But all Lucretius' work is in the language of poetry, so that we may quote some of it in this chapter. His epic begins with a glorification of Venus, however inappropriate that may be in the mouth of an atheist. These are his words (i, i):–

> Mother of Rome, delight of gods and men,
> kind lady Venus, thou who dost inhabit
> the sailing oceans and the fruitful earth
> and all that is beneath the gliding stars –
> since through thy power each race of living creatures
> begets itself and enters the light of the sun –
> thy coming calms the wind; the clouds of heaven
> vanish before thee; and the manifold earth
> puts forth sweet flowers, the level ocean smiles,
> and heaven shines with a broad peaceful light.
> When the first springtide lightens in the day
> and western winds unlock the gates of birth,
> then first the birds of the air acknowledge thee
> and thy dominion over their desires.
> Then herds of wild things gallop the happy fields,
> swim rushing rivers; captured and enchanted
> by sweet desire, they follow thee, their queen.
> Throughout the seas, the hills, the sweeping rivers,
> the leafy homes of birds, and the green plains,
> thou dost inspire all things with kindly love,
> and eagerly they multiply their race.

Despite this glorious invocation of the supreme godhead of

Venus, the poet later warns humanity (and especially men)
of the results of love. This he does almost like a disappointed amorist and hedonist; his warnings are sometimes closely
akin to the words of that trained voluptuary Ovid. Lucretius
says in Book iv (1052):–

> So then the lover, wounded by Venus' darts
> (be it a boy with womanish limbs who sends them
> or be they sped from a woman's radiant limbs),
> pursues what wounds him, eager to unite
> with it and cast his seed within its body;
> for his desire dumbly foretells the pleasure.
> This pleasure, then, is Venus; love is named
> Cupido, the Desire, from that Desire;
> whence flows the first delicious drop of love
> into men's hearts, and cold care afterwards.
> For when the lover loses his beloved,
> her image still remains, her name still sounds
> sweet in his ears. Avoid these images
> and shun the food of love! distract your mind!
> cast your collected seed in any body
> and do not harbour it by loving one
> and one alone – that brings unfailing sorrow.
> The ulcer lives, and feeds, and grows malignant,
> the anguish rises to a flood of madness,
> unless you strike elsewhere, to erase the wound
> and cure it while yet fresh, roaming abroad
> after a commoner Venus, or transfer
> elsewhere the motions and desires of your heart.
> But Venus is not barren to the loveless –
> rather she bears them blessings without pain.
> Pleasure is purer for the healthy man
> than for the lovesick – all a lover's ardours
> wander and waver even in possession,
> he cannot tell what pleasure first to enjoy . . .
> From lovely faces and fair coloured flesh
> nothing comes which the body may enjoy,
> but flimsy little images, hopeless hopes
> which the wind often seizes and carries away.
> As thirsty men, trying to drink in their sleep,
> can find no water to quench their burning limbs,
> but struggle for imaginary water
> in vain, and thirst among torrential streams,
> so Venus dupes lovers with images:
> they cannot satisfy themselves with gazing
> nor rub some satisfaction from these limbs
> though they caress and handle the whole body . . .
> Moreover strength is lost, the labour wastes them,
> moreover all their life is enslaved to another.
> Their wealth becomes carpets from Babylon,

> duty falls ill and reputation totters.
> But soft luxurious shoes laugh on her feet;
> enormous emeralds, glittering green,
> are set in gold; raiment of ocean-purple
> is worn constantly, drenched with Venus' sweat.
> A father leaves estates honestly earned,
> and they become turbans and tires and coifs,
> sweeping silks, and Oriental robes.
> Feasts are prepared, costly, luxurious,
> gaming and wine, perfumes and crowns and garlands –
> but all in vain. From the wellspring of joy
> rises a bitterness among the flowers –
> because the heart sees truth and gnaws itself
> for living slothfully in dens of vice;
> because a lady casts a doubtful word
> which hits and festers in the burning soul;
> or else because her glances are too free
> and stolen smiles linger upon her face.
>   These are the evils of a prosperous love.
> In adverse love they come in multitudes
> past counting, to be caught even with closed eyes.
> Better to watch beforehand, as I teach,
> beware, and be not drawn into the trap.
> For to avoid the gins and nets of Venus
> is not so hard as breaking them when caught,
> and struggling free from closely knotted meshes.

The poet now gives advice (just as Ovid does) how to escape the mischief by looking for 'defects of mind and body' in the beloved, which may break the lover's illusion. Finally he says:–

> But let her be as lovely as a dream,
> let Venus' majesty reign in her – yet,
> yet there are others! we once lived without her!
> we know she lives the same as the ugly women!

Still he concedes that

> the woman does not always feign her passion
> when she embraces the man's body with hers,
> sucking his lips to hers, drinking his kisses;
> she often loves truly and seeks to share
> the mutual joys which are the aim of love.

But it is significant for our view of Lucretius as a poet and a Roman that this 'aim of love' is the purely physical act of copulation, the aim which even the beasts strive to attain.

The poet proceeds to give a detailed account of the conception of a male or female child; and closes this section of the work with a truly Roman warning:–

> Sometimes without the heavenly arrows of Venus
> a woman of less beauty may be loved.
> A wife sometimes by her own acts and ways,
> by kindly manners and neat-fashioned dress,
> makes it an easy thing to live with her.

In ancient Rome, most marriages were prosaic and respectable unions of this nature, and most wives were strict and 'neat-fashioned' matrons.

We turn now to Catullus. If Catullus had always followed that homely middle-class morality he would have lived a less unhappy life. But we should then have known hardly anything of his life and love. As Hölderlin says, 'the heart's wave never breaks into such beautiful foam of spirit as when the dumb old rock of destiny opposes it.'

Catullus is the first Roman love-poet. He was the first Roman to give artistic (and truly national) expression to the experience of his inmost heart. He is more sympathetic to modern minds than all his famous successors; for he is a man, not a rhetorician, and he tells us frankly and beautifully of his passion. Gellius (*Noctes Atticae,* xix, 9) informs us that Catullus and his friend Calvus were the only early Roman poets whom the Greeks of Gellius' day thought fit to be placed beside Anacreon. All their contemporaries (nowadays scarcely known even by name) were men with neither charm nor profundity: their work was rough, hard, and inharmonious: it lacked the Greek magic. But whenever we think of Catullus's spiritual and artistic kinship with the Greeks, we shall pay less attention to his translations from Hellenistic poets like Callimachus and look rather to some of his exquisite lyrics. For these he may well have had Greek models, but we do not know what they were.

The famous love-scene between Septimius and Acme should be quoted (45):−

> Septimius held his Acme close,
> close to his heart, saying 'My dearest,
> unless I love you desperately,
> constantly, always, for ever, more than
> the fondest lover in the world,
> may I be dropped in the African desert
> to face a green-eyed lioness!'

> Love had been slow before, but now
> sneezed on the right to show his favour.
>   Now Acme turned her head softly,
>   kissing her lover's drunken eyes,
>   with crimson lips kissing them,
>   saying 'My darling Septimillus,
>   now let us worship Love for ever,
>   the God who has kindled a stronger and keener
>   love-flame within my gentle heart.'
> Love had been slow before, but now
> sneezed on the right to show his favour.
>   And now their God is favourable,
>   now they are both in love and beloved.
>   Septimius holds his Acme dearer
>   than all the wealth of the furthest Indies.
>   Acme loves Septimius
>   faithfully, gaily, deliciously.
>   Who ever saw a happier pair?
>   where is a kindlier God of love?

There is another love lyric almost equally charming (48):–

> Juventius, if I might kiss
> your honeysweet lips as I liked,
> I'd kiss them both five hundred
> thousands of kisses, have never enough,
> not even if our kisses grew
> thicker than barley in Africa.

These two examples show that Catullus was naturally bisexual, although, as we shall see, the heterosexual side of his nature predominated. In this discussion we are primarily interested in Catullus as the most vivid, true, and simple of Roman love-poets, rather than as the most original of Roman creative artists.

The art of Catullus is far purer, more spontaneous, and truer than that of any poet who followed him – or, as far as we know, of any who preceded him. It is true that modern taste sometimes finds his work very coarse and indecent. Nevertheless his very coarseness is naïve – unlike Ovid's lewd and sophisticated indecency. He was one of the great poets of the world, this ardent, unhappy lover, who did not dissolve into water sentimentally, but fought like a man against his hard but gracious fate.

The story which lies behind his most famous and beautiful poems is soon told. He was born in Verona in 87 B.C., and came to Rome while still a young man. There he met

and lived with other young men like himself, gay and energetic, easy and dissolute, but always devoted to poetry and
to the study of the best Greek models. That was the time
when Catiline and his party made their attempt at revolution; but Catullus and his friends remained aloof from politics. They must have lived a life like that of the young
Goethe in Strasbourg; and Catullus has often been compared to the young Goethe. We know he was capable of
depths of true friendship; and his only brother, who died in
early life, was truly loved and passionately lamented. His
circumstances must have been comfortable enough, despite
his occasional complaints. We hear of a house in Rome
with a large library, and of a country house on the borders
of the Tiburtine and Sabine country.

When Catullus was about twenty-six, he met the woman
who was to be his fate. He calls her Lesbia. Today, it is
generally accepted that the name is a screen for the famous
Clodia – sister of Cicero's enemy, P. Clodius Pulcher, and
wife of the distinguished but unimportant Q. Caecilius
Metellus Celer. Clodia, like many other figures in Roman
history, is known to us only through her enemies. Cicero*
gives her the scornful name of Quadrantaria, 'the twopenny
woman'. He also hints that she was guilty of incest with
her brother. In Catullus she appears as morose, fickle, capricious, and the lover of several men at once – and yet beautiful, bewitching, cultured, and capable of ardent love. How
else could such a woman become the destiny of such a vivid
soul as his? For Lesbia was his destiny. We can trace the
development of their love in Catullus's poetry, as if it were
an absorbing novel.

Perhaps the poet met her in the house of his friend Allius.
At least, a late elegy (68) praises the hospitable house of his
friend, where Catullus had snatched so many precious hours
with his mistress:–

> Dear Muses, let me tell the kindly friendship
>   of Allius, who helped me mightily –
> that the forgetful years, with growing darkness,
>   may not obscure the brightness of his deed ...
> You know the anguishes which cunning Venus
>   laid on me, how she broke into my life,

* Caelius so named her (*Quint.*, viii, 6, 53); Cicero refers to the name in
Pro Caelio, 26. – *Translators' Note.*

and how I burned like the Sicilian Etna,
    like the hot springs which name Thermopylae,
when my sad eyes dissolved away in weeping
    and gloomy rains were pining on my cheek.

But, like the water springing on a mountain
    beneath a mossy stone high on the peak
and rolling headlong down a rocky valley
    to meet the road and the crowding feet of men,
and cheer the traveller, fordone and sweating
    while the earth cracks in parching August sun –
or like the gentler breeze that comes to sailors
    after their ship has staggered in black gales,
after the gods of sea have heard their prayers –
    such was the help that Allius offered me.
Through walled preserves he made me a broad highway,
    he gave me both my lady and my home,
where we might love at last, and share our passion:
    there came my goddess, treading daintily,
and hesitating on the polished threshold,
    poising her white foot there, gleaming and still.

Still, Catullus was in love with a married woman, older than himself. He knew his fate from the beginning, but disregarded it in the blindness of passion. He says in the same poem (68):–

She will not be content with her one lover –
    still, I must bear my lady's little sins
(they are not many) rather than be tactless.
    Juno herself, the mighty queen of the sky,
beat down her blazing wrath when Jove deceived her
    although she could convict the Omnivolent . . .

She was not brought to me as bride to bridegroom,
    to a festal house perfumed with spikenard.
On one miraculous night she gave me favours
    silently filched from her husband's jealous arms.
It is enough if she will give Catullus
    the happy days she marks with a white stone.

It was then, at the beginning of his love, that he wrote the most famous of all his poems (5):–

My Lesbia, let us live and love!
Give not the half of a brass farthing
for scandal talked by grim old men.
Suns disappear and again return –
when our brief light burns down and dies
darkness remains and an endless sleep.
So kiss me now a thousand times,

> kiss me a hundred, a thousand more,
> again a hundred and a thousand.
> Then when we come to thousands of thousands,
> lose the account, forget the sum.
> Envious people could injure us
> if they but knew of our million kisses.

But soon his tone changes (70):–

> My woman says she'll never be the lover
> of any man, or even Jove himself.
> She says so. What a woman says to an eager lover,
> write in the water, write in the rushing waves.

The poet has learnt that unhappy love divides a heart
against itself. He writes (72):–

> You said you loved no other than Catullus,
> Lesbia, no one, even Jove himself.
> I loved you, Lesbia, not as a mistress only,
> I loved you as a father loves his sons.
> I know you now. My passion blazes hotter,
> and yet I hold you cheap and worthless now.
> *How can that be?* you ask. An injured lover
> loves more and more, but all affection's gone.

Or, in even clearer words (87, 75):–

> No living woman ever was loved
> as much as Lesbia was loved by me.
> Never a treaty, signed and sealed, was truer
> than was the faithful love I offered you.
> Now, Lesbia, your faults have brought my spirit
> to lose itself in its devotion deep.
> It cannot wish you well, were you an angel:
> it cannot leave you if you go to hell.

Yet, after this bitter disillusionment, Catullus seems to
have been reconciled to his mistress once more. He was
drowning in passion and grief – he clutched at every straw –
he was overwhelmed with delight when the sensual, heartless Lesbia turned to him again. In his brief ecstasy he wrote
songs like this (107):–

> Fulfilment after sore and hopeless longing –
> that is the heart's own dearest happiness.
> And this is happiness dearer than golden treasure,
> when Lesbia returns to my desire,
> returns unasked to my sore hopeless longing,
> on this bright day marked with a whiter stone.
> What happier man's alive? And how can heaven
> answer our prayers more graciously than this?

The perfidious woman promised him whatever he asked; and, as lovers do, he believed her (109):–

> My dearest, now you promise that our passion
> shall be for ever true, for ever gay.
> O God! grant that it may be truly promised
> and honourably said with her whole heart –
> that we may keep, enduring all our lifetime,
> the holy covenant of eternal love.

His next complaint is bitterer still, after another disillusionment (58):–

> O friend! My Lesbia, Lesbia,
> Lesbia, loved by Catullus
> more than himself and his dearest,
> stands in the streets and the alleys,
> and fingers the proud Roman rabble.

At last, in an effort to recover, he addresses his own weak soul, as if endeavouring to inspire it with a courage and resolution which it did not possess (8):–

> My poor Catullus, leave your folly!
> Count what is lost as lost, and abandon it.
> Yet once the sunshine lit your life:
> once, when you followed a willing mistress,
> and loved her as you'll love no other.
> Once there was laughter, once there was gaiety,
> once you shared love equally.
> Yes, once the sunshine lit your life.
> Now she refuses you. Harden your heart,
> make no pursuit; but cure yourself,
> bear it, be strong with a resolute will.
> Woman, farewell! Now I am strong,
> asking for nothing against your will.
> Yet you will grieve when left alone.
> Perjurer, think what a life awaits you!
> Who will admire you, who will court you?
> whom will you choose to be your next?
> whom will you kiss, and whose lips will you bite?
> Catullus! Take your stand, be resolute!

But to be resolute meant incessant effort; and the pain of that effort has never been so well expressed as in this couplet (85):–

> I hate and love. You ask how that can be?
> I know not, but I feel the agony.

One of Catullus's last poems (11) seems to show that, after dreadful struggles with his sweet and cruel passion, he

had conquered at last: he has brought himself to use these
hard words of Lesbia:—

> Go, friends, and take to my mistress
>   this evil greeting.
> Let her live in peace and adultery
> and lie in the arms of thousands
> and love never one, but succeed in
>   breaking their muscles.
> Let her look to my love no longer:
> it fell by her fault, as a flower
> falls on the edge of the meadow,
>   touched by the ploughshare.

But we may doubt whether Catullus's love died when it
fell. Perhaps his last thoughts of it are in the elegy (76)
whose closing words we quote:—

> O God, if you can help, if you can pity
> the helpless in the article of death,
> look on me now! reward a life of virtue!
> deliver me from this disease, my doom,
> the lethargy which now invades my body
> banishing happiness from my whole heart.
> I do not ask that she return my passion,
> nor that she should be chaste. She cannot. No,
> I pray for health and freedom from this sickness,
> grant me it, God! Reward my piety!

As we know, the poet died young. Did his unhappy love
break his heart, and kill him? Probably not. There are
many of his poems which tell of sexual experiences with
women of a lower rank that Clodia: although these affairs
may not have coincided with his love for her. He describes
them in powerful language, which must nowadays seem
coarse, but has never the same effect of calculated indecency
which characterizes Ovid's poetry. Catullus may seem to
have been naturally inclined towards women; but it is notable that he wrote tender verses to a beautiful boy. This
was 'Juventius', who is otherwise unknown, and whose very
name may be a pseudonym. Catullus's love for Juventius
may be explained as a natural preliminary to his love for
women. But modern psycho-analytical theory might lead
us to say that his disappointment in his love for Lesbia im-
pelled him to release the latent homosexual tendencies of
his nature. Both solutions are possible. We can at least be
sure that the affair was not a purely aesthetic and spiritual

one – that is proved by the sensuality of a little occasional poem (56). It is the form of a letter to Cato, telling how Catullus had caught a young rival with his mistress and punished him by turning the tables on him. Only a man of bisexual character could in this way transfer his sexual activity from a woman to a boy.

We cannot here discuss the singularly coarse poems in which Catullus attacks his personal enemies. And we can do no more than allude to the qualities of Catullus which do not appear in his erotic poetry. It is not for us to describe his sensitive nature-poetry, or his tasteful translations from the Greek.

We shall close this account of Catullus, by quoting a marriage poem of his: it is sane and beautiful, natural in the highest degree, and free from hypocrisy or sensuality. These are the last verses of the marriage song, which is conceived as a dialogue between choruses of boys and girls (62):–

Girls: A flower that grows in a secret garden,
        hidden from beasts, unbruised by the plough,
        reared by the rain, the sun, the breeze –
        many the boys and girls who desire it.
        If the flower is nipped and sheds its blossom,
        never a boy nor girl who desires it.
        So then a maiden, untouched and dear,
        when once she loses the flower of her body,
        no boys can enjoy her, no girls can love her.
Boys: A vine that grows in a desert country
        never rises nor bears a cluster:
        its body curves beneath its weight
        till its highest tendrils touch its root.
        Never a farmer or team will till it.
        But marry the vine to a sturdy elm,
        many the farmers and teams who will till it.
        So then a maiden, untouched and alone,
        when once she ripens and meets a mate,
        parents will prize her and husband love her.
        Maiden, do not fight with your husband:
        it is wrong to fight when your father gave you,
        your father and mother deserve obedience.
        Your parents share in your maidenhood,
        your mother one part, your father another,
        and you the last – do not fight with the others,
        they gave both dowry and rights to your husband.
        Hymen, come to us, holy Hymen!

It would seem clear that the character of Vergil was at least bisexual, if not completely homosexual. Such a character, however, did not hinder him from describing woman's love and woman's soul with the touch of a master. Paldamus calls the fourth book of the Aeneid (dealing with the unhappy love of Dido and Aeneas) the *Werther* of Latin literature. The comparison is not perfect, for the poem, unlike the novel, is not an idealized version of the author's own experiences; at least we know of nothing similar in Vergil's life. However that may be, it remains true that Vergil's greatness cannot be recognized from the scanty fragments of his work which we read in school. He is the greatest and most comprehensive poet of the Latin tongue.

The Aeneid is much more than an interesting but lengthy epic. It is a world-picture, of a dignity and scope equalled in only one novel of modern times. It is easy to understand why even modern Italy reverences Vergil among her greatest. However, we must here content ourselves with discussing his love-poetry.

Poets before him may have written of the love of Dido and Aeneas, for the story is an old one. Nevertheless, only one treatment of the story has survived – and that is Vergil's own. This cannot be accidental. The material is unimportant: the important thing is a master's treatment of it. Our special interest must be in the purely human and permanently significant elements in the tragedy, rather than in technical questions.

The fourth book begins thus:–

> The queen was wounded sorely: the deep passion
> fed on her lifeblood, burnt her with secret fire.
> She brooded on the hero's chivalry
> and noble birth; his face and words remained
> deep in her heart, and passion wrung her limbs.

In hesitating words, Dido discloses her passion to her sister Anna (who plays confidante, a character common in the tragedies of Euripides). She would willingly marry the stranger who has won her interest and her love by the stirring tale of his adventures and his destiny. But she cannot think of marriage after the death of the first husband whom she had so loved. Her sister endeavours to break down her scruples (32):–

> How can you wither in eternal youth
> alone, with neither love nor children dear?

The queen, she says, should think of her duty to the master-
less kingdom. The gods have sent Aeneas to make it famous
and powerful (54):–

> These words stirred glowing love into a blaze,
> strengthened her doubting heart, loosened her shame.

Dido's friendship with her guest grows closer. They visit
the temple together, join in offering sacrifices and in visiting
the treasures of the palace. Then Dido sinks back again into
her loneliness – what does she care for treasures and temples? (66):–

> The gentle flame eats at her very bones
> meanwhile: the silent wound lives in her breast.

She tries to confess her love to Aeneas, but modesty is too
much for her, and she breaks off. They meet constantly in
the evenings, and she hangs on his words with passionate
interest (80):–

> Then, when they parted, and the darkling moon
> concealed her light, and sinking stars brought sleep,
> she lingered in the empty palace, lying
> on the abandoned couch: she saw him still.
> Sometimes she kept his son (loving his image)
> and fondled him to deceive her guilty love.

Meanwhile, she forgets the duties of her rank, and cares
only for Aeneas. At last, on a hunting expedition, they are
overtaken by a storm and driven into a cave. There they
make their alliance (169):–

> That day was the first cause of death and anguish.
> Now Dido, careless of her name and fame,
> no longer purposes a secret love,
> but calls it marriage, and so shields her sin.

(Consider how Ovid would have treated this love-scene,
and how much he would have made of the opportunity for
sensual narrative and description: it is easy then to understand why Vergil was called 'maidenly'.)

Rumours now spread through the city (191):–

> Aeneas, Trojan-born, was come to Carthage
> and lovely Dido deigned to marry him;
> this winter-long they cherished each the other,
> rapt by their shameful lust, the realm forgotten.

But soon Aeneas breaks the bonds of love which have held him from his duty. Without the queen's knowledge he gives the order to make all preparations for departure. At first, he does not care to tell her of his decision (296):–

> But now the queen (who can deceive a lover?)
> foresaw deceit, and felt the coming change:
> she feared safety itself.

She rages through the city like a Bacchante, and at last returns to Aeneas. But her wrath is only increased by his protestations that his course is commanded by the destiny of his high mission (365):–

> 'Perjurer! You were born of the bristling rocks
> of Caucasus! tigresses gave you suck!
> Why hide my thoughts, or wait for greater wrongs?
> Did he groan while I wept, or drop his eyes?
> did he surrender to tears, pity his lover?
> Ah, what to say first? Surely mighty Juno
> and the father of heaven must look on this with anger!
> Nowhere honour and truth! I took him in
> a starving castaway, and made him king,
> redeemed his fleet from loss, his friends from death!

At last she breaks off her denunciations and rushes away: she is picked up in a swoon by her maids. Aeneas, shaken by grief, still continues his preparations. Even a visit from the faithful Anna fails to soften his heart (440):–

> His fate debars him, and God stops his ears.
> As when the Alpine gales endeavour to fell,
> with circling blasts, an oak of sturdy strength –
> the branches cry, the leafage strews the ground –
> still with its shaken trunk it stands unmoved,
> stretching its crest to heaven, its roots towards hell.
> So then the hero, buffeted with words,
> shakes, and his heart feels all the bitterness.
> Unmoved remains his will. Tears flow in vain.

Dido is terrified by omens and visions. She decides to die (465):–

> So in her madness
> she dreamt Aeneas led her on and always
> left her behind; she saw herself deserted,
> on lonely roads, seeking her friends in a waste land.

By some pretext, she orders a funeral pyre, which she decorates like a grave (506)

> with garlands and dark death leaves,
> then lays his garments and his word thereon
> and his own image – well she knows the future.

Once more in the lonely night she reflects despairingly on
the empty future, and at last makes her final decision to die.
Meanwhile Aeneas has been warned once more by Mercury
in a dream to speed his departure. He weighs anchor. At
dawn, Dido sees the fleet on the high seas. Furious, she
thinks first of revenge. Shall she send in pursuit? capture
the ship? kill his comrades and Ascanius, and (602)

> furnish the father's banquet with the son?

But she sees that it is too late (597):–

> The time was when you gave your sceptre!

She calls on Juno, Hecate, and the Furies to avenge her.
She invokes all curses on her faithless lover, prays for eternal enmity between her people and his successors, and
wishes that an avenger may rise from her bones. Then she
mounts the pyre and stabs herself with the sword of
Aeneas.

Meanwhile Aeneas sees from his distant ship the flames
of the burning pyre, and continues his journey 'with gloomy
forebodings'. Later, in the underworld, he meets the shade
of Dido. She turns away, unappeased even in death.

It is not within our province to follow his destiny to its
end. Our intention has only been to show Vergil's profound
and sensitive knowledge of women.

Bachofen gives an interpretation of the Aeneas-legend
which is extremely interesting, though it cannot be accepted
without qualification (*Primitive Religion and Ancient Symbols*). He considers that the epic is the highest poetic expression of 'the spiritual conquest of the Orient' which led to a
new epoch in the world's history. 'The Carthaginian episode
is decisive. It is the parting of the ways. The Tyrian woman
appears as an oriental queen, eager to subject man to her
sensual arts. She claims the mastery over Aeneas which
was claimed by Omphale over Heracles, Semiramis over
Ninus, Delilah over Samson – the old right over man's life
and supremacy which the Asiatic prostitute appropriated
for herself. Dido reproaches her runaway lover with perfidy – but her reproach is based on the traditional Asiatic

T—H

right. She can conceive of no other. But Aeneas represents
the new attitude, the advance in civilization which Rome
was to introduce. The roots of his past are in Asiatic culture, and (despite his resemblance to Heracles) in the same
religious beliefs which are the basis of Dido's claim. But his
face is towards his new home, and to the age which it is his
mission to establish. He will not falter for any tender memory, for any thought of his Asiatic origin ... In Italy, the
sensuality of Asia has no place; for Italy has been chosen
to bring forth a new age ... When the Trojan heroes arrive
at the mouth of the Tiber, Asia is doomed: Aeneas (who
appears again as a parallel to Heracles) is never again to
see his Assyrian ancestors and the wanton queen Dido, save
in the underworld at Cumae. They are nothing but idle
shadows, these figures from the Asiatic past. They can find
no new life for themselves and their extinct world in the
new land of Latium ... If you read the Aeneid for the sake
of the thought it contains, you will find the same conception throughout. The poem emphasizes both sides with the
same determination – both the bases of civilization: man's
attachment to his origins, and his development out of those
origins. The usual reading of the poem is very one-sided. It
is wrong to look at only one side of the picture – Asia's
kinship with the West. No less important is the emancipation of the Roman world from the bonds of Eastern tradition. The real moral of the epic is the lofty destiny which
brought the dying East to new life in the West. Rome was
founded in Asia; and at last Rome conquered Asia.'

Bachofen replies to his critics with these weighty words:
'We men of the nineteenth century generally find it enough
to know what to eat and drink and wear and enjoy. We are
hardly able to appreciate the strength which a nation derives
from lofty ideals, nor can we assess the significance which
such traditions as the Aeneas-legend must have for the
development of a nation. We imagine that these traditions
are the foolish inventions of authors, or fairy stories sophisticated in verse, or mythical renderings of historical events,
or problems for literary discussion. But they were part of
the life of antiquity. Like the legends of William Tell and
King Arthur, they had a deep and lasting influence on
national sentiment and national history. Vergil's poem is the

favourite book of the Roman nation, because the Romans see in it their own destiny and their own ideals.'

We turn to Horace. At the suggestion of his patron Augustus, he too joined in the Augustan reconstruction of Rome, by writing his famous odes (iii, 1–6). But his nature was radically different from that of his friend Vergil. We find him much less real and convincing in these moral homilies to his contemporaries than in his expressions of scepticism, hedonism, and the aesthetics of life and conduct. It is natural that the youth of today and of past ages should care little for this enlightened and cool-headed bachelor, who saw the limitations of life and accepted it in wise moderation. Unlike the violently youthful Catullus, he was never really young, and never enjoyed young love. We know his opinion of love – why plague yourself with love and its anguish when you can enjoy any pretty young slave or maid or prostitute? No man could speak in this way of love, if it were for him the exalted passion which has the power to make us immeasurably happy or immeasurably sad. And it is certainly true that all Horace's little love-poems, to Lalage, Chloe, Lydia, or Pyrrha, strike us as artificial and insubstantial, despite the severe grace of their language and structure. I have elsewhere tried to show that there is much more semblance of truth in the poet's account of his love for beautiful boys and youths. I should even venture to assert that the very reality of his liking for boys prevented him from deeply loving any woman. Horace was certainly bisexual, with a strong tendency towards homosexuality. That is why all the women he portrays or addresses seem to be so lifeless. No one ever doubted the reality of Catullus's Lesbia: every reader doubts the reality of Horace's Lalage, Chloe, and the others. It does not follow that Horace never had sexual relations with a woman; but love of that kind was never a passion for him. He could say 'I possess them, but they do not possess me'.

But the women who from time to time occupied his attention were certainly no more than slaves or harlots. His satires seem to be based on real experiences; and in them their graceful, fleeting, unreluctant figures constantly appear. On the journey to Brundisium he spends part of one

night waiting for a 'lying girl', falls asleep, and is deluded by
an erotic dream (*Sat.*, i, 5, 82). The well-known erotic satire
(12) gives what seem to us to be cynically exact instructions
for attaining brief sexual pleasure without danger to honour
or disturbance of comfort. Horace says (i, 2, 78):—

> Cease hunting married game: trouble and grief
> more often come to you than real enjoyment.

A prostitute is always available, and she is generally quite
as pretty, if not even prettier.

> Lying close to me, willing side to side,
> she is a princess, flaunts an ancient name.
> I need not fear a husband interrupting
> me in my pleasure, shouting, smashing locks,
> and the house a pandemonium, dogs barking,
> slams, cries, the woman jumping from bed,
> the confidante weeping with terror, afraid
> for her back, the wife for her dowry, me for myself.

These are not the words of a poet who honours or even
respects womanhood. In the same way, Horace speaks little
of really unhappy love for women. On the contrary, he
sometimes boasts of his own fickleness. We are again driven
to feel that this man, who never knew a deep, true, passionate love for women, had actually no need of women. A
woman was for him (as was the young male slave he loved)
no more than an object of momentary sensual enjoyment.

It is possible that the poet had bitter experience of
women's infidelity in his youth. The 15th epode points to
this. One of his low-born mistresses had sworn fidelity to
him, when

> night had come – the moon lit the calm skies
> among the lesser stars.

But she soon gave herself to more favoured suitors, who
were obviously richer. Horace prophesied that they would
suffer his own fate; then, he says, he will laugh in his turn.
And later he always laughed over his own misfortunes in
love. He says to young Lalage that she is only an unripe
grape, a heifer who will soon pursue her husband with bold
brow (*Odes*, ii, 5). He asks the fickle Pyrrha what slender,
perfumed youth is now her lover, for whom she binds her
yellow hair ... he himself thanks the gods that he has
escaped safe from the storm of perjury (*Odes*, i, 5). He

always records the fact with pleasure, when one of his old
loves who was once cold to him – Lydia – grows old in her
turn, is avoided by young men, and is compelled to go on to
the streets in search of vain adventures (*Odes,* i, 25). He
does not conceal his delight (*Odes,* iv, 13) when Lyce becomes an old woman, whose vanished charm cannot be re-
called by fine Coan garments and shining jewels. Better to
die young like his former love Cynara, instead of becoming
an old crow:

> for the laughter of ardent youth
> seeing the flame of your torch
> dropping away to ashes.

In *Odes,* i, 33, he advises his friend Tibullus not to complain
if the girl has left him for a younger lover. It is always so in
love.

> See, Lycoris' slender forehead
> beams on Cyrus, and Cyrus kindles
> only for Pholoe; but goats would
>   mate with the roaring wolves
> ere she would accept a lover.
> So Venus ordains: she loves to
> chain odd couples together –
>   cruel are Venus' jests.

(It happened, he says, that the freedwoman Myrtale, 'wilder
than the Adriatic strait', holds him enchained, although
Venus offers him 'a better love'.)

He writes to another friend (*Odes,* ii, 4) that it is no sin to
love a servant-maid – Achilles and other heroes of the Trojan war did likewise. Besides, the girl perhaps comes from a
royal family; and in any case she is beautiful:–

> arms and face and her smooth legs
> I commend with a clear heart,

with a clear heart, for he passed forty, and has lost interest.

We have the impression that, as Horace grew older, he
became more and more a spectator of life and love. This
was his attitude with regard to all conduct which was
guided by philosophy, and he tried to live up to it. He gives
a charming picture of such a life in the ode addressed to his
friend Quinctius Hirpinus (*Odes,* ii 11):–

> Thoughtful Quinctius, cease to ask
> what fierce Spain and the savage Goth

(barred from us by the Adriatic)
   threaten. Abandon forethought.
Life needs little, but graceful youth
soon will vanish, and beauty soon;
soon will drowsy and wrinkled age
   deaden our wanton loves.
Even the bright blossom of spring must fade,
even the moon's radiant face grows pale
soon: then why with eternal thoughts
   weary your mortal mind?
Come now, under this lofty plane
lying carelessly, take your ease,
rest, and garland your hair with flowers,
   perfume yourself, and drink,
while you may – for the god expels
gnawing care. Let a slave quench
our too ardent vintage in cool
   draughts from the passing brook.
Lyde, willing but coy, must come.
Bring her now, with her ivory lyre,
neatly knotting her hair in haste
   after the Spartan mode.

This ode shows everything which has still charm for the
ageing poet: friendship, wine, and not too modest girls,
bringing their music and their beauty to add to the delight
of a small open-air banquet. But in his heart, Horace has
long been beyond the reach of love, although he is once
more unexpectedly enthralled by a beautiful youth – the
Passion of which he sings so touchingly in the ode which we
have already mentioned (*Odes,* iv, 1).

To conclude, Horace was naturally bisexual. He never
disdained women, but enjoyed them sanely and temperately.
They never filled his heart, and he regards them and the
whole of sexual life with that wonderful humour which
gave him a magic power over all the confused and various
phenomena of life. For the man of ripe years, Horace
has more to say than any other Roman poet; but youth is
not attracted by his mature wisdom.

We now turn to Tibullus. Mörike characterizes him
thus:–

The changing breezes play over the corn,
bending the supple heads in delicate waves.
Love-sick Tibullus! so your melody wanders,
supple and exquisite, in the wind of God.

And Horace says of him (*Ep.*, i, 4):–

> You were never a soulless body: the gods
> gave you beauty and wealth and the power to enjoy.
> Nurses could wish no more than that their darling
> should have brains, and a tongue, and popularity,
> and fame, and health, and all these in abundance,
> and decent living from a well-lined purse!

Under the name of Tibullus a fair-sized collection of
elegies has been preserved. They vary greatly in content
and importance: the best are certainly Tibullus' own, while
many others must be by other authors. We shall accept the
attributions which are made by scholars, and confine our
attention to the poems which are his.

They are various enough. They show us a man who can
sing of his love for women, with real beauty and distinction,
and also a man who admires handsome boys. It is accordingly clear that Tibullus was bisexual in character.

It is difficult to determine the various times in his life
when he loved Delia, and when he loved the capricious boy
Marathus; but it matters little. We have not many particulars about his life in general. He belonged to a prosperous
knightly family, and grew up in the country. He was accordingly expected to serve some years in the army, but he was
– as he constantly says – not a born soldier (i, 1, 73): –

> Now I campaign in light love's army –
>   I still love breaking doors, and rows.
> Here I am general and bold warrior;
>   let other men die for a flag
> or let them plunder – with a little
>   I laugh at hunger and at wealth.

Still, he campaigned for many years, and saw many lands,
in the East and West of the Empire. Once during these cam-
paigns he suffered so gravely from wounds and privation
that he lay ill for some time in Corcyra. At this period he
had already had an affair with the freedwoman whom he
calls Delia (her real name being Plania). Filled with love
and longing for her, he renounces thoughts of war and
booty and wealth gained by valour (i, I, 51):–

> Perish the emeralds and ingots
>   rather than one girl weep for me!
> Messalla, you are right to battle
>   on sea and land for blood and spoil;

> but I am chained by a charming lover
>   and sit like watchdog at her door.
> I ask no praise, my Delia: let them
>   call me coward in your arms.
> When my last hour comes, let me see you
>   and hold you with my dying hand.

And he dreams of the rapture of calling Delia his own for
ever (i, I, 45): –

> How sweet to lie and hear the gale,
>   holding my mistress to my heart,
> or when the rainy south wind pours,
>   to sleep in safety from the storm!

Delia is to be a chaste wife, and keep his household (i, 5,
21):–

> I'll farm, if Delia guards the harvest
>   while the hot threshers clean the crop,
> and watches the full vats of vintage
>   when flying feet have pressed the grapes.
> She'll learn to count the herds; the prattling
>   slavelets will sit upon her knee,
> She'll offer grapes to the farmer-spirits
>   for wine, and ears for grain, and a feast
> for the flock's growth. She is the mistress,
>   and I'll be nothing in my house.

Such were his dreams of the future. They were unfulfilled.
Delia had no mind to be the wife of one man. Later, she
did marry a man whose wealth had attracted her, but she
remained the mistress of Tibullus and others. The poet
endeavoured to forget his old love and his disillusionment
by drinking and seeking new lovers (i, 5, 37):–

> I tried to drown my cares in winecups –
>   but sorrow turned my drink to tears.
> I took strange women – in the pleasure
>   I thought of Delia – Venus fled.
> The women left me, crying 'bewitched'.

But in the end he returned to her: as was not unusual in
those days, he was received as a lover, although she was
married (i, 6, 9): –

> I taught her to deceive her guardians –
>   she hoists me with my own petard.
> All her pretexts to sleep alone
>   and quiet skill in opening doors
> she learnt from me, with the herbs and juices
>   to hide the toothmarks made by love.

> Husband of my deceitful lady,
>   banish me too, and keep her pure.
> Beware! she must not talk to youths;
>   no loosened frock must show her breast;
> winks must not pass you; wine-dipped fingers
>   can write a word on table tops . . .
> I once pretended to admire her
>   signet, that I might press her hand;
> I made you sleep with stronger liquor
>   while I drank water and made love.
> Love commanded, Love resistless –
>   forgive me my unwilling wrongs.
> I am the man (I tell it boldly)
>   at whom your dog barked all night long.
> You don't deserve a wife! you're careless,
>   and care is more than bolted doors.

These verses, and others like them, show that Delia was nothing but a crafty and beautiful prostitute; she had saved herself by marrying one of her victims, but she could not abandon the delights of illicit love. We can understand her character well enough, but it cannot have been noble or inspiring.

Another of Tibullus' mistresses was called Nemesis. She was at his deathbed when he died (about the age of 30, according to Ovid); but even Tibullus can say little of her that is pleasant. She was more of the regular harlot than Delia, and her one aim was to get valuable presents out of her lovers (ii, 3, 49):–

> Alas, I see that girls love money!
>   Come, riches, if you'll buy me love;
> let Nemesis gleam in my jewels,
>   let all admire her in my gifts;
> she must wear clothes which Coan women
>   have interwoven with gold stripes;
> she must have troops of servants, darkened
>   by India's sun that drives too close.

And in the fourth elegy of the same book he complains (ii, 4, 11):–

> Now days are heavy, nights are heavier
>   all hours are dark with misery.
> Apollo and my songs are useless,
>   she asks for money with both hands.

We have said that Tibullus was not insensitive to the beauty of boys. Certainly he has left us a few elegies ad-

dressed to 'Marathus' which have never been interpreted to
mean anything else. Here is an extract from i, 9:–

> Why vow by gods, and then forswear them,
>   if you had meant to wound our love?
> Poor wretch! The silent-footed Furies
>   catch perjured victims, late but sure.
> Spare him, you spirits: charming liars
>   should have their first transgression free.

As far as this elegy allows us to conclude, Marathus was not
a boy, but a young man; seduced by the wealth of another
man, he had been unfaithful to Tibullus (i, 9, 11):—

> My boy was caught by gifts – ah, heaven,
>   turn all those gifts to water and dust!

The poet had warned Marathus often enough (*ib.*, 17):–

> 'gold must not corrupt your beauty –
>   evil things are often gilt' . . .
> So I spoke; now I blush to have spoken,
>   and to have fallen at your feet.
> You swore to me that golden ingots
>   and gems would never buy your faith.

Later in this remarkable poem, it appears that Marathus
himself had fallen in love with a girl. Tibullus wishes that,
in revenge for his sufferings, the girl may be false to Marathus, and that the seducer of Marathus may himself be
cuckolded by his wife (ib., 57):–

> You – may your bed be marked by others
>   and lovers find an open door!

From the poet's disdain, it appears clear that the seducer
was old (ib., 67):–

> Is it for you she parts her lovelocks,
>   drawing the close comb through her hair?
> and does your handsome face compel her
>   to wear gold lockets, purple robes?
> No, no! she does it for a lover
>   for whom she'd sell you, house and home.
> Small shame to her. A graceful lady
>   hates old embraces, gouty hands.

It was all the more shameful that Marathus should give
himself and his youth to those old embraces (ib., 75):–

> Yet my boy lies with him! now surely
>   my boy could love the savage beasts.

As the poem closes, Tibullus consoles himself with the
thought that there are other beautiful boys in the world . . .

In another elegy (i, 4), Priapus, as the god of boy-lovers,
advises his worshippers how to win the affection of boys
who are beautiful but cold:–

> Beware of boys! beware, and shun them:
>   for every one deserves your love –
> he for his brave and skilful driving
>   he as he swims so white and clean,
> and he again for his rude courage,
>   and he for modest blushing cheeks.
> But even if they deny their favours,
>   hope on, and they'll surrender soon.

The lover must always give way to the boy's whims (ib.,
39):–

> Whatever he may wish to venture,
>   consent: obedience makes love's way.

Eventually the boy will surrender (ib., 53):–

> then you may capture kisses –
>   he'll fight, but still they will be sweet.
> At first you'll seize them, then he'll give them,
>   at last he'll hang around your neck.

But boys have learnt that all their favours can, and must, be
paid for (ib., 57):–

> Alas, this artful generation!
>   even the youngest ask for gifts.

It was better when they admired poetry (ib., 61): –

> Love poets, boys, and love the Muses,
>   prize poems more than golden gifts.
> Songs gave the purple hair to Nisus,
>   songs polished Pelops' ivory bone. ——
> Who lives in songs will live for ever,
>   while earth has oaks and heaven stars.

The poem ends with a reference to Tibullus himself (ib.,
81):–

> Now Marathus consumes me slowly
>   with love, my arts and songs are vain,
> a laughing-stock! Dear boy, have mercy,
>   or my advice is empty words.

Finally, Elegy i, 8, is addressed partly to Marathus, now

suffering from his unrequited love for Pholoe, and partly
to the girl Pholoe herself. Tibullus describes the advantages
of Marathus' young love, in contrast to that of an older man.
The poem also expresses Tibullus' own satisfaction: he had
been spurned by Marathus, and Marathus is now tortured
by a coy mistress.

I feel that the whole business of Marathus seems inappropriate to the rest of the poet's nature. Scholars are sur-
prisingly ready to conclude that similar poems by other
authors (such as Horace, for example) are harmless *jeux
d'esprit* rather than serious revelations of the poet's soul.
Yes, as far as I am aware, it has never been held that these
Marathus poems might be no more than playful exercises
on a theme which had many Greek parallels. They appear
to me as exquisite trifles, with no real basis in experience.
It is of course impossible to prove this contention, but the
reader will form his own conclusions.

In the third* book of the corpus which bears the name of
Tibullus, there is a little collection of poems whose unity
of authorship is proved by their homogeneity of subject.
They all deal with the love of a woman Sulpicia for a man
Cerinthus. It is generally supposed that some of these
charming little pieces are the work of a real Roman girl,
Sulpicia – perhaps the daughter of Horace's friend Servius
Sulpicius Rufus; and that a poet (possibly, though not certainly, Tibullus) was led to compose additional poems
which made up a complete love-story. We shall quote a few
poems from both groups.

The girl is, very unwillingly, spending her birthday with
friends in the country. She writes (*Elegidia* 2):–

> My hateful birthday, in the boring country,
>   without Cerinthus, is a gloomy time.
> How sweet the city is! these country houses,
>   cold fields, and rivers cannot please a girl.
>
> Leave me in peace, Messalla you're too anxious,
>   too ready to go travelling too soon!
> I'll go, but leave in Rome my heart and liking,
>   since you refuse to let my will decide.

But fortunately the journey does not take place. Sulpicia

* Oxford Classical Text numbering.

spends her birthday in Rome with her lover, and writes
(*Elegidia* 3):–

> You know I am reprieved from the hateful journey?
>   Now I can spend my birthday here in Rome.
> We both must celebrate it as a birthday,
>   both you and I, this unexpected joy.

During an illness she writes to her lover (*Elegidia* 5):–

> Cerinthus, have you love and kindness for me,
>   now that the fever burns my tired limbs?
> I could not wish to conquer hateful illness
>   unless I knew my lover wished it too.
> And conquest will be vain, if my Cerinthus
>   can bear my sufferings with heart unmoved.

Her simple avowal in 6 is quite exquisite:–

> My life and light, I wish that all your passion
>   for me be less than it was yesterday,
> if ever I committed youthful folly
>   in which I find more to repent me now
> than this – last night I left my lover lonely
>   to hide the passion in my hungry heart.

The next poem celebrates in daring words the consummation of their love; but we may doubt whether it is to be
ascribed to Sulpicia herself or to Tibullus. It runs (*Elegidia*
1):–

> Love here at last! To hide it was more shameful
>   than to reveal it was an act of grace.
> Our Lady Venus, prayed to in my poems,
>   brought love to me and laid it in my breast.
> Venus has paid her promises! Let others
>   tell of my happiness if they have none.
> I will not set it down in secret writing
>   so that he may be first to read my love.
> No, I enjoy my sin! I hate pretences –
>   my love and I were both worthy of love!

This birthday poem on the other hand, is certainly the work
of Tibullus (*de Sulp.*, 5): –

> Juno, goddess of birthdays, take this incense
>   given by the soft hand of a poet-girl.
> Today she is your own, her joy and beauty
>   are yours, to decorate your sacred hearth.
> Goddess, for you she wishes to be lovely,
>   yet there's another whom she hopes to please.
> Grant us your favour! let no other part us,
>   but bind the youth to me with the same chains.

a happy union – there's no other maiden
    worthy of him, no other man of her.
And may their love escape their watchful guardians,
    may Cupid teach them manifold deceits.
Grant this, and come gleaming in robes of purple;
    see, thrice she offers holy bread and wine.
Her careful mother now dictates her prayers –
    she prays for other things in her secret heart.
She burns as these quick flames burn on the altar,
    and, if she could, she would not quench her fire.

As if to make a contrast to that poem, the poet makes
Sulpicia say (de Sulp., 4):–

The blessed day which brought me you, Cerinthus,
    will always be my festal holyday.
When you were born, the fates foretold your empire
    over all women, all to be your slaves.
And I burn with a hotter flame than others,
    loving my flames if I can burn you too.
Let love be shared, I pray you by your Spirit,
    and by your eyes, and by our dear deceits.
Great Genius, Spirit of birthday, take this incense,
    and hear his prayers if he thinks love of me.
But if he sighs for other loves, I pray you,
    most holy Spirit, leave this perjured hearth.
And you, be gentle, Venus, both together
    let us be slaves, or lift my servitude:
but let us both be bound in chains of iron
    which never any day of days can break.
His hopes are my hopes, but they are covered –
    he is ashamed to speak the word aloud.
So, birthday-Spirit, god who knowest all things,
    smile on him; silent prayers are prayers too.

Finally, the poet wishes (ii, 2, 17) that their love may end
in marriage and be blessed by children.

May love fly here on whirring pinions,
    and bring the golden chains of the marriage-tie,
the chains which never fall, till Time's old finger
    wrinkles your flesh and stripes your hair with grey.
May that winged omen come, and give you children,
    may little people play around your feet!

Besides these poems, Tibullus composed characteristic elegies in praise of country life and its manifold activities; but
we can speak of his work no further in this chapter. Similarly, we shall pass over the weak imitations of Tibullus
which appear as the Elegies of Lygdamus in the third book

of his works. They give us no new information about
Roman sexual life.

We must now endeavour to present a vivid portrait of
the greatest of Roman elegiac poets – Sextus Aurelius Propertius.

Although it is far from easy to make any reader without
a classical education understand the character and work of
a poet such as Horace or Vergil, it is even more difficult to
describe Propertius, that dark and thoughtful master of
the Latin speech. We cannot translate Propertius as he
stands. We can only attempt through carefully selected
paraphrases to make the meaning of his elegies comprehensible to the reader.

We know no more of his life than he tells us himself. He
came from Assisi; he was born in 50 B.C.; his parents died
when he was young; he lived almost exclusively in Rome,
on the rents of his country estates. He was one of the group
of poets who gathered around Maecenas, and Horace and
Vergil were his friends. He issued his first book of poems
when he was about 30 years of age; they were named
Cynthia, which was the pseudonym of his mistress, and they
form the first book of the corpus which has come down to
us under his name. He became famous, and was much read,
especially by cultured Roman ladies. Later he published
other elegies, and finally a small collection of patriotic
poems: Maecenas had encouraged him to write them, as he
had encouraged Horace to write the Roman Odes.

Only the love-elegies of Propertius are relevant in this
book. As we have said, they were chiefly inspired by a
woman whom the poet calls Cynthia: her real name is said
to have been Hostia. But we should be doing her too much
honour if we attempted to show her character developed
during her love affair with Propertius and what her nature
really was. The poet makes a point of repulsing inquisitive
readers; he says expressly (iii, 24, I) : –

> Your trust in beauty is at last confounded
>   although my worship made it high and proud.
> My passion, Cynthia, gave you that honour –
>   are you ashamed of shining in my songs?
> I praised you for a thousand different beauties:
>   love could imagine beauty where none was.

We shall not, therefore, attempt to give an exact picture of
Cynthia, for her character as it appears in the poems is
inconsistent and self-contradictory. Enough to know that
she was destined to fire the heart of this gifted and passionate man, to fan the hidden spark of poetry to a blaze, to
become his Muse. Through her he knew love in all its heights
and depths, in all its joys and sorrows, in its highest raptures and its cruellest disappointments; and he recorded
it all in unforgettable words. For the love of Propertius was
neither so youthful as that of Catullus, nor so coarse and
frivolous as that of Ovid: it was a real and tremendous
passion which filled his heart, a love as great as the love of
the *Nouvelle Héloïse* or *Werther*. Propertius lived a
passionate life, full of rapture, fury, and triumph; yet he
was not broken when he learnt the tragedy of his love. He
turned proudly away, and forced his heart to think, and
study, and be calm. From the beginning, his love was a tragedy – it could not be otherwise; his poet's heart aspired
to an immortal love and found only weak mortal lovers.
His was the fate of Lohengrin: the lover burns with the
highest ideal love, and longs to give himself completely and
for ever; but he expects true love and immutable loyalty
from his beloved. The beloved of Propertius was a common
prostitute: witty and refined, but a prostitute. Such was
Cynthia, as we read of her in her lover's poems.

She lived with her mother and sister in the notorious
quarter called the Suburra (iv. 7, 15). The poet actually
tells us that (ii, 14):–

> others plied the knocker, called their mistress –
> her head lay languid on the couch with me.

Indeed, he makes an offering to Venus when his mistress
grants him a whole night with her. And his general opinion
is expressed in ii, 32, 29:–

> if you have played a night or two with others,
> it is a trifle, not a grave reproach.

Is is strange that Cynthia was often the subject of malevolent gossip? Unfortunately, the gossip was not so profound as Propertius asserts. He had reason enough for jealousy when she went on a trip to Baiae – famous for its lax
morality – or visited the temples – which as we have said

often harboured assignations and flirtations. She could even
be bought for money (ii, 16):—

> Cynthia loves not power nor follows honour;
>   she judges every lover by his purse.

She had an affair with a rich praetor, among others.

She had, of course, the many-sided education which distinguishes women of her type from respectable matrons.
Not only could she dance, sing, and play the lyre, like others
of her class, but she was able to criticize poetry – indeed,
she composed poetry herself.

> You have majestic beauty, Pallas' graces,
>   your poet-grandsire fills your house with fame;

says Propertius in iii, 20.

We are told little of her personal appearance. She evidently belonged to the proud and dominating type, for the
poet often emphasizes her hard-heartedness in love, calling
her *dura puella*. She was very independent: she would wear
thin transparent dresses in public, and she would drive
along the Appian Way, managing the horses herself (iv, 8).
She gave way to furious fits of temper when her lover displeased her. But all these traits only increased the poet's
passion. Many of his remarks almost sound as if he had
masochistic tendencies, for example (iii, 8):—

> I relished fighting with you in the lamplight
>   last night, and hearing all your furious oaths.
> Why throw the table down when mad with liquor
>   and wildly hurl the wineglasses at me?
> Come, come, attack my hair in your savage temper,
>   and scar my features with your pretty nails!
> Dearest, threaten to burn my eyes to ashes,
>   split my robe wide open, and bare my breast!
> Surely all these are signs of a true passion,
>   without such passion women have no pain.
> The woman who has fits of savage scolding
>   is a true servant of the god of love.
> her watchers elbow you on every journey,
>   she follows you with a madwoman's care;
> she suffers from appalling dreams and visions,
>   she hates and fears a portrait of a girl.
> Now, I can diagnose these mental tortures,
>   I know the symptoms of a real love.
> Love is uncertain, if it never rages –
>   may my worst enemy have a placid girl!

> May those who know me see the marks of biting
>   and bruises which betray a happy love!
> In love I want to weep or see you weeping,
>   to agonize, or hear your agony . . .
> I hate a sleep never broken by sighing,
>   and I would always pine for an angry girl.

In love Propertius himself is almost feminine (in the usual sense of the word), for instance (ii, 5):–

> I would not tear your clothes if you betrayed me,
>   nor let my rage batter your bolted door,
> nor wrench your plaited hair out in my fury,
>   nor scar your tender flesh with brutal thumbs.
> These battles suit some clod, some country-bumpkin
>   who never wore the poet's ivy crown.
> Therefore I write a word to last your lifetime –
>   'Cynthia beautiful, Cynthia false.'
> Believe me, though you sneer at reputation,
>   that little line will blanch your faithless cheek.

Such, then, is the love of Cynthia and Propertius. She is the proud mistress, and his happiness lies quite simply in the enjoyment of her favours, even if these favours promise no eternal love. And he receives the gift of happiness almost humbly, while his occasional unfaithfulness rouses her, despite her own perfidy, to extremes of rage. The poet describes with great realism a scene of that kind: it makes the real character of their love clearer than any words of ours could make it (iv, 8). Cynthia has gone away for some time – although, as the poet rightly guesses,

> Juno the cause, but Venus more the cause.

For once he decides to have some enjoyment without his faithful mistress: he invites to dinner two pretty girls of easy virtue:–

> These I invited, to amuse my evening –
>   a fresh adventure with an unknown love.
> We had a triple couch in a secret garden . . .
>   and the arrangement? I between the two!

Everything was ready for a merry meal: with plenty of good wine, served by Lygadmus the cupbearer. But the lights burned dim; the atmosphere was gloomy; Propertius could not free himself from thoughts of the absent Cynthia. Then:–

> the hinges cried, the doors were suddenly creaking,
>   there was a murmur in the outer room.
> At once, Cynthia flung the doors wide open –
>   her hair undone, but handsome in her rage.
> The wineglass fell out of my loosened fingers,
>   my slack drunken lips grew suddenly pale.
> Eyes flashing, she raged with a woman's fury!
>   she was a sight as rare as a captured town!

The two girls fly in terror, pursued by the frenzied Cynthia, she scratches their faces and drives them out. Then she returns and attacks Propertius:–

> She wounds my face with angry random blows,
>   she bruises all my neck, her teeth leave bloodstains,
>   and most she strikes my eyes, the criminals.
> Then, when her arms were tired with my chastisement,
>   she caught the page-boy hiding behind the bed—
> he prayed me on my soul for mercy, grovelling –
>   but what could I do, I, a prisoner too?
> At last my pleading hands procured her mercy
>   and grudgingly she let me touch her feet.
> She cried 'if you wish peace and absolution,
>   here is the treaty which you must accept.
> THOU SHALT NOT be a dandy in the Forum
>   nor with the crowd in Pompey's colonnade.
> THOU SHALT NOT turn thy head to the ladies' boxes
>   nor linger by sedans with curtains drawn.
> And as for Lygdamus, who caused the trouble –
>   he must be sold with fetters on his feet'.
> This was the law. I answered 'it is binding'.
>   and she, my haughty sovereign, laughed with joy.
> Now every place touched by the foreign ladies
>   she censed and purified; she washed the sill,
> commanded me to change my dress twice over,
>   and touched my head three times with sulphur flame.
> And then the bed was changed, with all the covers,
>   and in my arms she ratified our peace.

Such is their love. It shows Propertius as an absurdly devoted lover – a slave, and the slave of an exciting but faithless prostitute. But despite all that, he was happy. And, most important of all, he remained the master of his passion. At times he is quite conscious that he is being fooled. That is the tragedy of his love; but it would have been a miserable and dispiriting affair if the poet had allowed this to break him. He stood firm. It is true that his jealous mistress forbade him to approach her for a long period – evidently after a similar discovery. (Of course we have no evidence for this incident.) He suffered considerably by the separation (iii, 16, 9):—

> For one betrayal, banished for a twelvemonth!
> My lady's hands are merciless to me.

After this twelvemonth, he was restored to favour, and the love affair lasted five years altogether. But Cynthia remained the imperious mistress who accords her favours when she fancies, and to any man she fancies. Once, for instance, her caprice led her to order Propertius (by letter) to come to her villa at Tibur in the middle of the night (iii, 16). The poet made the hazardous journey through the darkness, rejoicing that he should be allowed to come to her, and even rejoicing that if he met death on his journey he would be buried by his beloved. Although he himself was occasionally unfaithful, he was quite as jealous as his mistress (ii, 6, 9):—

> Portraits of youths, masculine names, annoy me;
>   I hate the cradle holding a baby *boy*;
> I hate her mother when she gives her kisses,
>   her sister, and the girl who sleeps with her;
> I hate them all – forgive me – I am timid
>   and I suspect a man in every smock.

He shared Cynthia's fears that Augustus' marriage laws might force them to marry or to separate, for a marriage between the famous poet and the prostitute would not have been possible without much difficulty. Neither of them, in fact, thought of marriage at all (ii, 7, I):—

> My Cynthia rejoiced when the law was lifted,
>   whose harsh decree had brought us both to tears:
> it might have separated us, but lovers
>   could not be parted even by God himself.
> Caesar is mighty. Yes, but mighty in battle –
>   his conquests could avail nothing in love.
> I would have parted head and neckbone, sooner
>   than waste my fire on any legal bride,
> or pass before your gates, a wedded husband,
>   and gaze, weeping, at what I had betrayed.
> My wedding-flutes, sadder than funeral trumpet –
>   they would have piped you to a dismal sleep! . . .
> How can I furnish boys for family triumphs?
>   My blood will never breed a soldier son –
> unless I followed Cynthia's encampments,
>   then Castor's charger would be tame for me.

> From Cynthia come my triumphs and my glories,
>   the glories which have reached the utmost pole.
> You are my only love; now love me only,
>   and love is more to me than fatherhood.

If she were the true love who he so earnestly desired, she would not (i, 2, I) have care to

> pace proudly forth with plaited tresses,
>   and move the delicate folds in silken robes.

And he reproaches her bitterly for that very fickleness — reproaches which she enjoyed, as the prize of her beauty, without taking them to heart. He says (i, 2, 3):—

> Why drench your hair with costly Syrian perfume,
>   and advertise yourself in foreign wares?
> Why kill with purchased pomp your native beauty
>   and not shine bright in your own loveliness?
> Believe my words, these beauty-aids are useless:
>   the naked god hates artificial grace . . .
> To please one lover is display enough . . .

The charming elegy, i, 3, is deservedly famous, it paints the picture of Cynthia sleeping:—

> I saw my Cynthia breathing quiet slumber,
>   resting her head on gentle yielding arms,
> while I dragged home my steps stumbling with Bacchus
>   and pages swung their torches through the dark.
> Senses were with me still; I tried to approach her,
>   resting a gentle knee on the dainty bed;
> for Love and Bacchus held me both together —
>   stern gods — and filled me with a double heat.
> They bade me slide an arm gently beneath her,
>   approach my hand, and kiss her, and fall to.
> And yet I did not dare disturb her slumber,
>   fearing her savage words, her well-known wrath.
> I stopped, and gazed, helpless and hesitating,
>   as Argus did on Io's monstrous horns.
> And now I stripped the garlands from my forehead
>   placing them on her temples as she slept,
> and now I shaped and curled her fallen tresses
>   or laid an apple in her hollow hand.
> But all my gifts were vain: sleep is ungrateful:
>   they rolled helplessly down from her sleeping breast.

At last the girl is awakened by a stray moonbeam. She is jealous and angry; she had spent the time embroidering and playing the lyre, and then cried herself to sleep. The poet leaves us to guess how peace was made.

In another poem, he comes to Cynthia in the early morning, to see if she has slept alone (ii, 29, 23):–

> Morning. I wished to see if my beloved
>   had slept alone. I found her as I wished.
> I stood amazed, she never was more lovely,
>   even once when she wore a crimson smock,
> going to tell her dream to holy Vesta
>   in case it boded harm for her and me.
> So lovely was she now, fresh from her sleeping –
>   delicious power of pure beauty, alone!

But he is not welcomed. Cynthia is furious at his suspicions and at his spying: she evades his kisses and runs away. Many of her fits of rage must have begun in that way.

We cannot give a detailed history of Propertius' love affair. It would only tarnish the vivid colours of his love and his poetry. It would, in fact, be pointless to ask whether this elegy of love triumphant (ii, 15) refers to Cynthia or another. Look through the translation to the soul of the piece, and hear how a Roman of that time described his highest rapture:–

> Happiness, happiness! blessed night! and bless you
>   bed, changed to heaven by my happiness!
> What happy talk we had, the lamp beside us!
>   and what a happy struggle in the dark!
> For now she wrestled with me, baring her bosom,
>   and now she closed her shift to make a truce.
> My eyes were heavy with sleep: she kissed them open
>   and whispered 'Lazy sluggard, lying still!'
> How often our arms slipped into new embraces!
>   how long my kisses lay upon your lips!
> Venus is spoilt by serving her in darkness;
>   surely you know, sight is the path of love.
> They say that Paris sighed for naked Helen
>   once when he saw her leave her husband's room.
> Endymion naked captured chaste Diana
>   and held the goddess naked in his arms.
> Now if you cling to clothes and sleep in nightgowns,
>   clothes will be torn, and you will feel my blows.
> And if my righteous anger takes me further
>   you will have bruises to take home with you.
> And drooping breasts must not prevent your pastime –
>   you have no secret child – you need not care.
> While fate allows us, feast our eyes in passion.
>   The coming night is long and has no dawn.
> Oh, that a chain would bind us, still embracing

LOVE IN ROMAN POETRY

> thus, irresolubly for evermore!
> Why, take example from the quiet turtles,
>   the doves, who make a perfect married pair!
> Folly to seek an end for this mad passion,
>   a real love can never reach an end.
> Sooner shall earth deceive the waiting farmer
>   with changeling crops, the sun drive quicker steeds,
> the rivers mount again towards their sources,
>   and fishes pant in the dry ocean-bed –
> sooner than I could change my burning passion
>   from her. I serve her now in life and death.
> But if she grants me other nights, and others,
>   one year is lengthened to a happy life.
> If she gives many, I become immortal!
>   for in one night anyone is divine.
> If all men sought to spend such quiet lifetimes
>   or sleep a peaceful slumber, full of wine,
> no cruel weapons would there be, nor warships,
>   nor would the sea of Actium toss our bones,
> nor would our city, ground by her own triumphs,
>   be tired of loosening her hair to mourn.
> Posterity can praise this life with justice:
>   our winecups are not blasphemous nor cruel.
> Only beware; leave not the feast in daylight!
>   if you gave all your kisses, they'd be few.
> And as the petals leave a withered garland
>   to float in the abandoned mixing-bowls,
> so now, for all our hopes, perhaps tomorrow
>   will end our little life and our long dreams.

The magic of these poems cannot be reproduced in translation. Any translator can only give the bare meaning, which may be enough to show imaginative readers that these are the noblest words of love ever uttered in the Latin tongue. We must add also that despite the vigour and passion of the emotion described, the poems give no impression of sensuality or indecency.

We have said that Propertius's liaison with Cynthia was broken off for a year by a quarrel of which we know nothing. Finally, after five years of Cynthia's continual unfaithfulness, Propertius took leave of her for ever, thus (iii, 25):–

> I was the laughter of your friends at dinner,
>   and every loose-tongued wit talked about me!
> Yet I spent five years in your faithful service:
>   you'll live to bite your nails, remembering me.
> Tears do not touch me now – by tears you caught me,
>   your sobs and tears are only strategy.

I shall weep as I leave you – tears of anger
   at you, who broke a happy comradeship.
Good-bye, threshold which wept to hear my anguish,
   and doors I never broke despite my rage.
But you, may bitter age and time attack you,
   bringing, the stealthy wrinkles to your face!
Then, as the mirror mocks your haggard beauty,
   may white hairs, as you pull them, multiply!
May haughty lovers bar the door upon you
   till you in age regret youth's insolence!
Beware of grim revenges on your beauty,
   doomed by the curses harboured in my song.

In the old phrase of the Nibelungenlied, this passion
ended in pain. Propertius's soul was deeply wounded. He
could not forget Cynthia. Keller's beautiful words are true
of his passion:–

Love, when at last you die,
   your loveliness will seem
the short reality
   of a delicious dream.

Later, after she was dead, he wrote a poem of sad forgiveness (iv, 7). The shade of Cynthia appears to the poet,
after she has been but a short while in her grave and has
not yet drunk deep of Lethe water; she reproaches him for
caring nothing about her funeral:–

O treacherous! always a faithful lover!
   Can you surrender thus to sleep, so soon? . . .
No watcher closed my eyes when I departed. . . .
Who saw you bowed and weeping on my body,
   in a black garment wet with burning tears?
Were you ashamed to pass the gates behind me?
   till there, my hearse need not have hastened so.
Or did you pray for wind to fan my burning? –
   O thankless! – or put perfumes on my pyre?
Was it too much to throw a worthless blossom,
   to sanctify my tomb by pouring wine?

And, she says, her faithful maids now belong to another
who persecutes them for remembering their dead mistress.
In a touching entreaty, she asks him to preserve at least her
old nurse and her favourite maid from the cruelty of the
new mistress.

Faithless Propertius! yet I cannot blame you:
   for in your poems I was long supreme.

And one comfort still remains:–

> Others possess you now, soon I shall own you;
>   you will be mine, and mix your bones with me.

This beautiful elegy sounds as if the poet knew that his life
would not be long; and he must have died about the age of
forty. He is without doubt the greatest love poet of Rome.

  In this work we cannot discuss the influence of ancient
poets on their successors in modern times. We must, however, note the fact that Propertius interested Goethe very
much, so that certain poems in his *Roman Elegies* are obviously modelled on the work of Propertius himself. Goethe
once spoke of Propertius in these terms: 'I have just re-read
most of the elegies of Propertius, and, as such works usually do, they have deeply affected me and made me eager
to produce something of the kind myself. But I must avoid
this, for I have other plans afoot' (28th November, 1798).
Goethe wrote these words after reading the translation
which his friend Knebel had made at his suggestion. He has
left a memorial of Propertius in the verses which introduce his elegy, *Hermann and Dorothea*:–

> Is it a crime, if still I am carried to heaven by Propertius?
>   if I receive as a friend Martial, the elegant rogue?
> if I refuse to abandon the ancients to lie in the schoolroom?
> if my companions have come with me from Rome into life?

  Are these words not a clear acknowledgment that the
great Romans were for Goethe more than mere subjects of
classical study? But what are they to us? A little Ovid is
taught in the schools. But the greatest and most human of
all the Roman elegiac poets – Propertius – is hardly even a
name to an educated man of today. For that reason I have
thought it necessary that this book should deal with him in
the greatest possible detail.

  Now we must continue our survey of Roman love-poetry.
We come next to a poet much better known and more widely
read – Ovid. But why should he be better known than his
friend Propertius? Why was he always more widely read?
Perhaps because men take more pleasure in an attitude to
love which is superficial, gracefully frivolous, and titillating

to the senses, than in the tragic seriousness with which Propertius spoke of his passion.

But we will not offer any criticism until we have attempted to paint a vivid picture of love as seen by Ovid. We may anticipate it by saying this: Ovid was in his way a great erotic poet, but in his work there is no flowering of the true, deep, and natural experience as there is in Catullus and Propertius. He must have had many erotic experiences, known and enjoyed love deeply; but we never feel in him as in the others, that love was the experience of a lifetime: we never feel that it shook his soul to its depths and compelled him to say what he felt. It is very significant for Ovid's character that it was he who wrote the *Art of Love* – a sophisticated manual of hedonism which is very nearly a frankly pornographic manual of the methods of physical love. In this book love is no longer the great and over-whelming divinity which sanctifies or ruins man's life. That idea would have appeared merely funny to Ovid. Love is rather a method for obtaining fleeting pleasure from a dis-gusting necessity. This attitude is nothing but absolute friv-olity.

Let us turn to Ovid's best known erotic work. As a young poet of twenty-two, polished, superficial, he produced his first work, the *Amores* or *Loves* (43 B.C.). It is generally agreed that these frivolous and graceful elegies do not des-cribe any deep spiritual experiences. The poet does describe a mistress in them – she bears a pseudonym, 'Corinna', derived from Greek lyric poetry; but as Ovid somewhere says, any one of several girls might think that she was meant. These skilful and elegant poems are no more than a collection of themes from Alexandrian poetry, which was then very widely known and influenced every Roman ele-giac poet. We can find in Ovid an imitation of Greek comedy in the long speech of a bawd to an intended victim (i, 8): or there is the cynical poem in which he says that he will not think of a woman's fidelity so long as he does not know the name of her other lover (iii, 14). There is also the hackneyed remark that greed and avarice make women false (i, 10) and a description of the vain attempts of a dis-appointed lover to break the chains he loves and hates (ii, 9; iii, 11b). There are, again, exhortations to enjoy life when one is young (ii, 9) and while one's strength is so inexhaustible that one cannot content oneself with one woman (ii, 4). The poet does not omit the popular theme of the lover's address to the dawn (i, 13) and a poem on the equally popular theme of the departure of a mistress for distant lands (ii, 11). In one poem the young poet trenches on obscenity (iii, 7), where he imagines himself in the miserable role of an impotent man.

But instead of giving further summaries we shall quote a translation of one of these poems. Its content is the same as that of Propertius, ii, 15 – the highest raptures of love's consummation. The poems themselves show better than any criticism the difference between Propertius' lofty passion and Ovid's skilful voluptuousness. Here is the poem (i, 5): –

> Hot summer; the day had passed its zenith;
> and I reclined at ease upon my bed.
> The window, partly closed and partly open,
> gave the dim light which glimmers in the woods,
> or fills the twilit air at the sun's setting,
> or comes when night is dead and day unborn.
> That is the kindest light for a modest maiden –
> it seems to give concealment to her shame.
>
> Corinna came to me, in a shift, ungirdled,
> her hair parted along her ivory neck.
> Semiramis looked thus, that lovely lady,
> and Lais, the beloved of all men.
> I tore her shift away, though it was flimsy,
> and though Corinna strove to wear it still.
> And while she struggled – with no mind for winning –
> she dropped her arms, and lost an easy fight.
> Now when she stood before my eyes, uncovered,
> I found her body faultless everywhere.
> What graceful arms I saw and touched! what shoulders!
> how sweet her breasts, ready for an embrace!
> beneath a moulded waist, what a smooth belly!
> what a rich flank, what a slender thigh!
> Why should I count her beauties? She was perfect:
> I pressed her naked body to my own.
> Who does not know the rest? It ends in slumber.
> Ah, may I often have such afternoons!

All in all, we can say that the tendency of the *Amores* is similar to that of Ovid's later masterpiece, *The Art of Love*. The poet says so himself (ii, I): –

> Girls who desire their bridegrooms – they should read me
>   and callow youths, touched by their strange first love . .
> Come, maidens, turn hither your lovely faces,
>   and hear the songs which bright Love teaches me.

In *Amores*, i, 8, 43, Ovid sums up his view of women –

> She is chaste who has no wooer:
>   unless she is a bumpkin, *she* will woo.

Finally, the young poet ventures on this wish (ii, 10):–

> Let soldiers steel their breasts and face the arrows,
>   and buy eternal glory with their blood.
> Let misers hunt and lie for wealth, and perish,
>   drinking the waves their keel has often ploughed.
> May I grow languid in the work of Venus,
>   when I die; may I perish in the act;
> and may a friend, weeping over my body,
>   say this of me: 'He died as he had lived'!

These words would seem to show that Ovid was a sophisticated voluptuary in his attitude to love. But that is not the
case. He was, as he tells us, thrice married, the first time at
an early age; but his married life was unhappy until his
third wife, a young widow of noble birth, brought him lasting happiness. We know nothing at all of any extramarital
relationships, and he himself asserts in *Tristia*, ii, 353:–

> My heart is different from my songs believe me,
>   my life is modest though my muse is gay.
> Most of my work is lies, imaginations,
>   and more licentious than its author was.
> A book is not a mirror of the spirit –
>   it brings an honest pleasure, light and pure.

We have no grounds for doubting the truth of this assertion. It is all the more interesting because we know nowadays that strongly erotic natures tend to sublimate those
lusts whose satisfaction might bring them into conflict with
morality; and that this sublimation is often accomplished
by the creation of works of art. We might well assume that
much of Ovid's frivolous verse was created by spiritual
necessities of this kind. In the long elegy which is the
second book of the *Tristia*, Ovid quotes many works by
other poets to prove that an author may describe murder
and other crimes realistically without having committed

any of them. Modern psychology goes further and says 'That is true, for the author could not describe these crimes so impressively if he had never fought with the impulse to commit them and sublimate the impulse by creating a work or art'.

In short, we have justification for assuming that Ovid was actually far from being the cunning voluptuary and seducer which he describes in his first poems. He was a hot-blooded young Roman, living in an age of great excitement, and he was a distinguished poet who possessed by nature a vivid erotic imagination and a deep knowledge of woman's heart. If it is objected that no young man could describe such things with such vivid realism without personal experience, we may reply that the objector shows no knowledge of the real nature of art. Besides, Ovid had as models not only the Alexandrians but also such poets as Catullus, Tibullus, and Propertius, and it is easily proved that he directly imitated them. We shall therefore give ready credence to his assertion that his erotic poetry is simply more or less playful imagination, with the reservation that his character influenced him in favour of erotic poetry – as such.

But his greatest work of this kind was not the juvenilia which we have been discussing. It was his far better known *Ars Amandi, The Art of Love*, of which Paldamus very justly says: 'Ovid provides a complete Manual of Amorous Tactics ... Lover and beloved are like rival chess players: they are both intent on the game, and their only interest is to see which will discover a weakness in his opponent and cry "Checkmate".' However, it should not be forgotten that Ovid says with much emphasis, in the introduction, that the work was not written for married women or chaste girls, but in order to give instructions about the pursuits of light ladies. It is not intended to show how to choose a good wife, but how to find an amusing 'friend'.* win her, enjoy her, keep her, and treat her in such a way as never to bore her or be mistreated by her. The point of the book, then, is pure eroticism: the art of enjoying woman – or rather woman's body – as fully and delightfully as possible. Perhaps no other classical book of the same type shows more clearly the true aim of erotic activity in ancient times – sexual

* *Amica*, lady-friend, is a Latin word for 'mistress'.

pleasure. That is the purpose of all the witty advice which the poet gives, that is presupposed in all his explanations of female psychology. And when he asserts that he is writing only of intercourse with 'friends', it is obvious and inevitable that all his discussions, counsels, warnings, and exhortations are true of intercourse with any woman whom a man can love.

But nowadays this manual of love gives us an unpleasant impression, despite its many gems of poetry and its real humanity. And that unpleasant impression is caused by the spirit of the whole book, the fundamental conception that man is a purely sexual being, and the total failure to recognize that woman is a spiritual being and man's co-partner in life. Everything which Ovid says about women (possibly from wide personal experience) would be correct if women were only things to give men pleasure, things which must be correctly treated to produce the maximum of satisfaction. The poet has no idea that woman is an independent spiritual being who shares man's sexual life on equal terms.

For this we must not blame only the fact that Rome regarded sexual activity as sensual satisfaction and woman as man's plaything: the attitude we have described is Ovid's own. Here there is a cleavage between Ovid's sober and faithful married life and his character as a frivolous and sophisticated voluptuary – the character which he chose to assume both in the *Amores* and in the *Ars Amandi*. We might imagine that his married life was less successful and pleasant, from a sexual point of view, than he had hoped – so that he was driven to write these books in order to give some reality to the unfulfilled dream of his strongly sensual nature. We might also follow the usual accounts of Roman literary history in saying that many other poets wrote similar *divertissements, and* that these two poems are no more than that. This is a convenient explanation, but it gives me personally no satisfaction. Behind these poems I see the living poet, compelled by his own nature and gifts to write *The Loves* and *The Art of Love* rather than solemn philosophical treatises.

The Art of Love has often been translated, into every modern language. We cannot here discuss the book in all its details. But we shall quote from it at length, to give the

reader some idea of its scope and character. The first book
gives instructions for winning a woman's love. Here are a
few lines (i, 93 sq.):–

> Like ants who come and go in lengthy columns,
>   bearing their small provisions in their mouths,
> like bees flying over their perfumed pastures
>   and skimming flowers and herbs and scented thyme –
> the finest women crowd to the arena:
>   their numbers often set my choice at fault.
> It is a place fatal to honest beauty,
>   where women go to see, and to be seen.

Next the poet gives a vivid but light-hearted version of the
legendary Rape of the Sabines (described more seriously
by Livy). We shall cite the whole of it, for it is an important
example of Ovid's treatment of legends which are sanctified
by their antiquity:–

> 'Twas Romulus first put danger in the circus,
>   when captured Sabines pleased his lonely men.
> There was no marble theatre, with awnings,
>   no stage perfumed with glowing saffron scent.
> The wooded Palatine gave up its leafage
>   to make an artless staging, unadorned.
> On seats cut from the turf, sat the young Romans,
>   crowning their unkempt hair with common leaves.
> They gazed around, while each marked down the maiden
>   whom he preferred, and made his secret plan.
> Meanwhile the Tuscan piper played his measures
>   and dancers smote the level earth in time.
> Amidst the cheers – then was no art in cheering –
>   the king unloosed his people on their prey.
> They darted forward, shouting lust and passion,
>   and clutched the maidens with impatient hands.
> As timid doves scatter before an eagle,
>   as tender lambs take flight before a wolf –
> so fled the maidens from their ardent suitors.
>   None kept the colour she had had before:
> their terror was the same, in different semblance:
>   some tore their hair, and others sat bemused,
> some called their mothers, some gave way in silence,
>   some wept or swooned, some fled and some remained.
> The ravished girls were led away to marriage;
>   their very shame made them more beautiful.
> And when one struggled hard against her captor,
>   he carried her away in eager arms,
> and said: 'Why spoil your pretty eyes by weeping?
>   Your father took your mother, I take you'
> Ah Romulus, you could reward a soldier!

> Give me such bounties, and I'll soldier too.
> Thus, even now, the theatre and circus
>   are dangerous for lovely girls. – Beware!

Ovid believes that is generally easy to win a girl's love (*A.A.*, i, 271):—

> The birds will leave their songs in spring, the crickets
>   be dumb in summer, dogs will flee from hares,
> sooner than women flee from tactful wooers.
>   Although she seems unwilling, yet she will.

And so (ib. 343):—

> Come then, take heart, you'll conquer every woman:
>   hardly one in ten thousand will refuse.
> Refuse, or not, they'll love you more for asking.

Ovid gives some interesting advice to lovers on their personal appearance (ib. 509):–

> Neglect suits a man's beauty. . . .
> Let cleanliness be yours, and healthy brownness.
>   Your toga must be neat, and free from stains;
> your tongue supple, your teeth unstained and shining,
>   your foot grasped steadily by your shoe;
> an ugly haircut must not spoil and stiffen
>   your hair; a skilful hand should clip your beard.

He adds similar advice for women (iii, 105):–

> Care brings you beauty, and neglect will kill it,
>   though it were lovelier than Venus' self.
> If our foremothers could neglect their beauty,
>   it was because our forefathers were rude. . . .
> These were the simple days. Now Rome is golden,
>   rich with the treasures of the conquered world. . . .
> Men are bewitched by elegance – your coiffure
>   should gain its beauty from incessant care.
> And styles are manifold. Consult your mirror
>   to choose the mode which decorates you best.
> A narrow face demands divided tresses. . . .
> Round faces need a knot above the forehead
>   to bind the hair and yet reveal the ears. . . .

Ovid now proceeds to a detailed discussion of fashions in hairdressing, and of the colours of women's dresses, which he says must suit the tone of their hair. He had much to say also about perfume and make-up; here he adds (iii, 209):–

> Your lover must not find the dressing-table
>   covered with lotions. Art conceals its art.

The poet adds instructions for concealing natural defects
(iii. 263):—

> If you are small, sit down, or you'll appear to,
>   even while you stand! Lie often at full length,
> and then conceal your stature while reclining
>   and cast a covering about your feet.
> A slender girl should dress in solid textures
>   and wear them loosely hanging from her neck.
> A pallid girl should clothe herself in purple. . . .

Even laughter and tears should be learnt and skilfully practised, to add to beauty (iii, 281):—

> Believe me, there are schools and styles of laughter,
>   even by laughter you increase your charm.
> Make your smile middle-sized, with two neat dimples,
>   and let your lower lip conceal its teeth;
> and do not strain your sides with constant laughter,
>   give your laugh lightness, femininity.
> One woman wrings her mouth in frightful giggles,
>   another laughs so that she seems to weep;
> another gives a horrid raucous braying,
>   like filthy donkeys grinding at the mill.
> Art is the queen of all! Even in weeping
>   there is an art, of manner, place, and time.

Walking is an important skill, and must be acquired by
beautiful women (iii, 209):—

> Never despise the art of graceful walking —
>   your walk can make a stranger fall in love.
> One girl moves delicately, catching the breezes
>   in flowing garments, stepping sure and proud.
> Another struts it like a blowsy farmer
>   And boldly straddles all across the way.
> Have moderation, moderation, always!
>   One is too rustic, one is too refined.

Ovid attaches great importance to refinement and culture both in men and in women. No doubt he remembers
that some of the *hetairai* in Greece were witty and well
educated, and hopes that similar refinement may be introduced into Italy. He gives this advice to men (ii, 112):—

> Add to your grace of body, gifts of wit.
> Beauty is frail, and with the passing seasons
>   it fades, its very life brings it to death. . . .
> Take earnest care to decorate your spirit
>   with wit and learning: speak both languages.

And this to women (iii, 329):—

T—I

Callimachus, you'll learn, and the Coan poet,
and the drunken songs of old Anacreon,
and Sappho too – most wanton of all singers –
and all the comic tricks of master and slave.
You should have read the songs of sweet Propertius,
and Gallus and Tibullus have their place;
with Varro's tale of Phryxus and his sister
their sorrow, and the wondrous golden fleece;
and exiled Aeneas, Rome's first beginnings,
the grandest poem of the Latin tongue.

Finally, he counsels every girl to master singing, dancing,
and other arts of amusement. But arguments, anger, and
bitter feeling should never enter into social life, nor into the
relation of lover and mistress (ii, 155):–

Quarrels for wives! they bring them as a dowry.
A mistress should be pleased and entertained.
For no necessity has made you bed-fellows;
you came together by the law of love.
So bring her flatteries and charming whispers,
soft words to make her happy when you meet.

Deception is always fair in love (i, 611):–

But you must act the lover, tell your passion,
use any artifice to be believed—
for every woman thinks she deserves a lover:
however hideous, she loves herself.
Yet often a pretender stops pretending,
and comes to feel the love he had assumed. . . .
Dupe your deceivers – they are mostly perjured,
and you can hoist them with their own petard.

When the lover reaches the critical point, he must abandon
shame (i, 663):–

A skilful lover blends his words with kisses –
and you must take them, if she will not give.
Perhaps she'll fight at first, and call it outrage:
for all her fighting, still she hopes to lose.
Only beware – you must not kiss her roughly
or make her weep at your brutality.
And after kisses, if you go no further,
you are unworthy even of a kiss.
Surely a kiss is near the last fulfilment!
To stop would be, not virtuous, but dull.
Although they call it force, they love the forcing,
they love to be compelled to give themselves.
If Venus takes a girl by storm, she loves it,
and takes outrage as gladly as a gift.
But if a girl escapes an ardent lover,
she may look happy, but she will be sad.

Elsewhere Ovid says 'Love hates the lazy', and he often
compares a love-affair to military service (e.g. *A.A.*, ii,
233).

He cares little for fidelity. If a woman is unfaithful, the
man is often to blame (ii, 367):–

> You give her time and place to be unfaithful –
>   surely your faithless wife took your advice!
> What can she do? A charming guest, no husband,
>   and all the terrors of a lonely bed!
> The husband is at fault, the wife is blameless,
>   she found a man convenient and polite.

The poet, then, would excuse a woman for adultery, if she
was – as so many are – a 'neglected wife'. And this is his
view of male morality (ii, 387):–

> I would not have you fettered to one lady –
>   Impossible – even to a bride!

But the other affairs should be conducted with some
subtlety, in case they are detected by the jealous wife (ii,
391):–

> Give all your gifts without her rival's knowledge.
>   Vary the times of your adultery;
> vary the places where you meet your mistress
>   in case a rival knows her secret too.
> And when you write, read over the whole letter –
>   for many women have a roving eye. . . .
> If any secret acts should be discovered,
>   deny them black, though they are clear as day.
> Neither be meek nor warmer than your custom;
>   meekness and warmth are often signs of guilt.
> Embrace her to make peace, and spare no efforts;
>   deny all other loves in her embrace.

In general a man can always reconcile a woman by making
love to her, however bitter their disputes have been (ii,
461):–

> When war's declared and bitter battle rages,
>   then an embrace will be an armistice.

A lover should pay little attention to rivals for the favour
of his mistress. In this connection, Ovid relates in detail
the well-known story of Venus' adultery with Mars (ii, 561).
The lesson he wishes to drive home is that it is quite useless
for a husband to spy on a faithless wife.

On the contrary – after Venus and Mars were discovered, they carried on their affair more openly than before:–

> they did more freely.
> what they had once concealed while shame survived.

Finally, at the end of the second and third books, the poet gives some profound advice on the technique of the sexual act and all its preliminaries. These verses have made the work of Ovid notorious ever since. According to modern standards, they are unsuitable for a poem, and would belong more properly to a textbook of sexual knowledge. Their reproduction in this book is, of course, out of the question. Only one passage may be mentioned: ii, 683 sq., in which Ovid deals with homosexuality. It is 'less attractive' to him, because in it sexual enjoyment is not mutual but one-sided. The remark shows the calm and non-moral attitude to homosexuality which was possessed by the Roman poets.

In this book we can only give short extracts from Ovid's *Art of Love*. But from them the reader can draw a fair conclusion as to the effect which the work must have had in its time, when the old strict morality was relaxing and Augustus was making well-meaning but practically ineffective attempts at reform. Ovid sometimes makes a weak attempt at excusing himself, by asserting that he has written the book only for those who have, or contemplate, liaisons with light ladies. For the book had an immediate popularity, and most certainly did not help to make Augustus' marriage reforms any more attractive to the Romans.

Ovid evidently found quite soon that people were not in general agreement about his *Art of Love*. In *Remedies for Love*, his next work – an unpleasant book, sometimes quite vulgar and ridiculous – he says (361) that:–

> Critics have lately pilloried my writings,
> because they held my Muse for wanton and gay.

He now pretends that such criticism, which he alleges to be 'carping', does not affect him in the least, but on the contrary only adds to his pride. But fundamentally it seems as if he wrote *Remedies for Love* (in Ribbeck's words) from a certain feeling of 'uneasiness, a stricken conscience'. The tone of the poem is purely frivolous, at times farcical and disgusting. The poet encourages the lover quite seriously to invent physical blemishes in his mistress; or to weaken his sexual powers by intercourse with other women, so as to become impotent with his own mistress; or to have intercourse with her so often that eventually he is nauseated . . . and so on, in the same filthy way. We do not care to continue our examination of such an ugly example of Ovid's work: its details are more akin to sexual physiology than to poetry.

The loveliest composition of this versatile poet – a work which is even today still read and known throughout the world – is the *Metamorphoses*, or *Transformations*. We mention them here because they introduce stories at least partly erotic, taken from the Greek legends of gods and heroes. Ovid here shows his powers of rapid and convincing narrative, vivid description, and almost naturalistic accuracy in the depiction of every conceivable character and situation from the idealistic point of view. It is not our task to analyse this immense work in detail but to show by a few examples how successful the poet has been in writing what are, in effect, erotic tales in verse.

Out of the abundant store in the *Metamorphoses*, we shall choose one or two which are not to be found in any of our school-editions. (Editors of school books even today believe that they must, from 'moral' considerations, avoid any suggestions of eroticism.) There is, for example, the charming tale – so often represented in painting and sculpture – of Apollo's love for the disdainful Daphne and his vain wooing (*Met.*, i, 463 sq.):–

> To him Cupid replied 'Phoebus, your shafts
> transfix all else, but mine wound you yourself.
> All living things yield to your godhead, you
> to me!' He spoke, and leapt on rosy pinions
> up to Parnassus' dark and holy peak:
> there from his deadly quiver chose two arrows,
> one shaft could bring, the other banish, love –
> the first was sharp with a bright golden barb,
> the other leaden-shafted, blunt, and cold.
> The leaden shaft sped to the heart of Daphne,
> the other pierced Apollo's inmost heart.
> Straightway the god was lover, and she fled –
> loving the hidden places of the woods,
> and the spoils of captured beasts – a virgin huntress.

Bound with one ribbon, lightly flew her hair.
Shunning her many lovers, hating men,
she wandered lonely through the pathless forest,
careless and ignorant of love and marriage.
Her father often said 'Daughter, you owe
a husband to yourself, grandsons to me'.
She shunned the marriage-torches like a crime,
with lovely blush of kindling modesty,
and, clinging to her father with soft arms,
said 'Grant me what Diana once obtained,
my dearest sire – a life of maidenhood'.
He granted it: her loveliness refused it,
for Phoebus loved her, craved to be her husband,
and hoped – for his own oracles deceived him.
As fiercely as the straw after a threshing
blazes up, or the hedge a traveller kindles,
leaving his torch beneath it at sunrise –
so the god's heart vanished away in fire,
blazing with love and fed with barren hope.
He saw her hair dangling carelessly down
and cried 'Ah, were it combed and dressed!' Her eyes
burning like stars, he saw; he saw her lips –
to see them was too little. Hands and fingers,
arms and her naked legs he saw and praised;
and more admired what was unseen. She fled
quicker than rapid breezes, never halting
even when he cried 'Stop, nymph! No enemy
pursues you here! stay, nymph! Lambs flee from wolves,
hinds from lions, the trembling doves from eagles,
fleeing their enemies: I am your lover.
Ah stop, in case you stumble! or the briars
mangle your lovely legs, and I be blamed.
These are rough deserts where you run so headlong!
Ah, flee more gently, I'll pursue more gently.
Ask your adorer's name! I am no shepherd
or mountaineer or shaggy countryman.
Know your pursuer, rash and headlong nymph,
then you will stay. Mine is the Delphic land,
Claros, and Tenedos, and Patara.
My father, Jupiter. I know what was,
what is, and will be. I give songs their music.
Sure is my arrow, surer than all others,
save one, which pierced me in my careless heart.
All medicines and drugs are of my finding,
I rule all herbs, and have the name of Saviour.
Alas, no herbs can remedy my love!
I that save others cannot save myself.'
Still he endeavoured to speak, but the quick nymph
fled from him and his disappointed pleading.
Beautiful even then – she was stripped by the wind,
her dress whirled out and beating in the breezes

which drove her hair up in a fan behind:
her beauty grew as she ran. The ardent god
grew angry when his flatteries were left;
love spurred him, and he followed her eagerly.
As when a greyhound sees in an empty field
a hare – it runs for its life, the dog for blood –
and every moment the dog closes and snaps,
flying behind the hare with outstretched muzzle,
the hare in doubt whether the jaws have gripped
or whether it escapes from the eager mouth –
so the nymph fled in terror, the god in hope
pursued, and still pursued, quickened by love,
giving the nymph no rest, clutching her back
as she fled, and breathing on her flying hair.
Exhausted, she grey pale, and was fordone
by the hot chase. She cried to Peneus stream
'Father, bring help, if you are god of the river:
and change this beauty which has ruined me!'
At once a languor swam throughout her limbs.
A film of bark covered her tender breast,
her hair grew into leaves, her arms to branches,
her rapid feet sank into slow roots,
the treetop was her face, whose beauty remained.
But still the god adored her: under his hand
he felt her bosom quiver beneath the bark,
and threw his arms around the branchy limbs,
kissing the tree – the tree shrank back from him.
He cried 'Daphne, you cannot be my spouse,
but you shall be my tree. My hair, my quiver,
my lyre shall always wear your garlands, Laurel.
Attend the Latin leaders, when the triumph
shouts through the streets or mounts the Capitol.
Faithfully guard the portals of Augustus
before his hall, and there support the oak.
And as my youthful head is never shorn,
so always wear the beauties of your leaves'.
Thus the god ended, and the new-made laurel
nodded its branches and its leafy head.

The impression we get from this tale is that the poet had
two aims in view: rapid and high-sounding rhetoric, and –
as in the *Art of Love* – the vivid description of womanly
beauty.

An interesting contrast to it is provided by the tale of
Vertumnus, the god whose appearance changed at his will,
and his courtship of the gardener-nymph Pomona (xiv, 623
sq.) : –

In Procas' time there was a nymph, Pomona,
a Latin tree-nymph, careful of her garden,

> and zealous for the growth and fruit of orchards
> (whence comes her name). She loved not woods nor rivers,
> but country scenes and branches low with fruit.
> No javelin filled her hand, but a hooked knife
> to clip the wantonness of wandering branches,
> or else to cleave the bark, setting a graft
> into the tree, to drink its alien sap.
> She would not let them thirst, but would divert
> the flowing rivulets to the thirsty roots.
> This was her only passion: love she shunned;
> fearing a rustic ravisher, she fenced
> her orchard and refused to see man's face.
> What would the leaping youthful satyrs do,
> and the horned Pans, begarlanded with pine,
> and old Silenus, younger than his years,
> and he whose scythe and loins both scare marauders,
> to grip Pomona? But Vertumnus loved her
> far more than they, and as unhappily.
> How many times he was a harvester,
> uncouth and rough, bearing a basket of grain!
> Often he bound his temples with fresh straw
> to seem a labourer fresh from tossing hay.
> Often he carried goads in his knotted hand –
> a carter who had just unyoked his team.
> A hook gave him the semblance of a pruner;
> a ladder made him seem an orchard-hand;
> a sword made him a soldier, and a rod
> an angler. All these semblances he found
> to gain admittance and enjoy his love.

Finally he transforms himself into an old woman who gives Pomona the fruits of her experience in the form of a spirited piece of rhetoric on the advantages of marriage over spinsterhood. Thus:–

> You flee from all your suitors and disdain them –
> a thousand men, and demigods, and gods,
> and all the deities of Alba's hills.
> If you are wise, and wish a noble marriage,
> listen to me who love you more than others
> (more than you think) – abandon common suitors
> and choose VERTUMNUS for your bedfellow.
> I pledge you him: I know him as he knows
> himself. He is no wanderer of the world –
> his home is here; he loves not, like your suitors,
> a newfound beauty; he will love you always,
> his first and last love, passion of his life.

But neither this impressive speech nor a myth told by the masquerading god has any effect on Pomona. He then appears in his real form, as a youth radiant with divinity:–

> As when the gleaming image of the sun
> conquers obstructing clouds and blazes clear –
> his power was ready, but his beauty won her,
> and she gave way, burning with his own passion.

The selections we have given are admirable examples of Roman rhetoric. But the next scene is like a passage from the Old Comedy: Juno the jealous wife and Jupiter amorous of Io. The god has seen the lovely girl and detained her by casting a darkness round the spot where he intends to possess her. Juno, for ever jealous, happens to glance at that part of the earth, and notices the unnatural darkness:–

> She gazed eagerly round after her spouse,
> as long experienced in his deceits.
> She saw him not in heaven: 'I am wrong,
> if I am not betrayed,' she cried, and sank
> to earth from the skies, and shook the clouds apart.
> Jove had perceived her coming, and had changed
> the lovely Io to a glossy heifer.

Another example. Mercury, in love with Herse, is about to visit his beloved, but first makes a neat toilet, like a young Roman gentleman (ii, 731):–

> He knows his beauty, and will not disguise it,
> but heightens it with seemly care and thought.
> He smooths his locks, and sets his cloak to rights
> to hang gracefully, showing its golden fringe,
> and polishes the divine sleepbringing wand,
> and settles on his feet the winged sandals.

The *Metamorphoses* also contain the curious and interesting story of the creation of the bisexual creature Hermaphrodite, from the union of the lovelorn nymph Salmacis with an innocent boy. We shall render this tale in prose, for it deserves a word-for-word translation. This is the story (iv. 288 ff.):–

'The Naiads brought up in the caves of Mount Ida a boy, born of Mercury and the divine Cytherea. It was easy to trace his mother and father in his appearance. Even his name was derived from both of them – Hermaphroditus, from Hermes and Aphrodite. When he was fifteen years old he deserted his fostering Mount Ida, left his ancestral hills, and wandered happily through unknown regions, seeing unknown streams; his eagerness lessened his fatigue. So he arrived at the cities of Lycia and their neighbours the

Carians. There he saw a pond whose water was clear and
transparent to the very bottom. In it were no bog-reeds, or
barren sedges, or sharp bulrushes: the water was crystal
clear. The borders of the pond were girt with living turf
and evergreen plants. It was the home of a Nymph. She
neither hunted, nor shot arrows, nor practised races. She
alone of all the Naiads was unknown to swift Diana. Her
sisters often said to her "Salmacis, take a javelin or a
painted quiver, and enliven your idle hours by hunting wild
beasts". But she neither took the javelin nor the painted
quiver nor spent her idle hours in sport. She bathed her
lovely body in the spring, and combed her hair, and asked
the waters what made her beautiful. Then, her body covered
with a transparent robe, she rested on soft leaves or in tender grass. Often she pulled flowers: this she was doing when
she first saw the boy and desired him.

'But she did not approach him, although she craved to,
until she had made herself beautiful, examined her dress,
adopted the right expression, and justified being called
beautiful. Then she began with these words: "You are
worthy, boy, of being thought some god. If you are a god,
then you could be Cupid. If you are only a mortal, then
blessed are your father and mother, and happy your brother, happy your sister (if you have a sister), and happy the
nurse who suckled you. But happiest of all is your bride, if
you are betrothed, if you think anyone worthy of marriage.
If you have a bride, then let me have your love in secret. If
you have none, then let me be the woman to enter your
marriage-bed." With these words the Naiad ended. The
youth blushed: he knew nothing of love. But even the blush
made him beautiful. ... The nymph besought him again
and again for at least a sister's kisses: she threw her arms
around his white neck. At that he cried: "Stop, or I flee and
leave both this land and you." Fear seized the nymph:
"You may possess this land freely, stranger." And she
turned away and looked as though she were departing. But
she hid behind some bushes, casting many glances backwards, and kneeled down there. As soon as he thought he
was alone, he ran boyishly here and there, and dipped his
foot ankle-depth in the laughing water. Soon, attracted by
the water's gentle warmth, he stripped his soft robe from

his lovely body. The nymph was amazed, and her passion quickened at the sight of his naked beauty. Her eyes burned like the image of the sun reflected from clear crystal. She was mad, and could scarcely control herself, could scarcely restrain her desire. She craved to embrace him then. But he, striking his body with his hollow palms, dived into the stream, and spreading his arms swam in the crystal water. It was as if ivory figures or white lilies were seen through gleaming glass. At that the nymph cried "I win! he is mine!" She threw off all her clothes, dived into the spring, caught the struggling boy, and stole his kisses. She touched him with her hand, caressed his breast – he bore it all unwillingly – and embraced him in every way. At last she encircled the lovely boy as he sought to escape – so a snake twists round an eagle which has caught it, so the ivy twines itself round a high tree trunk, and so the octopus holds fast an enemy with his many arms beneath the sea.

'Hermaphroditus resisted: he denied the nymph the joy she desired. But she would not let him go. Her entire body surrendered to him, she clung fast, and said: "Wicked boy, you may defend yourself, but you do not escape me. Command, O gods, that he may never be parted from me, nor I from him!" The gods fulfilled her wish. The two bodies merged into one, and one single form was left. Just as twigs are seen to grow into one when they are bound with the same piece of bark, so it was, as their limbs grew together in their close embrace. They were no longer two people, but one being of two sexes, so that it could be termed neither woman nor boy. It was neither and yet both.

'But when Hermaphrodite perceived that he had become half woman in the stream which he had entered as a man, he stretched out his arms and spoke in his altered voice: "Father and mother, grant your son this request. Whoever bathes in these waters, let him become half-male, let him become suddenly effeminate at their touch." And his parents fulfilled the wish of their two-sexed son, and endowed the spring with the horrible charm.'

None of Ovid's poetry shows his bisexual nature so clearly as this treatment of the Hermaphrodite myth – a myth whose material is naturally much older in origin. Although

Ovid may seem to be primarily susceptible to women, he is not altogether free from homosexual tendencies.

Modern students of sexual psychology and physiology find Narcissus, the lover of himself, an extremely important character. The Narcissus-myth is very old indeed: it is based, too, on a profound knowledge of certain common psychological facts. Just as the myth of Oedipus, who loved his mother and killed his father, is known to arise from a common sexual experience (modern psycho-analysis has sufficiently proved its origin), so the myth of Narcissus signifies 'the outward projection of the Ego, which is then chosen as the object of sexual desire' (Kaplan, *Outlines of Psychoanalysis* (1914), 209).

Ovid has treated the myth very charmingly. We shall quote a few passages to give an outline of the story (iii, 344 ff.).

Narcissus, even in his childhood, had charmed the nymphs with his beauty. A prophet predicted his fate at the beginning of his life. 'The youth,' he said, 'will reach a ripe age if he does not see himself.' In this enigmatic sentence the real nature of what we now call narcissism is clearly and significantly expressed. For the Narcissus-type sees only himself, and so completely that he overlooks all other possible objects for his love. Ovid relates:—

> To fifteen years Narcissus added one,
> and he could seem a boy and youth at once.
> Many the youths who desired him, many maidens,
> and yet such pride was in his tender beauty,
> never a youth attained him, never a maiden.

The Nymph Echo falls in love with him:—

> Now as she saw Narcissus wandering
> in the wild places, she loved and followed him
> secretly, burning more the more she followed . . .
> Often and often she would fain approach him
> with courtship and soft prayers. Nature forbade;
> Echo may not begin. She waited, ready
> to catch his words and answer with her own.
> And once Narcissus, straying from his friends,
> cried: 'Who is there?' and Echo answered 'there'.

After she had teased the boy for a little by repeating all

his words, she at last appeared, so that she might clasp his neck. But

> he fled, and fleeing cried: 'Off, your embraces!
> May I perish before you can possess me!'

The psychiatrist would say: 'This youth has repressed love: he fled – just as the poet here describes – from his first sensations of love.' And the poet now lets the logical sequence of events unfold.

> So he had mocked Echo, and other nymphs
> of mountain and river, so the men who loved him.
> And one he scorned cursed him, praying to heaven:
> 'So may he love, so may he be deluded!'
> To this just prayer Destiny assented.

Ovid proceeds to tell of the fulfilment of the curse of self-love:–

> There was a lucid spring, gleaming like silver,
> which neither shepherds nor the mountain goats
> nor other herds had touched: no savage beast
> nor bird had troubled it, nor falling branch.
> Around, the grass which the springwater fed,
> and woods which kept the place from burning sun.
> Here once, the boy, tired with hunting and heart,
> stretched out to rest, charmed by the lovely spring.
> He strove to quench his thirst, but other thirst
> was born – he was bewitched by his own beauty:
> loving a bodiless dream, and a body's shadow.
> He saw himself with wonder, motionless
> poised, like a statue carved of Parian stone.
> He lay watching his twin, his eyes like stars,
> his hair worthy of bright Apollo's head,
> smooth cheeks and ivory neck and lovely face,
> and all the crimson mingled with the snow.
> He wondered at his wondrous loveliness.
> Now he desired himself and loved his lover,
> and sued his suitor, kindling his own flames.
> How often, fruitlessly, he kissed the water!
> How often, to embrace that neck, he plunged
> his arms in the spring and could not catch himself!

At last he recognizes that he is consumed by love for himself, for a deceitful image – 'he has what he desires'. He wishes now 'to leave his own body':–

> A strange love-wish! I wish that my beloved
> would leave me! All my strength faints with anguish,
> my life is waning in its early years,
> Death is not cruel, if death ends my sorrow.

And so he dies

> as yellow wax dissolves
> before a little flame, or morning frosts
> under the glowing sun, so wasted by his love
> he faded slowly, gnawed by secret fires.

From his body grows 'a saffron-yellow flower, girt round with white leaves' – the narcissus.

Odi's penetrating knowledge of the heart of a woman in love is shown by the monologue which he gives to Medea (vii, 12):–

> Now, it is this,
> or somewhat like it, which is called – to love.
> Why should my father's orders seem too hard?
> And yet they are. Why should I fear for his life
> whom I have left a moment since, alive;
> Strike out these flames of love from your maiden breast,
> unhappy woman, if you can. I see
> the better course, approve it, follow the worse.
> Princess, why love a stranger? will you marry
> a man from another world? Yet your own country
> could give you lovers. Let him live, or die –
> the gods decide. But – let him live. That prayer
> need not be love. What crime has he committed?
> What kind heart is not moved by Jason's youth,
> nobility, and valour? by his beauty? –
> to leave his other merits. My own heart is moved. . . .
> I must not pray,
> but act. Am I to sell my father's kingdom,
> to save an unknown foreigner from death,
> who'll cast his sails in safety to the winds,
> and love another, while Medea suffers?
> If he could dare to leave me for another,
> death to the ingrate! Yet his face is loyal,
> his noble nature and his wondrous beauty
> forbid my fear of thanklessness and fraud.
> And he will pledge himself : as witnesses
> to our agreement I shall call the gods.
> All's safe – why fear it? On, without delay.
> Jason will always owe himself to you,
> and join you soon in holy marriage; then, in Greece,
> the mothers of the state will call you Saviour.

At last Medea banishes her doubts by thinking of her love for Jason – Jason whom she sees with the eyes of a lover. As Ovid says, within her heart 'justice, filial love, and modesty' were at war with her love. Although it seemed as

if these higher impulses would defeat love, yet it conquered
it at last:—

> At sight of him, the dying flames revived –
>   her cheeks blushed crimson and her face glowed hot.
> As when a little spark, smothered by ashes,
> takes food and energy from a passing breeze,
> starts up, and rises to its former might,
> so now Medea's languid waning love,
> blazed up again, fanned by your Jason's beauty.
> And he was handsomer than he was wont,
>   that day – too handsome to condemn his lover.

The story of Medea, which had already been wonderfully
dramatized by Euripides, was worked out by Ovid in a
tragedy which has unfortunately not survived. It is regret-
table that he made no further attempts at dramatic treatment of the psychology of a woman's inmost heart, for he
would have accomplished something memorable and important. However, the *Metamorphoses* contain many monologues which show women in dramatic parts.

Similarly, Ovid's *Heroides* are attempts – in dramatic or
rhetorical forms – to depict the souls of women in love.
They contain, for instance, letters to Aeneas from his deser-
ted mistress Dido, to Hippolytus from Phaedra, and to
Jason from Medea. These imaginary letters say less for
Ovid's originality than for his careful study of Greek and
Roman models such as Sophocles, Euripides, and Vergil.
They look like preliminary sketches for plays which were
never written. One example may be enough.

The tragedy of Phaedra, in love with her chaste and cold
stepson Hippolytus, is famous for its treatment by Euripides and Racine. Ovid represents her as writing to him in
these words (*Her.*, iv, 7 sq.):—

> Thrice striving to speak, my tongue, helpless,
>   stopped, and thrice the words died in my throat.
> Ah, when it can, shame should be joined to passion!
>   Now passion writes what shame forbore to speak.
> When passion orders, who is disobedient?
>   Passion is king, and rules even the gods.
> Passion commanded, as I hesitated,
>   'Write! and that iron man will melt at last.'
> The god of love kindled slow fires within me –
>   now may he pierce you with a sudden shaft.
> It is not wantonness that breaks my wedlock:
>   ask, you will find no scandal round my name.

Love, coming late, is stronger: now in secret
  he burns my heart, a gnawing hidden wound.
As the first yoke injures an ox's shoulders,
  as the unbroken horse detests the bit,
my unaccustomed heart hates its new burden
  and all my soul rebels at difficult love.
Love is an easy fault to learn in childhood,
  but for a late beginner it is hard.
So you shall have the firstfruits of my honour,
  and we shall share the joys of our first sin.

She comforts herself with the thought that all her race is
doomed to strange loves:–

Perhaps love is a debt which I inherit,
  and Venus takes a tribute from my race.
My family comes from Jove and fair Europa
  for whom he took the semblance of a bull.
And Pasiphae deceived a bull – my mother
  who travailed with her own iniquity.

The instant that Phaedra saw Hippolytus, she was overwhelmed with love for him:–

Then, then (and yet before) I found I loved you:
  passion struck deep into my deepest soul.
Your robe was white, your hair flower-garlanded,
  a modest blush tinted your sun-tanned face:
that face, which others called severe and savage,
  was not severe – for Phaedra it was brave.
Away, away, these youths who prink like women:
  moderate elegance becomes a man.
Severity, and hair dressed without fashion,
  and the dust of exercise became you well.
Ah, when you bend the neck of your ardent stallion,
  I love your skilful riding in the ring;
or when you hurl the spear with valiant muscles,
  your valour and your strength attract my gaze;
or when you hold the javelin iron-headed –
  anything that you do delights my eyes.
Only leave your hardness in the forest:
  let me not perish by your spear and strength.
Why practise all the arts of bold Diana
  and rob kind Venus of her bounden dues?

Phaedra adds the argument that her husband Theseus cares
little for her:–

Theseus is absent – long and timely absence!
  He lingers in Perithous' domain.
Theseus prefers – 'tis truth, though we deny it –
  Perithous to Phaedra and to you. . . .

Can you respect the bed of such a father?
    the bed he spurns himself, by his own acts?
Let not the love of stepson and stepmother
    affright you by parade of empty names.
Such honourable strictness, soon to perish,
    was dull even in Saturn's golden age.
But Jove made every pleasure honourable
    and by his incest justified all loves.
The bond of kinship fastens us more firmly
    if Venus rivets it with her own strength.
And yet her bonds are light, and may be secret:
    the name of kinship hides our common guilt.
Whoever sees our kisses will commend us,
    will call us kind stepmother, true stepson.
You need not brave closed doors and angry husbands,
    nor dupe a wary guardian in the dark.
One house has sheltered us, and still shall hold us:
    you kissed me openly, then kiss me still.
My arms are safe for you, your guilt is honour,
    even if you are discovered in my bed.
Banish delays, and hasten to our union,
    so may love spare you as he tortures me!
I do not scorn to supplicate you humbly –
    alas for humbled pride and haughtiness!
Yet I resolved to fight, not to surrender
    to guilt – can anything in love be sure?
Now I am conquered: hear my supplications!
    I am a queen, but lovers have no shame.
Modesty is undone, the battle's ended;
    forgive the truth, and tame your stubborn heart!

These quotations are only a part of Phaedra's long letter;
but they may be enough to show the tone of these experi-
ments. The women's writings reveal their character very
subtly and clearly; yet they are not heroines of Greek tragedy, but prostitutes of Augustan Rome. Many of their
remarks remind us of the *Art of Love*.

We shall close our brief survey of Ovid with a passage
from the *Metamorphoses*, which displays all Ovid's characteristic qualities – a light and piquant charm, as well as a
bright and glowing rhetoric. It is the story of Pygmalion
(*Met*., x, 244 sq.):–

Pygmalion loathed the vices given by nature
to women's hearts: he lived a lonely life,
shunning the thought of marriage and a spouse.
Meanwhile he carved the snow-white ivory
with happy skill: he gave it beauty greater
than any woman's: then grew amorous of it.

It was a maiden's figure – and it lived
(you thought) but dared not move for modesty.
So much did art conceal itself. The sculptor
marvelled, and loved his beautiful pretence.
Often he touched the body, wondering
if it were ivory or flesh – he would not
affirm it ivory. He gave it kisses,
thinking they were returned; and he embraced it,
feeling its body yield under his fingers,
fearing the limbs he pressed would show a bruise.
Sometimes he courted it with flatteries
and charming gifts – shells and rounded stones,
and little birds, and many-coloured flowers,
lilies, and painted balls, and amber tears
dropped from the trees: he clad it with fine clothes,
rings on its fingers, chains about its neck,
light pearls for earrings, pendants on its bosom.
All made it lovely; it was lovely naked.
He laid the statue on a purple couch,
calling it partner of his bed, laying its neck
on feather pillows, just as though it felt.

The festival of Venus crowded Cyprus;
and with broad horns gilded to do her honour,
the snowy heifers fell for sacrifice,
and incense fumed her altars. Then Pygmalion
did sacrifice, and prayed 'If the gods can give
whatever they may wish, grant me a wife'
(not venturing 'my ivory girl') 'like her'.
The golden goddess in her seat of power
knew what the prayer meant, and showed her favour:
her altar fire blased thrice, shooting aloft.

When he returned, he sought his ivory image,
lay on its couch and kissed it. It grew warm.
He kissed again, and touched the ivory breast.
The ivory softened, and its carven firmness
sank where he pressed it, yielded like the wax
which in the sunlight takes a thousand shapes
from moulding fingers, while use makes it useful.
Pygmalion was aghast, and feared his joy,
but like a lover touched his love again.
It was a body, beating pulse and heart.
Now he believed, and in an ardent prayer
gave thanks to Venus: pressed his mouth at last
to a living mouth. The maiden felt his kiss –
She blushed and trembled : when she raised her eyes
she saw her lover and heaven's light together.

Surely this myth provides clear proof that in ancient times love was thought of primarily as the enjoyment of a beautiful body.

Was it not a peculiar irony of fate that Ovid the love-poet should arouse the emperor's displeasure by his love-poems? Augustus' indignation was chiefly caused by *The Art of Love*, as well as by a certain incident of which we know no more than that it had serious effects for Ovid. He was compelled, in the prime of life, to retire from the pleasures of the capital to an exile on the Black Sea – in the inhospitable lands at the mouth of the Danube, where there was a small military colony, planted to protect the frontiers against the constant threat of invasion by the Sarmatians. We shall later discuss Ovid's banishment more carefully in connection with the history of Augustus' daughter Julia; for it is now believed that Ovid's fate was linked with hers. He died in Tomi, on the Black Sea, after ten years of this painful banishment. None of the many plaintive letters he wrote to his wife and his friends and the Emperor had any effect whatever. So ended the life of a richly gifted but dissolute man. His character and his end might be compared with those of Oscar Wilde: for both poets might have created still greater things had it not been for those unfortunate sexual tendencies which brought them to an early doom.

Our account of Augustan poetry would be incomplete if it did not include a mention of a collection of little poems known as the Priapeia. In our chapter dealing with religious and sexual life, we have described in some detail the nature and function of the god or spirit Priapus (p. 127). Men with a taste for improper wit sometimes visited the shrines or obscene statues of this lewd deity; and there, inspired by his statue, they versified (generally in the manner of Catullus) a series of equally obscene jokes. These verses were scratched up on the walls of these shrines, or even on the statue itself – just as nowadays similar but less witty inscriptions are scratched on walls in retired spots. A collection of the best of these poems was made and preserved until 1469, when it was printed for the first time as an appendix to a Roman edition of Vergil. This singular collection is an important document for the study of sexual life

under Augustus. However, we can give no examples of it
in our present volume. We may suggest its nature by re-
cording that the contents of these neatly turned verses:
they generally describe how the god with his gigantic phallus punished garden thieves in some gross way. Nowadays
it is generally assumed that such distinguished poets as
Tibullus, Ovid, Petronius, perhaps even Catullus, were
among the authors of these lewd jests. It is quite possible.
Even Goethe sometimes wrote very coarse verses; and the
Romans had less strict views on the artistic treatment of
sexual matters.

We must now make a brief mention of the Roman fabu-
list Phaedrus. He came from Macedonia and lived in Rome
as a freedman of Augustus. Later his life was almost ruined
by the enmity of Sejanus, the powerful favourite of Tiberius. We must refer to him because his fables contain some
interesting erotic material. For example, the woman in
labour who refused to go to bed (i, 18): –

> No one revisits a place if it hurt him.
> A woman once came to the time of her travail
> and lay on the ground making sore lamentation.
> Her husband attempted to get her to bed,
> where the burden of nature would leave her more gently.
> But 'How can I trust that perfidious place'
> she said 'where the seed of the trouble was sown?'

Or the comical anecdote of the two women who loved the
same man (ii, 2):–

> We learn by example this fact about women:
> they rob men who love them and men whom they love.
> A middle-aged woman enchanted a lover
> by hiding her years under smartness and chic;
> meanwhile a beautiful girl had ensnared him.
> Both in their efforts to make themselves like him
> pulled out all his hair, one by one, in their turn.
> He thought that the womanly touch would improve him –
> but instead he grew bald, for the middle-aged lady
> pulled out all the black hairs, the girl all the grey.

Again, there is some penetration in this (iv, 15):–

> Someone once asked how effeminate men
> and masculine women came into the world.
> Old Æsop replied that the Titan Prometheus

made men out of clay (which is broken by fortune):
and, making the portions which modesty hides,
in separate lots for the whole of one day,
in order to fix them to bodies that matched –
he was suddenly asked out to dinner by Bacchus.
Then, flooded with nectar throughout all his veins,
he came home again late, with a stumbling step.
With wits half asleep, in a drunken confusion,
he fitted the males with the feminine parts
and mixed up the masculine members with women.
Hence come perverted desires and delights.

Here is a final example (Appendix i, 27):–

A false-hearted harlot once flattered her lover,
and though he had often been injured before,
still he gave way to her flattering words.
Then the deceiver said, 'Others may tempt me
with presents – I love you far more than them all.'
The lover remembered her frequent deceits
and said, 'How I love to hear these dear avowals!
—not that you're faithful, but still you are charming.'

These examples may be enough to show that Phaedrus, besides the well-known animal fables, could write a graceful and comical erotic tale.

Petronius is called by Paldamus in *Roman Sexual Life* 'the only truly poetic spirit who wrote of love after the time of Augustus'. It is generally believed that Petronius was the man described by Tacitus (*Ann.*, xvi, 18) as follows: 'A little must be said of the past life of C. Petronius. He passed his days in sleep, his nights in the duties and pleasures of life. Others were distinguished for their diligence, but he for his indolence. He was not considered a glutton and spendthrift (like most of those who waste their property), but an aesthete of luxury. His acts and words were willingly accepted as marks of sincerity for their very laxity and carelessness. As pro-consul of Bithynia and later as consul, he showed that he was energetic and capable. Thereafter, he reverted to vice, or the affection of it; and was adopted among Nero's intimate friends, as the authority on taste. For the Emperor, surfeited with pleasure, thought nothing refined and charming unless Petronius had approved it. Therefore Tigellinus hated him as a rival who was more experienced in the 'science of pleasure.' In the end, Nero suspected Petronius of conspiring against him and Petronius, evidently through some sense of guilt, opened his veins. It is alleged that he left Nero an exact account 'of the indecencies of the Emperor, with the names of his accomplices male and female, and the novel details in every act of vice.' Accordingly it is quite possible that this man was the author of the brilliant but amoral novel, which, transmitted to us under the title *Book of Satires*, was so much admired by Nietzsche. Although the work was evidently fairly extensive, only some fragments from the fifteenth and sixteenth Books have been preserved. But these fragments are enough to show us that the *Book of Satires* is a work of real genius.

What is there so brilliant and so memorable in this incomplete novel of Nero's time? Ribbeck describes it as 'a broad and lifelike picture of the manners of the first century, crowded with characters from many classes of society'. It is true that it contains a wonderfully lifelike and detailed study of a Roman parvenu, the rich and gross snob Trimalchio – a character as richly human as Shakespeare's Falstaff or Cervantes' Don Quixote. But this is of less special interest to us than the book's extraordinarily varied picture of Roman sexual life. It shows not the high and noble passion which charms us in the work of Propertius, nor the exquisite refinement of Ovid. It shows rather an unrestrained sexuality which paid no respect to age or sex, but rushed wildly and without disguise into the sexual act – there to exhaust itself with a completeness physically impossible to modern Europeans. It would be as ridiculous to apply moral standards to this impulse as to a storm or a cyclone. We can only watch it and say to ourselves: 'This is how men once lived, these were their pleasures and their satisfactions.' We cannot in this volume discuss all the details of sexual life which are revealed in Petronius, although it would be interesting to develop from it a short essay on sexual knowledge in the Early Empire. We can discuss only the essentials, in so far as they have not been treated in any other chapter.

It seems to me that the most startling feature of the book is the easy and natural way in which Petronius ranks homosexuality beside love of women, as if it were neither different nor inferior. Encolpius, the narrator of the whole story, is himself a homosexual. Originally a condemned criminal, he escapes from the arena (having been sentenced to fight as a gladiator), and, after further crimes, sets out with his friend and confrère, Ascyltus, as a rogue errant. They take with them, for their pleasure, a pretty boy Giton, and love him alternately, jealous of each other's success. Petronius delights to relate their pleasures, and does it in bold, frank prose, which sometimes rises to spirited verse. Besides these three, Trimalchio himself, the most popular character in the novel, is an experienced homosexual. He was the favourite of a rich Roman for many years in his youth; inherited his property when he died; now, living a life of luxury and indulgence, he keeps several beautiful boy favourites as well as his wife. He is not restrained even by her jealousy. We shall quote one of the resulting scenes as a sample of the whole situation (74): '. . . Among the new waiters there was rather a handsome youngster: Trimalchio rushed at him and covered him with kisses. At this, his wife Fortunata wanted to be even with him and to assert her rights: she started to abuse him, calling him filthy scum for not restraining himself. She finished up by calling him a dirty dog. Trimalchio lost his temper and threw a cup in her face. She shrieked out as if she had lost an eye, and held her hands trembling to her face. Scintilla, her friend, was very upset also and threw her arms round Fortunata who was still shaking with sobs. An officious servant held a cold dish against her cheek, and Fortunata leant over it, groaning and weeping. But Trimalchio said 'What! Does that streetwalker not know her place? I took her off the streets and gave her a decent life, but she puffs herself like the frog in the fable! She doesn't know when to stop! She's not a woman, she's a lump of wood. Born in a slum, never dreams of a palace. As sure as I hope for heaven, I'll tame that foul-mouthed shrew!'

He goes on abusing his wife for some time, but is at last quietened. Then he becomes sentimental, begins to cry, and explains meanwhile that he didn't kiss the boy because he was beautiful but because he was a good, kind, honest servant.

Another character who appears in the novel is the poet Eumolpus. At his first appearance, Petronius makes him tell a sort of short story – its theme the seduction of a beautiful youth by his tutor, who eventually finds the boy more of a voluptuary than he is himself. The story is too coarse to be quoted here.

Later in the book, we are brought into one of the public baths of that time. This gives rise to the description of a scene in which a great crowd of bathers gathers around one man – 'Nature had given him such virility that his whole body seemed only to be an appendix to it.' (The possibility of such a scene shows how astonishingly frequent bisexual tendencies must have been.) Finally, the boy Giton attracts lewd stares from all men wherever he goes – as we are told time and again – although he was hardly a boy any longer, having reached the age of eighteen.

Petronius, is however, not exclusively interested in lovely boys. He shows a wide experience of the love of women, and describes it in glowing colours. For instance, Eumolpus relates with great spirit the old story of the widow of Ephesus – a tale which appears in other languages (and in Latin among Phedrus' *Fables*) but never so successfully. We give a version of this delightful tale (111):–

'There lived a lady in Ephesus, whose chastity was so famous that she attracted women from all the neighbouring countries to gaze upon her. When she buried her husband, she was not content with the usual custom of following the hearse with hair dishevelled and beating her naked breast in view of the public. She followed the dead man to the cemetery and began to watch and weep all day and night over the body, which was placed in an underground vault, in the Greek fashion. Neither her parents nor her relatives could dissuade her from tormenting herself in this way and starving herself to death. Finally, the town councillors were rebuffed, and left her, while everyone mourned for her as an exemplary character. She was then passing her fifth day without food. A devoted maid-servant sat beside her in her extremity, wept in sympathy, and refilled the lamp in the tomb whenever it sank. All the gossip of the city was of her – all classes acknowledged that she was the one true example of chastity and love.

'Meanwhile, the governor of the province ordered some robbers to be crucified at a place near the vault, where the lady was weeping over her husband's body. So next night the soldier who was posted to see that no one took a body down from the crosses for burial noticed a light shining among the tombstones and heard groans and lamentations. A natural weakness made him eager to see who it was and what was happening. He went down into the vault. When he saw a beautiful woman, he was dumbfounded, as if it had been a monster or a ghost from hell. He stood still in amazement. Then he saw the dead body lying there and noticed the woman's tears and her face covered with nail-marks. He realized the truth, that she could not bear the loss of her husband.

'So he brought his supper into the vault, and began to encourage the mourner to give up her useless grief, and to stop breaking her heart with vain lamentations: for all men had the same end, and the same resting-place – and all the usual thoughts which restore broken hearts. But the lady disregarded his comforting words. She struck her breast and tore it even more violently and rending her hair threw it on the dead body.

'However the soldier did not go. He continued to console her, and tried to give her some food. At last the maid, tempted by the smell of the wine, gave way. She accepted his well-meant invitations and helped herself. Then refreshed by wine and food, she began to attack her mistress's resolution. "What good will it be to you," she said, "if you perish with hunger? if you bury yourself alive? if you abandon your life prematurely, before Fate's hand is laid on it?

How can the dead feel this beyond the grave?

' "Why not begin life again? Why not abandon this womanish folly, and enjoy life and its blessings while you may? Even the body of your dead husband ought to persuade you to live."

'Everyone is glad to obey when he is urged to take food or keep alive. The woman was parched with several days' fasting. So she allowed her resolutions to be broken and filled herself with food as greedily as the maid, who had been the first to give way.

'Now, you know which temptation usually comes when

you have eaten and drunk well. The soldier had already persuaded the lady to keep her life, and he used the same gentle arguments to persuade her to surrender her virtue. Chaste as she was, she did not find him ugly or backward; and her maid encouraged his suit, saying

"Why fight a welcome love?
Remember to whose kingdom thou hast come!"

'I need not spin out this story. The woman gave way in this also, and the soldier's persuasions were again effective. So they passed that night together, and the next day; and the next day again. Meanwhile, the doors of the vault were closed, so that any friend or stranger who passed it thought that this model of chastity had expired on the body of her husband. The soldier was delighted with her beauty and the secret adventure. He bought every fine thing he could afford, and took it all into the vault as soon as night fell.

'The relatives of one of the crucified thieves saw that the watch was carelessly kept and took down the hanging body and burned it. The soldier's slackness had its result. Next day, when he saw one of the crosses empty, he was afraid of his punishment and told the lady what had happened. He said he would not wait for court martial, but punish his slackness with his own sword; and he asked her to give him a place to die in that tomb where her lover was to lie dead with her husband.

'But the lady was as kind as she was chaste. She said "God forbid that I should see the two men I have loved most both dead at once. I would rather hang up a dead man than kill a living one." Accordingly, she instructed him to take her dead husband's body out of its coffin, and hang it on the empty cross. The soldier followed this prudent suggestion, and next day the people wondered how the dead man had got on to the cross.'

This story postulates very realistic views of woman's nature. It is supplemented by a passage in which Petronius expatiates on women's sexual tastes (126). 'Some women are kindled to love by the dirt. Their passion is never roused unless they see a slave or groom in short garments. Others burn for a man from the arena, a mule-driver thick with dust, or an actor from the filthy exhibitions of the stage.'

We should read in connection with this, for explanation, Schopenhauer's famous chapter on the metaphysics of sexual love. In the same passage, Petronius gives an enchanting picture of a beautiful woman in these words: 'The woman was more perfect than any statue in the world. No words could express all her beauty, and anything I say will be too little. Her hair, curling of itself, poured over her shoulders, her forehead was small with the roots of her hair turning back from it. Her brows ran into the line of her cheek, and they almost met beside the borders of her eyes – her eyes which shone brighter than stars in the moonless sky. Her nostrils curved delicately, and she had lips like those which Praxiteles gave to Diana. And her chin! And her neck! And her hands! And her snowy feet within the slender gold sandal strap! They would dull the radiance of Parian marble.'

This is followed by passages which remind us of a modern operetta; the leading characters suddenly break into verse. For example, 'Circe' (the girl whose loveliness has just been described) 'clasped me in arms softer than down, and drew me on to the flower-strewn grass.

> Such flowers as blossomed on the peak of Ida
> at Jupiter's command, when willing love
> joined him to Juno in a flame of passion –
> roses and violets, tender galingale
> and snowy lilies laughed on the green bank –
> such was our flowery carpet, breathing Venus,
> and the day brightened on our secret love.

On this couch of flowers, we exchanged a thousand sweet kisses; then, seeking stronger pleasure . . .'

At a later point in this ardent love-scene, Petronius shows the fulfilment of the curse of Priapus (the sexual deity whom Encolpius had offended at some previous time). Suddenly the lover loses his powers – in fact, he becomes impotent, which is not surprising from a physiological point of view, after such a sensual life. Impotence is a favourite subject in the erotic literature of all ages – I shall mention only the description of it in Goethe's little epic *The Diary*. Petronius, as we might expect, describes this misfortune and its sequelae in vivid detail; his description contains some interesting information on the treatment of such cases in his

time. The most interesting element in the treatment is perhaps this. As well as eating certain foods and invoking the
help of special deities, the patient is obliged to take a
phallus smeared with oil, pepper, and nettleseed, and to
introduce it into his anus: this treatment is accompanied
by a light thrashing of the lower parts of his body with a
scourge of green nettles. This shows that the connection
between the sexual organs and the anal nerves was already
known. Or, in popular language, they knew of flagellation
for sexual purposes – although it is directly mentioned nowhere else in Roman literature, as far as I know. In the
same connection Petronius depicts a grossly sexual scene
in which three persons are concerned. Unfortunately, there
is a lacuna in the text here, just at those sentences which
would show without dispute whether this scene had any
connection with the revival of Encolpius' potency. It is
at least possible that the introduction of the scene was moti-
vated in that way.

Finally, there is a scene which must strike modern taste
and morality as hideous – a little girl, about seven years of
age, is deflowered by the youth Giton for the amusement
of guests at a party.

The above summary and extracts may be enough to give
the reader a rough idea of the novel. It would be entirely
wrong to conclude that all Petronius' contemporaries were
as grossly lewd as some characters and actions in the
Satiricon. The characters do not belong to the ruling
classes; they are coarse parvenus, freedmen, and slaves. And
we must remember that the author is attempting to give a
satiric picture of such people, in the style of the coarser
modern comic papers. It is therefore impossible to believe
that all his descriptions are true to life. Still, his attitude to
homosexuality is, as we said, surprising; and thus far the
Satiricon is a valuable document for the bisexual tendencies
of Petronius' contemporaries.

So much for the matter of the book. We may glance for
a moment at its style and construction, and ask whether it
is really possible for erotic tales to be aesthetically valid?
It may be said that the *Satiricon* is tolerable enough on the
hypothesis that it is a classical book; but that its frank
descriptions would nowadays be felt to indicate, not art,

but pornography. How did Petronius' own contemporaries regard the work? We do not quite know. In Ribbeck's words (*lib, cit.*, iii, 169): 'We can imagine the success which attended the recitation of these racy stories by Petronius, the distinguished master of good taste. At the shameless court of Nero; the delight which the street-scenes and the wanton servants would inspire in the Emperor himself, who loved to invade the lewd night life of his enormous city; the interests of lords and ladies in the delicate gradations of style, varying with the rank and character of the speaker, and in the idioms, vulgarities and solecisms which were the very voice of reality; and the amusement of the proud Romans at the vain efforts of provincial snobs to imitate them.'

Among the literary works of the Neronian period there are some dramas by Seneca, although it is not certain which Seneca is their author. They are all treatments of Greek subjects; but the style in which these subjects are handled is so interesting that we cannot omit discussing them here.

Almost all the dramas contain erotic themes, but it is not this which concerns us chiefly; rather the fact that their author (whoever he was) misses no opportunity of describing all sorts of horrible cruelties. The audiences which delighted in the bloody sports of the amphitheatre were charmed by the rhetorical treatment of wild passions and savage brutalities. The fundamental contrast between the high and noble feelings of the Periclean Greeks and the baseness of Nero's subjects and courtiers could not be better exemplified than by a comparison between the work of Sophocles and Euripides and the treatment of the same subjects by this Seneca. A few examples will allow the reader to form a picture of the works in question.

We have, for example, a *Medea*. Out of Medea's story Euripides fashioned one of his most subtle and thrilling tragedies. What does Seneca make of it? His treatment is almost identical – but what details he adds! Euripides, as we know, gives us a masterly portrayal of the conflict within a mother's heart. In Seneca, the deserted wife becomes a raging fury, who takes a hideous revenge on her faithless husband: first, she murders one of her children on the stage; then, interrupted in her cruelties, she takes its body and the surviving child into her dragon-chariot; there she murders the survivor, hurls the corpses down upon the moaning husband, and disappears.

The *Phaedra* deals with the same story as Euripides' play *Hippolytus* and degrades it. The nurse speaks like a Stoic rhetorician (195): 'The deity of Love was invented by shameful desire, tending towards vice; adding the title of a feigned godhead to its own madness, to make it more free. Are we to believe that Venus sends her son to wander throughout the world, and that he, flying aloft, launches arrows of wantonness from his tiny hand, and that he, the smallest of the gods, has such an empire? No, these follies are the invention of a mad heart, these, the godhead of Venus and the archer god. Whoever is carried away by prosperity and overflows with luxury always desires strange things. Then he is joined by the dreadful companion of good fortune – lust. He cares no longer for the usual meals, a sane and sensible dwelling, and a cheap cup. Why does this plague come less often to poor homes, and choose luxurious houses instead? Why does a pure love inhabit little houses? Why do the common people keep their emotions healthy and restrain themselves? and why do the rich who rely on power desire more than what is right? ... You see what is the duty of a mighty queen.'

This showy rhetorical argument is set off even more by unpleasant rhetorical description of scenes of horror. Here is part of the messenger's speech, announcing and describing the death of the innocent Hippolytus (1093 sq.): 'Far and wide he covered the fields with blood: his head dashed against the rocks and rebounded; the thorn-bushes tore out his hair; his fair face was ravaged by the hard stones, and all its ill-fated beauty was mangled and perished. His dying limbs were dragged along by the swift wheels. At length, as he whirled over it, a charred tree-trunk pierced his loins and impaled him on its stake. For a moment the chariot halted as its master was pierced and held fast; the team stopped, and then tore apart their hindrance and their master at one time. Then the half dead body was cut to pieces by the bushes – the rough barriers with their pointed thorns and every tree-trunk carried off a part of his body.'

Finally, the torn and bloody limbs of Hippolytus are brought on to the stage, and the leader of the Chorus gives directions for putting them together again.

Ribbeck calls the frightful tragedy of *Thyestes* 'a story after the Roman people's own heart'. With horrible particularity, it describes not only the murder of Thyestes' children but their dismemberment and their arrangement as a meal for their unsuspecting father. It is out of the question to give extracts from this tasteless and repulsive play. Yet it is characteristic of them all. For instance, the *Mad Hercules* kills his children in plain view of the audience. In *Oedipus,* Jocasta, the mother and wife of Oedipus, stabs herself on the stage, while the messenger relates with horrible realism how Oedipus tears his eyes out with his own fingers: as he related in the other play the torture and death-agony of Hercules.

The gloom and horror of these dramas is increased by vivid descriptions both of magical and necromantic ceremonies and of weird and haunted places where spirits dwell. Seneca's characters choose these surroundings to witness their atrocious crimes – for example, Atreus, when he murders Thyestes' children in the haunted valley.

In sum, it is clear that the author of these dramas has purposely used his effects to lash the quivering nerves of his readers or his audiences to a frenzy of excitement, and to give the fullest satisfaction to their desire for violent and thrilling sensations. It is accordingly all the stranger to discover, among these excitements and terrors, long rhetorical set-pieces in the spirit of the Stoa. Still, the plays (however unpleasant) are perhaps a true reflection of the spiritual movements of Nero's time: for according to Tacitus and Suetonius, that age saw both the crass and disgusting sensuality of rich parvenus, and the earnest efforts of noble souls to find a new humanity and a new religion. Stoicism gave these efforts the philosophical support, the rational basis which they needed. The showy and emotional rhetoric, in which Stoic ideas are embodied by the author of these plays, is tasteless and ill-conceived. Yet sometimes profound and noble thoughts appear among the rhetoric, like pearls in a foul-smelling heap of dirt. However, it is beyond the scope of our work to elaborate this point of view.

There is another drama, of a very different kind, which has come down to us under the name of Seneca. It is *Octavia*: and its theme is the unhappy life and death of the princess Octavia who was married to Nero against her will. It is really what is now called a historical play; for although it compresses facts for artistic reasons, the facts are purely historical. Its plot is that of a love-drama: the noble Octavia is in her youth unwillingly married to the cruel Nero and is then divorced in favour of her beautiful servant, Poppaea Sabina; there is a popular rising, but the indignant people are crushed; Octavia herself, who is innocent of any part of the revolt, is nevertheless banished to a lonely island and there done to death. The plot develops quickly, with considerable skill in suspense. But, curiously enough, the poet has neglected great possibilities which lay ready to his hand – for instance, a meeting between the two women, or a confrontation of Nero by his former wife. Besides, Octavia's character is much as Tacitus describes it: she plays the passive part of the pure and suffering woman. Not a dramatic figure: and her whole part is one long complaint against her unhappy fate and Nero's cruelty. A real dramatist could have made a great play out of this material. Striking contrasts are ready for him to use: Nero, the sensual tyrant – Octavia, the pure sufferer, doomed in utter innocence to exile and death – Seneca, the noble philosopher, advising his former ward and pupil on sane moderation and respect for the marriage bond – the attractive and vicious Poppaea, using her beauty to conquer the pitifully weak Nero – the people, rising in just indignation to defend Octavia; and finally, the brutal suppression of the rebellious people, and the despair of Octavia, her renunciation of this world and her prayer to be released by death (Octavia's despair was one of the elements which Schopenhauer thought necessary in a real tragedy). This would have made a magnificent play. However, the poet (whoever he was) made nothing more of it than a dramatic poem for reading, not for performance: all its effects disappear (like the effects in the other dramas of Seneca) in a flood of lyricism or rhetoric. But the *Octavia* has none of the shocking lapses of taste, none of the frightful horrors which deform the other tragedies we have discussed.

We shall now give a few extracts from the *Octavia*. Here is the scene in which Seneca attempts to convert his former pupil Nero (533 sq.):

SENECA: Soon young divinities will throng your palace,
born of the glory of the Claudian house
who shares, like Juno, her own brother's bed.

NERO: Her mother's sins make her race dubitable;
her heart has never linked itself with mine.

SENECA: The loyalties of youth conceal themselves
while modesty muffles the flame of love.

NERO: Such my belief – a long and vain belief –
though the unfriendly heart and face at war
with me revealed how deep her hatred lay.
At length my pain has blazed up into vengeance.
I have a consort whom her rank and beauty
make worthy of my bed: Venus would yield to her,
Venus, and royal Juno, and armed Minerva.

SENECA: Virtue and loyalty and the pure heart –
these things should please a husband: these alone,
the glories of the soul, live to eternity.
The flower of beauty fades from day to day.

NERO: God has united every high perfection
in her: the fates created her for me.

SENECA: Unless you yield lightly, love will leave you.

NERO: Love, whom the lord of lightning cannot rule!
the tyrant of the sky! who enters the sea,
explores the underworld, drags gods from heaven!

SENECA: That love is winged, cruel, and divine
is man's delusion: man gives love his arrows,
his bow, his sacred power, his cruel torch,
his birth from Venus and the craftsman god.
Love is a force of the mind, a warm enchantment
of souls. He springs from youth and luxury
and he is fostered on wealth's ample bosom.
Unless you nourish him and warm him, love
will lose his short-lived power, and sink, and die.

NERO: I say that love is the prime cause of life,
the source of all delight – he is immortal,
for humankind still procreates itself
through love, the kindly god, who tames the beasts
Come, love, and bear the torches at my bridal,
and light Poppaea to my royal bed!

SENECA: That bridal is opposed by enemies –
the people's loyalty, and your own duty.

NERO: Where others find no bar, am I forbidden?

SENECA: The people asks the highest of the highest.

NERO: Then I shall show my strength – this random favour
may break, and leave the people's foolish heart.

SENECA: Rather give way, with calmness, to your people.

NERO: An evil rule, where mobs dictate to rulers!

SENECA: Yet when their prayers are vain, anger is just.
NERO: When prayers fail, are they to turn to violence?
SENECA: Denial is a hard thing.
NERO: Revolt is worse.
SENECA: Then let the prince give way.
NERO: And seem to be conquered?
SENECA: Rumour is foolish.
NERO: Yet it brands a man.
SENECA: It fears the highest men.
NERO: Still, it attacks them.
SENECA: Rumour is easy to crush. Your father's kindness,
        your consort's youth and modesty, must crush it.
NERO: Enough, enough. Your are importunate.
      Must I not act till Seneca approves?
      The people's hopes and prayers wait on me;
      she carries in her womb a sacred pledge –
      so let us mark to-morrow for our bridal!

Another of the scenes in *Octavia* might well have been
extremely effective if it had been skilfully treated. Poppaea
tells her nurse how her sleep had been troubled by evil and
ominous dreams; she is filled with dark forebodings of
approaching evil. Unfortunately, this scene also (like many
others in the drama) is not fully worked out, but only
hinted at. Here is an extract (690):–

NURSE: Why do you hasten trembling from your bed,
       my child? what hiding-place do you seek? Your face
       is terror-stricken and your cheeks are wet.
       The day for which our prayers implored the gods
       has dawned at last: Caesar is in your arms,
       wedded to you, and captured by your beauty,
       bound hand and foot and heart, delivered to you
       by Cupid's mother, the almighty Venus.
       Ah, you were beautiful on that high couch
       in the palace hall! Your loveliness astonished
       the senate, when you burnt the holy incense,
       sprinkling the altar with the sacred wine,
       wearing the delicate marriage-veil of saffron.
       The emperor himself clung to your side,
       proudly receiving the loud joyful prayers
       the people thrust upon him – gay and noble,
       he took you as the hero Peleus took
       Thetis, the nymph who left the foaming sea
       to be a mortal's bride, while ocean's gods
       and the lords of heaven looked on applaudingly.
       What sudden change disfigures now your beauty?
       Why your pale face and tearful eyes? Come, tell me.
POPPAEA: Ah, nurse, I am distracted by a night
         of horrid visions, dreams that shook my mind

and stunned my sense. After that joyful day
died into night, and heaven was clothed with stars,
I sank, folded in Nero's close embrace,
into a gentle slumber – but not long!
For dismal faces thronged my bridal chamber:
with hair dishevelled, weeping piteously,
the Roman matrons came, beating their breasts;
the trumpet shouted terribly; blazing torches
all stained with blood, in Agrippina's hands –
and she glared dreadfully on me, shaking her torch!
Gripped by these fears, I followed stumblingly,
and suddenly the earth before me yawned
in a vast abyss – I whirled into the depths,
and found myself, amazed, on my bridal bed,
sitting exhausted. There approached me then
Crispinus, my dead husband of the past[ii]
and my dead son. Crispinus would embrace me
and sup the kisses which were long denied him –
but Nero rushed trembling into my house
and plunged a sword deep in Crispinus' breast.
At length these terrors struck my sleep away:
an awful trembling shakes me to the soul,
my heart surges, my voice was numbed by fear
until your love and loyalty gave me speech.
What dreadful thing is sent to me by hell?
Why should I see my husband's blood and death?

The Chorus is at one time infuriated by Nero's cruel
tyranny and at another time inspired by the unconquerable
power of love. It sings of love thus (806):–

Why fight a war in vain?
Love's arrows pierce all armour:
love's fire will quench your flames,
the fire which weakens the lightning
and makes Jove prisoner.
Attack him – you will rue it
and pay in blood, for his rage
is terrible and tyrannous.
Love ordered fierce Achilles
to harp at home, deserting
the Greeks: love broke Atrides,
love overturned the kingdom
of Priam, sacked great cities:
and now my heart is pale
for the god's violent purpose!

Let us quote, in conclusion, part of Seneca's opening
monologue. Through this speech we can hear the underlying note of the whole tragedy (377):–

Why flatter me, queen Fortune, with deceitful
smiles and soft acts? why break through my contentment
and thus exalt me? So that this vast height
may show me greater dangers, heavier falls?
I lived a happier life, hidden from envy
among the desert rocks of Corsica.
My soul was free, and busied with itself,
while study and sweet learning held me all.
Ah, what delight to gaze at the mightiest
work made by the great Mother and Creator –
the sky, the holy chariot of the sun,
the motions of the universe, the night
coming in turn with moon and wandering stars,
and the far-shining beauty of the heavens!
If all its beauty ages, and it falls
back into sightless chaos, then doomsday
has come at last, to crush impious man
under the ruins of heaven, and re-create
a better race, bringing a second youth,
a second Golden Age to all the world. . . .
Now vice has gathered in an avalanche
to burst upon us – ah, the heavy time,
when crime is master, blasphemy, outrage,
and filthy lust stalk raving through the earth!
Now spendthrift greed grasps at the mighty treasures
of the whole world, to throw them to the winds!

However imperfect the *Octavia* may be from a technical
point of view, we have thought it worth quoting, because
it is not merely a cento of borrowings from Greek models:
although it has some indebtedness to Greek drama. Its subject makes it unique; and we could wish that some modern
author of genius might avail himself of the same subject to
write a really great tragedy. Later in this book we shall have
to refer to the *Octavia* again for the picture which it gives
of the manners of the Neronian court.

The dramas attributed to Seneca are not alone in their
cultivation of swelling rhetoric and grisly horrors. Rhetoric
and horror were the form and matter of Silver Age poetry;
and they were translated into epic by Seneca's nephew
Lucan, in his grandiose poem of the Civil War, *Pharsalia*.
It contains no charming descriptions of erotic scenes; and
even avoids such situations where an opportunity for them
might have occurred. But Lucan expends all his energy on
depicting the horrors of war with a circumstantial vividness

which at times becomes positively repulsive. Here, for
instance, are some incidents from the naval battles at Mar-
seilles (iii, 635 ff.):—

> A hooked iron hand, snatching the ship,
> pierced Lycidas and would have whipped him down
> into the deep, but comrades clung to him.
> He burst in sunder: the blood, not starting slow
> as from a wound, poured out of every vein
> together, and the various paths of life
> were stopped by water. None of all who died
> lost life by such wide channels. Loins and legs,
> empty of vital organs, rushed to doom;
> but where the lungs and heart remained, beating,
> there death was checked, and, struggling long and sore,
> conquered the trunk at last, and won the man. . . .
>   Then death appeared
> in unexampled shape – the battle-rams
> of two opposing ships transfixed a swimmer.
> At the appalling shock his breast was cloven;
> his ground and shattered limbs could not prevent
> the rams from clashing, and his mangled belly
> rushed through his mouth, vomiting blood and flesh. . . .
> Tyrrhenus, standing high on the lofty prow,
> was struck by Lygdamus, a master slinger:
> the bullet struck and smashed his hollow temples.
> The blood burst every ligament: the eyes
> started out of his head, and he stood blind,
> amazed, thinking this the shadow of death.

Lucan does not confine himself to battle-scenes for the
exercise of his talent for grisly description. At the appearance of the Thessalian witch Erichtho, his imagination
probes deep in crime and terror (vi, 515 ff.):—

>   Her face of blasphemy
> is drawn and ghastly: piled with unkempt hag-locks,
> it is enveloped by the pallor of hell
> and never sees the sun; when rain and black
> storm-clouds conceal the stars, the witch comes forth
> from rifled tombs to catch the meteors.
> The growing seeds shrivel and parch at her tread,
> the wholesome air grows poisonous when she breathes.
> No gods, no helpful deities, no hymns,
> no sacrificial animals, have power
> in her grim rites: flames from the funeral pyre
> burn incense robbed from tombs upon her altars.
> The gods grant every curse at her first prayer,
> in terror lest she chant a second spell.

Souls yet alive, that still control their bodies,
she buries in the tomb: fate owes them life
but death unwilling takes them. Funerals
she leads back from the grave, makes corpses live.
She snatches from the pyre the smoking ashes
and burning bones of youths, the ritual torch
from the parent's hand; she gathers smoky fragments
of the burnt coffin, and the shroud as it wavers
into ash, and the cinders of the corpse.
Or, when stone coffins hold the dead, draining
the secret moisture of corruption, slowly
hardening the corpse, she rages on its limbs,
plunging her hands in its eyes, gnawing the growths
of the withered nails. The deadly hangman's noose
she bites apart, and robs the gibbeted corpse
and strips the cross and ravages the flesh
beaten by rain and the bones cooked by the sun.
The nails driven through the hands, the black decay
dripping from every limb, the distilled poison
she gathers, wrenching and chewing the stubborn muscles.
The corpse that lies exposed on the naked earth
she will not wound, but waits for the ravenous wolves
and snatches the torn flesh from their eager throats.
Her hands shrink not from murder, if she needs
new blood bursting fresh from the open throat.

Enough. It would be easy to add other frightful pictures
to those we have quoted; but in the midst of war, blood,
and murder, Lucan sometimes turns to other subjects. The
second book contains a little incident which is told in a
really charming and idyllic style, though with the deadly
earnestness of the convinced Stoic: it is the return of Marcia
to her first husband Cato, after the death of Hortensius, to
whom Cato had given her (ii, 326 ff.):–

Meanwhile, as chilly night gave way to dawn,
a knocking sounded: leaving her husband's tomb,
there entered Marcia, filled with pious grief.
A nobler husband took her maidenhood,
then, when the rich reward of marriage grew
to a third child, another home received her
to fill it too with offspring, a fertile mother
linking the houses. Now, her husband's ashes
laid in the urn, she came in pitiful stress,
tearing dishevelled locks, beating her bosom
with blow on blow, defiled by funeral ash –
for thus she would please Cato. She addressed him:
'While strong and fertile blood was in me, Cato,
I did your bidding, gave two husbands children.
My womb is tired now: let me return to you

and let no other husband take me. Grant
again our early union; let my tomb
bear the vain title *Marcia, wife of Cato*.
Let future ages know whether I left you
as a gift or as a castaway from marriage.
You will not share prosperity and peace
with me; I come to share your cares and labours.
So let me follow your camp. Must I be left
further than Pompey's wife from the civil war?'
Her pleading moved her husband's heart. The crisis,
the fates crying *To arms* were strange for marriage;
yet simple union and a sober wedlock,
with gods alone to witness, pleased their thought.
No crowned threshold, and hanging garlands of joy,
no gay white ribbon linking door and posts,
no torch-procession, couch with ivory dais,
no coverlet of gold embroidery,
no towering marriage-crown, no solemn entrance
of the bride, stepping across the threshold lightly;
no saffron veil shielding her downcast face –
a flimsy garment for her modesty –
no jewelled belt girding her flowing garments,
necklace, or scarf resting light on her shoulders
and flying freely from her slender arms.
She kept the state of grief: she gave her husband
only the embrace a mother gives her sons.
Her simple robe was veiled with funeral weeds.
There was no marriage-jesting, and the husband
did not submit to the gay old Sabine songs.
No kin, no family faces, smiled on them;
they wed in silence, with one witness – Brutus.
And Cato neither freed his solemn face
of shaggy hair, nor would admit a smile –
when he first saw the fatal weapons raised,
he suffered his unshorn grey locks to hang
over his brow, and his beard mourned on his cheeks;
for he alone, free of ambition and hate,
wept for the human race – nor did he now
resume his nuptial rights: even a just love
his strength refused. Such was the rule of Cato,
such his unyielding will – to keep sure limits,
to follow nature, spend his life for his country,
to live not for himself but for the world.
To conquer hunger was a feast; a palace
for him was a plain roof; a precious garment
for him was the rough-haired toga of the Roman
in time of peace; the only use of love
was offspring: he begot and loved for Rome.
Justice and rigid honour – these he worshipped,
and virtue serving the world. No act of Cato
was touched by pleasure and the greedy self.

We have quoted this passage as a true and touching picture of the Stoic conception of love and marriage. (It is easy to see the influence of such conceptions on early Christianity.) Appropriately enough, Lucan cares nothing for Cleopatra: he sees in her only the shameless wanton who captivated even the mighty Caesar.

> On the Leucadian sea, the chance hung doubtful -
> a foreign woman might have ruled the world.
> Such daring gained she on the night when first
> a Roman general loved a queen of Egypt.
> Who would not pardon you for your mad passion,
> Antony, when Caesar's heart of iron
> was melted? in the midst of rage and madness,
> within the palace trod by Pompey's ghost,
> soiled with the blood of Pharsalus, he loved
> amid his cares: between the clash of battles
> he sought unlawful love and bastard children. . . .
> Her unchaste beauty gave her victory –
> from a bribed judge she bought a night of sin.

So, in the tenth book (66 ff.), he writes of the Egyptian enchantress, without a word of her physical charm: Lucan, the stern young Stoic, despised such things. Instead, he often dilates upon commonplaces of Stoic teaching: he praises the carefree sleep of the poor (v, 527 ff.) and condemns luxury and sensuality (iv, 373 ff.).

The life and work of Persius also fall within the reign of Nero. Persius lived the life of a scholar and a recluse, in a circle of friends who all had Stoic sympathies like himself, and died of a gastric complaint at the age of twenty-nine or thirty. His six satires are scarcely important enough to be mentioned in this book, were it not for a very charming piece of autobiography which occurs in Satire V.

We have said elsewhere that very few Roman men succeeded in sublimating the homosexual impulse. An ancient biographer expressly mentions Persius's 'slim figure and fine soft features'. It is known also that he lost his father at an early age, grew up among the women of his family, and never had sexual knowledge of a woman – this would explain the coarsely expressed distaste for heterosexual love which occurs here and there in his poetry. I should be inclined to conjecture that he confined his affections entirely to men: we are not of course entitled to speak of

homosexuality in default of some proof. Let us see what he
says himself (v, 19 ff.):—

> My energy's not spent on tragic trifles
> to swell my page with a ton of weighty nothing.
> My talk is private. Take my heart and sift it –
> the Muse empowers me – look, I offer my heart,
> the great part which is yours, dear friend Cornutus,
> examine it! sound it with practised hand
> to tell the solid from the showy plaster.
> Now I should pray to have a hundred throats
> to say how deep within my intricate soul
> you're fixed, and to explain in candid words
> the incommunicable depths of my heart.
> When first I put off childish things, quitting
> the restraints which awed my youth, when friends grew
>   courteous
> and my fresh manhood gave me liberty
> to gaze with freedom on the worst of the City;
> in dubious paths, where errant ignorance
> amazes the faltering mind, I confided
> myself to you, Cornutus. All my childish
> experience of life you cherished, tenderly
> as Socrates; and imperceptibly
> your canon smoothed my twists of character,
> while my spirit, stressed by reason, struggled in
> subjection, shaped and plastic from your hand.
> Yes, I remember spending summer suns
> with you, and culling the first bloom of night
> to feast together. We dispose our work
> and rest in unison: gravity we loosen
> before a modest table. Never doubt it –
> by certain law our lives consentient
> have an agreement, hang upon one star.
> They must be hung in equal scales of the Balance
> by the truthful Fates – or the hour when friends are born
> gives to the Twins our allied destinies
> and our star Jove repels the hostile Saturn –
> some star of friendship fuses me with you.

The importance of this touching confession of gratitude
from pupil to master is that Persius says that when he grew
up he was able to look on the Suburra (where prostitutes
generally lived) but preferred to give himself up to philosophy under the guidance of his beloved and honoured
master. If Persius says that his teacher loved him with the
love of Socrates, he is at the very least thinking of highly
spiritualized form of homosexuality. We need hardly say
that it was too high a love to have contained any conscious
expression of sex.

The finest tribute which Persius can pay to his teacher
is this (v, 63 ff.):–

> You grow pale over the midnight page,
> you weed young ears, and sow them with Stoic fruit,
> kind gardener of youth. Come young, come old!
> Find here the goal of your hearts and a solace for age.

These words might well be thrown in the path of those who
imagine that old age should stretch from education till
death, and who constantly preach 'the education of the
young by the young'.

Epic poetry after the age of Nero is largely in the style
and taste of Nero's age. Its chief representatives are
Valerius Flaccus, Silius Italicus, and Statius: in them all
Ribbeck traces a penchant for demoniac characters and
scenes, for the dark powers of evil and madness, for the
horrors of the underworld, and for vivid descriptions of
huge battles and bizarre and repulsive modes of death.

The least profitable of these for our inquiry is Valerius
Flaccus, who attempted a translation of the epic of the
Argonauts composed by Apollonius of Rhodes. The translation has not been preserved in its entirety, but breaks off
abruptly at the point where Medea begins to suspect the
faithlessness of Jason. The plot is, of course, the famous
one of the voyage of the Argonauts and the theft of the
Golden Fleece by Medea's help; but our special interest is
in a few small scenes which are peculiar to the Roman poet,
and are characteristic of him and his age. For example,
Peleus says good-bye to his little son, Achilles, in the evening before Argo sails – just as the Roman must have said
good-bye to his dear ones when he left them to fight for
Rome's empire in Asia or remote Gaul. The scene is brief,
but full of deep and tender feeling. The faithful centaur,
the Chiron, teacher of young Achilles, gallops down from
the mountains and shows the father his son calling to him.
'When the boy saw that his father knew his voice and saw
him hasten towards him with outspread arms, he sprang to
him and clasped his neck long and eagerly.' The boy gazes
with admiration at the heroes: he listens to their sublime
converse, and is allowed to see and touch the lion-skin of
Heracles. Peleus kisses his son tenderly, and implores

heaven's blessing on his head; and then he gives Chiron the
last instructions for the boy's education – he is to learn
war and the arts of fighting, and be practised in hunting and
spear-throwing (i, 255 ff.).

As well as scenes of tender affection, the epic contains
descriptions of hideous battles, which are – when compared
with the corresponding scenes in Apollonius's original – an
interesting commentary on Roman taste. (Such scenes, for
instance, are iii, 15–361, and vi, 317–85.) It is particularly
interesting to find that the Roman poet works out Medea's
character with much deeper insight than the Greek: both
of them depict truly and subtly the conflict in her soul between her new-born love for Jason and her loyalty to her
kinsfolk, but Valerius Flaccus describes the birth and
development of her love with much more skill. He belongs
to a later age, and has learnt to see woman with the experience and insight of Ovid and Propertius.

A work of a different kind is the *Punica* of Silius Italicus,
a historical, or rather a national epic. The *Punica* was conceived as a continuation of the *Aeneid*: it sings of the
heroic labours of the Roman people and its leaders in the
war with Hannibal. We mention it here because it resembles
Lucan's poem (and to some extent uses the same technical
devices) in holding up to the weak and undistinguished
present the mirror of the magnificent past. The whole poem
is filled with Stoic beliefs and attitudes.

> Ah, Roman, may you bear success as bravely
> as then you bore defeat! be that the last!
> may heaven never test the Trojan race
> with other wars so mighty! Cease to weep
> over thy fortune, Rome; adore thy wounds –
> they are thy laurels; and no future age
> will see thee greater. Thy success will drown thee,
> only thy great defeats will save thy glory.

That is the poet's cry (ix, 346) while he describes the
battle of Cannae. The words are enough to show the lofty
spiritual impulse which fills the whole epic. His Stoic condemnation of his age even leads him to close his Homeric
description of Cannae with the words (x, 657 ff.):–

> Such was Rome then. If she must lose her virtue
> after thy death, Carthage, thou shouldst have lived!

As we should expect, the poem is filled with the clash of arms and the blaze of furious battle: and such scenes are depicted with all the technical skill which we saw in the work of Seneca and Lucan.

Here are a few examples. The heroic Scaevola, in the battle of Cannae, is struck in the face by a rock hurled by a Carthaginian (ix, 397):–

> Beneath the blow his jaws shattered,
> his face was torn away; thick with his mangled
> brain, blood rushed through his nostrils; in black gore,
> from crushed head and smashed sockets, dripped his eyes.

Even more frightful than that is the scene in which the Carthaginians torture the slave who murdered Hasdrubal (i, 169 ff.):–

> The furious Carthaginians, wild with grief
> (a race hungry for cruelty), hurry their tortures:
> fire, red-hot glowing steel, the searching lash
> to mangle the quivering flesh with a thousand cuts,
> the torturer's cruel hands, agony poured deep
> into the body, flames blazing within
> the open wound – horror! His limbs were strained
> with savage skill, and grew to the full extent
> that torture willed; the blood left his veins,
> his bones boiled and smoked in his melting limbs.
> His mind remained untouched. He laughed at pain
> as if he watched it, flouted the tormentors
> for their fatigue, cried to be crucified.

It is interesting to compare this terrible scene with the account in Livy xxi, where we find the calm matter-of-fact statement that the murderer laughed in the midst of his tortures, because his agony was overborne by his delight at the accomplishment of his task. But all the details of horror are peculiar to Silius, who must have known the tastes and demands of his readers.

In the same way, we must think of Silius and his time when we read the encomium (xv, 274 ff.) of Laelius on Scipio: Laelius praises his friend because, after the army captured a maiden betrothed to a Spanish chieftain, he took her as his own share of the booty and sent her back untouched to her bridegroom. To the Roman of Domitian's time this would appear as a splendid and heroic act.

> Laelius cried: 'Revered and glorious leader,
> praise to thy purity! The high renown

> of heroes famed in legend yields to thee.
> Great Agamemnon launched a thousand ships,
> Achilles brought the North to aid the South,
> but love of women broke their fair compact.
> In every tent that thronged the Trojan plain
> there was a captive mistress. Thou alone hast kept
> thy foreign maiden purer than Cassandra.'

The poet cares little for historical verisimilitude when he wishes to bring his beliefs home to the reader. Hannibal, leaving his wife, speaks like a Roman Stoic (iii, 133):–

> 'My loyal wife, give up thy sad forebodings.
> In peace and war, our term of life is fated:
> our birth brought forth our death.'

And Silius really becomes a Stoic homilist in his presentiment of the moral conflict in the soul of the young Scipio (xv, 20 ff.) as he deliberates whether he shall undertake the difficult command in Spain. As in the famous parable of Heracles at the cross-roads (related in Xenophon), Virtue and Pleasure appear to Scipio: they enter on a rhetorical contest before him, like a grave Stoic against a smiling Epicurean, each trying to inspire him with one of these contradictory ideals. Pleasure concludes with a moral commonplace:–

> 'Give heed to this. Thy mortal life runs fast,
> and has no second birth; the days fly; death
> is a mounting tide; and none of all thy treasures
> may go with thee to the shades. At the death-hour
> who has not wept for hours of pleasure missed?'

Virtue opposes her thus:–

> 'Neither the wrath of the gods nor the enemy spears
> do such despite to me as thou, smooth pleasure.
> Thy friends are drunkenness and luxury,
> and infamy flaps round thee on black pinions.
> With me go honour, praise, and smiling glory,
> honour, and victory white with snowy wings:
> the laurelled triumph raises me to the stars.'

Scipio follows Virtue, as he was bound to do; but Pleasure has the last word, and prophesies:–

> 'My time will come, the time
> when Rome will strive to do me eager homage,
> obsequiously honouring me alone.'

Silius works out the conception of Virtue in many memorable scenes – scenes which are now unjustly ignored:

apart from professional scholars, no one reads the *Punica*
any longer. Yet it is an important and valuable poem. It
shows us, for example, the standard-bearer who spends his
failing strength on rescuing the eagle from the enemy; he
is desperately wounded, and sinks fainting to the ground;
and at last rouses himself to bury his charge in the earth; his
last spark of life flickers out when he achieves his task, and
he sinks for ever into a holy sleep. That is the faithfulness
unto death which Silius gloomily says is now known only
by name (i, 329). Another episode (xiv, 148 ff.) bears witness to the gentle humanity of the Stoic creed. An Etruscan
soldier, captured by a Carthaginian at the Trasimene Lake,
was kindly treated and sent back to his home. He rejoined
the Roman army, and fought against the Carthaginians in
Sicily; where by chance he met his former captor, and
struck him down without recognizing him. The Carthaginian tore off the helmet which concealed his face, and asked
for mercy, in amazement, the Etruscan recognized his
friend.

> The Etruscan warrior sank his sword, and thus,
> between his groans and starting tears, he spoke:
> 'Ah, do not supplicate! Thy life is safe.
> To save an enemy is my duty. First
> and last to keep faith – that is the mark and function
> of a good soldier: thou hast given me life
> before, and saved me; thou wert still to be saved.
> I should be worthy to accept a cruel
> fate, worthy to be hurled to deepest hell,
> if my right hand refused to make thy way
> through fire and flowing water.' So he spoke,
> and lifted him, paying his life with a life.

The same spirit breathes in the utterance of Honour (xiii,
281 ff.):–

> From lofty heaven
> pure Honour looked, and stirred their traitor hearts.
> Her voice stole secretly into their ears:
> 'Put up your cruel swords! maintain the bond!
> and keep your Honour chaste – she is more powerful
> than kings enthroned. Who breaks a solemn pact
> in doubtful times, when his friend's hopes are light,
> he shall have neither home nor wife nor life for ever
> free from incessant pain: on land and sea
> driven, by day and night driven and tortured,
> fleeing from outraged Honour and her vengeance.'

These words express an almost Christian attitude of man

to man: it is easy to understand why scholars constantly assert that the most genuinely Christian doctrines are derived in the end from Roman Stoicism. The *Punica* contains, in the midst of its bloodthirsty descriptions of agony and death, many gentle and humane utterances, and we know that its author was a friend of the Stoic Cornutus, whom we have already met as the tutor and friend of Persius. Even today we may sum it up in Ribbeck's words: 'A kindly and enlightened spirit breathes through the poem; and its author is inspired by the principles which made Rome great.' To this we must add the qualification that the kindly spirit was first produced by Stoic philosophy, and that Rome was made great by very different qualities.

The third epic poet of Domitian's time is Statius. He was born in Naples, but came to Rome in his youth, where he acquired an excellent education. His reading did not make him a moralist: he took the world as it was. His interests and aspirations lay in the imperial court, and he made himself popular in the houses of rich nobles by his astonishing talent for graceful improvisation. He could throw off a charming occasional poem on any subject – from the beautiful bay of Sorrento to the first haircut of the imperial page Earinus; he could produce, at the request of an acquaintance, an elaborate marriage-song full of mythological allusions, or a pathetic elegy for a dead kinsman. These amiable trifles he later collected under the title *Silvae*: we shall deal with them in a subsequent page.

Statius was especially famed for his epic the *Thebaid*, which treated the old Greek story of the Seven Against Thebes with all the technical adroitness of the Silver Age. The plot is, as Ribbeck says, 'a melodrama of crime and bloodshed', and the epic does not sustain comparison with the favourite national epic of the Romans, Vergil's *Aeneid*, although Statius flattered himself that he had created something almost as great. Nevertheless, among the battles and horrors, there are occasional scenes which show the charm characteristic of Statius's other work. Here, for example, is an evocation of the young hero Parthenopaeus – still almost a boy, he is described with all the grace and delicacy which Statius could command (iv, 251 ff.):–

Of all the warriors facing war's grim hazard
none had so fair a face, such welcome beauty:
noble his heart too, if he grew to strength.
What guardians of the woods, what god of the river,
what forest-nymph did he not captivate?
Diana, in the woods of Maenalus,
seeing his light foot on the grass, forgave
his errant mother; and, they say, she fastened
upon his shoulder arrow-case and shafts.
Forth he sprang, pierced with the love of war,
burning to hear the clash of arms and the trumpets,
to soil his yellow hair with dust, and ride
a captured steed; he hated the woods, ashamed
to bear no arrows stained with human blood.

He appears again in vi, 561 ff.:–

Now for Parthenopaeus
the wandering murmurs of the circus call.
His mother's speed is famed – who does not know
the fame of Atalanta, and the footprints
untouched by all her suitors? With her fame
she loads her son; now he, among the glades
of Mount Lycaeus, catches the timid hinds
on foot, and overtakes the flying spear.
At last he comes, leaping over the crowds
nimbly, and frees his cloak from its golden clasp.
His limbs shine brightly forth, his naked body
laughs with its beauty, shoulders and smooth breast
reveal a frame as lovely as his face.
He scorns the praise of his beauty: his admirers
he shuns. And now, taking the sacred olives,
he darkens all his skin with supple oil.

The death of this youth is touchingly described in a later
book.

The epic is true to its time. Scenes of crime and bloodshed constantly occur. An important example is the murder
of the Lemnians by their wives, in Book v. Polyxo there
rouses her companions against man's injustice in words
which remind us of Aristophanes' Lysistrata (v, 104 ff.):–

An act inspired by heaven and righteous anger,
you widowed Lemnians – courage, forget
your sex! – I am preparing. If you hate
homes for ever empty, youth neglected
and wasting away, and dismal barren years,
I know a way – and heaven offers help –
to give our loves new life. Take courage, courage
as great as your grief: assure me first of that.
Three winters now have whitened – who is bound

in the sacred rites of marriage? who has panted
with a husband's love? whom has the birth-god helped? –
tell me, whose prayers live and grow within her
during her term of months? Yet beasts and birds
can couple freely. Cowards! A Greek father
armed his daughters for vengeance, traitorously
drenching in blood the bridegrooms' careless slumber.

The speech incites the women to swear a dreadful oath to
murder their husbands (v, 152):–

Then in a forest grove – Minerva's peak
is shaded by its blackness; above it looms
the mountain; sunlight dies in its twofold darkness –
they plighted troth to kill. Warlike Enyo
and Ceres of the dead and the nether goddesses
left hell to witness it; secret among them
moved Venus, Venus armed and kindling their fury.
Unhallowed sacrifice! A woman brought
her child; they girt themselves, their hands and hearts
met eagerly; they pierced its heart (astonished
at the strange steel); in blood they pledged the sweet
crime, while the child's new ghost haunted its mother.

The husbands return home, suspecting nothing (v, 186):–

Throughout their houses, and in sacred groves
they feasted richly, emptied copious gold
of its deep draughts; and all the Thracian battles,
the toils of war on Rhodope and Haemus,
were told again. And still the murderous wives,
adorned and beautiful, lay among garlands
at the rich board. Venus on this last night
made the husbands kind: she gave them a brief peace,
kindled in them a vain and fleeting passion.

Night falls: the women turn from love to murder. (Such
a theme was admirably suited to the age when Statius
wrote.) Two details from the whole scene of sadistic cruelty
may be enough to exemplify it all (v, 207 ff.):–

Elymus, gay with garlands,
sunk in the piled cushions, asleep, panted
ferment of wine. His wife stood over him
parting his garments for a stab, but sleep
left him when he was touched by the finger of death.
Confused, with eyes uncertainly awake,
he clasped his enemy. Close in his embrace
she drove the dagger through his back, to touch
her own breast. The crime was done. His head
fell back; his eyes breathed love still, and his passion
murmured her name; his arms died on her neck.

And this (v, 252 ff.):–

> Dead faces pressed the cushions; open breasts
> showed the sword-hilt; fragments of mighty spears
> lay there, and garments mangled on the bodies,
> winebowls upturned, and the banquet swimming in slaughter,
> and the wine in torrents out of gaping throats,
> mingled with blood, gushing back to the cups;
> a crowd of youths; old men beyond the scope
> of armed outrage; upon their groaning fathers
> half-murdered children, at the gate of life
> sobbing their souls away.

Scenes of this kind follow, one upon another, until the most repulsive of all (viii, 751 ff.) – the bloodthirsty Tydeus makes his men hack his enemy's head off, and tears it in mad rage with his teeth.

But we must not leave the *Thebaid* with that revolting picture fresh in our minds: it would be wrong to leave our readers with the impression that the whole epic is composed of such a scene, for they would find it impossible to believe that the poet had other tones at his command. Here is a different instance – a sad love-scene, with a woman's character tenderly depicted (viii, 636 ff.):–

> So they conversed, when suddenly a tumult
> startled the quiet house. Toilfully rescued,
> they brought home Atys, bloodless but alive.
> His hand was on his wound, his head drooped
> over the shield, his hair fell back from his forehead.
> Jocasta saw him first: trembling, she called
> his dear Ismene – for his dying voice
> uttered that prayer alone, that name quivered
> on his cold lips. The slave-girls shrieked, the maiden
> raised her hands to her face: despite her shame,
> she was compelled; her lover's dying wish
> was satisfied, to see her near. Four times
> in the agony of death he raised his eyes
> at her name; he would not look on heaven
> but gazed on his love, gazed, and was not sated.
> And then – his mother absent, and his father
> blessed in death – they grant her the sad duty,
> to close his eyes. At last, with none to witness,
> she spoke her love, and drowned her eyes in tears.

That was the conduct of a noble Roman girl, trained to show no emotion – a girl of a type which, of course, still existed in the poet's time.

We possess also a valuable fragment of an *Achilleid* by Statius. It is most unfortunate that the work was not completed, for the fragment shows us the poet at his best. He tells of the youth of Achilles: the boy, living in the tutelage of the centaur Chiron, with his friend Patroclus as companion, rushing off to hunt or plunging in the river, under Chiron's eye, or singing old songs of heroes to the lyre after a meal is over. Thetis his mother, full of anxiety, attempts to keep him from the Trojan war by taking him in a girl's clothes to the court of Lycomedes. There he lives as a girl among the other girls; but soon his manhood stirs in him, he falls in love with Deidamia, the fairest of his companions, and, in a nocturnal love-scene, reveals his identity and possesses her. The poem goes on to tell how the envoys of the Greeks arrive, and by a stratagem unmasks the young hero. He joins them; and, after telling Deidamia's father who he is, asks for her hand; as his suit is granted, he gives the old man a grandson to protect. He himself is bound for that war from which he is never to return.

As Ribbeck says, Statius has here employed the charming Hellenistic art of miniature-painting. And his occasional poems, the *Silvae*, are instinct with the same spirit.

Statius, the light-hearted South Italian, the nimble and cultured versifier, lived in the same world as Martial and Juvenal; but saw it in very different colours from the gloom which fills their pictures of it. We feel that he enjoyed the brilliant exterior of that rich and showy society, but never cared to look more deeply into the problems of his time. Enough for him to reproduce and heighten its bright colours – country house or statue, bath or garden, he could write an elegant description of any such superficial beauty. There is, of course, a hymn of praise to the emperor for asking him to dinner (*Silvae*, iv, 2). Particularly interesting for our inquiry are the marriage-poems and funeral elegies, which contain a good deal more of the personal element than the others. The elegies express his sympathy with bereaved friends, in words full of tact and delicacy (e.g. ii, 1; iii, 3) and sometimes in exquisite pieces of miniature painting (e.g. ii, 1, 50 ff.); the marriage-songs sometimes contain complete stories full of mythological allusion (e.g.

i, 2). Unfortunately, lack of space forbids us to give further examples of these carefully wrought poems, unique as they are in their own sphere; it is to be hoped that a modern poet will one day reveal them to a world which has ceased to know their beauty. (One point is made quite clear to any reader of the marriage-songs – even in the Rome of Domitian there still existed the pure and noble love of husband and wife.)

A better known contemporary of Statius is the poet Martial. If we speak of him here, our interest is neither in the brilliant epigrammatist to whom Lessing has done such generous justice nor in the cutting satirist who is so often mentioned by other critics. We must consider Martial principally as an authority on sexual life in Rome, for which he is a mine of information. His treatment of the matter is, in fact, so candid and unvarnished that in this work we must refrain from reporting all that he says: we must content ourselves with a few indications.

Martial knows and speaks of all possible varieties of sexual conduct: from the normal love of man and woman to the most sophisticated and bizarre practices of voluptuaries. Nevertheless, it would be wrong to conclude from this that Martial himself was a violent sensualist. Lessing, in his essay on the Epigram, has already asked this question and answered it in the negative, Martial himself protests, in almost the words used by Catullus and Ovid, 'my page is wanton, but my life is pure' (i, 4). And he says more expressly elsewhere (i, 35):–

> I write indelicate verses
> which can't be read in a schoolroom –
> do I, my friend? But my poems
> (just like an amorous husband)
> must have some spermatozoa.
> Am I to sing of a marriage
> without some suitable joking?

And, with justice, he throws the rebuke back in the face of his age (iii, 86):–

> I warned you not to read my wanton poems,
> you pure young lady – but you're reading them.
> Still, chastity, you watch the coarsest farces;
> my poems are no coarser. So, read on!

Martial sums up his poetic aims in the epigram viii, 3:–

> Speak! Would you change motley for tragic purple,
>   or sing harsh wars in equally harsh tones,
> and then be lectured on by hoarse professors,
>   hated by tall maidens and gallant boys?
> Leave that to overweighted minds and morals,
>   let them mix ink with sweat and midnight oil.
> The purest Roman wit must salt your poems:
>   there let life read and recognize itself.

But the foundation of these aims is that mentioned in x, 33:–

> to spare the person and to tell the vice.

When Martial gives names, they are all pseudonyms.

What do we know of Martial's own life? First, he came from the little Spanish town of Bilbilis, and he himself knew well that he was not Roman by blood (x, 65):–

> Why call me brother! I come from
> the Spanish Celts and the Tagus.
> You think our features resemble?
> Your hair is curly and shining,
> my Spanish locks are unruly;
> you're smooth with daily depiling,
> my thighs and shanks are abristle.

He came to Rome in the year 64, and tried to win a position and an income as a barrister; but he soon gave up the law, because he was more attracted by poetry. Still, it was a hard struggle for him to keep his head above water: he complains bitterly (evidently from experience) that a poet can hardly live in Rome (iii, 38). He was compelled to spend years of his life as a client, a rich man's dependant. He had to court nobles and rich men, to amuse them at dinner by smart remarks or witty poems, to call on them early in the morning in the hope of an invitation to dinner that night, and to degrade himself in other ways. It was while he frequented senators and knights in this way that he wrote his first poems (obviously by request) and circulated copies of them among his patrons – in this way becoming known before he published his first book of collected poetry. 'His epigrams were like a piquant liqueur, with its stimulating action on the nerves – the stronger the better' (Ribbeck). He met many of the best known poets of the time: he

admired Silius Italicus, and Juvenal was a good friend to
him. Lucan's widow, Polla Argentaria, was 'a queen' for
him (x, 64) – that is, she was one of those to whom he was
indebted for some mark of favour. But he remained a poor
man, living on the third floor of a large block of flats in a
noisy part of Rome, where he was disturbed early in the
morning by the sound of the neighbouring schoolmaster's
birch or his loud voice scolding his pupils. He had a little
farm in the Sabine country, but the soil was barren and un-
productive, and the rain came through the farmhouse roof.
If he asked a few friends to dinner in Rome – which can
have been seldom enough – the bill of fare was very simple:
usually a few harmless vegetables, with perhaps a roast kid,
and/or tunny fish, eggs, cheese, and fruit (x, 48; xi, 52). He
often had to go without a coat, and was compelled to
humble himself by asking one of his rich friends to give
him one (viii, 28). It was natural that he should attach himself to the great men of Rome, including of course the
greatest of all – the emperor Domitian: on every possible
occasion he wrote *at* the emperor with a servility which is
often disgusting. But it is clear that his flattery had no success, for we never hear him offering Domitian thanks for
any gift.

In later years he spent some time in the country round
Aquilegia, with a friend – no doubt on a holiday from his
tedious existence as a dependant. At bottom, he demanded
little of life. He writes thus to his friend Julius Martialis
(x, 47):–

> To bring yourself to be happy
> acquire the following blessings:
> a nice inherited income,
> a kindly farm with a kitchen,
> no business worries or lawsuits,
> good health, a gentleman's muscles,
> a wise simplicity, friendships,
> a plain but generous table,
> your evenings sober but jolly,
> your bed amusing but modest,
> and nights that pass in a moment;
> to be yourself without envy,
> to fear not death, nor to wish it.

But life refused him all these blessings. Lessing has proved

that he was never married, and if he sometimes speaks of
an *uxor* (wife), it is nowhere an indication of his own marriage. But Ribbeck's judgment is too cruel: 'Happiness and
pain Martial knew, but he seems never to have known heart-
felt love even for a moment.' At the very least, Martial had
some close women friends; besides them he had an exceptionally deep feeling for the beauty of young boys, and sings
of their charms in various poems. We must agree that in
Martial's character (which was naturally bisexual) the
homosexual side came out very strongly. We find an occasional mention of a boy with the pseudonym Dindymus
(x, 42):–

> So soft the bloom upon your cheek, so doubtful,
>   it fades before a sunbeam or a breath.
> Such is the delicate down on growing quinces
>   that gleam even from a maiden's gentle touch.
> When I have pressed your lips with a dozen kisses,
>   my tender Dindymus, I grow a beard.

He appears again in an exhortation to enjoy the Saturnalia
(xi, 6):–

> In Saturn's holiday fortnight
> when cards and dice are dictators,
> allow me, Rome, in your motley,
> to write some frivolous verses.
> You laugh? Enough. I'm permitted.
> Aroint ye, cares that infest us!
> Whatever comes to my mind, I'll
> discuss without cogitation.
> Here, boy, let's have a few flagons –
> the vintage Nero made love on –
> but, Dindymus, fill them faster.
> I'm useless sober; in liquor
> a dozen poets inspire me.
> Now kiss me – kiss like Catullus,
> and if you kiss me as often,
> I'll give you what he gave Lesbia.

Martial is enchanted by the perfume of these same kisses
(xi, 8):–

> The oriental tree distilling balsam,
>   the last waft of a drooping saffron-bloom,
> the scent of ripening apples in the cupboard,
>   an orchard when its trees laugh with the spring,
> the silken perfumes of the empress' wardrobe,
>   amber lying warm in a maiden's hand,

> a distant drift of spilt Falernian vintage,
>   Sicilian gardens murmuring with bees,
> heaven's altars, Cosmus' alabaster,
>   a garland newly dropped by a noble head –
> why should I tell them? Take them all together,
>   they are the perfume of his morning kiss.

In xi, 73, there is a coarse acknowledgment, which we cannot overlook in our judgment of the man:–

> You always swear to come when I invite you;
>   you fix the time and you appoint the place.
> I am deluded, after hours of waiting
>   I have to find a substitute for you.
> Deceiver, this I wish, in expiation –
>   carry a one-eyed lady's parasol!

(The same sort of substitute is mentioned in ii, 43, 14.)
Obviously Martial was not particularly devoted to the love
of woman; and there is another significant confession in
ix, 67:–

> For a whole night, I had a wanton mistress:
>   her lewd inventions were beyond compare.
> Exhausted, then, I asked for something boyish,
>   she gave it me before I'd said my say.

If anyone is shocked by this, let him remember that no less
a person than Goethe once wrote:–

> When I've enough of the girl, she'll play the boy for me, too.

But in this love of boys there is a very strong aesthetic
element. Thus, he can always turn a neat epigram on Domitian's beautiful cupbearer, the boy who was sung by Statius
also; and there is no better way to compare the styles of
the two poets than by contrasting Martial's brief and graceful epigrams with the longwinded prize-poem of Statius on
this subject. Here is one of Martial's poems (ix, 12 [13]):–

> Your name speaks of the tender year's beginning,
>   when bees harvest the brief delights of spring,
> your name deserves that Venus' brush should paint it,
>   that she herself should sew it into silk,
> your name should be inscribed in the stones of India,
>   or carved in amber smooth from the nymph's hand,
> or else designed by the scholar-cranes in heaven –
>   your name alone should live in Caesar's house.

Here are a few adroit lines on the boy's hair, offered to a
god (ix, 16):–

> His master loves him most of all the palace,
>   this boy, who marks the springtime by his name;
> the glass, his beauty's mentor, and his ringlets
>   he now has sanctified to the healing god.
> Fortunate land, to whom such boons are granted –
>   boons rarer than the locks of Ganymede!

Martial (like Catullus in his marriage-song) denies a married man the right to love boys (xii, 97):–

> Although your wife is a prize who
> would satisfy any husband –
> rank, riches, chastity, learning –
> you take your pleasure with youngsters
> and pay them out of her dowry.

And here is another to the same effect (xi, 78):–

> Come, take the good of feminine embraces
>   and learn the work you never knew before.
> The veil is on the loom, the bride is ready,
>   and soon your wife will cut your darlings' hair.
> Once, fearing the attack of a new weapon,
>   she will allow you reminiscences;
> her nurse and mother will forbid them later,
>   crying 'She is your wife, and not your boy.'

Perhaps Martial was, in the end, dissuaded from marriage
by considerations of that kind. At least he says (xi, 104):
'Wife, leave my house, or cultivate my morals.' And he
describes vividly the qualifications which he would demand
of a mistress, but unfortunately not of a chaste and respectable wife. The poem could well be quoted in a modern
treatise on the Art of Marriage. . . .

And there were other deterrents (viii, 12):–

> Why do I refuse a wife who's wealthy,
> you ask? I will not 'honour and obey'.
> The wife, my friend, must rank below the husband;
> then wife and husband make an equal pair.

We must of course not imagine that Martial's knowledge
of women was purely theoretical. That was certainly not
the case. He had loved women; but, in order to love
women, one need not be a marrying man. Still, he speaks

little of his own affairs with them. We might mention the
poem ii, 31:–

> Yes, I have often had Chrestina. Is she good?
> Ah, Marianus, better than the best!

And iii, 33:–

> I like a freeborn woman. If I cannot,
>   my next selection is a freed slave girl.
> And last a slave; her I prefer to either
>   if beauty makes her seem to be freeborn.

He can even say gallant things to a lady he respected, like
his patroness Polla (xi, 89):–

> Polla, why do you send me virgin garlands?
>   I had preferred a rose wreath crushed by you.

Towards the end of his life, Martial returned to his home
in Spain, after his travelling expenses had been paid by his
friend and patron, Pliny. It was a beautiful close for his life;
but it seems to have been too brief, for Pliny mentions in a
letter that he is affected by the death of his dear Martial, and
this only a few years after he had gone to Spain. Still, he
spent a few quiet and happy years there. He speaks of a
woman named Marcella, who had given him an estate
which delighted him so much that he would not exchange
it for the gardens of the Phaeacians (xii, 31). But we have no
ground for seeing more than a patroness in Marcella – certainly not to imagine that Martial married her, although
Lessing believed that he did. Martial was never married.
The last we hear of him is perhaps the comfortable letter to
his friend Juvenal in Rome (xii, 18):–

> Perhaps you're anxiously roaming
> the noisy streets of Suburra,
> perhaps the hill of Diana;
> you pass the gates of the mighty
> and fan yourself with your toga,
> and curse the Caelian mountains.
> Now after so many winters
> my native Bilbilis takes me
> and makes me into a rustic.
> With not too strenuous labour
> on unpronounceable Spanish
> estates, I sleep to excess here,
> and snore till hours after sunrise,
> and now recover the sleep lost
> for thirty years in the City.

> A toga? Never; we pick up
> the nearest coat from the hallstand.
> I rise, to stand at a blazing
> fire always fed with an oak log
> and crowned with pots for my dinner.
> A keeper follows me – you could
> enjoy him deep in the forest.
> The foreman gives out the rations
> and begs me shorten the slaves' hair.
> Ah here I'll live and I'll die here!

There is no mention of a wife in this; and the cutting of the hair of the handsome slave-boys is because they are being converted into real servants and slaves.

We must close our survey of Martial. We have spent some care on the details of his private life, and have found again the truth expressed by Lessing: 'the most important accounts of the life of any writer of ancient times are important in so far as they can illuminate his work.' The inference to be drawn from our account of Martial's life is that his eyes were open to all the doubtful and unpleasant elements in the character of his age; he had plenty of opportunities to study these elements; but he himself was certainly not the man to experience in person many of the disgusting things about which he wrote.

A younger contemporary of Martial was the satirist Juvenal. About the life of this man, even fewer facts are known. Lessing's remark is entirely true for him: the life of this poet is his poetry. From the poem itself, it appears that Juvenal came from the Volscian city of Aquinum, but knew life in Rome very well. He did not begin to write until he was past his prime. His attitude to the international city of Rome with all its lusts and vices was that of the Roman provincial of the old school – he judged it and condemned it. His insight is profound and acute, although it entirely lacks humour: none of the evils of his age was hidden from him, from the freed slave swaggering through the streets in all the ostentation of new wealth to the insinuating legacy-hunter; from the man who was equally ready to give children to a woman or pleasure to another man, to the masculine warrior-woman brandishing her spear in the arena.

And above all he knew and condemned all the aberrations of sexual conduct. That is why he is so important for our inquiry. We need not say much more of him in this place, because we have used, throughout our earlier chapters, the abundant evidence provided by his satires. And some of his information (which, like Martial, he gives in frank and unequivocal words) cannot be closely examined in a volume of this character. We may say this of the spiritual outlook which is responsible for his condemnations: it is a direct contrast to that of Martial. In all Martial's criticisms of the sexual conduct of his contemporaries, he remains the friend and admirer of the beauty of boys and women. But Juvenal's whole attitude is one of unqualified pessimism and disgust; even for the poetry of Propertius and Catullus he has not the slightest sympathy. These words begin the famous sixth satire:–

> Chastity may have lived, in the Golden Age,
> upon this earth; when a cold cavern was
> a little homestead and enclosed the fire,
> the gods, the flocks, and the master in one cell;
> when the rough highland wife still made a bed
> of leaves and straw and the hides of her rough neighbours
> the beasts. Unlike you, Cynthia, or you
> whose shining eyes clouded for a dead sparrow,
> she had rich dugs to feed gigantic children,
> she was fiercer than her acorn-belching husband.

That, Juvenal believes, was the only time when women were chaste and marriage was inviolate; as soon as civilization developed in the slightest degree, chastity fled.

> It is a hoary custom now, to shake
> a stranger's bed and spurn the gods of marriage.
> The Iron Age produced all other crimes,
> but even in an earlier Age appeared adultery.

A really clever man, therefore, never marries. Juvenal goes so far as to recommend his hearers, if they wish to shorten their lives by sensual pleasure, to take it with a boy rather than with a woman (vi, 33) – a recommendation which seems to indicate a strong element of homosexuality in his character. Thereafter he enters on the distorted and terrible Dream of Bad Women; we shall not describe it here in detail, because we have used much of its information in previous chapters. There is in it no saving grace of humour (as there is, for instance, in Horace), and no touch of love for humanity: the reader turns away in horror from the icy prejudice of Juvenal's moral judgments. It is almost as if Cato had returned from the age of Hannibal, or Camillus from the early Republic, to pass judgment on the Romans of Domitian's time. The judge makes one very significant remark (which we have already quoted elsewhere): it occurs at vi, 292:–

> The lingering disease of peace and galloping
> luxury now avenge the world we conquered.
> No crime, no shape of lust is absent, since
> Rome lost her poverty.

The old complaint of Rome's excessive wealth and power. ... But few of the Jeremiahs recognized that it was necessary to raise the Romans (now that their business of making war had ceased) to greater heights of *humanity*.

Juvenal was naturally a convinced woman-hater: he detested and despised not the women of any particular age, but women in general. He discloses that feeling in such verses as vi, 161 ff.:–

> 'Does none of all that multitude seem worthy?'
> Let her be lovely, rich, and fertile – let
> busts of old kinsmen throng her hall – let her
> be purer than the Sabine peacemakers –
> she is a rare bird, strange as a black swan!
> Yet who could bear a wife with every virtue?

Similarly he condemns physical beauty as such – not only beauty in women, but even good looks in boys – for he sees that it will only attract seducers (x, 289 ff.). And the knot in his homespun country wisdom is the prayer of his ancestors: *mens sana in corpore sano,* 'a sound mind in a sound body'. To it he adds the moralist's commonplace (x, 364):–

> Virtue alone guides men to a peaceful life.

One general remark. Juvenal, for all his misogyny and pessimism, is basically a member of the Stoic and aristocratic opposition: all that opposition, like its greatest leader Tacitus, hated the Empire and felt itself bound to describe

life under the emperors in the darkest possible colours.
That should be remembered by every reader of the satires
of Juvenal.

Lastly, we must examine a curious and versatile author of
the second century A.D. This is Apuleius; we have already
seen some examples of his work. Since this chapter deals
only with Roman sexual life, we cannot investigate
Apuleius's special peculiarity – his relationship to the
oriental mysticism of the Isis-cult and other religious phenomena of his time. Still, we shall find enough to interest us
in his work.

He was born in the African military colony of Madaura,
and grew up in Carthage, which was then a centre of
rhetorical education. He travelled for years in Greece,
visited Alexandria and went to Rome itself before returning to his home in Africa. His travels gave him an admirable opportunity for writing – they made him acquainted
with the whole of contemporary culture in all its elements,
from rhetoric to mysticism, from the art of telling simple
old folk-tales in affected and enigmatic language to the
simple pleasure of relating coarse and amusing anecdotes.
This breadth of experience is reflected in his principal
work, the *Metamorphoses* or *Transformations*. It is a work
full of restless variation. The general framework is comparatively simply and easily grasped; but it is filled with a
multitude of episodes, charming short stories, little melo-
dramas, and gross anecdotes, in which every reader will
find something to his taste. The style is a peculiar mixture
of barbaric exuberance and recherché grace – we can
scarcely hope to reproduce its effect in translation. In discussing the contents of the book we must confine ourselves
to the very varied erotic themes which it introduces in
quick succession.

The framework is almost wholly borrowed from an old
Greek story, which Lucian also used in his short story,
Lucius, or the Ass. It describes the adventures of one
Lucius. He visits Thessaly to see witchcraft at close
quarters. With the help of the servant-girl of one of the
witches, he is changed (by mistake) into an ass; but he can
recover human form if he eats roses. In the search for roses,

he meets with a succession of wild adventures, which are the real contents of the book. At last the poor creature finds his roses, eats them, resumes his shape, and immediately becomes a convert to the cult of Isis, who had shown him in a dream how to obtain release.

So much for the main plot. But we must examine some of the manifold stories, adventures, and pictures which the versatile Apuleius has packed into his book. To tell them all would be to retell the whole *Metamorphoses,* so that we must content ourselves with a small selection. We shall begin with the best known of all – the fragrant tale of *Cupid and Psyche,* which is based on a very ancient Indo-Germanic fairy tale. We cannot here describe the whole plot, especially since it is probably well known to our readers. The form which Apuleius gives it is characteristic of his art. Clearly, he wanted to accommodate the material to contemporary taste and to make it acceptable to Roman readers. Therefore he converted the simple folk-tale into an extravaganza filled and overloaded with an exuberant variety of colour and detail, as if a modern author were to take a naïve story from Grimm and turn it into an elaborate ballet. An extract will make our meaning clear.

Like Elsa in Lohengrin, Psyche had been commanded to surrender herself to the husband who came to her only in the darkness of night, to trust him and not to attempt to discover his identity. But her innate curiosity is too much for her; and her wicked sisters have insinuated that her husband is a hideous monster. What does she do? Here is Apuleius's description (v, 21):–

'Night had come and her husband had arrived and after a short skirmish in the fields of love had sunk deep into slumber. Then Psyche, weak in body and mind but succoured by the malignance of fate, confirmed her strength and brought forth the lamp and seized the razor, changing her sex by her own boldness. But when at the approach of light the secrets of her bed were revealed, she saw the gentlest and sweetest of all savage monsters, Cupid himself, the beautiful god in beautiful repose; and at his sight even the light of the lamp grew gay and brilliant and the razor's sacrilegious blade gleamed bright. But Psyche was overborne at the sight and no longer commanded her heart; weak

and trembling with a swooning paleness, she sank down
on her haunches and sought to hide the steel, but in her
own bosom: which she would surely have done had not
the steel in terror of such a crime slipped from her rash
hands and flown away. And now in her exhaustion, overcome by her own safety, she gazed again and again at the
beauty of the divine face, and her heart recovered its
strength. She saw the delightful locks of his golden head
steeped in ambrosia, and, wandering over his milky neck
and crimson cheek, the curls of his hair in beauteous confusion, backwards and frontwise hanging, by whose excessive and blazing splendour the very light of the lamp was
made to tremble and weaken: from the shoulders of the
winged god sprang dewy wings with flashing white bloom,
and though the other feathers were at rest the utmost delicate tips pulsed tremulously in restless excitement; the rest
of his body was smooth and delightful, and Venus would
not be ashamed to have given birth to such beauty. Before
the feet of the bed lay the bow and the quiver and the
arrows, the kindly missiles of the great god. While Psyche,
with her insatiable curiosity, gazed at these things and
handled and admired her husband's weapons, she drew one
arrow from the quiver and, essaying its furthest point with
the tip of her thumb, chanced to press too hard as her finger
still trembled and pierced it to a little depth, so that the
surface of his skin was dewed by tiny drops of rose-red
blood. Thus unwittingly Psyche fell of her own act into
love with Love. Then as she burnt more and more with
desire for Cupid and leaning over him gazed desperately
on his face, as she hastily redoubled wide-lipped wanton
kisses she grew to fear for the length of his sleep. But while
overwhelmed by her great blessing and heartsick for love
she quaked and trembled, suddenly the lamp – whether by
horrid perfidy or by guilty envy, or because it too desired
to touch and kiss a body so beautiful – poured from the
point of its light a drop of burning oil, on the god's right
shoulder. Ah! bold rash lamp, wretched attendant of love,
you burn the god of fire himself, though it was some lover
who discovered you that he might enjoy his delight the
longer even in night-time! Thus burnt, the god sprang up
and, seeing the ruin of his trust disclosed, straight flew

silently away from the kisses and hands of his unhappy spouse.'

But after Psyche had borne her various tests and punishments, she is reunited to Cupid by Jupiter himself. This scene also is very characteristic of Apuleius (vi, 22):—

'Then Jupiter, pinching Cupid's cheek and raising his hand to his lips, kissed it and made answer: "My son and master, although thou hast never kept the honour decreed to me by the consent of the gods, but with thy incessant blows hast wounded this my breast, which disposes the laws of the elements and the changes of the stars, and hast defiled me by frequent falls into earthly lust, and against the laws, even the Julian law, and the public order, hast injured my fame and reputation with shameful adulteries, making my serene face suffer sordid change into serpents and fires and beasts and birds and the field-cattle, nevertheless, mindful of my moderation and that thou hast grown up between my hands, I will accomplish all . . ." '

And Cupid is at last married to Psyche, which Apuleius expresses by saying: 'duly she came into Cupid's hand.' (The phrase derives from Roman law, and our chapter on Marriage should be consulted: p. 25 ff.)

The Roman touch can also be traced in the employment of the usual lifeless allegories. E.g., Venus punishes Psyche by giving her *Sollicitudo* and *Tristities* (Care and Melancholy) to be her servants; and before the gate of Venus Psyche is met by a servant of the goddess, called *Consuetudo* (Habit).

We shall quote another of the episodes as an example: this story comes from Book ix (5), and was used by Boccaccio:—

'A man oppressed by slender poverty sustained his life by the small rewards he gained for his carpenter work. But he had a wife, poor also like himself but reputable for her uttermost wantonness. On a certain day while he set out in the morning season to an undertaking, at once a bold adulterer crept secretly into his abode. And while they were at the business of wrestling in Venus' grip and had no forebodings, the husband still ignorant and suspecting no such thing came unexpectedly back to his abode. Now, the doors being closed and bolted, he praised his wife's modesty and knocked at the door, announcing his presence by a whistle.

T—L

Then the woman, in her cunning and polished skill for misdeeds of the kind, loosened the man from her tenacious
embrace and hid him undetected in a barrel which stood in
a corner half broken but still empty, and opening the house
received her husband at his entry with harsh words: "So
thus you walk about idle and leisured, with hands pocketed,
instead of providing for our life by going to your accustomed work and getting us some victual? While I, poore
wretch, night through and day long twist my sinews making wool, that a lamp at least may shine within our little
cell! How much happier than I is neighbour Daphne, who
drowned in wine and early luncheon rolls and wallows
with her lovers!" The husband thus disappointed said:
"What is all this? Although our contractor, intent on legal
business, has made this day a holiday for us, yet I have
provided for this day's dinner. See, if you please, that barrel which is never full, and vainly keeps its space and in
fact provides nothing except a hindrance to our intercourse.
That I have sold a person for five denarii, and he is now
here to give the price and take his goods away with him.
Come then, be active and grant me your hand for this short
moment, that the barrel be rolled out and made over to the
buyer forthwith."

'The deceitful woman at once broke into a daring laughter. "Mighty merchandising," she said, "and a man of mark
have I got in marriage; he has sold for a smaller sum a thing
which I, a woman confined within my dwelling, have sold
this long while for seven denarii." The husband, joyful
with the addition in the price, said "And who is the man
who has bespoke it?" She replied, "He climbed into the
barrel to test its firmness with great care."

'And the other falling in with her speech rose quickly up
and said: "Do you wish, madam, to know the truth? The
barrel is too old and variously battered with gaping chinks";
and, turning with a fine pretence to the husband, "Come,
come, assist me to a lamp forthwith, so that I may carefully
clean off the dirt withinsides and distinguish whether the
barrel is right for use – unless you think I find cash growing
on tree-branches." With no delay and no suspicion, the acute
and brilliant husband, kindling a lamp, said "Hence, brother
and stand by at your leisure, until I scrutinize carefully and

report the matter to you"; and with the word he stripped and bearing down the light began to scrape off the old filth of a crazy barrel. And now the lover, that limb of elegance, bent the carpenter's wife over the barrel and over-stooping her finished his work in peace. She meanwhile put her head down into the barrel and treated her husband comically with harlotry cunning: she pointed out this and that and the other and the other again to be cleaned, until both pieces of work were finished and the miserable carpenter taking his seven denarii was compelled to carry the barrel on his neck to the abode of the adulterer.'

In book viii, the tale of Charite and her Tlepolemus is a complete little novel in itself. The *Metamorphoses* do not lack their share of the horrors which contemporary taste demanded: a slave is bound naked to a tree, smeared with honey, and left to the ants whose nest is there. 'As soon as they savoured the sweet honeyed odour of his body, they clung deep to him with small but continuous and multitudinous bitings and thus through a long space of torment consuming the flesh and the very inwards they devoured the man, stripping his limbs so that only bones deprived of meat and gleaming with excessive whiteness still adhered to the mortal tree' (viii, 22). Compare with that the following speech (vi, 31): 'Be it your will then on the morrow to cut the throat of this ass and, emptying him of all his entrails, to sew into the midst of his belly, naked, the maiden he preferred to us, so that only her face is left protrusive and the rest of the girl's body is imprisoned in the beast embrace; then let us expose on some rugged rock the ass thus bestuffed and insewn, and commit it to the sun's burning heats. Thus both will suffer what you have rightly ordained – the ass that death which he has long merited, and the girl the bites of beasts when the worms mangle her limbs, and the ardours of fire when the sun's excessive heat burns in the ass's womb, and the torment of the gibbet when dogs and vultures draw out her inmost entrails. Count also her other pangs and tortures: alive she will inhabit the belly of a dead animal, and she will suffer the immoderate stench as the heat torments her nostrils, and she will waste away in mortal hunger from long starvation, and she will have no hands free to compass death for herself.'

We must mention these sadistic imaginations, although they and their kind occur only now and then in the book. A final example of the same spirit is the scene in Book x, where the author tells with evident enjoyment how the ass (not yet transformed back to human shape) has sexual intercourse with a lascivious woman, and how a woman condemned for a crime is sentenced to have intercourse with the ass in public before being thrown to the wild beasts.

Ribbeck is correct in his judgement of the work as a whole: he calls it 'a kaleidoscope of sensuality and barbarity, with the power to madden or enervate those who gaze at it'. We must add, in conclusion, that a number of very obscene little poems have been handed down under the name of Apuleius: we shall not discuss them here.

We do not wish, however, to leave the reader with a one-sided view of this remarkable author. It should be mentioned, therefore, that he left a few unimportant philosophical essays, and also a technically brilliant *Apologia*, or Speech in Self-defence, against a charge of magic which had been levelled at him. Towards the end of his life he was in charge of the cult of the emperor in his own province, and was therefore a very distinguished person.

Chapter Six.

Men and Women of the Imperial Age

IN this chapter we shall attempt to examine some of the most famous characters of the Empire, with special reference to their sexual life. We shall at once meet the objection that even well-attested individual traits in the personality of any historical figure are so uncertain that a complete sketch of his character must be extremely subjective: this being particularly true for his sexual experience and outlook, which are the most intimate side of his life. Another consideration is that historians and poets have left us very different and often contradictory descriptions of such men as Tiberius and Nero. That may be. But let us be quite honest. Is the same objection not valid for every description of historical fact? How much do we know of any period of history which is truly *objective*? Is not every famous historical description a more or less subjective re-creation of the facts by the historian? I am not referring to such authors as Livy or Tacitus, whose objectivity is still a matter of dispute. But is the work of Mommsen, or Birt, or Gregorovius, a really objective account of the facts? Surely the famous lines from *Faust* may be applied to these historians: 'What you call the spirit of the time is the master's spirit which reflects the time.'

It may be permissible for us, then, to attempt a few portraits of the famous men and women of Rome. These portraits will be as objective – that is, as well documented – as our present knowledge permits. We shall of course confine ourselves in cases where the extant evidence allows us to draw valid references. It would be extremely interesting to learn something of the sexual life of Jugurtha, Catiline, or Hannibal; but all we actually *know* of their sexual life is so vague or unimportant that the truth can only be conjectured. In contrast to this, the abundant evidence for the sexual life of Caligula or Nero makes it impossible to resist the temptation to construct character-studies of them by interpreting the ancient evidence in the light of modern sexual psychology. Even these character-studies may seem to be subjective; many of our readers may shake their heads over them; it does not matter. We know that our whole work is an initial attempt which is certain to provoke objections on many sides. But that is to be expected by one who explores a new realm of thought. Later historians will perhaps follow us, will perhaps go further, having greater knowledge and more skill in presenting it: and all for the use and benefit of human knowledge, whose very nature compels it to remain imperfect. We hope that this chapter will be so regarded. The characters it describes are subjectively chosen; perhaps the selection may be enlarged and completed in later editions. In its composition, the author has received much valuable assistance from a book named *Portraits of the Caesars,* by Dr Ernst Müller. The author, a man of profound classical learning, attempts in this book to establish the character of certain great historical figures by using every portrait, on coins and in sculpture, to which he had access. His use of the numismatic material is exceptionally happy; it often leads him to astonishing results, sometimes corroborating personal characteristics, which are attested by the literary evidence, and sometimes contradicting that evidence. We cannot here enter upon the very minute and accurate arguments which Müller brings forward, or even discuss their validity. We shall content ourselves with using his results, and emphasize our dependence on them wherever we do so. I may say that in my opinion Dr Müller has opened a path to new and unexpected discoveries in the whole of Roman civilization – in fact, in all the civilization of the ancient world.

And now let us turn to the individual portraits which we must study.

Caesar

It is no accident that these portraits are all taken from the Imperial age. The historians of the Empire are the first whose work contains material suitable for our purpose. Certainly everything we read of Julius Caesar's sexual life is so uncertain and unimportant that we cannot attempt a detailed portrait of that great man. We hear that in his youth he was loved by the King Nicomedes. We know that Cleopatra fascinated him for a time. And we know that he married Cinna's daughter Cornelia and (after Cornelia's death) Sulla's grand-daughter Pompeia; he divorced her because she was suspected of adultery with Clodius (Suetonius, *Julius*, 6) and at last married Calpurnia, daughter of Piso. We need not wonder that Suetonius, that jackdaw of gossip, says (Suet., *Jul.*, 50): 'It is generally held that he spent much energy and money on his lusts, and seduced many women of high rank.' It is the very vagueness of the statement which shows that Suetonius's reports are, fundamentally, mere gossip and scandal, and that they become no more valuable for being occasionally furnished with a few names. Besides, are we better off for knowing that the great man gave his love to this or that woman outside the confines of his marriage? We cannot and must not judge a great Roman general and statesman as if he were a middle-class Christian gentleman. If greater lapses from mass-morality had been known in Caesar's life, Suetonius would have enumerated and described them with avidity. It may be evidence for the normal constitution of Caesar's sexual nature that Suetonius has no more to say.

It is much more interesting and important to learn (Suet., 45) that Caesar was an epileptic, and twice had an attack during a public meeting. This epilepsy could not have been inherited directly from him (he left no heirs except a son by Cleopatra, who died young); nevertheless it is remarkable that clear cases of epilepsy occur in the later generations of the Julian house. These later Julii were related to Caesar through his sister, and Caligula and Britannicus at least are known to have been sufferers. Can we not infer from this that even the elder Julii showed certain factors of degeneration? If we add the fact that in the Julian house marriage of near relatives was a common thing, we can see the first elements of the manifold degeneracy which comes to manifest itself in individual characters.

Augustus

We have more details about the private life of Caesar's heir, his grand-nephew Octavian, who was to become the Emperor Augustus. Portraits of Augustus on coins and statues show a certain spiritual kinship with the great Caesar. They had many qualities in common – efficient and capable statesmanship, relentless energy, clear vision, penetrating intellect, and an unquestioned genius for handling men and affairs. Their physical natures also must have been similar; and this is corroborated by Müller from coin-portraits. For Augustus, the reformer of Roman morality and Roman marriage laws, was himself no pattern of righteousness. It is true that Suetonius writes (*Aug.*, 71): 'Of all these scandals or accusations, whichever they were, he refuted the charge of homosexuality, most easily, by the chastity of his life then and later.' Still, he does not omit to mention that Augustus was accused in his youth of 'being effeminate', of 'earning his adoption by his uncle Caesar through unchastity', of 'selling his honour to Aulus Hirtius in Spain after it had been first stained by Caesar', and of the other crimes with which a great and unpopular man is sometimes charged. But we may assume that Augustus, at any rate, can never be charged with having had any sort of sexual relations with men. For this reason – all descriptions of his character agree that he was a *man* through and through, entirely devoted to women and devoid of any traces of bisexual tendencies. We know that he was married three times. 'In his youth he was betrothed to the daughter of P. Servilius Isauricus. However, when he made up his first quarrel with Antony, both armies demanded that the two generals should be united by some family tie; so that Augustus married Antony's step-daughter Claudia (daughter of Fulvia and Publius Clodius), although she was almost too young for marriage. Then he quarrelled with his mother-in-law, Fulvia, and divorced the girl before the marriage was consummated. Not long afterwards he contracted a marriage with Scribonia. She had been married to two men of consular rank, and had borne children to one of them. But he divorced her also, "because," as he wrote, "he was sick of her crabbed character". Immediately after this he made Livia Drusilla leave her husband Tiberius Nero, although she was pregnant; he loved and respected her alone for the rest of his life.' Thus Suetonius (*Aug.*, 62). According to Cassius Dio (48, 34), Augustus put Scribonia away because he had fallen in love with Livia. These are the facts we know about his regular marriages.

Suetonius, however, adds this (69): 'Not even his friends deny that he often committed adultery: but they plead his motive was not lust but policy, since he could more easily discover the plans of his enemies by making love to their wives. Marcus Antonius threw in his teeth not only that he married Livia in a hurry, but that he once openly took the wife of an ex-consul from her husband's dining room into a bedroom and brought her back again with her ears red and hair dishevelled; also that he put Scribonia away because she was too free in complaining about the influence of his concubine; also that assignations were sought for him by his friends, who stripped and inspected married women and maidens, as if the whore-monger Toranius had been selling them.' And we are told of a letter which Antonius wrote to Augustus, excusing his liaison with Cleopatra by charging Augustus also with adultery: 'not content with Drusilla you have also your Tertulla, Terentilla, Rufilla, or your Salvia Titisenia. What does it matter where or with whom you take your pleasure?'

We may well believe that Augustus acted on this easy principle when choosing women to satisfy his lust. His marriage with Scribonia was dictated primarily by political motives. Scribonius' brother, after being an adherent of Pompey, supported Sextus Pompeius his young successor. If Sextus had joined the triumvir Antony, Octavian's position would have been in danger. But Octavian had perceived the danger and anticipated it by courting (through Maecenas) Scribonia, the sister of Scribonius. Her brother agreed, and she married Octavian when he was 23, and she a twice-married woman in the 30's. To one of her husbands she had borne children – one of them the noble Cornelia, whose early death inspired Propertius' famous funeral poem (iv, 11). The elegy tells us that although Augustus was then separated from Scribonia, he had shown sincere grief at Cornelia's death; which allows us to assume that he separated from his wife without any quarrel. Still, it was brutal to divorce her for the beautiful and alluring wife of Tiberius Claudius Nero, Livia, who was only 17. Scribonia had just borne Octavian's first child Julia. Besides, this second marriage was in a way the curse of the whole family of Augustus. It sowed the seed of dangerous jealousies, dissensions, and rivalries of the two houses – the Julii who were descended from Scribonia's daughter Julia, and the Claudii, who were Livia's kinsmen. (This can be seen more clearly in the genealogical table of the two houses which appears at the end of the book.) Nevertheless it is certain that Augustus married Livia from no political motives, but from deep passion, and she may have suited a young man better than Scribonia, who was much older – and is called by Seneca (*Ep.*, 70) a *gravis femina,* a serious and respectable woman.

There is an excellent but too little known book by that very distinguished scholar Adolf Stahr, called *Pictures from Classical Antiquity*. (Unfortunately this book is now out of print.) In volume iii, Stahr tells the affecting story of Scribonia, and likens her tragic fate to that of Niobe, for she saw, one after another, her daughter Julia, Augustus' only child, a girl of great promise, and her grandchildren, Caius and Lucius Caesar, languishing in exile or carried off by an early death. Meanwhile, Tiberius, the son of her hated rival, Livia, became Emperor of the world. Stahr conjectures, perhaps rightly, that the dreadful dissensions in the Imperial family found their last expression in the memoirs of the younger Agrippina, Scribonia's great-grandchild; and that the malevolent and one-sided pictures given by Agrippina were later used by Tacitus. Of such deep moment for the future was the love and marriage of Augustus.

However, Roman society was not offended by the triumvir's marriage with Livia, for marriages of this kind were common enough. But anecdotes about this event were told everywhere. Cassius Dio relates (48, 44): 'Livia was in her sixth month of pregnancy by her husband, Nero. When Octavian in perplexity asked the High Priests whether it were permissible to marry a pregnant woman, they answered: "if the pregnancy were doubtful, the marriage must be postponed, but if it is known the marriage can proceed without objection." Perhaps this was the regulation which their books recorded; but if the regulation had not existed it would have been necessary to invent it. Livia's own husband gave her a portion as if he had been her father. At the wedding banquet a comical thing happened; one of the beautiful naked pages who sometimes attended ladies of the time saw that Livia was reclining at table at a place beside Octavian at some distance from Nero; he ran up to her and said, "What are you doing here, my lady? The master is over there!" pointing to Nero.'

According to all appearances, the marriage of Augustus and Livia was a truly happy one. Tacitus describes her with a good deal of unfavourable bias. Cassius Dio, however, says that she had only a good and calming influence on Augustus' sometimes irritable nature (55, 14 ff). Still, his remark (54, 19) that Augustus was 'also in love with the beautiful wife of his friend Maecenas' is probably more than a baseless invention. Augustus was always susceptible to a pretty face, and he knew very well that his own life, especially his youth, had never been a pattern of morality. On this account another of Cassius' remarks (54, 16) may be considered very near the truth. At the time when Augustus published his laws against immorality, he had to decide the case of a young man who had lived with a woman in adultery and later married her. 'Augustus was in a dilemma – he could neither overlook the affair, or inflict a punishment. After much time and thought, he gave this reply: "The civil wars have had many terrible consequences; let us forget them and see that nothing similar happens in the future".'

The greatest trial which came to him from his own household, the trial which darkened his old age, was the frightful disappointment caused him by his beloved daughter Julia. We cannot understand the case unless we pay a little closer attention to the character of this strange woman.

The Elder Julia

Suetonius (*Aug.*, 64) speaks thus of her youth. 'He brought

up his daughter and grand-daughters to spin wool; they
were forbidden to do or say anything secret which could
not be published in the daily news-bulletin; they were not
allowed to associate with people outside his own household
– he once wrote a letter to a distinguished and virtuous
young man called L. Vinicius saying that he had committed
a misdemeanour by coming to Baiae to call on Julia.' It is
clear that Julia grew up in a confinement something like
purdah, in the company of her grave and matronly aunt
Octavia and her stepmother Livia, who can hardly have
been a gay companion. And it is quite possible that this unnatural and perverted restraint awoke in her the impulse to
live in complete freedom. When she grew to womanhood,
she was not allowed to choose a husband after her own
heart – the daughter of the triumvir had to give way to the
requirements of diplomacy. Her first husband was a boy of
seventeen, Augustus' nephew Marcellus; he was a scion of
the Julian house and Augustus intended him to inherit his
power. Julia was then fourteen years old. However, she
was not his wife for long. Marcellus was clearly a weakly
youth, and died at eighteen of a fever which could not be
cured even by a course of treatment at Baiae (Serv., *Comm.
Aen.*, vi, 885). Everyone knows the grief of Marcellus'
mother and of his uncle Augustus; and the panegyries of
the dead boy which were sung by all the Augustan poets,
especially by Vergil (*Aen.*, vi, 860). However, the young
widow was thrust into another diplomatic marriage – this
time to the great general and statesman Agrippa, 'the Bis-
marck of the Augustan age'. Maecenas had advised the
alliance, and Augustus hoped that it would establish his
dynasty once and for all. Certainly Julia's own inclinations
were not consulted. She was married to a man more than
twice her age, who had to divorce his own wife, Octavia's
daughter. Still, her husband's importance must have flattered her own ambition.

The marriage lasted ten years, during which time she
bore five children – the young princes Caius and Lucius,
two daughters named Julia and Agrippina, as well as an
evil and degenerate boy called Agrippa Postumus, who was
born after her husband's death. Despite the birth of five
children, we may doubt whether it was a happy marriage.

The characters of husband and wife were totally different. All ancient testimony (coins and statues as well as literature) shows that Agrippa was a serious-minded Roman of the old peasant type. Pliny (*N.H.*, xxxv, 4[9]) says that he was more of a rustic than an elegant. And since he had no pedigree, he was not accepted in aristocratic Roman society – despite his great political services to the nation, and despite his expenditure of gigantic sums on beautifying the city by the constructions of temples, baths, colonnades, and gardens. He was far from being an inspired and subtle hedonist. And his political duties often called him away from Rome and his young wife's side. Julia, on the other hand, was the spoiled child of the imperial house; young, very beautiful, lively and spirited, full of keen intellectual and artistic enthusiasm, and full of a youthful eagerness to enjoy life and love.

We know that during her marriage to Agrippa, she carried on a liaison with a certain Sempronius Gracchus, and did not give it up after the divorce. Tacitus mentions this (*Ann.*, i, 53): 'Sempronius Gracchus was a man of the old nobility: he was a versatile character, a glib villain, who had debauched Agrippa's wife Julia.' But Macrobius has left us a good deal of interesting information about Julia, and his remark is much more revealing (*Sat.*, ii, 5). According to him, she was once asked why all her children looked like her husband in spite of her frequent adulteries. She replied, cynically: *numquam eni mnisi naui plena tollo vectorem*, which means that she did not give herself to her lovers until she knew she was pregnant by her husband. (Our translation is free, because the actual words are extremely coarse.) It would seem, then, that her manner of life was no secret. We may remind our readers that just at this time Ovid's frivolous *Art of Love* was popular among the gay youth of Rome – that is, in the very circles where Julia took her pleasure behind her husband's back. And did it not describe how to seduce the young wife of an ageing husband? We have good ground for the assumption that Agrippa (whose illnesses and toils had soon brought him to old age) knew of his wife's misdemeanours, but avoided scandal and kept quiet. He died at the age of 51, worn out by a life of titanic toil in the service of his master.

Even now Julia was not to be free.

Her father may have had an inkling of her real character. At any rate, he made a long search for a suitable husband, and thought of several relatives who were knights. Finally, he made his choice, and was certainly influenced in it by Livia, who knew that the time had come to exalt her son. Julia was married to the Emperor's stepson Tiberius. Politically, the marriage had good reasons. From the point of view of character, it was absolutely impossible. For some years Tiberius had been happily married to a grand-daughter of Atticus (the well-known banker, who was Cicero's friend). He had one child, and was expecting another. He was now compelled to accede to the requirements of the state – or rather to the ambition of his mother and stepfather. He broke off his happy marriage, and was bound to a wife whom he despised. As we learn from Suetonius (*Tiberius,* 7), Julia, even during her marriage with Agrippa, had cast her eyes on the young, handsome, and interesting prince Tiberius, and had made vain efforts to get him into her toils. It is easy to imagine how this young, popular, beautiful and voluptuous princess must have thought of the man who had dared to prefer the simple daughter of a banker. Nevertheless the marriage with Julia seems to have been happy enough to begin with. A son was born who died very young. After that the marriage must quickly have become impossible. Julia obviously detested her husband and paid less and less attention to her position and reputation. She gave herself up entirely to pleasure, which was the real bent of her character. Tiberius soon learned the truth, and left her for ever (Suet., *Tib.,* 7). He even imposed a voluntary exile on himself. He had been delegated to put down a revolt in Armenia – certainly to the great joy of Julia and for the advancement of his more favoured rivals, the boy princes Caius and Lucius. But Tiberius saw through the intrigue; and suddenly announced that he was not well enough to carry out the Emperor's orders; he asked for leave of absence, to be spent on a quiet island where he could give himself up to his studies. It is obvious, however, that the most weighty reason for Tiberius's absence in Rhodes was his wish to separate from his faithless and hostile wife. Even Tacitus, the deadly enemy of Tiberius, does him justice in his consideration of this unhappy marriage: he says (*An.*, vi, 51): 'Tiberius was in the greatest danger because of his marriage with Julia; he had either to tolerate her adulteries or else to separate from her.' Augustus did not understand the real reason for his stepson's exile; he took it as 'insulting' to himself (Plin., *N.H.*, vii, 45 [46]), and was angry with Tiberius for years.

Suetonius's account of Tiberius's resolution is as follows (*Tib.*, 10): 'In the prime of life and health he suddenly decided to retire and to remove himself as far as possible from human society – whether from disgust with his wife, whom he dared neither to accuse nor to divorce, and whom he could bear no longer, or in order to keep and even increase his prestige by absence, and to avoid boring people by his constant presence, in case the State ever needed him ... Under the excuse that he had had enough of office and sought a rest from labour, he asked for leave of absence; and did not give way even to the earnest prayers of his mother, nor to the complaints of his stepfather, who said in the Senate that he was being deserted. In fact, when they insisted on keeping him he refused all food for four days. When at last he was given leave to depart, he left his wife and son at Rome and hurried down to Ostia. He would not even speak to those who had escorted him and only kissed a few at his departure.' Suetonius goes to say that he lived quietly in Rhodes, as a private person. In fact, he was deeply wounded and, being a proud Roman gentleman, endeavoured to pass over his enormous disappointments.

After her separation from Tiberius, Julia threw shame to the winds. Macrobius says that when she was 38 'she would have thought, if she had been reasonable, that she would soon be an old woman'. Also, she must still have played her part of the proud princess of the Imperial house – and in this she resembled her father from whom she inherited so many traits which were her undoing. Macrobius relates that a worthy old gentleman once expostulated with her on the luxury of her table and her household, and cited her father's example of temperance: she replied proudly, 'Although my father may forget that he is the Emperor, I must be mindful that I am the Emperor's daughter.' The same author emphasizes her 'gentle and humane character, and her broad moral outlook, which won affection for her wherever her lusts were not known'. Stahr says (*lib. cit.*), with much justice: 'Such was Roman society of the Augustan age, and such it appears to us in its fine flower, the Princess Julia – a conjunction of contradictory elements; the finest culture and the coarsest materialism, the most enchanting physical beauty and the crudest sensuality, brilliant aesthetic refinement and cynical immorality.'

All ancient sources agree in describing Julia's conduct after her husband's departure; but the authors relate the story with varying emphasis. Velleius Paterculus (ii, 100) says, 'His daughter Julia, entirely forgetting what she owed to her father and her husband, exceeded in lust and debauchery the utmost limits of shamelessness. She considered her sins should be equivalent to her high position, and considered anything that pleased her was permissible.' Seneca's account is even worse (*De ben.*, vi, 32). 'She counted her lovers in scores. At night, she revelled through the city streets; she chose for the scene of her embraces the very Forum and the platform from which her father had promulgated his law against adultery. She made daily rendezvous at the statue of Marsyas, for she had now turned from adulteress to whore, and permitted herself any licence with unknown lovers.' This account perhaps derives from the original decree of Augustus. It is so dreadful that it might sound exaggerated if it were not confirmed by Pliny (*N.H.*, xxi, 3[6]). He says: 'The only Roman example of this licentious practice was provided by the daughter of Augustus, who in her nightly revels used to crown the statue of Marsyas – this being mentioned in her divine father's letter of complaint.' Until then, Augustus had disregarded all warnings about his daughter's evil tendencies. Cassius Dio says (55,10): 'For men in high positions know everything but their own private affairs; nothing which they themselves do is unknown to their household, but they know nothing of what their household does. When Augustus learnt what was happening he was so enraged that he did not keep it at home, but told the Senate about it.' Suetonius writes (*Aug.*, 65): 'He bore death in his family more easily than disgrace. He was not overwhelmed by the deaths of Caius

and Lucius; but he informed the Senate about Julia's misdeeds by a letter read in his absence by the Quaestor. For a
long time he avoided appearing in public because he was
ashamed to be seen, and even thought of having her killed.
Certainly, when a freedwoman called Phoebe, one of Julia's
accomplices, hanged herself, he said he would rather have
been Phoebe's father.' It says little for Julia's pride that she
did not take this way of escape from disgrace.

She was banished to the little island of Pandateria – a
deserted rock six miles from the Campanian coast, today
named Vandotina, and belonged to the Ponza group. Her
mother, Scribonia, was allowed to share her frightful sentence. Julia was guarded like a dangerous prisoner. Such
care must have been due to the fact that a number of her
male associates were banished at the same time under suspicion of a political conspiracy against the Emperor. Among
these was the son of the triumvir Antony, a young man who
had been favoured by the Emperor and even taken into his
own household. The whole case must have affected a
wide circle of society; Cassius Dio (55, 10) says: 'Although
in consequence of this case many other women were liable
to similar charges, Augustus did not allow them all to be
prosecuted; he limited the time concerned in such a way as
to avoid troubling himself about offences which had occurred before he took power.' Special orders were given that
no men – even slaves – should approach Julia in her banishment without special permission from the Emperor. She
was also forbidden the use of wine and every ordinary comfort. The behaviour of Tiberius, whom she had betrayed, is
truly affecting and is sufficient evidence to contradict the
infamous calumnies in the *Annals* of the vindictive Tacitus.
Suetonius (*Tib.*, 11) tells us that Tiberius wrote many letters
to Augustus, imploring Julia's father to be lenient, at the
same time allowing her to keep any gifts he had given her.
Augustus was inexorable. He said, 'Fire and water will mix
before she comes back to Rome' (Cassius Dio, 55, 13). The
only concession he made after five years was to grant Julia
a pleasanter place of exile; she was allowed to leave her
comfortless island for the little fort of Rhegium (Reggio),
opposite Sicily. But even there she was guarded with the
same care. Her mother did not desert her in her misery, but

closed her eyes when she was at last released from her pitiful existence. Tiberius had increased the rigours of her cap-
tivity; her spirit was broken, and she died scarcely fifty-one
years old. There is a notable judgment by Tacitus (always a
stern critic) on the offences of Julia and her daughter (*Annals*, iii, 24):– 'Augustus called the common guilt of men
and women by the impressive names of sacrilege and *lèse-
majesté*, and thus exceeded the leniency of his ancestors
and the laws which he himself had enacted.'

(Is Tacitus offended by the Emperor's disregard for the
old aristocracy in dealing with these cases? It is at least
possible.)

The gravest blow ever inflicted on the moral reformer
Augustus was the disgrace of Julia, his own daughter.

The Younger Julia

The case of Julia's daughter (called the younger Julia) is
only a recurrence of 'the tempest which raged in the Emperor's own house' (Velleius, ii, 100). The younger Julia also
was found guilty of adultery and banished to the lonely island of Trimerus on the coast of Apulia. There she lived
for twenty years, supplied with food and drink by Livia, the
enemy of her mother, who was evidently in sympathy with
her.

In this way Augustus was compelled to treat his nearest
relatives. Yet Suetonius (*Aug.*, 71) says of him: 'He could
not free himself from lust – they say that in his later years
he had a special liking for virgins, who were procured for
him even by his wife.' Tacitus says that Livia was generally
complaisant (*Annals*. v, 1). It is clear that in such matters
she had 'modern' ideas, as Tacitus says of her more in blame
than in praise: 'Her friendly and complaisant disposition
went beyond the limit which would have been approved by
ladies of the old school.'

The fate of his daughter and grand-daughter must have
taught Augustus – that cold, scheming, and ambitious politician – that a man who sacrifices the laws of humanity to
passionless self-interest must always pay the penalty. He
himself was convinced that at bottom he was no more than
an actor in the play of life; and this is shown by his last

words, which are almost identical in Suetonius (*Aug.*, 99) and Cassius Dio (56, 30): 'He asked his friends if they thought that he had played the farce of life well, adding the verses:–

> The comedy is ended: clap your hands
> and send us home with favour and rejoicing.'

Cassius Dio adds: 'So he derided the whole of human life.'

Ovid

In this connection we must say something of the fate of Ovid. As we have said, he must have been connected with the catastrophe which overtook the younger Julia. We can never know the truth. No other writer mentions the affair, and none of Ovid's frequent allusions to it is intelligible. As he recognized (*Tristia*, ii), he had aroused the Emperor's displeasure long before his banishment by his frivolous *Art of Love* which obviously ran counter to all Augustus's work as a reformer. And although at the end of his *Metamorphoses* he had extolled the Emperor as the conqueror of Mutina and Actium, and as the peacemaker who had re-created political and social order, nevertheless this was not enough to soften the Emperor's resentment; especially as he could hardly have read the *Metamorphoses* at the time. Their publication was followed almost immediately by the fall of the elder Julia. Her daughter was sent into exile a few years later for a similar offence; and Ovid must have met his fate at the same time. He was exiled to Tomi, in the same year, A.D. 8.

What was the real ground of his exile? As we have said, Ovid only alludes to it indirectly. He met with 'the wrath of the injured prince' (*Tristia*, iv, 10). Without knowing it, he saw a crime (*Tristia,* iii, 5); chance made him privy to a deadly sin (*Tristia,* iii, 6); his acquaintance with persons of high rank was fatal to him without his knowing the real truth of the matter (*Tristia,* iii 4; i, 2; i, 5). He knows that his *Art of Love* excited the Emperor's displeasure; as we have seen, he attempts to vindicate himself in detail (*Tristia,* ii). All these allusions allow us to conclude that Ovid may have been a friend of Silanus, who seduced the younger

Julia, and may have abetted their criminal association in some way; that he was perhaps in the same house when they were caught; that a copy of the *Art of Love* was perhaps found there and brought to the Emperor; so that Ovid appeared as the spiritual instigator of the adultery. In this way, at least, we might explain the inexorable wrath of Augustus.

Tiberius

The character of Tiberius, the successor of Augustus, is even today a subject of dispute. However, we shall not discuss him, since his nature does not appear interesting from a sexual point of view; he seems to be a perfectly normal man. Everything that is said of his sexual lusts by ancient writers and especially by the malevolent Tacitus and Suetonius, is classed by modern scholars as pure invention. Tiberius was a man of high intellectual and moral standards; he lived only for the welfare of the state; his life had been full of grave disappointments which he had borne bravely. Such a man does not give way – especially in his old age – to the excesses described in these vulgar and ridiculous stories. Such a supposition is psychologically impossible. Those who do not understand this impossibility, but, with an eye for sensation, make uncritical transcriptions from the ancient authors, need not be considered as serious scholars. Tiberius' character is certainly puzzling; especially in his last years, he was reserved and unfathomable – but he was never a debauchee. We may add that this opinion is fully confirmed by the portraits of Tiberius on coins and statues. (Compare, on this subject, the work of Müller mentioned above.)

Caligula

Tiberius's successor was a man of very different nature. This was Caius Caesar, generally known by his nickname of Caligula.

All the classical accounts of this, the strangest of the Julio-Claudian house, agree that he combined all the elements of madness, cruelty, coarseness, and vileness which have been attributed in turn to the most unbalanced of the Caesars. Our special interest is in his sexual character, which we must try not only to condemn but to understand and appreciate. We must start from the certainty that Caligula was a man tainted with hereditary degeneracy, and that the absolute power which he enjoyed strengthened and developed the worst features of his character. He was the son of Germanicus (through whom he belonged to the Claudii) and of the elder Agrippina, a daughter of the libertine Julia, the daughter of Augustus. From his great grandfather Antonius he had inherited a tendency to extravagant vice; and from the Julii, ambition and sensuality, as well as the family affliction of epilepsy. Such modern scholars as Müller and von Delius describe Caligula as 'weak-minded' and diagnose his case as one of *dementia praecox* or youthful insanity; and they draw inferences from his portraits in coins and statues to stupidity, coarseness, despotism, and cruelty, coupled with a furious energy generally expressed in crime. An interesting fact about Caligula is that his real nature was only gradually revealed. Müller considers this a significant indication of the diseased state of his whole mind. As he says (*loc. cit.*), 'Caligula did not become mentally unbalanced until he had reigned for some months. It is clear that his first attack of *dementia praecox* occurred then; before that time, his reign had been mild and he had been adored by the Roman people as the son of Germanicus, but after that he was raving mad.'

The picture is fairly consistent. As Müller admits, Suetonius's account is psychologically correct. As a boy, Caligula committed incest with his sister (Suet., *Cal.*, 24). It cannot have been good for him to grow up in a camp where, as a general favourite of the uncultured soldiers, he must have been thoroughly spoilt. In his adolescence, he came under the eye of his grandfather, Tiberius: but it was clearly too late to produce any good results. It is clear that he always played the part of a dutiful and upright young man, but Tiberius knew character too well to be deceived by this pretence. His comprehension of Caligula's character often gave him cause for anxiety, an anxiety which appeared in such sentences as 'there was never a better slave or a

worse master than Caligula' and 'I am nurturing a viper for
Rome, and a Phaethon for the world' (Suet., *Cal.*, 10 and
11). The clearest indication of his whole character is his
extraordinary passion for cruelty, his unconcealed sadism.
'Standing near the image of Jupiter, he asked the actor Apelles whether Jupiter or Caligula was the greater. When
Apelles hesitated he had him cut to pieces with the lash,
praising his voice as he pled for mercy, remarking on the
melodiousness of his groans. Whenever he kissed the neck
of his wife or mistress, he used to say, "This lovely neck
will be chopped as soon as I say so." Sometimes he used to
boast that he would have Caesonia tortured to see why he
loved her so much.' Again (Suet., 32): 'At a merry party he
once burst into fits of laughter. The Consuls who were near
him politely asked why; he said "Because if I nodded once
I could have your throats cut".' Again (Suet., 26): 'His
quaestor was accused of conspiring against him; he was
stripped and flogged, and the soldiers stood on his clothes
to get more purchase for flogging.' Again (Suet., 27): 'An
overseer of games and beast-fights was flogged with chains
before him for days on end, and was not put to death until
Caligula was offended by the smell of the gangrene in his
brain. The author of an Atellane farce, who had written one
line containing a *double entendre*, was burnt alive in the
middle of the amphitheatre. A Roman knight who had been
thrown to the beasts cried out that he was innocent. Caligula had him brought out of the arena, cut his tongue out
and sent him in again.'

Perhaps these instances will be enough. Suetonius describes many similar actions and traits: by them all we are
reminded of the fact that Caligula 'praised his own callous-
ness more than anything else in his character' – that is, he
was proud of sadism and considered it as truly Roman.
When his grandmother Antonia warned him, he justified
himself by saying, 'Remember that I have power to do
anything to anyone.' As generally happens, absolute despotism and sadism went together in him – compare his
famous wish that the Roman people had only one head
for him to cut off when he liked. He could not repress
these sadistic desires even during his games or banquets:
then too men were tortured before his eyes and sometimes

beheaded (Suet., 32). Even in his 'good' period 'he could not repress his savage and vicious nature, but took much pleasure in attending punishments and executions' (Suet., 11). Our chapter on sadism will be enough to show our readers that, among the sadistically inclined Roman people, a man was bound to appear in whose character this type of degeneration would be fully developed.

All Caligula's sexual extravagance and vice can easily be deduced from what we know of his sadistic nature. Suetonius says with much point (35): 'In effect, there was nobody – however low his rank and condition – whose happiness was not disturbed by Caligula.' He was irresistibly attracted by every pretty young woman whom he did not possess – even by his own sisters, with whom he committed the most shocking acts of incest. He used to debauch women of high rank, whom he left like fruit he had tasted and thrown away. At last he found in Caesonia a wife whose natural sensuality and dissoluteness were an excellent match for the tendencies of his own nature. She was the woman who held him fast, and her nature was such that he often showed her to the soldiers wearing the military cloak, shield, and helmet, and to his friends quite naked (Suet., 25). The daughter who was born of this marriage he considered his own child, because 'she was so savage even in childhood that she used to attack with her nails the faces and eyes of the children who played with her' (ib.).

It is not at all surprising that he was accused of having sexual relations with men – the chief of whom were the pantomime actor, Mnester, and Valerius Catullus, a young man of consular family.

The last feature in his character is his astonishing extravagance. In a few months he entirely exhausted the treasury which Tiberius had filled by years of economy. We know of his luxurious yachts, his palaces, his manor houses, his crazy excavations, and his habit of rolling on heaps of gold (Suet., 37, 42). Like Nero, he appeared as athlete, charioteer, singer and dancer, although these characteristics were in him not so strongly marked. 'On the day before the games his soldiers proclaimed a general silence throughout the neighbourhood, so that his horse, Incitatus, would not be disturbed; he also gave it a marble stall, an ivory manger,

and purple trappings, and jewelled necklaces, and a house
and furniture and a staff of servants for itself' (Suet., 55).

It was a real deliverance for Rome when some officers
did away with this degenerate from motives of personal
revenge. Suetonius mentions as an exceptional circumstance
in the murder that some of the conspirators drove their
swords through his sexual organs. This may be an invention.
Still it is certain that Caligula was, first and foremost, a
sexual degenerate. His wife Caesonia and his little daughter met their deaths at the same time.

Claudius

Caligula's successor, Claudius, was fifty years old when he
became Emperor. Both modern scholars (such as Müller)
and ancient authors show that he cannot have been intel-
lectually sound, although many of the facts which are
related about him may well be exaggerated. Müller's judgment is based on all existing statues and coin-portraits:
according to it Claudius had periods of intellectual weakness, and in old age suffered from a mild form of senile
dementia. Even those who are not psychologists must be
struck by the expression of Claudius in all these portraits –
it is grave, bad-tempered, and sad.

Claudius must be discussed in this chapter because he
possessed certain sexual peculiarities which seem to point
to other phenomena of degeneracy. We must remember in
the first place that his descent gave him the characteristics
of Antonius, of the Julian family, and of the Claudian house.
There is a very important remark in Suetonius about his
education – a remark to which I consider that too little
attention has been paid. Suetonius says (*Claudius*, 2): 'For
many years (even after he had come of age) he was superintended by a tutor. He complains in one of his books that
this man was a foreigner who had once been a stable boy,
and that he had been given the post in order to suppress
Claudius himself as cruelly as possible on any pretext.' The
weak and sickly youth must, then, have been brought up
under the rod. This will explain much of his nature, as it
later developed, especially his weak reliance on other
people, and notably on women. In addition, his inclinations

in youth were towards a life of quiet scholarship; this cannot have made him attractive to his ambitious relatives. It is worth quoting some of the letters of Augustus to Livia which deal with Claudius (Suet., *Claud.*, 4): 'Tiberius and I are both of the same opinion: we must make a decision once and for all about Claudius's future. If he is, so to speak all there, why should he not be taken through all the stages of office through which his brother has passed?' (His brother was, of course, Germanicus – a man of very different gifts). 'However, if we think that he is wanting physically and mentally, we must not let either him or ourselves be laughed at by those people who enjoy turning up their noses at this kind of thing.' And in another letter, Augustus says: 'I wish he would choose, less vaguely and impractically, somebody whose gestures, dress, and gait he might copy.' And in a third letter Augustus expresses his surprise that he enjoyed hearing Claudius deliver a speech, 'for I cannot see how a man who talks so badly can say the right things well in a speech!'

It seems that we must regard the young Claudius as a quiet, shy, and scholarly boy, who was so repressed as a child that he could never develop freely and who was utterly unsuited for all the duties expected of him as a young prince. It is in keeping with this that Claudius 'after giving up hope of political success, withdrew into private life, hiding himself in his country house near Rome or in a remote part of Campania' (Suet., 5). But other remarks of his biographer show that he cannot have been a complete idiot. He was consul under Caligula; and, when chosen by the soldiers to be Emperor after Caligula's murder, he showed many excellent qualities. (We cannot enter upon a description of his merits, since it is not our intention to give a complete history of all the Emperors.)

Like Tiberius, Claudius has long been misunderstood, but justice is being gradually done to him now. We shall therefore turn to those sides of his character which seem more difficult to understand. We need not discuss whether the passage of Suetonius, dealing with Claudius's sadism (quote in the chapter on sadism) must be taken as it stands without qualifications. On the contrary, Claudius often appears a gentle and amiable man – for example, as we have said above, he published a decree that sick and abandoned slaves should have their freedom, and that the killing of such a slave should count as murder.

What we know about his sexual life is certain and indisputable. 'His passion for women was immoderate, and he cared nothing for men' (Suet, *Claud.,* 33). We must cite the whole of Suetonius's chapter 26, which deals with his relations to women: it contains several important facts.

'When he was quite young he was betrothed to two women – Amelia Lepida, great-granddaughter of Augustus, and Livia Medullina, also called Camilla, since she belonged to the old family of the dictator Camillus. Amelia he divorced while she still a virgin because her parents had offended Augustus. Camilla fell ill, and died on the very day appointed for her marriage. After this he married two wives – Plautia Urgulanilla, whose father had won a triumph, and later Aelia Paetina, whose father had been a consul. He divorced them both, the latter for some light offence, the former because she was disgraced by sensuality and suspected of murder. After this he married Valeria Messalina, the daughter of his cousin Messala Barbatus. He found out that in addition to her other disgraceful crimes she had publicly married Caius Silius, even signing over the dowry before witnesses. He executed her, and asserted in public before the Praetorian Guard that since his marriages were all unlucky he would remain a bachelor, and if he did not he would not refuse to be stabbed to death by their own hands. However, he could not resist the temptation to negotiate marriages, even with Paetina whom he had once divorced, and with Lollia Paulina, the widow of Caius Caesar. But Agrippina, the daughter of his brother Germanicus, enchanted him by such means as the kiss of kinship and opportune flattery. Accordingly, he induced some senators to move at the next meeting of the senate that the Emperor should be constrained to marry Agrippina, as if it had been a matter of great public importance, and that marriage between uncle and niece, hitherto considered incest, should be generally allowed. And with hardly a day's interval he completed the marriage. Nobody followed his example, except one non-commissioned officer, whose wedding he and Agrippina both attended, and one freedman.'

It is easy to believe that, as Suetonius says elsewhere (29), 'Claudius was in the hands of his freedmen and his wives, and was not their Emperor but their servant.' The whole matter is psychologically clear. The greater a man's sexual needs are, the greater his dependence on women throughout his life – especially when he is, as Claudius was, no heroic figure, but a quiet scholar and an awkward and impractical man.

We shall pay no further attention here to that interesting erotic character, Messalina, since a book on her has recently appeared. But we shall make a closer acquaintance later in this book with Agrippina, the mother of Nero. All we shall say here is that Agrippina's marriage was only an ambitious scheme to gain power and to secure the throne for her own son, Nero. It is quite credible that she murdered Claudius, when she feared that Britannicus, the son of Claudius and Messalina, might be preferred to Nero. But it is equally probable that Claudius died a natural death. He had suffered for years from digestive trouble, and was not such a moderate eater and drinker as his illness required.

He was a man of considerable culture. He knew Greek well. He wrote several works on history, including two on the Etruscans and the Carthaginians, which were considered so important in Alexandria that they were read in the public hall every year. He must have understood the real nature of all his wives, for he said of them (Suet., 43) 'that he was fated to have wives who were all adulterous, and who all suffered for it.'

Nero

Of all the Roman Emperors, it is Nero who has been most discussed by scholars and described in literature. Nevertheless, historians are still in doubt about his character. It would seem that today they tend to see the good and valuable elements in his character more than their predecessors – this is done, for example, by Stahr, the scholar whose translation of Tacitus we have already had occasion to mention. We ourselves shall not merely repeat the opinions of others, but carefully examine all the evidence, in the light of the results of modern sexual science, and thus, among the confused traditions, discover a sound core of truth. If we employ psycho-analytical words and ideas in discussing Nero's character, it is because we believe that his character is best explained in terms of psycho-analysis. We need not repeat that our character sketch of this Emperor is, so to speak, purely subjective.

It is certain that Nero was afflicted with a grave hereditary taint. In addition, he was capable (as every man and woman is) of departure from the sexual norm, in any direction. Psycho-analysts say that everyone is 'polymorphically perverse' (i.e. potentially abnormal in many ways), and the remark is clearly true of Nero. We shall see that, in the peculiar conditions of the imperial family, the young Nero developed sexual characteristics so numerous and so conflicting that it is astonishing to find them all in one and the same person. A preliminary summary would be this – Nero was a good husband, who nevertheless had strongly homosexual tendencies; in addition, he had many extra-marital relations with women; his character also contained sadistic elements, although they were less important than modern scholars often believe.

Cruelty was, as we have shown, a deep-rooted feature in the Roman national character; but Nero's descent gave him a special inclination to sadism. His father's father was a savage and heartless man. He presented the beast-hunts which were popular amusements at that time, not only in the circus but in every possible part of the city; he loved the cruel gladiatorial games, and conducted them so cruelly that he had to be stopped by a decree of the Emperor Augustus. Nero's father was even worse. According to Suetonius (*Nero*, 5), this man, while on a tour of the East with Caligula, had one of his own freedmen put to death for refusing to drink as much as he ordered. On the Appian Way he deliberately killed a child by driving too quickly. He was quite capable of knocking an eye out of the man who argued with him. He was also guilty of avarice, adultery, incest. Such was Nero's descent on one side. On the other, it was little better. His mother was the younger Agrippina, who is described as wildly ambitious and also as wildly sensual, the mistress of many men. She was the daughter of the younger Julia – banished by Augustus for sensuality – and the taint was in her from birth. We can understand why Nero's father, when congratulated on the birth of his son, replied that any child of his by Agrippina must be a monster and a curse to the state.

Nero's ancestry, as we have described it, accounts for the grossness, ambition, sensuality, and cruelty of his nature. They were intensified by lack of control in the decisive years of childhood. He lost his father at the age of three; and his mother was banished shortly afterwards; so that he was brought up by his aunt Lepida and two 'tutors', a dancer and a barber (Suet., 6). When his mother returned from exile, Nero was subjected to her evil influence until his eleventh year. Suetonius tells us that 'her power and popularity made him so distinguished that – as rumour had it – Messalina, the wife of Claudius, sent emissaries to strangle him at his siesta, as a rival to Britannicus'. Messalina may well be credited with these intentions. We can understand, then, that Nero grew up among singular surroundings and relationships. He was not guided and controlled by a prudent father; instead, he was under the influence of two women – his aunt, and his mother, a woman as masterful as any man – and in addition to them, in his early youth, two men whose standards were obviously low, the dancer and the barber. It is surely possible that Nero's early association with the dancer may have awakened in him his inborn passion for sport and the stage; while his association with his mother may have been responsible for the tragic end of that relationship – Agrippina, still given up to sensual pleasures, was eventually murdered by her son.

We must not disregard a note in Suetonius (7) to the effect that 'when Nero was still very young, more of a child than a boy, he joined in the Game of Troy during the shows in the circus: he did this repeatedly, with great success' – that is, he made a public appearance on the stage, just as he did in later times, when he shocked the aristocratic senators.

In his eleventh year, after the Emperor Claudius adopted him, he was handed over to the philosopher Seneca to be educated. When Seneca was entrusted with this duty, he visualized it in a very interesting way: on the very next night, he dreamt he had Caligula for a pupil. If Nero had been a good and harmless boy, we could not explain why the great

psychologist Seneca should have dreamt of his task in this
way. 'Nero soon made the dream come true,' Suetonius
goes on, 'by showing the savagery of his nature as soon as
he could.' We cannot imagine that his education would be
very rigorous. For example, corporal punishment was (as
we know from other evidence) entirely prohibited in the
case of a prince of the imperial household, though it was
usual in the education of other young Romans. We have
little exact knowledge of the way in which he spent the few
years before his accession to power. Suetonius says that he
'was taught the usual subjects, and music also'; that (22) he
took great pleasure in horse-races; and that, 'although it
was forbidden, he spoke chiefly of the circus: once, when
he was saying gloomily to his schoolmates that a Green
charioteer had slipped and been dragged along, he was
scolded by the master, and replied that he had been talking
of Hector.'

We know little of the rest of his boyhood. I believe that
Suetonius's remark (7) is important – the biographer says
that Nero attempted to make Claudius believe that Britannicus was illegitimate. (Britannicus was Nero's stepbrother,
three years younger than he was.) We can well imagine that
his mother Agrippina took every opportunity of impres-
sing him with the idea that he would one day be the master
of the world. As for the influence of Seneca, good or bad,
we shall say this: Seneca has in previous centuries been regarded almost as a saint. At best he was a refined and well-
read man, but also weak and hedonistic: his real motto was
Live and let live. We can understand, then, how it came
about that, according to Tacitus, Seneca did not only tolerate Nero's love-affairs but sometimes actually assisted them.

What of Nero's sexual life in his youth. We must first
notice that when he was barely sixteen he was married to
his unsympathetic step-sister Octavia – a marriage which
must from the very beginning have been defective in the
most important point of all, the sexual requirements of the
partners in it. It is easily comprehensible that Nero with his
strong sexual tendencies can have found no satisfaction
whatever in marital relations of this kind. Perhaps his ambitious mother had encouraged the marriage for her own
ends – knowing that it would not diminish her influence

over her son. We have a clear impression that Nero and his mother stood in an erotic relationship which may have been unconscious. There was no real father to come between them; and the unscrupulous Agrippina may have hoped to satisfy her reckless ambition for ever by acquiring power of this kind over her son. That would explain the constantly recurring rumours of incest between Agrippina and Nero. And on that hypothesis we can understand why the first really satisfying liaison which Nero entered after his uncomfortable marriage should have aroused the most terrible fury in his mother's heart. She felt instinctively that her power over her son was over. Tacitus sees the matter with the acuteness of a great psychologist, and says (*Ann.*, xiii, 13): 'But Agrippina complained with womanly jealousy and rage that she had a freedwoman for a rival, a maid for a daughter-in-law, and so forth. She could not wait for her son's repentance or his satiety; the more scandalous her accusations, the hotter was his passion, till at last he gave way completely to his love and, throwing off allegiance to his mother, put himself in the charge of Seneca.'

But even in early life Nero must have been acquainted with the other type of love – homosexuality. There was nothing very shocking about it in those days. We know from Catullus that it was perfectly common for a young Roman to have sexual relations with a handsome male slave (called a *concubinus*) until his marriage. Why should such a sensual youth as Nero have been the exception, and refrained? It is striking that Cassius Dio (61, 10) should tell us directly that Nero was introduced to a taste for boy-favourites by his tutor Seneca, whose inclinations lay in the same direction. We may consider this to be one of the malevolent fictions which later authors invented in order to traduce unsympathetic Emperors. Yet it is quite conceivable that Cassius Dio may be speaking the truth. As we are told, Nero shortly after coming to power poisoned his stepbrother Britannicus. This unfortunate boy was scarcely fourteen years old, but was naturally distrusted by Nero as a possible pretender to the imperial power. But other sources mention that he was a handsome and well-grown boy, and Tacitus (*Annals*, xiii, 17) mentions the story that Nero had sexual intercourse with him before poisoning him – that is, he used him for

purposes which were then unworthy of a free person but
were permissible on the persons of slaves without reproach
from current morality. Moreover, all our evidence agrees
in stating that Nero had immoral connections with boys of
free birth: the emphasis being on the word *free*. Tacitus
mentions also that Nero had a homosexual affection for the
actor Paris. Finally, all authors agree in telling the story –
which modern minds find so absurd – of Nero's 'marriage'
with a male favourite (the male favourite's name was either
Pythagoras of Sporus). Whatever be the truth of any of
these assertions, one thing is certain: Nero was fundamentally bisexual, like Horace, Catullus and many another
famous Roman.

In this connection it is apposite to quote the remark of
Suetonius (29): 'I have learned from several sources that
Nero was convinced that no one was chaste or pure in any
part of his or her body, and that most merely dissimulated
their vice, under a clever pretence.' This assertion shows
such a deep knowledge of the human heart that we are
almost inclined to attribute it to the experience of Suetonius, rather than to Nero who died at thirty-one. Does it not
seem to be reminiscent of Schopenhauer?

With regard to Nero's homosexual tendencies, we may
remind our readers of Freud's assertion that the homosexual
element in a child's character is increased when its mother
shows male characteristics. (This occurs in the essay *From
Leonardo da Vinci's Childhood*.)

It is my belief that another and very peculiar characteristic of Nero, which is mentioned by all our sources, belongs
to this side of his character. Tacitus says (*Ann.*, xiii, 25):
'In the year 56 there was peace abroad. Civil life was dis-
figured by Nero's lewd revels through the city streets,
brothels and inns: he wore a slave's dress to preserve his
incognito, and with him went accomplices who stole things
from shops and wounded those whom they encountered.
His disguise was so complete that he was sometimes beaten
himself and carried the marks on his face.' This curious
kind of double life is characteristic of many modern homo-
sexuals. I am not sure whether we are justified in diagnosing
Nero's case as one of schizophrenia, but there must have
been something of this kind at the bottom of his character.

Accounts of Nero tell us that 'he practised wantonness, lust, extravagance, greed and cruelty in a modified form, and, in secret, as if they had been the errors of youth' (Suet., 26); but, they add, everyone was certain that these vices were produced not by his education, but by his disposition. This is undoubtedly correct. We still find in some history books the picture of Nero as a 'good' Emperor at the beginning of his reign, changing into an unspeakable monster at the end; but this picture has no foundation in historical fact. Nero was the same throughout his life. That has been proved for us by what we have seen of his youth. But his mother, and after her Seneca, must have been able to manage him in such a way that for some time he presented a fair deceiving face to the general body of citizens. As he threw off the bonds laid on him by his mother and by his tutor and minister Seneca, he revealed more and more clearly that character which has been described to us sometimes with gross fantasy and sometimes with terrible truth.

As a politician, he is nowadays regarded as adroit and prudent (especially in the field of foreign politics), but we need not concern ourselves with that here. We shall proceed to the investigation of his adult sexual life.

We have said that Nero had both wife and mistress, and at the same time displayed homosexual characteristics. It is also stated that the first years of his reign were free from acts of tyranny or cruelty. It was then that he made the famous remark 'I am sorry I ever learned to write' when he had to sign a death warrant. According to Tacitus, Nero's hitherto good character began to degenerate into licentiousness, cruelty, and lust when he was first seized by a passion for the notorious Sabina Poppaea. She was already married, and some years older than Nero. She had great beauty, great sophistication, and no morals. Here is Tacitus's description of her (*Ann.*, xiii, 45): 'This woman had every quality but virtue. Her mother had exceeded all the women of her time in loveliness, and had bequeathed her daughter both her reputation and her beauty. Her wealth was equal to her high rank. In conversation she was charming and witty. She made a pretence of modesty and a practice of sensuality. She was seldom seen in public: when she was, her face was partly veiled to increase the interest of those who saw her,

or else because the fashion suited her. She paid no attention to her reputation, for she did not differentiate between
her husband and her lovers. She was a slave neither to her
own passion nor to another's, and transferred her favours
wherever she saw an advantage for herself.' One of her say-
ings is well-known, 'Rather die than see my beauty fade.'
And her beauty seems to have been fabulous. She was married to a Roman knight; but she must have had a court of
young admirers among whom was that gay hedonist who
became the Emperor Otho. This man had spared no efforts
to insinuate himself into Nero's society. Nero, young as he
was, and unfamiliar with this mode of life, must have found
in Otho what Dorian Gray found in Henry in Oscar Wilde's
novel. According to Suetonius, Otho was Nero's companion
when he wandered forth flown with insolence and wine. It
was Otho who opened his eyes to the beauty of Poppaea.
And he was the rival whom Nero at last supplanted in Poppaea's affection; and his reward was to lose the woman he
loved so much and to see her carried off by a more powerful competitor. His behaviour to Nero in this affair is remarkable. Although he was deeply in love with Poppaea,
he committed the great imprudence of praising his wife
before his friend and naturally of arousing Nero's vanity
and desire thereby. Poppaea herself had, from the beginning, only one aim, which she pursued with cool calcula-
tion – to become Empress of Rome. That was the price
for which she was willing to surrender to Nero. And her
tactics were marvellously adroit. Sometimes she was the
amorous and yielding mistress, sometimes the haughty and
reserved lady; and when Nero attempted to keep her with
him, she cried out indignantly that she was a married woman
and could not gamble away her honour – besides, her heart
belonged to Otho, who understood how to live better than
all others (Tacitus, *Ann.*, xiii, 46). At other times, she would
pretend that Nero's visits were unwelcome, and would admit
him only when her husband was present. This kind of treatment naturally kindled the young Emperor's passion to a
blaze.

Otho did not appear to surrender his wife to Nero. Accordingly, he was removed from the court and finally sent
to govern a distant province. Nero had now only one aim:

to break the bonds which hindered him from marrying Poppaeà. These bonds were in the first place his unhappy marriage to Octavia, and in the second place his own mother, who knew that Poppaea would banish all other womanly influence from the court. Stahr, in his admirable book, *Agrippina, mother of Nero,* says: 'Once again, a life and death struggle broke out between two women of Imperial Rome – one had everything to lose, and the other everything to win. One was on the defensive, while the other attacked.' It is easy to understand which of these women would be victorious – that one whose allies were youth, beauty, the arts of seduction, intelligence, sophistication, and calculating purpose. When Poppaea derisively called Nero 'a mother's boy, who was bound to obey orders' (Tac., *Ann.,* xiv, 1), she was using the best possible tactics – for Nero had long rebelled against the guardianship of the mother whom he had once obeyed in everything. And if, as we have said, there had been an unconscious erotic basis beneath Nero's affection for Agrippina, it is easily comprehensible that when he felt he had found a real love, all his repulsion for his incestuous mother was given full expression. But what is comical in the situation is this: Poppaea was older than Nero and she was a complete woman in every sense of the word; accordingly she was nothing to him but the reflection* of the mother he hated. This would explain Poppaea's tremendous influence on Nero's character, as well as the fact that his consort Octavia (a different type of woman) awoke practically no sexual emotions in him. We can see the importance of this projection of the mother's influence in the remark that Nero chose a prostitute to be his mistress because she resembled his mother (Suet., 28).

I should account for Nero's matricide in the light of these facts. The historical truth of the murder has never been doubted, although we may well believe that the romantic accompaniments which Tacitus describes are no more than pure invention. The accounts of Nero's life agree that his real nature did not reveal itself until after his mother's death: until then, however little he had loved her, he had at least feared her. It is quite credible, also, that Nero

* Or Imago, as modern psycho-analysts term it.

retained so much filial feeling that his blood-guilt weighed heavy on his conscience, and that he was haunted by 'a sound of trumpets, heard on the surrounding hills, and the wailing of mourners around Agrippina's grave' (Tac., *Ann.*, xiv, 10).

His divorce from his wife Octavia was less hasty than his mother's murder. It is a terrible story nevertheless. This unfortunate woman, who had never been really Nero's wife, could be moved neither by persuasion nor by threats to consent to a separation. She was therefore falsely accused of adultery with a flute player. However, when her servants were questioned under torture, they did not corroborate it. One of her faithful maids was long tormented by the prefect Tigellinus (Nero's base accomplice who had replaced Seneca after his retirement); and in the midst of her tortures cried out that Octavia's body was purer than Tigellinus's mouth.

After the failure of this attempt, Octavia was compelled to leave Rome, and was detained in Campania under a military guard. Then something very unexpected happened. The common people openly expressed their displeasure at the Emperor's conduct. When the rumour spread that Octavia was returning from banishment, they rushed to the Capitol, offered sacrifices of gratitude to the gods, threw down Poppaea's statues and decorated those of the beloved Octavia with flowers. Nero now began to hate his wife. He called out his soldiers, cleared the people off the streets, and intimidated them by a show of power. And Poppaea, who now recognized the dangers impending over herself and her ambitious plans, used all her influence on the weak and cowardly Emperor to make him end this intolerable situation. The death of Octavia was certain. Her enemies fabricated a story that she had committed adultery with the murderer of Agrippina, and he was threatened with death if he would not confirm the story. The so-called proof of her guilt were made public. She was banished to the desert island of Pandataria, so ill-omened for her family, and there she was horribly murdered.

Now, at last, Nero could, without hindrance, make Poppaea his Empress; and this he did without delay. However, that ambitious and heartless woman did not enjoy her dignity for long. She died three years later, as rumour said, after being kicked, while pregnant, by Nero in a fit of temper. Thus the report, which cannot be implicitly believed.

Hitherto we have said little of Nero's artistic attainments. This side of his nature has an important bearing on any estimate of his sexual character, and must therefore be discussed. As has been said, Nero had been well educated in all branches of art and knowledge, and must accordingly have had a certain talent. Suetonius (52) says: 'He loved poetry and wrote verses with ease and pleasure. He did not, as many think, publish the works of others as his own. I have seen notebooks and documents of his containing certain of his best known verses written in his own hand, so that it was easy to see that they were not borrowed or taken down from someone else's dictation, but worked out by himself with all the signs of poetic creation – they were full of erasures, insertions, and additions. He also had great enthusiasm for painting and carving.'

It is known that he also had a passionate interest in everything connected with racing and chariot running in the Greek style. And, however exaggerated may be the accounts of ancient authors, it is still germane to our discussion to consider his public appearances as actor, singer, charioteer, boxer, and fighter. The psychologist Stekel boldly asserts that 'the emperor who had such artistic ambitions would never have been bloodthirsty if he had possessed the power of poetic creation'. According to this theory, Nero was neurotic, 'a talented man who failed of his ambition'. If so, the opinion expressed above – that Nero never escaped from his mother-complex – would be confirmed. All Nero's dilettantism, all his amateurish attempts to shine in one art or another, would be simply explained. Nero was *compelled* to be a great criminal, because he could not sublimate his impulses by creating great works of art. That was the tragedy of his life.

A modern Italian poet, named Pietro Cossa, has tried like many another poet before him to bring Nero back to life on the stage. It is he who sums up Nero's nature in one line: 'His heart is Roman, but his mind is Greek.' These words express the whole tragic conflict which this singular man was fated to endure in his own heart. It is easy to

imagine how enraptured Nero was by everything Greek, and
especially by the Greek games, coarsened as they were by
Roman pomp and ostentation; how flattered his immoderate vanity was when he heard himself applauded by thousands as a singer or an actor or a victor in the games – yet
in his heart he was a miserable weakling, tortured by re-
morse. History has other examples of the prince who
appears as a magnificent despot, while his heart is fainting
with despair. All the details of Nero's homosexuality (true
or exaggerated) would correspond very well with this Hellenism in his character. Men of this type are not naturally
prudent and farsighted financiers; they cannot keep their
money, but dissipate it in brilliant festivities and all sorts of
extravagances. Nero seems to have been wildly extravagant. And none of his sexual deeds or misdeeds did him so
much harm in the eyes of the people as his wastefulness;
for he was compelled to refill his treasury, which was at that
time hardly separated from the treasury of the state, by
doubtful means, such as debasement of the currency and
even downright plundering of the provinces. I am inclined
to use this purely aesthetic outlook of Nero in order to
explain the attribution to him of the famous burning of
Rome. It is perfectly credible that when he gazed from his
palace on the flames of the blazing city, he let fall imprudent
remarks about the dreadful beauty of the sight – and that
these remarks were taken to mean that he had instigated the
burning either to enjoy its beauty or else to construct his
new palace on the ruins. I myself would not attribute the
burning of Rome to Nero. If he was not responsible, the
famous chapter in Tacitus (*Ann.*, xv, 44) about the persecution of the Christians after the fire loses much of its claim
to validity. No Christian author mentions the persecution;
which makes it all the more probable that the chapter is an
invention interpolated by Christians to give some historical
evidence for the existence of Christ. This by the way. But
Suetonius mentions a persecution of Christians at that time,
although only in brief and general terms. He knows nothing
of the details which are given in Tacitus. We must not disregard the fact that he, the greatest gossip among historians, says nothing of these matters.

We may say, also, that Nero's aestheticism was the factor

which made him so detested by the still powerful senate –
so detested that the senators joined in one conspiracy after
another, and finally allowed him to meet his end when some
of the frontier armies revolted. We read in Cassius Dio:
'It was insufferable to hear of it, far less to see it, when a
Roman, a senator, a patrician, a pontiff, a Caesar, an Emperor, an Augustus, put his name on the list of competitors,
exercised his voice, practised various songs, appeared with
long hair and smooth chin, with robe thrown back, presented himself in the lists with only one or two attendants,
stared savagely at his opponents, defied his rivals with abu-
sive words, and bribed the overseers of the games and the
attendants in fear of being rebuked by them and being
whipped out of the lists – all this to win a prize for lyre-
playing ... and to lose his imperial honour!' It should be
noted that the same author says (62, 10): 'The common
people and the soldiers watched this, and did not object,
but praised it.'

His weak-willed aestheticism and love of pleasure are
reflected in his inglorious conduct when his throne began to
totter. The account of Suetonius can in this case be accepted
because of its close correspondence with Nero's real character. He writes (47): 'When the revolt of the other armies
was announced, he was at dinner. He tore up the dispatches,
threw over the table, dashed to the ground two goblets
which he loved and used to call the Homeric cups because
of their designs, and then procured some poison from Lu-
custa which he put in a golden jar. Then he went to the
Servilian Gardens. There he sent the most faithful of his
freedmen to Ostia to get the fleet ready, and meanwhile
tried to induce the tribunes and centurions of the Guard to
join him in flight.' When they refused, he conceived the
maddest schemes – all, in fact, except the obvious one of
resistance. He had the idea of going to the Forum in mourning clothes and using all his eloquence to awake the people's
pity. But even he had to admit that such a course would lay
him open to being murdered by his enemies. Finally, he fled
to the country estate of one of his freedmen, and hid himself in a remote part of it, continually complaining of the
misery of his life. Finally he directed everything necessary
for his funeral to be prepared; bursting into tears at every

stage of the preparations, and crying out 'What an artist perishes in me!'

Still he shrank, like the coward he was, from killing himself. At last a messenger arrived with the terrible news that the senate had made him an outlaw, and that he was to be brought back to Rome and flogged to death. Nero was overpowered by horror. He could not endure the physical pain which he had calmly inflicted on thousands of his fellowmen. He heard the troopers riding up to arrest him – and even now the aesthete could not refrain from citing a line of Homer:

> Listen! there falls on my hearing the thunder of galloping
> horses!

At last he accomplished the task of dying. With the help of his secretary (who had fled with him) he thrust a dagger into his throat.

His body was not mutilated, as he had feared. His mistress Acte and two of his faithful nurses gave it honourable burial, and even brought it home to the tomb of his family. It is clear that he was not hated by the common people; for a long time his grave was covered with flowers, and a false Nero who impersonated him soon after his death found many to believe that he was the real Emperor.

We may summarize his character in this way. Nero suffered from a dreadful hereditary taint. The development of his nature was strongly affected by his irregular education in childhood and by the long and powerful influence of his mother. To these factors we must add his versatile and artistic disposition, which he was never able to organize, despite his amateur efforts in many different arts.

He appears, then, as a neurotic man, weak and cowardly at bottom (as aesthetic men often are). Sexually, he found satisfaction in many different ways, because he could always command the fulfilment of any of his desires. He was certainly bisexual by nature. He was not a sadist through and through, as he is often described. Above all else he was a man who never freed himself from his maternal fixation.

His character has always appeared differently to different men. This can be seen in the variety of works which deal with him and his age – sometimes Nero is a cold cynic and a heartless aesthete (as in Cossa's play), sometimes a devilish Antichrist (as in Sienkiewicz's famous romance *Quo Vadis?*), and sometimes (as in Wilbrand's book) the tyrant who perishes in the pitiful madness of despotic power. It seems to me that there is no such thing as an artistic re-creation of the real Nero; for we do not yet know what Nero really was.

Domitian

Among Nero's successors, the most interesting for us is the enigmatic Domitian. History books usually describe him as 'the cruel and malignant Emperor'; however, it seems that scholars are gradually coming to a different estimate of him. Müller calls him 'crazy' and 'unbalanced'; his craziness would be enough to explain his notorious cruelty. Still, Müller is prepared to admit that 'Domitian's portraits on coins and statues show no direct trace of a cruel nature'. It is therefore possible that much of the cruelty of which he is accused is the malevolent invention of historians who sympathized with the senatorial party. The senate hated him because he was not so susceptible to their flatteries as his predecessor Titus had been. It is fairly well established that apart from his supposed cruelty he was an energetic Emperor who paid careful attention to every department of administration and was nevertheless a keen and intelligent patron of the arts.

What was his sexual nature? Suetonius (1) says it was well known that a certain ex-praetor possessed and showed a letter from Domitian promising to spend a night with him. This, of course, may be the usual scandal about an unpopular young man; for Domitian's usual reputation was that of a great lover of women. He carried off his wife Domitia from her husband, 'after seducing many other wives'. Later he divorced this woman for having a love-affair with the actor Paris, but took her back shortly afterwards, 'because' as Suetonius (3) maliciously conjectures 'he could not bear to be separated from her'. It is not disputed that Domitian paid quite as much attention as Augustus to the morals of his subjects: we have referred to this in earlier chapters. He forbade the castration of boys, and reduced the price of eunuchs in order to diminish the incentives to buy them.

He also attempted to revive the unpopular Scantinian law against homosexual intercourse with boys of free birth, and he inflicted the severe penalty of former times on guilty Vestals and their lovers.

Surely it is quite possible that these measures (which were obviously far from popular) were enough to give Domitian a reputation for cruelty. We can be sure that he was not a sadist in the usual sense of the word; for once, as Suetonius (11) expressly tells us, he reprieved some criminals who had been condemned in the old manner to the dreadful death by flogging, and allowed them to choose their own death, 'because he shrank from that atrocious punishment'. On this account we must refuse credence to the report (Suet., 10) that he invented a new method of torture which consisted in burning the sexual organs of his victims. But there is another remark which is more worthy of notice – it is found in both Suetonius and Cassius Dio without much variation. Domitian, we are told, took pleasure in killing flies. Even more surprising is a report in Cassius Dio (which is not found in any other author). We shall quote it in full (67, 9):—

'Domitian had a room hung entirely with black – ceiling, walls, and floor – and furnished with black benches without cushions. His guests were shown into this room at night, with no attendants. There was a slab of stone beside each of them, like a tombstone, bearing that guest's name; and the slabs were lit by the little lamps which are hung on tombs. Then there appeared beautiful boys, naked, and painted black like spectres: they moved round the guests in an uncanny dance, and then stood one at the feet of each of the guests. Now food and drink were brought in, as for the banquet of the dead – all black and in black dishes. The guests shook with terror: they expected the deathblow to fall at any moment; the room was as silent as a grave; only Domitian spoke, and he talked only of murder and a sudden death. At last he dismissed them. But before he did so, he sent away his servants who had been waiting in the courtyard so that the guests were carried or driven home by total strangers – which increased their terror. Finally, when they had all reached home, and partially recovered, a messenger from the Emperor was announced. Every guest thought his last hour had struck. But instead, each of the guests received his gravestone (which was of silver) and then other gifts, including the valuable dishes of costly workmanship which had been set before him at the banquet, and finally even the boy who had played his wraith, now washed clean and beautifully dressed. These were their compensations for the death-agony they had suffered all the preceding night. Such were the feats which Domitian gave to celebrate his victories (as he said) – or rather (as the people said) in honour of those who lost their lives, both in Dacia and in Rome.'

Yet, for all this, we must remember what we have seen in the chapter on literature: Domitian's age loved sensational presentments of gloom and horror. However tasteless this may appear to us, it was fashionable then. If we remember this, we shall see that even Domitian's notorious funeral feast is no clear proof of sadism in him. Nor can we infer the cruelty of his nature from the fact that he killed his wife's lover, Paris, and then, despite a reconciliation with his wife, made his niece Julia his mistress.

We must not forget the remark of Suetonius (*Domit.,* 9): 'In the beginning he shrank from any form of bloodshed.' It can hardly be denied that, like Tiberius, he was driven by the cruel experiences of his later life to be constantly on his guard with a harshness which was sometimes excessive. In his last years, his unfathomable cunning became more and more noticeable. He was capable of inviting an erring official to talk with him, and even to sup with him, and then of dismissing him in such a way the man retired happy and carefree. Next day the man would be executed. This was not a sign of a kind or humane character, yet similar conduct is not unknown to history.

Towards the end of his life, Domitian must have been a strange and almost uncanny companion, with his distrustful nature and his constant fear of conspiracies. This fear was sometimes justified, and was natural enough to any Emperor who thought how his predecessors had died. If, in the end, even his wife Domitia (who had betrayed him with the actor Paris) was privy to his murder, we cannot take this as a criticism of Domitian's own character. The mistress of a pantomimist was not a high-souled woman. Domitian has often been misjudged, and it is hard not to feel some sympathy with him when we read (Suet., 21):– 'He often gave sumptuous banquets, but they were hurried. They never lasted beyond sunset, and were never followed by revels. For, between sunset and sleep, he always walked alone in a secret place.' With this we may compare a few words in Cassius Dio (67, 1):– 'He never had a genuine affection for any human being, except one or two women.'

In this connection, we must discuss a further point. Domitian is well known as a particularly cruel and unjust persecutor of the Stoic philosophers. We have elsewhere discussed the part played by Stoic philosophy in the Imperial age; here we must discuss the real nature of this particular persecution. In the first place, we must observe that there had been persecutions before Domitian's time, even under his humane predecessor, Vespasian. At least, we read in Suetonius (*Vesp.*, 13):– 'Vespasian bore without anger the obstinacy of philosophers. ... Demetrius, the cynic, after he had been condemned (to exile), met Vespasian on the road, and refused to rise or to greet him, but yelped out some abuse. Vespasian contented himself with calling him a dog.' Cassius Dio (65, 12) tells the story with more detail:–

'Helvidius Priscus was the son-in-law of Thrasea; he had been educated in Stoic doctrine, and imitated Thrasea's freedom of speech, sometimes unseasonably. During his praetorship, he did nothing to honour the Emperor and never ceased to abuse him. On this account the tribunes once arrested him and put him in the charge of their attendants. Vespasian broke down at this, and left the senate-house in tears, saying: "I will be succeeded by my son or by no one" ... Vespasian hated Helvidius Priscus not so much because of himself and his friends whom Helvidius insulted, but because the man was seditious and pandered to the mob and was for ever denouncing monarchy and praising democracy. He acted on his words, and formed a league of sympathizers, as if it were the function of philosophy to abuse the rulers, and stir up the masses, and overthrow the constitution, and bring about revolution. Being Thrasea's son-in-law, he attempted to copy him, but fell far short of doing so. For Thrasea had lived under Nero, whom he disliked;

yet he had never said or done anything insulting to Nero, except that he refused to share in his conduct. But Helvidius had a grudge against Vespasian, and never left him alone in public or in private; he courted death by his behaviour, and he was due to pay the penalty for not knowing his own place. A great number of people (including Demetrius, the cynic philosopher) were induced by Stoic doctrines to teach in public many doctrines unsuitable for the times; they covered their acts with the name of philosophy. Mucianus, therefore, persuaded Vespasian to expel all such people from Rome, although he himself was prompted more by anger than by a love for logic and philosophy. He made a long and remarkable speech to the Emperor against the Stoics. "They are full," he said "of vain ostentation. If one of them grows his beard long, raises his eyebrows, wears a coarse mantle thrown back and no shoes, he at once lays claim to wisdom, bravery, and justice, and gives himself great airs even although (as they say) he can neither swim a stroke nor write a line. They look down on everybody else. They call a nobleman a nincompoop, a common man a lout, a handsome man wanton and an ugly man a dolt, a rich man greedy and a poor man slavish." Vespasian immediately expelled all the philosophers from Rome, except Musonius. Demetrius and Hostilianus he banished to islands. Hostilianus paid no attention whatever when he heard about the banishment (he was teaching somebody at the time) but ran down monarchy even more bitterly. However, he left Rome at once. But Demetrius would not give way even then. Vespasian ordered this message to be given to him: "You are trying hard to get me to kill you, but I do not kill a dog that barks at me".'

These accounts are enough to show that the Stoics, like the later Christians, did not only abuse the emperor, but 'preached doctrines contrary to the existing regime'; and that they won adherents to these doctrines and sought to draw attention to themselves by their appearance and behaviour. Domitian, then, did no more than carry out the course of action which Vespasian had begun. Adherents of Thrasea and Helvidius were executed (Cas. Dio, 67, 13), others were banished. Others were condemned by Domitian to death or to the confiscation of their property, be-

cause they 'despised the gods . . . a crime for which many of
those who sympathized with Judaism were condemned'.
Do these accusations not resemble the reproaches which
were later levelled against the Christians? Are they not
almost identical with them? In our chapter on literature,
we have tried to indicate the real importance of Stoicism,
as distinguished from the ridiculous affectations of its
adherents: it was a secret doctrine, widespread among the
best spirits of the age, the real seekers after truth. Perhaps
we shall one day follow Drews and Bruno Bauer in emphasizing the organic connection between these Stoics and the
first Roman Christianity – or shall we say the first Christianity? Such an idea is of course not admitted by official
theology. Yet it might at least be admitted that many of
the deepest and most human teachings of the Gospel are
found in Roman Stoicism. The consequences of that admission must be left to scholars. Today, these questions
are too important to be ignored.

Antinous

We turn now the melancholy and pathetic figure of Antinous, the beautiful boy loved by Hadrian. The riddle of
his character can, I believe, soonest be solved if we emphasize above all the religious element in it. But first let us take
the facts as they are given by our sources.

Cassius Dio (69, 11) writes: 'Hadrian travelled through
Palestine to Egypt. There he sacrificed to Pompey's spirit,
and wrote this verse on him:–

'Unburied lay the man who built a thousand temples.'

He gave orders that Pompey's grave, which had fallen into
ruin, should be repaired. There also he built the city of
Antinous. Antinous was a Bithyian, from the city which is
called Claudiopolis. He was Hadrian's male concubine, and
he died in Egypt – either through falling into the Nile, as
Hadrian declared, or because he was offered as a sacrifice,
which is probably the truth, because Hadrian was so inquisitive that he meddled with soothsaying and magical arts.
Either because of his love for Antinous, or because Antinous had died for his sake (for his purposes he needed the

voluntary self-sacrifice of a life), Hadrian honoured the dead youth so much that he built a city in the place where he had died, naming it after him. He placed statues and busts of Antinous in almost every city throughout the Empire. He wished even to see a special star of Antinous in the heavens, and he was pleased when his companions helped him to concoct the story that Antinous' soul had become a star never seen before in all the sky.'

Another account is equally sensational – that of Spartianus, one of the six 'historians of the emperors'. (We shall later make the acquaintance of the worst of these, Lampridius.) These authors are characterized by their use of excellent evidence, which they mingle freely with foolish and worthless gossip. Spartianus writes in his biolgraphy of Hadrian (chap. 14): 'After his tour of Arabia, Hadrian visited Pelusium, where he repaired Pompey's tomb with great splendour. During a voyage on the Nile, he lost his favourite Antinous, and lamented him in a womanly manner.' (The word is *muliebriter*, which Birt well translates *tenderly*, like a mother mourning for her child.) 'With regard to the death of Antinous, there are various reports. Some say that he sacrificed himself or was sacrificed for Hadrian. Others give a different reason, which can easily be guessed from Antinous' beauty and Hadrian's sensuality. The Greeks deified him, which gave Hadrian much pleasure, and attributed oracles to him which were said to be really written by Hadrian himself. For Hadrian paid much attention to poetry as well as to science: he was very learned in arithmetic, geometry, and painting. He had also some claims to distinction as a singer and harpist. In sensual pleasure he knew no bounds. He himself wrote many love-poems about his favourites. He was also very experienced in strategy and the use of arms. . . . He was at once serious and gay, friendly and dignified, wanton and irresolute, thrifty and generous; he could affect emotion or conceal it, he was both cruel and gentle, in fact at all times and in all things he was versatile and varied.'

The third piece of evidence about Antinous which is extant occurs in a much later but valuable author, Sextus Aurelius Victor (*History of the Emperors,* 14): 'Hadrian as usual in time of peace, retired for rest to his estate at

Tibur, and put Lucius Aelius Caesar in charge of Rome.
In Tibur he built palaces and gave himself up to banquets,
sculpture and painting, as is the way of rich men with their
fortunes: he paid great attention to all luxuries and sensual
delights. This gave rise to scandals. It was said that he had
had sexual connections with youths, and had been ardently
devoted to Antinous, which was the reason why he founded
a city in the youth's name and raised statues to him.
Others think these were acts of piety and religion. Hadrian,
they say, had wished to prolong his own life, and had been
asked by magicians for a substitute who was willing to die
for him; all others refused, but Antinous gave himself up,
and that, they say, is the reason for the acts of duty which
have been mentioned. I shall leave the matter undecided,
although in my opinion a friendship between two persons
of different age is always suspicious when one of them has
a lascivious temperament.'

Another important piece of evidence about this enigmatic youth has lately been discovered. This is quoted by
Birt (*Roman Portraits*, 301). This is a papyrus found in
Egypt which contains forty lines of poetry describing a
lion hunt in which Hadrian and Antinous took part, and
where Hadrian rescued his favourite from the claws of a
savage lion. It is possible to conclude from this papyrus
that the relation of the middle-aged emperor to the youth
was not that of a coarse voluptuary to his plaything. And
such a conclusion would be confirmed by the fact that
the emperor did not shrink from instituting a cult of the
boy after his death, and even of founding a sort of new
religion on the young life which had been so brief. Is it
conceivable that anyone could have instituted a cult for
anything so despised by the Romans as a male concubine?
No, the beautiful youth from Bithynia must have stood in
that ideal relationship to Hadrian which Plato in his Sym-
posium calls Eros. Hadrian had more than an admiration
for Greek things; his heart was truly Greek. The relation
of the two must have been purely spiritual. The Emperor
was bewitched by the beauty of Antinous as soon as he saw
him in his native country; and from that year (A.D. 124) he
made him his constant companion. As Socrates admired
Alcibiades – for wisdom loves what is beautiful – so the

wise Hadrian loved what was most worthy of love and adored it like a god. Is this so hard to understand? Must we think of a purely sexual relationship, like the ancient historians, who could understand neither Hadrian nor his favourite?

In my view, the best and profoundest commentary on Hadrian's love for Antinous, and especially for the deification of the youth after his death, is to be found in a modern work, little known by general readers. This is the wonderful sequence of poems named *Maximin* by Stefan George, the latest of Plato's descendants. There George says:

> In thee I see the God
> whom I accept with awe,
> the God of my devotion.

This is the fire which burned in Hadrian when he first saw Antinous. And Hadrian must often have cried, like the modern poet:

> The spring returns again!
> Thou hallowest earth and air
> and us, by thy regard –
> my faltering thanks are thine.

And still more often after the death of his beloved:

> Heavy the air, and desolate the days.
> How can I worship you in fitting way?
> How may I light your beacon through our days?
> My only pleasure is to hide away
> in earth the pomp and ashes of my days.
> Only my sorrow points me down each way,
> as, blank of song or act, vanish the days.
> Lift out of mist and darkness my life's way,
> accept the sacrifice of my dead days.

Then came the revelation. Filled with new strength, he could cry:

> Adore your city, which brought forth a God.
> Adore your time, in which a God has lived!

I would very gladly transcribe the whole of these simple and yet extraordinarily profound poems, for they illuminate the whole experience of Hadrian. He had really felt the innermost meaning of Platonism. The youth who had died so early became a god, who spoke thus to his worshippers:

> Lift up your heads, ye gates!
> The candle's feeble glimmer must be quenched,
> the requiem is sung!

And the Emperor could say of himself at the end of his earthly life:

> Thy name now journeys high and far,
> raising our souls to purity. . . .
> Against a dark eternity
> I kindle and exalt thy star.

I have no doubt that these last verses can be taken to mean that Hadrian had (as the historians say) given for his favourite a place among the stars. This lofty interpretation, high above worldly gossip, is the real clue to the love of Hadrian and Antinous. It explains the lives of these strange men so far as the inmost life of the soul can ever be explained.

Every wise and sympathetic reader must feel certain that Hadrian could never have caused or even approved the self-sacrifice of his young friend. Antinous died young, in the flower and hope of his life. We do not know the details of his death, and we do not need to know them. But such a death made it easy for myths to be woven about his life and fate. The depth of such a love as this and the Greek mysticism of Hadrian's many-sided character explain why he founded the city of Antinoöpolis, at the place of Antinous's death, and made him the patron deity of the city. In that city he became Osiris, the young Egyptian god, as he became the Greek Dionysus at other centres of his cult. For we find him worshipped in many other places besides his own city; so many that his statues are common in museums of antiquity. It was a peculiar cult, modelled on that of Adonis, or, in the opinion of some scholars, on that of Christ. Today we possess full information about it. French scholars have excavated the greater part of Antinoöpolis. The mummies of his priests have been found, and we know that the greatest of their rites was a 'mystery play, the Passion of Antinous, in which ceremonial dances or moving images annually represented his death and resurrection' (Birt, *lib. cit.*) It is now certain that Roman historians have misunderstood the deepest meaning of this cult. It will always be memorable that the love of a mighty emperor for a beautiful Greek youth developed into a religion which had, for many years and in many cities, its own altars and its own beautiful statues.

The face of Antinous was the last of the idealizations produced by Roman art under the influence of Hellenism. All those who have seen those statues of the youth with the full soft lips, curling hair, and the cheeks of a child, have wondered what is the real meaning of that earnest gaze. The most improbable theories have been constructed to explain it. It seems to me that the simple humanity of Birt's explanation is the only true one. Antinous' face expresses the eternal sorrow for youth which passes, beauty which fades, and perfection which dies at last.

Heliogabalus

One of the most enigmatic figures in the late empire is the boy Heliogabalus (or, as he is sometimes called, Elagabal). He was associated with an oriental deity, and cannot be understood apart from it; so that everything we can say of Heliogabalus might have been said in our discussion of the religious ideas of the Romans. Still, we have so much vivid and concrete information about the boy, that it seems more suitable to discuss him in connection with the other scarcely less interesting characters of Imperial times.

In order to understand his life, we must be clear on one point: in him three inconsistent elements are united. He is a fourteen-year-old boy. He is the priest of a cult 'which combined deep mysticism and wild obscenity without reconciling them', as Dieterich says. Finally, he is the Roman Emperor who made the crazy attempt to introduce to Rome his own Syrian cult, and in fact to put it in the place of all other religions. We can understand at once that the character which contained such dissimilar elements had something tragic about it.

But besides that, Heliogabalus was predisposed by his inherited character to a life of licentiousness and sensuality. He was a Syrian, a grand-nephew of the Emperor Septimius Severus and the Syrian woman Julia Domna. The historian of that time, Herodian, whose *History* seems to tell the truth about Heliogabalus, says of him (v, 3, 7): 'He was in the flower of his youth, and in beauty he surpassed all others of the same age. Since he combined youth, beauty, and fine dress, he made men think of a beautiful picture of the young Bacchus.' Descending, as he did, more from the Semitic than from the Roman stock, he must have had that almost feminine beauty which won the special admiration of men of his time. Herodian continues (v, 3, 8): 'When he did sacrifice and danced in the foreign way around the altar to the sound of flutes and pipes and other instruments, he took the eyes of all the men – especially of the soldiers, who knew that he was of royal birth. His youthful beauty fascinated those who saw him ... The soldiers used frequently to come into the city, and, visiting the temple to attend service there, took pleasure in watching the young man.'

With the help of these soldiers, and at the instigation of his ambitious grandmother Maesa, he declared himself Roman Emperor in the Syrian town of Emesa or Hemesa, where he was born. After a short stay in Nicomedia, he came to Rome, urged on as ever by his grandmother. He was still faithful in his allegiance to his god, and 'made a great display of the priesthood of that native god whose acolyte he had been. He wore very costly clothes: a purple robe embroidered with gold, necklaces, and bracelets, and a crown of gold, in the form of a turban, ornamented with precious stones. His costume was something between the priestly robes of Phoenicia and the luxurious dress of the Medes. He detested Greek and Roman clothes; he said they were made of wool, a cheap material; he himself liked nothing but silk. When he appeared in public, it was to the sound of flutes and kettledrums, as if he were worshipping his god' (Herodian, v, 5, 3). His prudent grandmother, who wished through him to recover her power in the imperial court, warned him that such a costume was not likely to please the Romans, 'who were unaccustomed to such a dress and would think its splendour more suitable for a woman than a man'. But Heliogabalus knew little of life, and cared nothing for the advice of his experienced grandmother: he listened only to his flatterers, who, of course, never told him the truth. Still, he caused a picture of himself to be painted, wearing priestly robes as he appeared at the sacrifice. This was sent on ahead to Rome, and was hung in the Senate above the goddess of Victory, in order that offerings and libations could be made to it, and also in order that the Romans might become accustomed to the foreign appearance of their new Emperor.

At the same time he ordained that every sacrifice to any god should be accompanied by an invocation of 'the new god Elagabal'.

What god was this, whom the boy-Emperor served so faithfully? Even today there are conflicting opinions of his nature. Wissowa thinks he was the Syrian sun-god, better known as Baal. In Emesa he was worshipped in the form of a conical black stone (a phallus?). In Rome, according to Wissowa, he had been known since A.D. 158, under the name of *Sol Inuictus Deus*, the Unconquerable Sun-god. After this god, the young Emperor named himself Elagabal, although his real name was Bassianus. (The word Elagabal passed into Heliogabalus in Greek, because the Greek for *sun* is *helios*). The new god was given his own priesthood, and several temples – one on the Palatine near the imperial palace, and another in the suburbs of Rome. In one of these temples the Emperor assembled the symbols of all other existing deities in order to show that the cult of Heliogabalus embraced the secrets of all other religions (so Lampridius tells us). This, of course, was far from extraordinary then, in the age of syncretism, when all the gods were confused with each other. Alexander Severus, for example, had in his house images of all known gods, and even, it is alleged, of Christ as well. Heliogabalus, however, did not stop at this. He conceived the idea (which we should call an absurd fancy) of marrying his god to a goddess-consort. This is mentioned in Dieterich's essay, *The Decline of Ancient Religion,* p. 496 (ed. 1911, in the book named *Essays and Papers*). He writes: 'Senseless as it may seem, this ceremony conceals the profound religious idea of the marriage of the Divine King and the Divine Queen, who unite in a $\iota\epsilon\rho\grave{o}\varsigma$ $\gamma\acute{a}\mu o\varsigma$ to bless and fructify the earth. Heliogabalus found his Queen in the great Carthaginian goddess, who is sometimes called Juno, sometimes the

Heavenly Virgin, *uirgo caelestis*, and sometimes the simple title of Queen, *regina*. Her magnificent statue was brought to Rome to be the bride in the colossal marriage-ceremony which the young Emperor celebrated.'

We see, then, that the basis of the Emperor's religious innovations was the worship of a Syrian sun-god. This is what Herodian says of the cult (v, 5, 8): 'He built a huge and magnificent temple to the god, surrounded by numerous altars. Every morning he visited it at dawn; he slaughtered hecatombs of oxen and multitudes of sheep, and laid them on the altars, pouring over them all kinds of perfumes, and drenching the ground before the altars with many flagons of the finest and oldest wine, so that streams of blood and wine flowed everywhere. He danced round the altars to the sound of various instruments, and Syrian women danced with him, running round and clashing cymbals and beating kettledrums. Around him stood the whole senate and the whole order of knights, in their ceremonial attire. The entrails of the sacrificed animals and the perfumes were carried high above the worshippers' heads, in golden vessels; they were not carried by slaves or common people, but by the prefects of the garrisons and the most important ministers of state. These men wore long robes reaching to their feet and covering their arms, in the Phoenician fashion, with one stripe of purple down the middle of the robe; and they were shod with linen shoes, like oriental priests. Heliogabalus thought it the greatest honour he could bestow to allow any man to take part in the ceremony.' In the summer, the stone image of the god was transferred in solemn procession to another temple (v, 6, 6). 'He placed the god on a chariot ornamented with gold and the finest jewels, and so took him out of Rome into the suburbs. The chariot was drawn by a team of six great white horses without spot, with golden harness and with coloured breastplates. There was no driver; the reins were wound round the god, for he drove himself. Heliogabalus ran ahead of the chariot, stepping backwards, keeping his face turned to the god, and holding the bits of the horses. He went backwards all the way, gazing on the god's face. So that he should not stumble or slip (not seeing where he put his feet) the way was strewn thickly with golden sand,

and men-at-arms held him, one on each side, to keep him safe as he ran. On each side ran a multitude of the common people, bearing torches, and throwing wreaths and hand-fuls of flowers. In the procession went the images of all the other gods, and every precious and costly offering, and all the symbols of sovereignty and the imperial treasures, and the knights, and the whole army. So Heliogabalus took the god to his new home.'

In this connection we must cite the fact that Heliogabalus (sexually precocious as he was) married one of the Vestal Virgins, saying 'It is an appropriate act of religion for a priest to wed a priestess'. This was his second marriage, and there were others to follow. Not long afterwards, he repudiated this Vestal wife (who must have been much older than he) and married a grand-daughter of Marcus Aurelius.

Why was Heliogabalus able to hold the imperial throne for only four years? Historians give very different answers to that question. Herodian, the most matter-of-fact of them, says that the army put him on the throne, was dis-illusioned, and overthrew him. His grandmother, whose ambition had been responsible for his ascent to power, soon saw that his strange life and conduct displeased the army – especially when he copied Nero (whom he seems to have resembled in some ways) by appearing in public as a dancer and a charioteer, and by using paint 'to disfigure a face which Nature had made beautiful' (Herodian). Maesa's cun-ning and experience led her to fear that by his eventual fall she would lose her own power. She found a brilliant and dangerous solution. Heliogabalus had a cousin twelve years old, named Alexianus, whose character seemed to be much more suitable for the imperial duties and dignity. Alexia-nus, therefore, was 'adopted by Heliogabalus and given a share of the Empire ... Heliogabalus himself should now be able to devote himself to his worship and his priesthood, devoted as he was to mystical rites and orgies and the ser-vice of his god'; meanwhile, someone else must attend to the duties of this world, and for that duty Alexianus was best fitted. Accordingly, Alexianus was adopted to share the throne, under the name of Alexander. His adroit mother, Mammaea, saw to it that he had tutors to educate

him both in Greek and Roman letters and in the most
reasonable kinds of sport and physical exercise. Heliogabalus attempted to inspire him with adoration for his own
god. He endeavoured to dismiss the tutors. Perceiving that
the army was beginning to transfer its affection to the upright and sensible Alexianus, he attempted his life; however, the women of the court, Mammaea and Maesa the
grandmother, shielded the boy from the danger which
threatened him.

The Emperor's effeminate life came to infuriate the army
more and more. 'They were disgusted when they saw his
face made up more elaborately than any honest woman's,
and himself effeminately ornamented with golden necklaces and dainty clothes, dancing for all the world to see.
So their minds began to incline towards Alexander: they
placed more hope in him, because he was being decently
and soberly brought up' (Herodian, v, 8, 1). When Heliogabalus committed the folly of depriving his cousin of the
title Caesar, which he had lately given him, the soldiers
became even more enraged. At last they broke out in open
revolt. Heliogabalus was killed, along with Soaemis, his
detested mother, and his whole household. His body and
that of Soaemis were dragged on hooks through the city
and thrown into the Tiber. The well-beloved youth Alexander succeeded to the throne, under the guardianship of
his mother and grandmother. That is the story as told by
Herodian.

We have two other accounts of Heliogabalus, which
differ greatly from the one just quoted. The first is that of
Cassius Dio, who was a contemporary; and the second that
of Lampridius, a cheap and sensational writer from a later
age. Both accounts contrast with Herodian's simple and
matter-of-fact history by emphasizing the phallic element
in Heliogabalus' life. The contrast may be explained in
several ways. The simplest solution (which appears in all
history books) is of course that Cassius Dio and Lampridius give the real truth about the life of this 'degenerate
scoundrel'. Convenient as that view may be, I do not share
it – at least not in all its implications. It is doubtless true
that this half-Semitic youth, suddenly raised to the mightiest throne in the world, may have permitted himself to act

in a way reminiscent of Nero. For instance, these authors tell us that shortly after his accession he put to death a great number of men who had deserved well of him, including his tutor, who had done him great service in the war with the previous Emperor Macrinus. And this is the description which Dio gives: 'He murdered this man because he insisted on making him behave moderately and reasonably; and he himself struck the first blow, because none of the soldiers would begin the butchery' (Cassius Dio, 80, 6). Our first comment on this must be that such an act can hardly have taken place without the consent of Heliogabalus' mother, who is described as a cruel and vicious woman. She and the ambitious grandmother must have played a part in his Government similar to that of Agrippina with the young Nero. The heartless ingratitude shown in the savage murder of Heliogabalus' tutor can be psychologically explained in this way: the youth was conscious of his new-found manhood, and, in the attempt to break finally with all the old restraining influences, grasped at his sword. Yet perhaps the whole incident is only a malicious and baseless piece of scandal – the kind of scandal which would multiply rapidly as soon as the Emperor was overthrown and murdered. I believe also that all the other atrocities (especially the sexual ones) mentioned in Cassius Dio and Lampridius may be interpreted in a very different sense – although no one to my knowledge has yet attempted to do so. Possibly my interpretation is mistaken; but I shall try to substantiate it. Here it is.

As Dieterich says (in the passage quoted above) the cult of Heliogabalus' Syrian deity had elements of gross obscenity. We know that the entrance of his temple in Syria was flanked by two colossal phalli, said to have been set up by Bacchus himself; and the symbol of the god of Emesa was nothing but a 'great conical black stone' like a phallus. Can we not believe that the cult introduced by Heliogabalus was simply a phallic cult – especially since phallic cults appear throughout the ancient world in very different forms? The young priest of such a cult will involuntarily see himself as *feminine*. It is in harmony with this theory that, as we read, Heliogabalus wished to castrate himself, and then confined himself to circumcision,

but always appeared at the dances in honour of his deity
in more or less feminine attire. He saw himself as the female
principle, in contrast to the god of pure masculinity. We
can see clearly that Heliogabalus conceived his deity as
the male principle; the divine marriage which he carried
out is evidence enough.

Now, if he was, so to speak, a woman carried away by
worship of masculinity, everything else explains itself. It
is easy to see why this 'infamous' youth sought out men of
remarkable phallic endowments, and eventually 'married'
one whose qualifications were exceptional. The scenes of
jealousy which occurred between these lovers are only
further developments of the same fantastic idea. It may
well be the case that feminine characteristics (in fact the
bisexual element) were unusually developed in his nature:
this is indicated by the remark in Cassius Dio (80, 14) that
he not only danced in the orchestra at his festivals, but had
an extraordinary 'dancing walk' in daily life. The same
characteristic occurs in modern biographies of homosexual
men.

Finally, we must notice a trace of masochism in his character – mentioned by Cassius Dio. We are told (among the
other reports which seem to be so questionable) that Heliogabalus was often thrashed by a jealous lover, and bore the
marks on his body. Cassius proceeds (80, 15, 4): 'His affection for this lover was not a casual impulse, but a strong
and deeply-rooted love: harsh treatment did not rouse his
indignation, but rather increased his passion; he wished to
give his lover the title of Caesar.'

We should like to imagine Heliogabalus as a pretty boy,
whose charm lay in his tender grace and his soft womanly
features. But if, as generally believed, there is any truth in
the portraits of him which appear on Roman coins (and
we know that coin-portraits generally reveal character),
then we are confronted with another enigma. The coins
which bear his head show a very ugly youth, almost adult
in years, with strongly Semitic features, oriental ringlets,
bleary eyes, a projecting underlip, and a great hooked nose
– in fact, the very opposite of 'a young Bacchus'. But these
very Syrian features (almost negroid, in fact) are enough to
explain the sensual character of so young a man.

At all events, we can see, from all the above facts and descriptions, that the riddle of Heliogabalus is not yet solved. I believe that the solution will not be found by treating as historical facts all the absurd and vulgar stories related by Lampridius, or by composing a sensational novel out of them, as the Dutch author Couperus has done. The matter is more complex than that. In my opinion, Herodian's biography approximates most nearly to a true description of that strange Syrian youth: I have accordingly based my account on his testimony.

Chapter Seven

The Fall of Rome and its Causes

In early Christian writings, and in the works of historians and moralists ever since, it is constantly asserted that the fall of Rome was a natural consequence of the sexual degeneracy, luxury, and dissipation of its people. In this chapter we will attempt to discover how much of that assertion is valid, and how much we must discard.

Leave the noisy streets of modern Rome, and make your way into the holy silence of the ruined Forum. Gaze on the old walls, on the pillars ivory-white against the blue of heaven; then raise your eyes to the Palatine, where, among the fallen stones of the imperial palace the soft blue of flowering trees stands out against the black pine crests. Or walk along the Via Sacra, beneath the colossal arch, which celebrates Titus' conquest of the Jews; and approach with awe the vast Flavian amphitheatre, rising like a rugged mountain wall before you. Despite yourself, you will be gripped by the thought which Hölderlin has expressed thus:

'Nations and brave cities are seized by the desire of death.
After the years have seen its work progress
after it has sought the best,
it meets at last a holy end.'

In Rome, as in hardly any other place in the world, the problem of the birth and passing of men and nations becomes a real and urgent one. If such a nation as Rome, whose Empire seemed established to eternity, sank at last into the dust, like the creature of a day, what can be the meaning and purpose of our life, our work, our hopes, and our beliefs?

We should be wrong to think that these questions and these thoughts are in any sense modern, and that the Romans themselves never reflected on them. Men were not slow to see that empires, however great and powerful they are, may yet be doomed to fall. As early as the time of the third Punic war, the historian Polybius meditates on the changing fortunes of the nations of the world: and it is clear that even although he does not say so, he does not believe that Rome will be eternal. Everyone knows the impressive scene from Book 38, preserved by Appian, where we see the proud conqueror of Carthage, among the ruins of Rome's ancient rival, reflecting gloomily upon the chances and changes of human fortune: he quotes two famous lines from the Iliad:

> The day will come when holy Troy shall perish,
> and Priam, king of the spear, and all his people.

and in them prefigures the fate of his own fatherland. And Polybius adds: 'Only a great, complete, and memorable soul could, at the climax of victory over his enemies, think of his own fate and the fickleness of fortune, and in the midst of his own happiness remember that happiness passes.'

There is an exceptionally interesting passage (generally neglected by modern writers) in a letter addressed to Cicero: in it Servius Sulpicius, one of his friends, tries to console him on the early death of his daughter (Cic., Ad fam., iv, 5):

'I shall tell you of something which brought some consolation to me, in the hope that it may lighten your own grief. On my return from Asia, I was sailing from Aegina to Megara. I looked at the countries surrounding me. Behind me was Aegina, ahead was Megara, on the right was the Piraeus, and on the left Corinth – once flourishing cities, they now lay prostrate and ruined. My thoughts were these: "To think that we creatures of a day should find it hard to bear if one of us dies or is killed (and yet our life must be short) when here in one place lie the unburied corpses of so many cities! Come, Servius, control yourself and remember that you are human." Believe me, my friend, these reflections greatly helped to strengthen me. And you also would do well to fix your mind upon them. Not long since, in one short time, many famous men perished, and this Roman Empire suffered great loss, and all the provinces were shaken. If one girl has lost her life, why must you grieve so heavily? If she had not died at this time, she must have met her end a few yers later, for she was mortal.'

Would any Roman write like this who believed that the Empire would last for ever? As the Republic passes away and the Principate comes into being, we hear such voices more often. Horace, in the famous Roman Ode, iii, 6, proclaims that the world is deteriorating with every new generation. Lucan, the poet of the Neronian age, perceives danger in the excessive size of the Empire, and in the 'envy of fate'. Other authors see spiritual decadence around them. Velleius Paterculus, writing under Tiberius, points out the degeneracy of art, saying (i, 17), 'It is hard for perfection to be constant. What cannot go forward must go back.' And this, he says, has happened in Rome to rhetoric, sculpture, painting, and engraving.

Tacitus, in his *Dialogue on Oratory*, singles out the decline of rhetoric (*Dial.* 28): 'Everyone knows that eloquence and the other arts have declined from their ancient glory – and not because they lacked men to practise them, but through the idleness of the younger generation, the negligence of the elder, the ignorance of teachers, and the disappearance of the old morality. This evil was born in Rome itself, infected Italy, and is now invading the provinces.'

Even Seneca, who usually points to the good of any age, is forced to acknowledge that the Roman Empire entered its old age when it lost its freedom in the principate (ap. Lactant., *Div. inst.*, vii, 15).

The second century historian Florus compares the development of the Roman people with the development of a man (i, 1): 'If we consider the Roman people as a man, and reflect on the whole course of its life – its birth, its growth, its prime, and its old age – we shall find that it passed through four stages. The first, under the Kings, lasted for 400 years, during which Rome struggled with its own neighbours. This was its infancy. The next age lasted from the Consulship of Brutus and Collatinus to the Consulship of

Appius Claudius and Quintus Fulvius – 150 years, in which Italy was subdued. This was a time full of virile and martial energy and might be called Rome's youth. Next come 150 years until Augustus, during which Rome subdued the whole world. This was the early manhood of the nation, the prime and flower of its life. From Augustus to the present age are almost two hundred years, in which the idleness of the Emperors has withered the Empire in old age.' Florus also sees in Rome's power and immensity one of the causes of her decline (i, 47; or iii, 12): 'Perhaps it would have been better for Rome to content herself with Sicily and Africa, or even to do without these provinces and rule all Italy, rather than to grow to such a magnitude that she is overwhelmed by her own power. What caused the madness of civil war, except excessive prosperity? We were corrupted first by the conquest of Syria, and then by Asia, the legacy of Attalus. That wealth and power struck at the root of morality, and made the nation sink and drown in the cesspool of its own vices ... Whence came the slave-wars if not from the abundance of our troops of slaves? What caused the gladiators to arm against their masters if not the extravagance lavished on gaining popularity among the commons by giving them games and shows as a favour, and raising even the execution of our enemies to an art. To turn to more blatant vices, is not political ambition excited by this wealth of ours? Hence the storms raised by Marius and Sulla. And do costly and magnificent banquets and largesse freely spent not change the greatest wealth into poverty? It was that poverty which set Catiline against his country. And last of all, is it not excessive riches which create the desire to be sole ruler of the Empire? Riches, then, armed Caesar and Pompey with the torches of the Furies to destroy their country.'

Last of all, Zosimus writes of the same matter. He was an historian writing under Honorius. He was not, however, a Christian, but a convinced adherent of the old state religion. He had seen the invasions of the Goths and Vandals, and he considered the fall of the Empire (or, as he calls it, the transference of power to the Germans) to be a consequence of the infidelity of Rome to the creed of its fathers. His remarks were so unpopular among the Christians that

scholars have attributed the mutilation of his text to its
pagan contents. However, they are in many respects an important supplement to Christian thought and writing of the
time. His opinion on the decline of Rome appears in the
passages dealing with Theodosius (iv, 59):

'The Senate still adhered to the tradition of its ancestors
and could not be induced to subscribe to blasphemy against
the gods. Theodosius called a meeting of the Senate, and
made a speech exhorting them to abandon what he called
their errors, and to choose the Christian faith; which
meant forgiveness for every sin and every impiety. No one
was converted by his speech: no one was willing to leave
the traditions which had been handed down since the foundation of Rome, or to prefer the foolish doctrine of the
Christians. They said that by upholding the traditional religion they had kept Rome safe from conquest for 1200
years, but that if they changed the old beliefs for the new
ones they could not tell what would happen. Theodosius
replied that the common people were oppressed by paying for sacrifices and religious ceremonies, and that he
wished to do away with them because he disliked the custom and because military emergencies called for more
money. Although the senators replied that the holy rites
would not only be duly performed unless they were paid
for by the State, the law about sacrifices was repealed, and
all the ancestral traditions of Rome fell into disregard. And
so the Roman power and empire was gradually mutilated
and became the home of the barbarians – or rather, having
lost all its inhabitants, it came to such a condition that no
one knows even the sites where its cities once stood.'

In another place (ii, 7) Zosimus says that after Diocletian neglected the rites 'the Empire gradually fell away, and
imperceptibly sank into barbarity'.

We cannot wonder that Christian writers, on the other
hand, always represent the degeneracy or the fall of Rome
as achieved through God's will. It will be enought to allude
to the most important and interesting of these authors –
the early writer, Minucius Felix (at the end of the second
century), Augustine himself (in the fourth and fifth centuries), and Augustine's follower, the historian Orosius.
Whatever may be our opinions of these writers, who of

course judge Roman life entirely from their own religious point of view, we may perhaps still learn a valuable lesson from them. We may learn to avoid the error of many distinguished modern scholars, and refuse to idealize the Roman Empire and its gigantic organization. One truth was recognized by the Christian authors more than by others. The Roman Empire actually was, as Minucius says, 'built up and extended by plunder, murder, crime, and infamy' – as we have tried to show in the chapter on cruelty in Rome. Augustine in his work *On the City of God* goes further and thinks more deeply. He cites a multitude of examples to prove that an empire based on such outrage and injustice, contained the germs of decay. The noble central thought of the whole work is perhaps expressed most clearly in these sentences (iv, 33): 'God alone creates and imparts happiness, because he is the only true god. God gives earthly power to the good and to the bad – yet not at random, as it were by chance (because he is God, and not fortune), but in accordance with a scheme of times and events which is known to himself and hidden to us. He is not governed by this scheme like a servant; he rules it like a master, arranges it, and controls it. But happiness he gives only to the good.' Augustine agrees with the greatest of his pagan predecessors that 'the marvellous achievements of Rome had two springs – freedom and the passion for glory'. But he has another thought in which I see the great advance made by his philosophy of history. For him, the great successes of Roman policy are no proof of great humanity among the Romans; for we must not forget, as he says, that the Empire grew up through the injustice of those against whom it waged righteous wars. In other words, it is only because the nations overthrown by Rome were even worse than Rome that they gave way before its power. Augustine's thoughts on the whole question of imperialism are so interesting and so easily intelligible in modern times, that I shall quote them here: 'War and conquests of other nations appear to the bad to be happiness, to the good merely a necessity. This necessity can be called happiness, only because things would be even worse if the just were conquered by the unjust. But without doubt, it is a greater happiness to live in harmony with a good neighbour than to overthrow

a bad neighbour in war. It is only the wicked who go so far
as to wish for an object of hate or fear in order to find an
enemy to conquer.' That is the verdict of a real Christian
on imperialistic policy, and in it is expressed the great
advance in political thought for which Christianity is alone
responsible. Augustine could not believe that the Roman
Empire would last for ever, because, as a devout Christian,
he was convinced that in the words of the Bible 'heaven
and earth shall pass away'.

Orosius, the Christian historian who was Augustine's
spiritual disciple, believed that the first symptoms of the
inclinatio imperii, the decline of the Empire, had shown
themselves as early as the murder of Julius Caesar.

The view of all these Christian writers, then, was that
Roman Christianity must take over as an inheritance from
pagan Rome its task of moulding the history of the world,
and for ever carry on that task on a new basis, a basis which
was truly better and more in accordance with the divine
will. These were the views which influenced men during
the time of the German invasions, when the spiritual
leadership of the world was given over to the Christians as
the physical mastery of the world fell to the invaders. But
the scope of our book forbids us to follow these developments any further.

The results of our investigation, so far, are these. Many
ancient writers felt that some internal change was opera-
ting within the Roman Empire, and they had expressed this
idea in many different ways. But it became a widespread
belief as Christianity on the spiritual side and the barbarian
on the political side gradually took over the internally de-
caying *imperium Romanum.*

Yet even now we cannot see clearly what causes were
responsible for this collapse, change, decline, or development, whichever it may be. And especially we do not know
the importance of the part played in it by degeneration in
sexual life: we do not even know if sexual degeneration
played any part whatever. We shall try, therefore, to discard all general conceptions of historical process and all
philosophies of life; to use our evidence as objectively as
may be; and so to find some indication of the causes which
initiated or influenced this development.

It might be said that the Roman stock was composed of very different elements (perhaps including the alien blood of Etruria). And the suggestion might be made that a nation with such an origin may reign and conquer for some time, and yet – when the conquests which kindled its ambition at last come to an end – may be bound to degenerate, because it is not a complete whole in itself. But ethnological questions are exceedingly difficult; I shall not discuss them here. Nevertheless, it is certain that after Rome encountered Carthage, and Greece, and Asia Minor, a multitude of different stocks poured into Italy, and mingled with the pure native breed. That was a grave change from the old ideals: for the Empire had been built on the solidarity of the ancient aristocratic families. In addition to this, the best blood of Italy was sapped by constant and savage warfare, and nothing was gained to compensate that loss. And the institution of colonies of veterans was a bad remedy for depopulation, since the ex-service men who settled in them were probably not representatives of the sound old Roman stock. Even at the end of the Republic the percentage of pure Romans in these colonies was small; and long before the Empire officially came to an end, they suffered changes and importations which diminished even that small proportion of pure stock.

We have said elsewhere that, as early as the end of the Republic, the old families of Rome were suffering diminution by the increasing childlessness of each generation. This was even then so serious as to compel Augustus to take steps against it (in his marriage laws) although his measures had little success.

In the second half of the second century A.D. the whole Empire was attacked and devastated by a plague, of which Zosimus says (i, 26): 'With the same violence as the war which had broken out everywhere, the plague fell on cities and villages alike, and destroyed the few survivors of the human race. Never in any previous time had it destroyed so many people.' This refers to the year 250 or so. Zosimus says again of the year 268 (i, 46): 'All the invading Scythians had been infected by the plague: some of them died in Thrace and others in Macedonia. Those who escaped were either enrolled in the Roman legions, or else presented with land, which they cultivated with care and eagerness. The plague broke out in the Roman army also, and many died, including the Emperor.' The provinces which were depopulated by the plague were less able to resist the urgent danger of the German invasions.

We cannot here trace the whole development of Roman policy during the last years of the Empire: it would in any case be superfluous to rewrite a well-known piece of history. It may be permissible, however, to remind our readers of a few of the central facts.

In A.D. 251 the Emperor Decius fell in battle against the Goths, who had made their way from the East as far as Thrace and Asia Minor. In 260 the Tithe-land between the Rhine and the Limes (the frontier beyond the Rhine) was lost to the Alemanni. During this time, Roman territory was penetrated by thousands of peaceful German immigrants. They were settled within the Empire as *coloni*; as *foederati* they took over the task of defending the frontier, and multitudes of them were incorporated in the Roman armies. Probus (276–82) – the man who encouraged vine-growing on the Rhine and Moselle – and other Emperors of the same stamp attempted to rejuvenate and improve the army by these measures. Clearly the statesmen of the time were scarcely conscious of the gravity of the step. The same policy was further developed under Constantine (306–37). When the Vandals, hard pressed by the Goths, begged for admittance into the Empire, Constantine settled them in Pannonia.

That was the position when the Mongolian tribes called the Huns began to push westward (*c.* 375): the last stage of the long war between Romans and Germans had commenced. Driven by the Huns, the Western Goths likewise sought admittance to the Empire. Valens allowed them to cross the Danube. Shortly afterwards they were misused by Roman officials, and took arms. The Romans were heavily defeated at Adrianople, and Valens himself was killed. Yet the Empire was saved once more, by Theodosius. (Christianity had of course been the state-religion since the time of Constantine.) He allied the Goths with Rome as *foederati*, and attempted to blend the races by admitting Goths to join the army and to hold official posts.

But after his death the Empire fell apart into two Empires, Eastern and Western, nominally governed by Theodosius' sons Arcadius and Honorius, but really by their Germanic generals Alaric and Stilicho. During their wars, there was one event which had not occurred since the Gallic invasion of 387 B.C. – Rome was besieged by an enemy, taken, and sacked. Alaric, the Western Goth, took Rome in A.D. 410. We learn from Zosimus that, throughout the siege, the public games were still held in the city!

Different Germanic races occupied other parts of the Empire. The Vandals established themselves in North Africa, the Franks in Belgium, the Anglo-Saxons in Britain. But the most dangerous enemies of Rome were the Huns, who had already burst into Gaul under the leadership of the terrible Attila. Only the energetic co-operation of the Western Goths and the Romans under Aetius succeeded in halting their advance, at the famous and bloody battle of Châlons in 451. But the march of destiny could not be stopped. In 455 the Vandals invaded Rome from the sea and plundered the city for two weeks. And finally the 16-year-old Emperor Romulus (derisively called Augustulus) was overthrown by Odoacer, a German whom the German army had chosen as their ruler. This event took place in the year 476. It is usually singled out of the crowded history of centuries as marking 'the fall of the Western Empire'. It is certainly true that thenceforth the Western Empire was the battleground and the prize of warring Germanic peoples. As we know, the Eastern Empire survived for some centuries more; it sometimes claimed to rule the West also, but was never able to uphold its claim for long. The West, as an Empire of the true Roman nation, had disappeared for ever.

The external political relations of Rome, which we have described, may have contributed to bringing about the end of the Empire; but they were not alone responsible. In history, there is never a single cause for any decisive change. I take leave to doubt whether it can ever be possible for us to comprehend the fullest implications and the remotest causes of any change so enormous as the fall of the Roman Empire. There are always certain irrational factors which are hidden from our thought, and must always

remain hidden. In history, as well as in other studies, we
must think of Goethe's 'First Phenomena', whose existence
we can know but whose nature we can never understand.
It must be enough for us here to know those causes which
can be known and comprehended by unbiased research.

For example, in the change which we are discussing, the
economic factor, also was of great importance, although it
has hitherto been largely disregarded. The whole matter
was, as far as I know, first explained by Max Weber, in a
remarkably fine essay, *The Social Causes of the Decline of
Ancient Civilization* (in a book published in 1924, and entitled *Collected Papers on Social and Economic History*).
Every classical scholar owes it to himself to study this
illuminating work with great care. It is of course not within the scope of our book to give a full analysis of Weber's
essay; we must content ourselves with employing its results
where we believe them to be sound.

According to Weber, the course of the development of
ancient civilization was as follows. It was primarily an urban civilization. The city consumed what it produced itself.
There was no commerce except in coastal cities; and such
commerce was concerned chiefly with certain articles of
great value, and very little with commodities of daily use.
There was very little commerce in inland cities; natural
economy prevailed. Therefore a higher type of civilization
arose only in the coastal cities. That civilization was ultimately based on slave-labour, and was impossible without
a huge supply of slaves, constantly renewed by great wars.
'A war in ancient times is also a slave-hunt. War brings a
steady supply of material to the slave-markets, and allows
the use of forced labour and the accumulation of vast
populations.' The slave-market, then, was the 'necessary
condition' of the existence of this civilization. If the supply
of slaves ever shrank, the effect on the civilization would be
'the same as the effect caused on blast-furnaces by the exhaustion of coalmines'. Yet that happened when Tiberius
stopped the wars of expansion at the Rhine. The supply of
men and women to the slave-markets fell off. There was an
enormous shortage of labour. The great plantations which
had been worked by slave-labour became gradually deserted. The slave barracks were transformed into settlements

of peasants bound to serve the lord of the manor – that is, there was a widespread change to a natural economy. Weber closes his essay with these words: 'Civilization has become rural. The economic development of antiquity has come full circle. Its spiritual achievement is, to all appearance, obliterated. With the disappearance of trade, the splendid marble cities too have disappeared, and all the spiritual refinements which depended on it – art, and literature, and science, and the subtle forms of commercial law. And in the manors of *possessores* and *seniores* there is as yet no echo of the songs of troubadour and minnesinger ...' Yet that change contained some consolation, and pointed towards a better future. 'The multitudes of serfs and slaves recovered the rights of the family and of property; they were gradually raised from the status of "talking furniture" to a real humanity; and their family life was surrounded by the rising power of Christianity with rigid moral sanctions ... The cultured and elegant aristocracies reverted to barbarism.'

According to this account, which seems to me to be well grounded, ancient civilization fell because it did not understand how to use the mass of mankind otherwise than as slaves to the pleasure and profit of a small class of conquerors and exploiters. But Weber rejects the common opinion that 'the supposed luxury and the real immorality of the upper classes' or 'the emancipation of women and the relaxation of the marriage bond among the ruling classes destroyed ancient civilization. That civilization was de-destroyed by more important factors than the guilt of individuals.'

It cannot be doubted that, as well as the purely economic causes of the decline of ancient civilization, there were spiritual causes at work – causes usually summed up as 'the rise of Christianity'. The old state could not be preserved by a religious attitude to life – an attitude which did not only condemn the Empire and the principate by which it was governed, but set up, in opposition to the existing scheme of human life, the new, almost ascetic ideal of overcoming this world.

We shall choose a few striking features to allow us to realize the true nature of this doctrine. Does it not assert

the ideal which Rome had lacked for so long – the value of
humanity in itself? Be like the Creator (it says), who makes
no distinction between the good and the bad, the just and
the unjust, when he dispenses benefits – 'for he maketh his
sun to rise on the evil as on the good, and maketh it to
rain on the just and on the unjust.' This God alone is the
Master, the Lord. Before him *all* men are brothers. They
exist in order to help one another to bear one another's
burdens, and to love one another – that is, one man must
be tolerant and forgiving to another, be reconciled to him,
and do good to him even if he is an enemy. In the face of
this brave new world of high spiritual purpose, all the
wealth, all the power, all the splendour of this world have
no meaning – except that their purpose is to be used by
one man to help his less fortunate and happy fellow-
creatures. The highest in that new world is not he who has
most power but he who serves others and humbles himself. And injuries must not be followed by revenge: whosoever shall smite thee on thy right cheek, turn to him the
other also. And property is to be of no importance: him
that taketh away thy coat forbid not to take thy cloak also.
We must strive to be like God. But God is neither the jealous and revengeful god of Judaea, nor the deities of old
mythology endowed with human caprice and human weakness, nor a Roman Emperor with all his sins and lusts, nor
a cold and bloodless philosophical idea. God is the Father,
the loving Father of mankind, who embraces his children
even when they return after wandering far from his love.

Such is the new gospel. In itself it is perhaps no more
than the assertion of humanity pure and simple, as it always
lay in the heart of man ready for expression; but until that
time the message had never been so straightforward and so
clearly uttered. For our purposes it is quite superfluous
and unimportant to know whether these profound thoughts
were spoken, at least in part, by a historical person, Jesus
(as I tend to believe they were); or, as many scholars believe, were 'floating in the air', and developed with their
accompaniments as a natural opposition to the horror, violence, and madness of Roman sadism. It is enough for us to
know that this new doctrine *existed* – this new attitude to
life, this inner conquest of life and all its terrors.

By this time we scarcely need to emphasize the fact that through the new gospel, the Roman state and its ideals were denied and rejected. For instance, Nietzsche (who in later life was certainly little inclined towards Christianity) writes as follows in his *Antichrist* (*Works*, viii, 305): 'Those holy anarchists made it an act of piety to destroy "the world" – that is, the Roman Empire – to raze it until one stone was not left on another, until the Germans and other boors became its overlords.' Nietzsche overlooks only this one fact – in the original gospel there is no word of the destruction of an Empire or anything else. But the whole Empire (and modern, as well as ancient Empires, be it said) is described in one word as being entirely unimportant. *My kingdom,* it is said, *is not of this world.* And that does not mean *my kingdom is Cloudcuckooland* or *Utopia.* It means *my kingdom is the kingdom of love, of virtue, of the spirit, and it lives in the heart of every man who is inspired by these things.*

Another passage of Nietzsche contains so much beauty and so much real comprehension of what can truly be called Christianity that we must quote some part of it. (It is taken from *The Will to Power*, ed. Brahn, 1921.) 'Jesus aimed directly at the ideal condition – the kingdom of heaven in men's hearts. He did not find the means to that condition in the observances of the Jewish church ... The ideal Christian life consists of love and humility; of that depth of feeling which will not shut out even the lowest; of absolute refusal to maintain one's own rights to defend oneself, or to conquer as a personal triumph; of belief in happiness here on earth despite poverty, opposition, and death; of the forgiving spirit which puts away anger and disdain; of the refusal to be rewarded or to consider anyone as one's debtor. It is a life without a spiritual and religious master – a proud life rich with the will to poverty and service ... *The thief on the cross.* The thief, while he suffered a painful death, decided "This alone is right – to suffer and die like this Jesus, kindly and submissively, without revolt or enmity"; and so he accepted the gospel and was in Paradise.'

Nietzsche, then, considers that the core of Jesus' teaching is first and foremost a rule of life. Yet these new views of

life (so simple and so revolutionary), of life and of our attitude to life and of our attitude to our fellow men – this
Gospel or Good News was not inherited by the simple
childlike people to whom it was addressed. Instead, it
reached men who had long lost their primitive simplicity
among the thorns and subtleties of Greek philosophy and
Hellenistic-Roman civilization. And that misdirection was
one of the greatest tragedies in the history of the world.
Thereby, the new hearers of the gospel refined it into a
system of philosophy and theology so complex that men
bitterly disputed the meaning of a sentence or a word in it.
The disputes lasted for centuries, and in some cases continue at the present day; and their effect on the disputants
was to make them entirely forget what Jesus really meant.
We must remember, in this connection, what Nietzsche
says so forcibly: 'The Church is exactly the thing against
which Jesus preached, and against which he taught his dis-
ciples to fight ... What is Christ-like in the ecclesiastical
sense is really Antichristlike – it is simply things and persons instead of symbols, it is simply history instead of the
eternal verities, it is simply forms and rites and dogmas
instead of a rule and practice of life. Absolute indifference
to dogmas, cults, priests, and theology – that is Christ-
like! ... The kingdom of heaven is a condition of the heart
(it is said of children that theirs is the kingdom of heaven),
not something above the earth. The kingdom of God will
come not in the chronological and historical sense, nor at
some date in the calendar, in such a way that it is here
today although it was not here yesterday. The kingdom of
God comes as a change of heart in individuals – something
which always comes and always is yet to come.'

That is the real teaching of Jesus. I am certain that among
the oldest followers of Jesus there must have been many
who lived according to that teaching. But as it became
more and more widely known, as the so-called educated
classes of the time sought to interest themselves in it (instead of simply living by it), so the fabric of alien elements
was woven more and more tightly round it, gripping and
immobilizing its simple central doctrines like ivy on a tree.
At last the Christian system became a hotch-potch of these
old truths and countless new importations – Greek philo-

sophy, mysticism, and innumerable popular customs from peoples near and far. And that became the official religion of Rome, under the latest Emperors; thus it entered its fateful alliance with Power – with that outlook which was at first diametrically opposed to everything Jesus meant and taught.

We cannot and must not here follow the course of its development any further. Our purpose was only to assert, as far as possible, that true Christian ideals cannot be allied to a mighty power like the Roman Empire, and that they did in fact play their part in undermining that structure from within and eventually in causing its disintegration.

It has been held by some authors (especially by Ferrero in *The Decline of Ancient Civilization*) that, among all the other causes of this disintegration, we must not underestimate the importance of the deteriorating organization and administration of the Empire. Ferrero believes that after Alexander Severus the Senate lost all its power, and thus made way for the arbitrary despotism of the army and of the Emperors who were set on the throne by the army. The 'good' Emperors – those from Vespasian to Marcus Aurelius – reigned with the active co-operation of the Senate; and so, he considers, the whole empire was benefited. He writes: 'The century during which that aristocracy controlled the destinies of the world was marked by unbroken economic prosperity. Both the Senate and the Emperor were respected and obeyed, without any of the discussions and conflicts between these authorities which have been elaborated by those historical writers who wish somehow or other to see a monarchy in the first two centuries of the principate.'

But Ferrero can give no reasons why a regime so beneficial to the Empire should not have lasted longer, except 'gradual deterioration' resulting from 'internal exhaustion' – and, in the end, Stoic and Christian doctrines, whose 'fundamental hypothesis of the equality of all men and nations before the moral law' broke through 'the armour of the principles of aristocracy and nationalism'. Ferrero, then, is forced to acknowledge that a falling-off in organization cannot have been so powerful a factor in the decay of the Empire as his other writings would lead us to assume.

All the causes which he quotes must certainly have contributed to the great effect. But they were not the principal cause, any more than Diocletian's bureaucracy, which cost so much money and necessitated such heavy taxes, thereby helping to paralyse the economic life of the world. The condition of affairs which we have described was produced by *all* the above-mentioned causes, acting not individually but collectively.

And what, we may now ask, was the effect of the degeneracy (or rather the new development) of Roman morality? Certainly it was not so important as is affirmed by many historians who follow Augustine's account. On the contrary, it would seem to be true that the Romans changed their attitude to love, marriage, and sexual life as the conditions of their world changed. When everything else that was stable in a man's life becomes doubtful and insecure his sexual life is apt to have its aberrations also. On the other hand, the man who has found in Jesus' teaching a new attitude to life and humanity learns new opinions and new values in love also; and that change is far from being a degeneration.

We have found, then, that it is untrue to say that ancient civilization was ruined by its own immorality. The real causes of its downfall, and of the transformation generally known as the decline of the ancient world, are of a different nature and belong to other sides of human life.

Conclusion

IN any work of this kind, whose purpose is to describe the civilization and the intimate personal life of our predecessors the ancient Romans, the author's philosophy of life must constantly appear, like the background of a bright and vari-coloured picture. The reader is of course bound to become aware of the author's general attitude to the life of antiquity; but he is bound to become aware also of his attitude to the problems of human life in general. Any attempt to conceal that attitude would produce, not a living work, but an arid collection of evidence; and the book would be no less arid for the fact that the passages chosen were translated instead of being left in the original. And, in fact, the author of this work did not choose to conceal his outlook; for the work is in some sort a confession of faith. We have said elsewhere that if we are charged with failing to write 'objectively', we plead guilty, and answer that we do not believe that any work of history can be absolutely objective. Ultimately, things and even historical facts are given their value by men; and the value varies enormously, according as it is given by Tacitus or Suetonius or a modern historian. Our estimates of the evidence throughout this book have been made from our own subjective point of view. Is it not, therefore, permissible and even desirable to set that point of view before the reader? It would be impossible to conceal it, as we have said. Any author, however objective, betrays his own individuality by his approach to ancient civilization, to the Roman Empire, to the ideal of Imperialism ... And we may say that Nietzsche's

Aphorisms or any greater works dealing with antiquity reveal more of the author than of his subject. Yet I cannot consider that to be an indictment. It is merely a proof that the author in question did not see ancient civilization as the dry material of scholarship, but as something living with which he must grapple in order to repel it or to strengthen himself. In sum, ancient civilization is linked with him by becoming a part of his own philosophy of life. Scholars and historians may shake their heads at this; headshaking never troubled Nietzsche. The carter was always busy when the king built a palace. Needless to say, it is far from our mind to compare this book with any work of a mind so great as Nietzsche. But his example is perhaps enough to show what our purpose is: to understand a part of history in order to throw a little light on our own path.

These reasons may perhaps make it permissible for the author himself to explain the background of his book, from his own knowledge of his intentions and his general outlook on life. Otherwise, certain chapters of it (such as those dealing with the fall of Rome and its causes, and religion and philosophy in relation to sexual life) may be less comprehensible than their writer intended.

Modern moralists often complain that men nowadays 'stand rootless in an empty eternity'. That feeling of helplessness and ignorance in the face of life is reflected in the search in which so many of us are engaged, the search for a rock to cling to, for secure ground beneath our feet. No one knows the origin or the destiny of this rapid and unstable existence; the world's last mysteries are being solved by inventions and discoveries which bring us neither greater happiness nor deeper knowledge. Uncertainty, and indecision, and aimlessness, and helplessness – that is the condition of man in the modern world, in this godless, empty, 'civilized' world. Hence it comes that men are ever seeking after some new thing in every branch of life, from education to economics, from dietetics to religion. That is the picture which moralists draw, and each individual reacts differently to it; the masses shout louder for bread and circuses, while the *soi-disant* educated classes lament that they are the last outposts of civilization against an invading world of barbarism.

But the true philosopher, his spirit undisturbed by the senseless rush of our fleeting life, stands gazing calmly on the seas which surge and ebb and whirl madly around him. He laughs: ironically? or humorously? or in deep sympathy with his fellow-men, doomed as they are to wear themselves away in sound and fury? He looks up – above him burns the eternal sun, in his hair play the eternal winds; but at his feet is the wild raging of the sea. Will it rage and storm thus for ever? ... No. When the winds sink and the tempest is calmed, then at last it will lie at peace, and the sun will mirror itself upon the waveless blue.

Yet its peace will not last. Again and again storms will gather and billows will mount as the elements strive and rage together. There is no rest in the world of Becoming and Passing-away. And every storm will be watched by a silent thinker, angry, or amazed, or wild with grief, or calm and smiling: or perhaps he will cry, like Goethe's Lynceus, 'be it as it will, it was beautiful!'

The same Lynceus cries from his tower those words less often quoted: 'What dismal horror fronts me from the darkness of the world?' And he sees the cloistered happiness of old Philemon and Baucis vanish away in smoke and flame ... a symbol for us to lay to heart. Often and often such cloistered happiness today goes up in flames, and the men and women who were happy sink into ruin or death. Today? Not only today, but for ever, in every place where men live and pursue happiness.

And we may still listen to the grave voice of Schopenhauer, as he points a way for us through the gloom: 'There is only one innate error and that is the belief that we are here in order to be happy. It is innate in us because it is linked with our very life, and our whole being is only an echo of it, our very body is marked with its stamp. We are no more than the will to life; and the repeated satisfaction of all our will is what we envisage in the idea of happiness. As long as we persevere in this innate error, and are confirmed in it by optimistic creeds, the world appears full of contradictions. In every step, in every act great or small, we must learn that this world and this life are not so arranged as to preserve happiness ... So, then, everything in life tends to bring us back from that original error, and to convince us that the aim of our existence is not to be happy. If we gaze more closely and more calmly at life, its real purpose appears to be that we should *not* be happy in it. Life is so constructed that it will disgust and revolt us, and force us to recoil as if from a delusion, so that at least our heart may be cured of its mad desire to enjoy and to live, and may be turned away from the world.'

A comfortless philosophy! So, at least, it will be called by the high-souled humanists of today. And comfortless it is for modern civilization. It considers with indifference or repulsion all the marvellous achievements of that civilization, from the newest aeroplane and the latest dance to the deadliest poison-gas, and discards them all: none of them can do anything to secure true peace of heart. The philosopher proceeds – and thus lightens the darkness which, they say, obscures his vision of the world – 'Suffering is actually the process of purification. In most cases men are sanctified only by suffering – that is, brought back from the delusion of the will to live.'

I confess that ever since my early youth I have admired this tragic philosophy because of the thought which Schopenhauer expresses in these words: 'Only in my philosophy are the evils of the world acknowledged to their full extent: they can be so acknowledged because the question of their origin has the same answer as the question of the origin of this world.' That is the enormous and inestimable advance made by this philosophy, as compared with Goethe's finest humanism, with all the classical age, and the whole of the creed of liberalism. Schopenhauer somewhere counters his opponents, the optimists, in words as brief as they are vivid: 'The world is not a peep-show.' The world is an ethical problem, for ever insoluble to us. To that view thinkers are at least beginning to return. Schopenhauer proceeds: 'In my philosophy, the will comes to self-knowledge by becoming objective (as always happens); and thus its abrogation, its change and redemption become possible. Accordingly, only in my philosophy is ethics securely grounded and completely worked out in harmony with the profound and sublime religions – not merely Judaism and Islam, but Brahmanism, Buddhism, and Christianity.'

This sublime philosophy may be accused of having absolute nihilism as its end and goal – an accusation which even now is constantly put forward in speech and writing. But the accusation may be answered. Nothingness or Nirvana is a state which our reason cannot comprehend; it is the state in which the will to life changes and denies itself. In his earliest thought, Schopenhauer gave it a positive character, naming it 'the better consciousness'; later, he wondered whether it might be named 'God' – but he discarded that name in the end in order to leave no trace of vagueness. It is a state whose influence on the soul is so strong that from it alone springs every act which we call ethical, moral, good, or noble. It is simply the Irrational. E. von Hartmann names it the Unconscious; and I would call it the state of being which is for ever beyond the reach of our reason, but is for that reason truly divine; the state from which comes everything which exists, towards which everything strives, in which everything finds eternal rest, and where everything has its ultimate meaning, its real strength, its true being. Call it First Being or what you will – whosoever knows himself to be safe within it, his life has found a secure haven, his efforts have meaning and direction, his destiny (however dark it may be) has a goal, his whole humanity stands firm in the face of the vast Nothingness and does not falter and tremble like that of the common man. That is the man who has faith. He knows that his life was not given him so that he might enjoy it, nor yet that he might dream it away in idleness or in weeping and wailing over the miseries of the world. It is of him and for him that Schopenhauer said these words (so truly modern): 'A happy life is impossible. The highest that man can achieve is a heroic life. And a heroic life is lived by any man, in any sphere and at any time, who fights against overwhelming difficulties for the good of all men, and at last conquers, though scantily rewarded, or rewarded not at all. He stands at last, like the prince in Gozzi's *Recorvo*, turned to stone; but his mien is noble and his bearing proud. His memory lives after him, and he is revered as a hero. His will – mortified by toil and effort, failure and ingratitude, throughout his life – dies away in Nirvana.'

One word more. What can this philosophy give to the man who is inspired by it?

First, the courage to see the reality of the world as it is – that is, without the deceitful lustre of any charming idealism: the lustre vanishes as soon as such a philosophy meets and must conquer the hard reality of the world – especially of the modern world.

Second, a profoundly earnest attitude to life, an attitude founded on a truly ethical basis. We have pointed out above that every optimistic view of the world wavers as soon as it is made the basis of an ethical system. Everything truly ethical is, as we said, in some sort a denial of what is natural, of what is given through the senses. Yet only the man whose life rests upon this ethical foundation can stand fast amid the storm of events, however grim it may be. And he feels himself safe against infinity. He does not feel, as so many do, 'I am faced by nothingness!' He feels 'I am not *faced* by anything, because I myself have found a resting place in infinity. I have the power to realize it; by thought, in everything which I call beautiful, good, true, pure, noble, great – by act, in moral conduct. I know that I cannot speak of these things otherwise than the mystic speaks of his God. I know that all these forces, or powers, manifest themselves differently in every human heart. But I feel, I experience their existence – I know that they are the only reality and the whole meaning of my life. And last of all, this. Instead of losing myself in barren speculation, I know this Divinity, as I may still name it. I experience it every day and every hour, through loving actions, through self-sacrifice for other men, through renunciation of the so-called delights of the world. They are delights only for the man who is still far distant from that which has manifested itself in me as Divine, and manifests itself in every minute of my existence.' In this way, we do not lose ourselves in unmeaning Nothingness, but find ourselves for ever, in the unfathomable depths of the Self which we have thus established and fulfilled.

THE JULIO-CLAUDIAN HOUSE

OCTAVIUS married ATIA

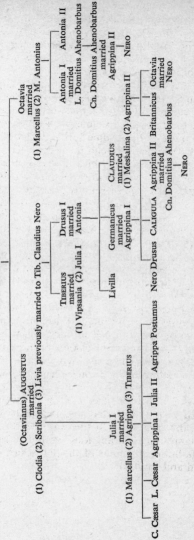

Index

MODERN AUTHORS

BACHOFEN:
The Legend of Tanaquil, *19*, *26*, **135**
Primitive Religion and Ancient Symbols, **139–40**, **209–11**
The Right of the Mother, **19**
unspecified, **31**, **134–5**, *145*

BECKER AND MARQUARDT:
Roman Private Antiquities, *29*, **31**, **32**, *41*, **46**

BIRT:
Roman Portraits, **351**, **352**, **354**, *355*
unspecified, **37**, **110**

BLOCH:
Origin of Syphilis, ii, 514, **119**; 652, *72*
unspecified, *139*

BLÜHER:
The Role of Sexual Life, ii, 26, **69**, *70*

BURCKHARDT:
The Age of Constantine **119**, **156**, **157**

COSSA unspecified, **341**, *345*
COUPERUS unspecified, *363*

DIETERICH:
The Decline of Ancient Religion, **355**, **357**, *361*

FERRERO:
The Decline of Ancient Civilization, *379*, **379–80**

FREUD:
From Leonardo da Vinci's Childhood, *366*

FRIEDLÄNDER:
History of Roman Morals, *79*
History of Roman Morals, i, 521, *37*; ii, 111, **186–7**; ii, 420, **117**, ii, *427*, *113*; v, *423*, *62*
unspecified, *73*

GEORGE:
Maximin, **353–4**

GOETHE:
The Diary, *267*
Faust, **309**
Hermann and Dorothea (Introduction), **233**
Letter of 28th November, 1798, **233**
Roman Elegies, *233*
Werther, *206*, *224*
unspecified, *158*, *296*, *374*

GOZZI:
Recorvo (referred to in SCHOPENHAUER), *385*

GREGOROVIUS:
Hadrian, *145 n.*

GURLITT:
Erotica Plautina, 15, **67**

HÖLDERLIN unspecified, **198**, **364**

KAPLAN:
Outlines of Psychoanalysis, **252**

KARLOWA:
History of Roman Law, **26**, *27*

KELLER unspecified, **232**

LESSING:
Emilia Galotti, *21*
The Epigram, *292*
Laocoon, **161**
unspecified, **298**, **299**

LICHT:
Sexual Life in Ancient Greece, **16**, *71*

Famous Authors in Panther Books